MW00484446

MEDIA EFFECTS

MEDIA EFFECTS

W. James Potter
University of California, Santa Barbara

Los Angeles | London | New Delhi
Singapore | Washington DC

Los Angeles | London | New Delhi
Singapore | Washington DC

FOR INFORMATION:

SAGE Publications, Inc.
2455 Teller Road
Thousand Oaks, California 91320
E-mail: order@sagepub.com

SAGE Publications Ltd.
1 Oliver's Yard
55 City Road
London EC1Y 1SP
United Kingdom

SAGE Publications India Pvt. Ltd.
B 1/I 1 Mohan Cooperative Industrial Area
Mathura Road, New Delhi 110 044
India

SAGE Publications Asia-Pacific Pte. Ltd.
33 Pekin Street #02-01
Far East Square
Singapore 048763

Acquisitions Editor: Matthew Byrnie
Editorial Assistant: Elizabeth Borders
Production Editor: Astrid Virding
Copy Editor: Pam Suwinsky
Typesetter: C&M Digitals (P) Ltd.
Proofreader: Dennis W. Webb
Indexer: Ellen Slavitz
Cover Designer: Bryan Fishman
Marketing Manager: Liz Thornton
Permissions Editor: Karen Ehrmann

Copyright © 2012 by SAGE Publications, Inc.

All rights reserved. No part of this book may be
reproduced or utilized in any form or by any means,
electronic or mechanical, including photocopying,
recording, or by any information storage and retrieval
system, without permission in writing from the
publisher.

Printed in the United States of America

Library of Congress Cataloging-in-Publication Data

Potter, W. James.

Media effects / W. James Potter.

p. cm.
Includes bibliographical references and index.

ISBN 978-1-4129-6469-2 (pbk. : acid-free paper)

1. Mass media—Influence. 2. Mass media—Social aspects.
3. Mass media—Physiological aspects.
4. Mass media—Psychological aspects.
I. Title.

P94.P68 2013 302.23—dc23   2011030164

This book is printed on acid-free paper.

12 13 14 15 16 10 9 8 7 6 5 4 3 2 1

Brief Contents

Detailed Contents

Preface

Media effects is a very popular topic of discussion. People like to speculate about how society is being harmed by certain kinds of media messages, such as violence, sexual portrayals, bad language, negative stereotypes, superficial news, manipulative advertising, depictions of unhealthy behaviors, and the list goes on. Fortunately, scholars have produced a very large research literature that reveals that the media do, in fact, exert all kinds of influences on us. Some of that influence has been found to be relatively weak, while other influences have been found to be much stronger. Some of that influence occurs infrequently, but other influences are exerted continually in our everyday lives. Some of that influence comes at us directly as we encounter particular media messages, while other influences have been found to come at us indirectly through our institutions and society.

This research literature has great utility in informing our speculations about media effects; that is, we can use the literature to help guide our discussions away from areas where criticism is faulty. However, few people really understand the important patterns of findings in this literature; therefore many discussions about media effects are based on unfounded beliefs rather than on solid knowledge.

Why do so few people understand the nature of media effects? The answer is that this research literature is so large and complex that it is a very challenging task to read through it all without getting lost in the complicated details. Whenever I journey into this country—that is, read through the media effects literature—I often get lost. I wonder how a particular research study or even a line of research fits into the overall literature. It is rather like several people are showing me pictures of their vacations in a foreign country in random order and I wonder how all those places are related to one another. I often feel frustrated that I am not able to absorb the meaning of the different studies in a way that would help me see the big picture. And I think that this journey would be so much more rewarding and efficient if I had a map.

Where can we find such a map that shows the big picture of media effects? I have been looking for one for decades and have become convinced that one does not yet exist. Of course, there are maps of various neighborhoods; that is, there are scholars who have written very useful books and review articles on particular subtopics, such as the effects of exposure to violence, sexual portrayals, television news, and stereotypes, to name just a few. And there are scholars who have written books on multiple topics about media effects, but those books always leave me with questions such as "Are there other issues that we should be concerned about that are not on this author's agenda?" and "What have those writers overlooked?" In short, I wondered about the full set of media effects.

I suspect that you feel the same way; that is, as you read through even a few studies in this very large literature, you can feel disoriented. Like me, you want a map that would provide the full picture of media effects. Such a map would provide a clear structure to help you navigate through this territory efficiently and provide you with a set of categories to help organize your learning.

This book provides such a big picture map of media effects. It took me more than two decades to develop such a map. During that time, I have been taking notes, making outlines, and drawing graphics to help me and my students better understanding various parts of the media effects phenomenon. Eventually all this thinking coalesced into two Media Effects Templates—one for media influences on individuals and the other to organize media influences on macro units, such as the public, institutions, and society. These are the maps that organize the media effects literature and structure this book.

My hope is that you, the readers of this book, will find my overall approach and organizational tools as helpful to you as these have been to me and my students over the years. Of course, I realize that careful readers of this text will undoubtedly find places where my organizational scheme has limits to its utility. I do not claim this is a perfect organization of such a large literature created by so many different kinds of scholars using so many different ideas defined in many different ways. However, I do believe that it is complete in presenting the big picture. To illustrate what I mean by this claim, I return to a geographical analogy. In order to produce a good map of the United States, we need to create a visual that shows all 50 states and illustrates their locations relative to one another. Such a map, however, is limited in how much detail it can provide; it cannot show the dimensions of Aunt Martha's backyard in Des Moines and at the same time keep the viewer's attention on the overall structure of the United States. This book attempts to keep the focus on the big picture, and therefore details are sacrificed at times. Not every study in this large literature is acknowledged, and when I do describe a research study, I foreground the findings and necessarily ignore many of the details that would help you understand how those findings were generated. If you're looking for more details, you'll find many citations of research studies provided in exhibits. The citations refer you to individual research studies that can be easily accessed through your university's library with an electronic search of scholarly journals.

In trying to keep the focus on the big picture of media effects, the book treats the characteristics of history, methods, and theory as background. While these characteristics are important, they are not foregrounded in this book. I am assuming that most readers of this book have not lived with the phenomenon long enough to care much about how thinking and research has changed over time. Also, I am not assuming that readers are experts in research methods, so I do not require you to make fine discriminations among which study's findings are more valid based on an explication of researchers' skill with methods. And I realize that many readers may regard theory as being too abstract, so I try to foreground the practical utility of the predictions the theories make rather than the technical terms used by the theoreticians. By foregrounding *effects*—rather than history, methods, or theories—the book will focus your attention on what the effects are, how they manifest themselves, and the factors that are likely to bring these effects into being. These characteristics should make the text much more relevant to your experience and thereby more interesting to you.

OVERVIEW OF BOOK

The book is organized into four major parts. The first part provides a fundamental examination of the basic ideas underlying this entire book. This first part is composed of five chapters.

Chapter 1 makes the case for why the study of media effects is so important. This argument is built from three ideas. First, there is a huge amount of information manufactured each year in our culture, and a great deal of it is disseminated through the media. Second, each of us is continually being affected by media content in our everyday lives. Third, scholars have generated a great deal of knowledge about media effects, so there is something important to learn.

Chapter 2 introduces the five main ideas that underlie the entire book. These ideas are mass media, effect, media influence, audience, and algorithm. Each of these ideas is defined, then analyzed, so that you can understand *why* each is defined the way it is.

Chapter 3 lays out a scheme that will be used to organize the very large number of media effects. Called the "Media Effects Templates," one of these templates organizes all possible effects on individuals, and the second one organizes the effects on larger social structures, such as the public, institutions, and society. Chapter 4 clarifies how the media exercise their influence. Chapter 5 explains the role of theories and how they have helped—and sometimes have failed to help—us to understand the nature of media effects.

Part II focuses attention on media effects on individuals. It consists of six chapters, one for each type of effect: physiological, cognitive, belief, attitudinal, affective, and behavioral.

Part III shifts attention onto media effects on macro-level units. Chapter 12 examines media effects on the public. Chapter 13 lays out the media effects on a variety of institutions, and Chapter 14 examines the effect of the media society and well as on the media themselves.

Part IV returns to the big picture of media effects. Now I have discussed the range of individual level and macro effects, I focus on several big picture issues in Chapter 15.

PEDAGOGICAL AIDS

In Parts II and III, where the wide range of media effects is presented, each chapter presents several pedagogical features that will help you understand the material better and incorporate this understanding into your way of thinking. First, each of these chapters presents exhibits in which sets of effects are outlined in summary form, and each effect is indicated by at least one citation for a research study that examined that particular effect. Also, each of these chapters concludes with a list of questions that will help you review the important material presented in that chapter as well as to direct your thinking to analyze your own experiences to look for evidence of these effects in your everyday lives. The chapters in Part II, on individual-level effects, also contain colored boxes that present anecdotes that illustrate some of the effects.

ANCILLARIES

The password-protected instructor's site at www.sagepub.com/potterme contains PowerPoint presentations, classroom assignments, and Web and video resources for use in the classroom.

The open-access student study site at www.sagepub.com/potterme contains SAGE Journal articles and Web and video resources to enhance student learning.

ACKNOWLEDGMENTS

I have been teaching about media effects in various courses for almost three decades now and have learned so much from the students in those courses at Western Michigan University, Florida State University, Indiana University, University of California-Los Angeles, Stanford University, and the University of California at Santa Barbara. I thank those thousands of students for every question, every puzzled look, and every smile of satisfaction from an insight gained.

I thank the reviewers whom SAGE called on to critique an earlier manuscript that enabled me to make many revisions and produce what you see in these pages. The reviewers include William Beauchamp (Southern Methodist University), Joseph R. Blaney (Illinois State University), Brad J. Bushman (University of Michigan (USA) and VU University Amsterdam (The Netherlands)), Sahara Byrne (Cornell University), Margaret U. D'Silva (University of Louisville), Dolores Flamiano (James Madison University), Tom German (Muskingum College), Jim Grubbs (University of Illinois Springfield), Charles H. Ingold (University of Northern Colorado), Christopher O. Keller (Cameron University), Kenneth A. Lachlan (Boston College), Michaela D. E. Meyer (Christopher Newport University), David Tewksbury (University of Illinois at Urbana-Champaign), and Shuhua Zhou (University of Alabama). I learned so much from these media effects scholars and teachers. I hope I did justice to their many helpful insights.

I am grateful for the support of numerous SAGE staff. First, I thank Todd Armstrong, who encouraged me to begin this project and signed me to a contract, then Matt Byrnie who took over for Todd and shepherded it through the revision and production processes. I also thank their very helpful assistants, Deya Saoud and Nathan Davidson. Finally, a big thanks to the skillful people in the SAGE production department (especially Astrid Virding), to Pam Suwinsky, who did an excellent job copyediting this entire manuscript, and to the marketing department.

SAGE would like to thank Professor Margaret D'Silva of the University of Louisville for her careful work on the PowerPoint presentations that accompany this book, as well as Chan Thai of the University of California at Santa Barbara for her work on the class assignments, web and video resources, and SAGE journal articles.

If you like this book, I share the credit of success with all the people I mentioned above. If you find a mistake, a shortcoming, or a misinterpretation, then it is my fault for not fully assimilating all the high-quality help I have been privileged to experience.

Organizing Thinking About Media Effects

This book begins with a set of five introductory chapters. Chapter 1 shows you why it is so important to study how the media are constantly influencing us in many ways. We live in a culture that is saturated with information, and much of that information comes to us through the media, both directly and indirectly. For most of us, the media exert the single most dominant influence on our lives. Therefore, understanding the nature of that influence is of paramount importance to being a truly educated person in our information-saturated culture.

Chapter 2 introduces and defines the key terms that will be used throughout the book. These key terms are *audience, exposure, information-processing tasks,* and *algorithms.* Another key term is *media effect,* which is so important it gets its own chapter that reveals the wide range of things that should be considered media effects. This task is undertaken in Chapter 3.

In Chapter 4, media influence is introduced, with a distinction between baselines and fluctuations as well as a distinction between manifestation and process effects. Understanding these distinctions is crucial to appreciating how the media exert their continual influence on every one of us.

Part I of the book concludes with Chapter 5, where I list the most visible theories that attempt explanations of media effects. While these theories have made important contributions in identifying media effects and predicting when they will occur, most of our knowledge about media effects has been generated by research studies that have not relied on these, or any, theories. Therefore it is essential that we not limit ourselves to media theories if we want to understand the full range of media effects.

Each chapter begins with an outline that serves as a study guide for the key ideas in that chapter. Each chapter concludes with two sets of questions. Review Questions test your comprehension of the material you read in the chapter. Further Thinking Questions stimulate you to translate the ideas in the chapter into your own experience and encourage you to internalize the information so you can use it in your everyday lives. Each of these features is designed to help you keep your focus on the big picture on each chapter.

Source: ©iStockphoto.com/fotosipsak

CHAPTER 1

Why Study Media Effects?

Why Study Media Effects?

You may be thinking that the question of this chapter is such an obvious one that it is silly to attempt an answer. Isn't it obvious that the hundreds of films, thousands of songs, tens of thousands of TV shows, and billions of Internet sites must be having some effect? Also, if advertisers did not think their messages had effects, why do they spend hundreds of billions of dollars each year on making and distributing such messages? In our everyday lives, we see other people being affected by the media all the time. Of course there are media effects!

Yes, there are media effects. But the things you regard as examples of media effects when you observe them in your everyday life may not be stimulated by the media at all. Also, there are many, many effects that the media are responsible for—either in part or in full—that we never notice or even think about. And many of those large numbers of effects are not just happening to other people; they are happening to you every day.

It is the purpose of this book to move you beyond the obvious that is likely to be based on faulty beliefs about media effects. The purpose is to get you to see the more complete "big picture" of media effects that has been constructed from a very large literature of scientific studies. When you see the big picture, you will realize that the topic of media effects has far more facets and is far more interesting than you may have thought. Also, when you understand the full spectrum of media effects and how they occur, you will feel much more powerful in your ability to control those effects in your day-to-day life.

This chapter focuses you on the big picture of media effects by emphasizing three trends: media message saturation, the growing challenge of coping, and the growth of knowledge about media effects. Taken together, these three trends make now the most important time for you to start studying media effects.

MEDIA MESSAGE SATURATION

Our culture is saturated with information. And much of that information comes to us through a flood of messages from the media. As Table 1.1 reveals, there will be 175,000 book titles published in this one year in just the United States. Throughout the world, radio stations send out 65.5 million hours of original programming each year, and television adds another 48 million hours.

Source: © iStockphoto/Chris Schmidt

With personal computers, we have access to even more information than ever when we connect to the Internet. By early 2011, the Internet had over 13.6 billion pages that were indexed and therefore available through search engines (WorldWideWebSize.com, 2011). If you started visiting these 13.6 billion Web pages right now and visited a new one every second all day with no breaks and no sleep, it would take you 42 years to get through just the first 10% of these Web pages. Of course, over the course of those 42 years, the number of websites is likely to have increased several thousand times, because the amount of information that is produced not only grows each year, but the *rate of its growth* accelerates each year.

High Degree of Exposure

We love our media, as evidenced by how much time we spend with them. A recent comprehensive study of media use found that by the end of 2010, the average American was spending 11 hours with the media each and every day—and this figure continues to grow (Phillips, 2010). Of this total time, television and video (not including online video) accounted for about 40% while Internet and mobile accounted for an additional 31%. The increase in media use is driven by younger people who are shifting away from traditional

Table 1.1 Number of Media Vehicles

Medium	United States	World
Books (titles per year)	175,000	968,735
Radio stations	13,261	47,776
TV broadcast stations	1,884	33,071
Newspapers	2,386	22,643
Mass market periodicals	20,000	80,000
Scholarly journals	10,500	40,000
Newsletters	10,000	40,000
Archived office pages	3×10^9	7.5×10^9

Source: Adapted from Potter (2011).

media (such as newspapers, magazines, and books that use print on paper) and toward electronic forms of media. A report generated by the Kaiser Family Foundation in 2005 characterized your generation (people 8 to 18 years old) as the "M Generation" for your focus so strongly on media use. This report found that children and adolescents were spending 49 minutes per day with video games and another 62 minutes with the computer. Furthermore, most of your generation frequently multitasks by exposing yourselves to several media at a time (Kaiser Family Foundation, 2005). Also, computer use is especially high among college students. In the United States there are now 17.4 million college students, and more than half of you arrive on campus as freshmen with laptop computers. The typical college student has been found to spend more than 3.5 hours a day on the computer e-mailing, instant messaging, and Web surfing. And you likely spend an additional 7.5 hours every day engaged with other media, such as books, magazines, recordings, radio, film, and television (Siebert, 2006).

It is clear that the media are an extremely important part of everyone's lives, especially people in your generation. The media organizations themselves realize this and continue to provide more and more messages in a wider range of channels with each new year.

Accelerating Production of Information

Not only is information easily available to almost anyone today, but information also keeps getting produced at an ever-increasing rate. More information has been generated since you were born than the sum total of all information throughout all recorded history up until the time of your birth. It is estimated that 80% to 90% of all scientists who have ever lived on this planet are alive today and producing scientific information at an exponentially growing rate; there are now more than 100,000 scientific scholarly journals; they publish more than 6 million articles each year (Shermer, 2002), and those numbers continue to grow. Also in the past 40 years, the number of people in this country who identify them-selves as artists increased from about 700,000 to 2.2 million, the number of musicians grew from 100,000 to more than 200,000, and the number of authors and writers increased fivefold to more than 190,000 (U.S. Census Bureau, 2011a). These fast-growing numbers of artists, musicians, and authors are pumping even more messages through our media chan-nels every day.

How much information is produced each year? In 2002, researchers at the University of California at Berkeley conducted a huge project that resulted in the estimate that in that single year, 2002, there were 5 exabytes of information produced worldwide (Lyman & Varian, 2003). This means that the amount of information produced in 2002 was 500,000 times the amount of all the holdings in the Library of Congress. As if that is not scary enough, Lyman and Varian estimated that the rate of growth of information increases at 30% each year. However, Lyman and Varian were wrong—they greatly *under*estimated the amount of information produced. Infoniac.com (2008, March 13) estimated that in 2007, there were 281 exabytes of information produced in that one year. The biggest drivers of this accelerating increase in information are the growing popularity of social networking and digital television and cameras that are not only used by hobbyists by in surveillance of public places.

Impossible to Keep Up

There is now so much information already in our culture that it is impossible to keep up with all of it. To illustrate this point, let's focus on just one medium: books. Until about two centuries ago, the majority of the population could not read, and even if it could, there were few books available. In the early 1300s, the Sorbonne Library in Paris con-tained only 1,338 books and yet was thought to be the largest library in Europe. Only elites had access to those books. Today, there are many libraries with more than 8 million books, and they lend out their books to millions of people every year. With literacy rates high, the ease of buying books from websites, and the availability of free public libraries in every town, *access* to books is no problem.

Source: ©iStockphoto.com/kertlis

Time, however, is a big problem. If you were to try to read only the new books published this year, you would have to read a book every 3 minutes for 24 hours each day with no breaks over the entire year—that is 20 books per hour and 480 books each and every day. All that effort would be needed just to keep up with the *new titles published in the United States alone!* You would have no time left to read any of the other 66 million book titles in existence world-wide. And this example is limited to only books!

We live in an environment that is far different from any environment humans have ever experienced. And the environment changes at an ever-increasing pace. This is due to the accelerating generation of information and the sharing of that information through the increasing number of media channels and the heavy traffic of media vehicles traversing those channels. Messages are being delivered to everyone, everywhere, continually. We are all saturated with information, and each year the media are more aggressive in seeking our attention. It is a hopeless expectation to keep up with all the available information. The most important challenge now lies in making good selections when the media are continually offering us thousands of messages on any given topic.

THE CHALLENGE OF COPING

Source: Noel Hendrickson/Digital Vision/Thinkstock

How do we meet the challenge of making selections from among the overwhelming number of messages in the constantly increasing flood of information? The answer to this question is, We put our minds on "automatic pilot" where our minds automatically filter out almost all message options. I realize that this might sound strange, but think about it. We cannot possibly think about every available message and consciously decide whether to pay attention to each one. There are too many messages to consider. So our minds have developed routines that guide this filtering process very quickly and efficiently so we don't have to spend much, if any, mental effort.

To illustrate this automatic processing, consider what we do when we go to the supermarket to buy food. Let's say we walk into the store with a list of a dozen items we need to buy. We rush through the aisles, and 15 minutes later we walk out of the store with our dozen items. In this scenario, how many decisions had we made? Our first guess is to say 12 decisions, because we needed to have made a decision to buy each of our dozen items. But what about all the items we decided *not* to buy? The average supermarket today has about 40,000 items on its shelves. So we actually made 40,000 decisions in the relatively short time we were in the supermarket—12 decisions to buy a product and 39,988 decisions not to buy a product. That is 45 decisions for each and every second we were in the store; that is indeed some fast thinking! Of course, we did not consider each product, weigh its merits relative to other products, and pick the best option. Instead, we relied on automatic programs running in our minds that guided us to certain products and brands while ignoring all others. These automatic programs are what enable our minds to work so quickly and efficiently.

Our culture is a grand supermarket of media messages. Those messages are everywhere whether we realize it or not, except that there are far more messages in our culture than there are products in any supermarket. To navigate our way efficiently day-to-day through our information-saturated culture, we rely on automatic processing. Psychologists refer to this automatic processing of information as *automaticity*. Automaticity is a state wherein our minds operate without any conscious effort from us. Thus the human mind is able to perform many mundane tasks routinely with remarkable efficiency. Once you have learned a sequence—such as tying your shoes, brushing your teeth, driving to school, or playing a song on the guitar—you can perform it over and over again with very little effort compared to the effort it took you to learn it in the first place. As we learn to do something, we are writing the instructions like a computer code in our minds. Once that code is written, it can later be loaded into our minds and run automatically to guide us through any previously learned task with very little thought.

In our everyday lives, the media offer us thousands of choices for exposures. With automatic processing, we experience a great deal of media messages without paying much attention to them. Every once in a while something in the message or in our environment triggers our conscious attention to a media message. To illustrate this, imagine yourself driving in your car with the radio playing while you are talking to your friend. Your attention is on the conversation with your friend instead of on the music coming from the car radio. Then your favorite song starts playing, and your attention shifts from the conversation to the music. Or perhaps your conversation is interrupted when your friend notices that the radio is playing her favorite song, and she starts singing along with the music. In both scenarios, you are being exposed to a stream of media messages from your car radio without paying conscious attention to them, but then something happens to trigger your conscious attention to the music from the radio.

The huge advantage of automatic processing of information is that it helps us get through a great many decisions with almost no effort. However, there are some serious disadvantages. When our minds are on automatic pilot, we may be missing a lot of messages that might be helpful or enjoyable to us. We might not have programmed all the triggers we need to help us get out of automatic processing when a useful message comes our way. Returning to the supermarket example, let's say you are very health conscious. Had you been less concerned with efficiency (getting through your shopping list as quickly as possible), you would have considered a wider range of products and read their labels for ingredients. Not all low-fat products have the same fat content; not all products with vitamins added include the same vitamins or the same proportions. Or perhaps you are very price conscious. Had you been less concerned with efficiency, you would have considered a wider variety of competing products and looked more carefully at the unit pricing, so you could get more value for your money. When we are too concerned with efficiency, we lose opportunities to expand our experience and to put ourselves in a position to make better decisions that can make us healthier, wealthier, and happier.

MEDIA INFLUENCE IS PERVASIVE AND CONSTANT

Because we spend so much of our time with automatic processing of media messages, the media exert a continual influence on us without our conscious realization. We typically follow our habits day after day because it is easier to do that than to have to rethink everything every day. But this raises an important question: Who has programmed the computer code that governs our automatic routines?

The answer to this question is that *we* have programmed some of our code but that there are also other forces that have been programming our code. Those other influences include our parents, our friends, society in general with its social norms, the educational system, along with a variety of other institutions (such as religion, politics, criminal justice system, government, and so on), and the media. Each of these is continually exerting an influence on how we think, how we feel, and how we behave. Some of this influence is obvious and easy to notice, but most of it occurs subtly and shapes our mental codes unconsciously. When we are not consciously paying attention to these influences, they quietly shape our mental codes without our being aware of it. This is especially the case with the media, because there are so many messages and because we open ourselves up to so much media exposure. Over time, this exposure becomes a habit that we never think about consciously. For many of us, we turn on the radio every time we get in our cars, turn on the television as soon as we get home, and turn on our computers when we get up in the morning. Once we open these channels—the radio, the television, the computer—storytellers pump messages into our subconscious. Advertisers continually program the way we think about ourselves. Advertisers program an uneasy self-consciousness into our minds so that we are on the lookout for products that will make us look, feel, and smell better. Advertisers have programmed many of us into a shopping habit. Do you realize that Americas spend more time shopping than do people in any other country? Americans go to shopping centers about once a week, more often than they go to houses of worship, and Americans now have more shopping centers than high schools. In a survey of teenage girls, 93 % said that shopping was their favorite activity (Schwartz, 2004). Advertising works by programming our automatic routines so that we shop even when it would be in our best interest to do other things.

The media are continually programming and re-programming our mental codes. They are adding information, altering our existing information structures, stimulating responses, and reinforcing certain patterns of thinking and acting. The media are thus exerting an influence on us whether we are aware of it or not.

Furthermore, media influence is constant. The media influence on us does not stop when we stop exposing ourselves to media messages. As long as the media have an influence on programming our mental codes, their influence shapes how we think and act any time those mental codes are automatically running in our conscious or unconscious minds. So when you go into the supermarket to buy food, you may not be looking at coupons from newspapers or magazines; you may not be looking at TV monitors or listening to radio or an iPod. But your purchasing decisions are being shaped by the "shopping code" running automatically in your mind, and much of your shopping code has been programmed by advertisers who have sent their messages to you through all kinds of media year after year—for your entire life.

HUGE KNOWLEDGE BASE ABOUT MEDIA EFFECTS

Scholars have generated a very large number or research studies that examine media effects. Estimates place the number of published studies in communication journals at about 6,200 (Potter & Riddle, 2006). There are also likely to be media effects studies published in scholarly journals outside of communication, such as in social science (psychology, sociology, anthropology, political science, economics), as well as humanistic (film studies, English, comparative literature) and applied fields (such as education, business, law, and health). Furthermore there are likely to be many books and governmental reports published on this popular topic. When we take all these additional outlets into consideration, there may be more than 10,000 published studies on the topic and an untold number of unpublished studies in the form of convention presentations and working papers.

All of this careful research activity has generated a very long list of media effects. This literature is now so large that many scholars have a difficult time organizing it all, so they often focus only on a small handful of more visible effects, such as the effect of violence on unstable people or the effect of sexual portrayals on impressionable teenagers. While these two effects are important, it is a serious mistake to limit our examination of media effects to a small number. Instead, we need to develop an appreciation for the wide range of effects that show up in the full spectrum of the population. Many of these effects are subtle to observe at any given time, but this does not make them unimportant. To the contrary, many of the most influential effects on each of us are those that occur during our everyday lives and sneak in "under the radar" so that we are unaware of how they are changing our habits and the way we think until someone points it out.

The purpose of this book is to ignore neither the common everyday effects nor the high-profile dramatic effects. This book will give you a map of the full range of media effects and to do it in a way to help you recognize those effects in yourself as well as in other people.

In the next four chapters, I show you some tools—basic terms, definitions, and ways of thinking about media effects—to help you as a reader get ready to process all this evidence without losing sight of the big picture—that is, the map of media effects. These tools will help you navigate through all the detail in Chapters 6 through 14.

By the end of the book, you should really appreciate the saying, "Knowledge is power," because you will have the knowledge that few people in our culture have, that is, an accurate vision of the big picture of media influence on you, your friends, and society. If you use that knowledge, you can powerfully control the effects in your life as well in the lives of other people.

SUMMARY

By this point in the chapter, you should have three ideas fixed well in your mind. First, you should realize that there is a great deal of information being produced each year and that production of new information continues to grow at an accelerating rate. We cannot avoid massive exposure to media messages in our information-saturated culture. Second, this continual flood of information influences us whether we pay conscious attention to it or not. And third, there is a large base of knowledge that clearly demonstrates that there is a wide range of media effects that are continually occurring in all kinds of people across the full span of our population.

Review Questions

1. Why is keeping your focus on the big picture of media effects so important?

2. List some indicators of media message saturation.

3. What is the most important challenge in coping with the flood of information?

4. What is automaticity?

5. In what way is media influence pervasive and constant?

6. Why is it difficult to organize the findings in the research literature on media effects?

Further Thinking Questions

1. Think about your own media message exposures.

   - What are your favorite media? Why are those your favorites?
   - What are your favorite types of messages (news, action/adventure movies, situation comedies, games, vampire stories, romances, reality competitions, sports, or others)? Why are these your favorites?
   - How much time do you spend with all the media on an average week?

2. Think about the automatic routines you use unconsciously to filter media messages.

   • How well do these routines work for you?
   • Can you think of any changes you should make to these routines?

3. Before you read any further in this book, think about the media effects that have been happening to you in your everyday life.

   • Take out a sheet of paper and draw a vertical line down the middle. Label the left side "Negative Effects" and the right side "Positive Effects." See how many effects you can list in each column.
   • When you are finished, put the paper aside. Then refer back to it as you read through Chapters 6 through 12.

Defining Key Ideas

Source: ©iStockphoto.com/Destonian

Nature of Audience Members
The Human Mind as Machine
Interpretive Beings
Media Exposure
Exposure and Attention
Physical Exposure
Perceptual Exposure
Psychological Exposure
Attention
Exposure States
Attentional State
Automatic State
Transported State
Self-Reflexive State
Information-Processing Tasks
Filtering
Meaning Matching
Meaning Construction

Defining Key Ideas

This chapter lays the foundation for the rest of the book. First we deal with the nature of media audience members, then we move onto the defining the key ideas of media exposure, information-processing tasks, and algorithm. Because each of these terms is difficult to define in a precise manner, many people avoid defining them, assuming that everyone will know what they are talking about. This is a mistake. While many of these terms may seem familiar, they are likely to have a wide variety of meanings among scholars and especially among people in everyday language. Therefore, it is important in this textbook to define the key foundational terms clearly. Once you understand how these key terms are defined, the rest of the book will be easier to read.

NATURE OF AUDIENCE MEMBERS

The most fundamental starting place for examining media effects is to consider the nature of humans and how they process meaning from media messages. Scholars who conduct research on media effects have engaged in a longstanding debate about the nature of humans when they encounter media messages. One side of the debate argues that the human mind is like a machine that automatically processes meaning from the outside, then stores those learned meanings in the brain. When people encounter a media message, their minds decode the symbols automatically and everyone arrives at the same meaning. The other side of the debate argues that people are interpretive beings who have the freedom to construct any kind of meaning they want out of any message. Let's examine each of these two positions in a bit more detail.

The Human Mind as Machine

One view of the human mind is that it operates as a machine that is wonderfully efficient at making sense of all the chaos of stimuli we encounter every day in our lives. It is able to process the mass of stimuli very quickly and arrive at standard meanings that are shared by other humans. If people did not share meaning, communication would not be possible. When we talk to people, we must assume that they will have the same meaning for words as we do. We all need to learn these common meanings, so when we are toddlers and our parents teach us to talk, they are helping us memorize certain common meanings for the sounds of words. In school, when we learn to read, we must memorize the meanings of the vocabulary words. The more words we can recognize and the better we can access those meanings, the better we can read. So the human mind must acquire many common meanings for words, pictures, sounds, smells, and sensations.

The human mind is very fast in accessing those learned meanings when it encounters stimuli. For example, the average person reads at about 300 words a minute. This means that as our eyes scan over a printed page or a screen, we are able to recognize 300 words and access the meaning of each of those words within a minute. That is very fast!

As we go through our everyday experiences, we encounter all kinds of images, words, and sounds delivered by the media. If our minds were not able to process all this information quickly, we would become paralyzed by the first few messages we experience at the beginning of a day. To avoid this paralysis, we "boot up" some mental code and let it run automatically. This allows us to navigate through thousands of messages every day with almost no effort. Thus mental codes allow our minds to be very powerful information processors.

Interpretive Beings

Another view of the human mind is that people are interpretive beings who continually create meaning for themselves. We have a great deal of freedom to think for ourselves, and this allows for a wide variety of opinions, experiences, and lifestyles. We are able to break our habits and routines any time we want and do something in a completely different way. We can listen to someone talk to us and reject his or her meaning because we interpret things in a very different way. We can go to the movies with four friends, and afterward find out that the five of us had five totally different interpretations of the movie.

We as humans have the power to reject the common meanings and wander off in a completely new direction of meaning. People are creating new stories all the time. People are fantasizing about things that never existed. People make up the truth and lie in order to get their way.

The debate about whether humans are machines or interpretive, creative beings has generated a very large body of research literature both by behaviorist social scientists (who examine the commonalities among people) as well as by humanistic scholars (who focus more on the uniquenesses across people). This has been especially important because media effects researchers have found times when people act rather like machines (that is, there are certain factors that affect all people the same way) and other times when people act very different from one another (that is, where everyone constructs a different interpretation of the same media message). In the upcoming chapters, you will see many examples of both.

MEDIA EXPOSURE

Now it is time to examine the issue of media exposure. What does it mean to be exposed to a media message? In this section you will see that exposure includes some things you might not have considered before. That is, exposure is not the same thing as attention, and furthermore there is a range of exposure states that we use to experience media messages. With some of these states, it seems we are not paying attention to media messages at all, yet those messages still have a way of getting into our minds and later affecting us in all sorts of ways.

Exposure and Attention

In everyday language, *exposure* is a term that is often used synonymously with the term *attention;* but when we study media effects, we need to be more precise and draw an important distinction between the two terms. This distinction says that there are three kinds of exposure: physical, perceptual, and psychological. Only when all three conditions of exposure are met can there be attention.

Physical Exposure. Physical exposure requires some sort of proximity (both in time and space) to a message. This means that the media message and the person must occupy the same physical space at the same time in order for this type of exposure to take place. Thus space and time are regarded as barriers to exposure. If a magazine is lying face-up on a table in a room and Harry walks through that room, Harry is physically exposed to the message on the cover of the magazine but not to any of the messages inside the magazine unless Harry picks it up and flips through the pages. Also, if Harry does not walk through that room when the magazine is on the table, there is no physical exposure to any of the magazine's messages. Likewise if a radio program is playing in a room over the lunch hour, then is turned off at 1 p.m., anyone who walks through that room after 1 p.m. is not physically exposed to that radio program.

Perceptual Exposure. The perceptual consideration refers to a human's sensory bandwidth or the ability to receive appropriate sensory input through the visual and auditory senses. There are limits to the abilities of a human's sense organs. For example, human sensitivity to sound frequency extends from around 16 Hz and 20,000 Hz, but sounds are heard best when they are between 1,000 Hz and 4,000 Hz (Metallinos, 1996; Plack, 2005). A dog whistle is pitched at a frequency higher than 20,000 Hz, so humans cannot perceive that sound, that is, it is outside their range of human sensitivity to sounds. Any auditory or visual signal that occurs outside of a person's sense organs ability to perceive it is nonexposure.

The perceptual criterion, however, has a feature beyond simple bandwidth; we must also consider the connection between the sensory input and the processing in the brain. There are instances when the sensory input gets to the brain in one form, but then the brain transforms the raw stimuli into another form. For example, when we watch a movie in a theater, we are exposed to individual static images projected at about 24 images per second. But humans cannot perceive 24 individual images in a given second, so our brains miss seeing the 24 individual static pictures and instead "see" motion. Also with film projection, there is a brief time between each of those 24 individual images every second when the screen is blank, but the eye–brain connection is not quick enough to process the blanks, so we do not "see" those blanks as blanks; instead we only see smooth motion. If the projection rate of images were to slow down to under 10 images per second, we would begin to see a flutter; that is, our brains would begin to see the blanks, because the replacement of still images is slow enough for the eye–brain connection to begin processing them.

The same limits are applied to watching television, where the screen appears to present motion pictures in a full range of color. But the television screen itself presents hundreds of thousands of glowing dots called *pixels,* each of which continues through cycles of glowing with one of three colors, then fading, then glowing and fading, over and over, dozens of times each second. As humans, we are not capable of seeing the individual pixels, so instead we perceive more than the three colors as our brains blur the three colors together in all kinds of combinations so we see the full spectrum of colors. Also, the pixel cycles of glowing and fading occur too fast for us to see them, and instead our brains perceive the total picture on the screen.

Stimuli that are outside the boundaries of human perception are called subliminal. Subliminal messages can leave no psychological trace because they cannot be physically perceived; that is, humans lack the sensory organs to take in stimuli and/or the hard wiring in the brain to be sensitive to them.

There is a widespread misconception that the mass media put people at risk for "subliminal communication." This belief is based on confusing "subliminal" with "subconscious." There is an important distinction that needs to be made between subliminal and subconscious, because they are two very different things and they have two very different implications for exposure. Subliminal refers to being outside a human's ability to sense or perceive; thus it is always regarded as nonexposure. However, once media stimuli cross over the subliminal line and are able to be sensed and perceived by humans, it is regarded as exposure. But this does not mean that all exposure is conscious, and this brings us to the third criterion in our definition: psychological.

Psychological Exposure. In order for psychological exposure to occur, there must be some trace element created in a person's mind. This element can be an image, a sound, an emotion, a pattern, and so on. It can last for a brief time (several seconds in short-term memory then cleared out) or a lifetime (when cataloged into long-term memory). It can enter the mind consciously (often called the *central route*) where people are fully aware of the elements in the exposure, or it can enter the mind unconsciously (often called the *peripheral route*) where people are unaware that elements are being entered into their minds (see Petty & Cacioppo, 1986). Thus there is a great variety of elements that potentially can meet this criterion for psychological exposure.

Attention. In order for attention to occur, a person must first clear all three of the exposure hurdles described: physical, perceptual, and psychological exposure. However, these three things alone do not guarantee attention; something else must also occur. That something else is conscious awareness of the media message. As you can now see, there are a lot of things that have to happen in order for us to pay attention to a media message. For this reason, attention rarely occurs compared to all the opportunities for attention that are presented to us continually each day. Harold Pashler, who wrote *The Psychology of Attention* (1998), explains that at any given moment, awareness encompasses only a tiny proportion of the stimuli impinging on a person's sensory systems. Furthermore, while we are paying attention to one thing, our attention can be distracted away to another thing. Pashler says there are times when "attention is directed or grabbed without any voluntary choice having taken place, even against strong wishes to the contrary" (p. 3). Thus when we are paying attention to a conversation with our roommate, our attention can be grabbed by an image that pops up on our computer screen and we shift our attention away from our roommate to the screen.

Exposure States

There are big differences in how we experience the exposure to media messages, depending on the psychological state we are in when we encounter a message. There are four possible exposure states: attentional, automatic, transported, and self-reflexive. Each of these states is qualitatively different from the other three; that is, you will have a different experience with a given media message depending on which state you are in when you encounter that message. Let's take a closer look at these four exposure states.

Attentional State. When you are in the attentional state, you are conscious of being exposed to media messages, and you pay attention to the message as you are exposed to it. Often you have done some work to find the message, such as looking up TV shows in a channel guide or searching through websites on the Internet. This does not necessarily mean that you have a high level of concentration, although that is possible. The key feature of the attentional state is that you have a conscious awareness of the messages during exposures.

Within the attentional state there is a range of attention depending on how much of your mental resources you devote to the exposure. At minimum, you must be aware of the message and consciously track it, but there is a fair degree of variation in the degree of concentration, which can range from partial to quite extensive processing depending on the number of elements handled and the depth of analysis employed.

Automatic State. When you are in the automatic state of exposure, you are not consciously aware of those messages in your physical environment. Let's say you are reading this book and concentrating on what the words mean, but at the same time you have a radio playing songs in the background, the TV is on in the next room, and your computer screen is showing pop-up ads. Your mind is on automatic pilot as it screens out all those sounds and sights that are not on the page of the book you are reading, yet your mind is monitoring those sounds and sights unconsciously so it can screen them all out; during this automatic monitoring, certain sounds and images are recorded in your unconscious mind, so you were continually exposed to those messages even though you were not paying attention to them. This screening-out continues automatically with no effort until some element in a message breaks through your automatic filtering process and captures your attention, such as your favorite song coming on the radio; you shift your attention away from the book and start singing along with the song.

In the automatic processing state, message elements are physically perceived but processed automatically in an unconscious manner. This exposure state resides above the threshold of human sense perception but below the threshold of conscious awareness.

Source: Thinkstock Images/Comstock/Thinkstock

The person is in a perceptual flow that continues until an interruption stops the exposure or "bumps" the person's perceptual processing into a different state of exposure, or until the media message moves outside of a person's physical or perceptual ability to be exposed to it.

In the automatic state, people can look active to outside observers, but they are not thinking about what they are doing. People in the automatic state can be flipping through the pages of a magazine or clicking through the channels on a TV. While there is evidence of behavior, this does not necessarily mean that people's minds are engaged and that they are making decisions. Rather the decisions are happening to them automatically.

Exposure to much of the media, especially radio and television, is in the automatic state. People have no conscious awareness of the exposure when it is taking place, nor do they have a recollection of many of the details in the experience if they are asked about it later.

Transported State. When you are in the transported exposure state, you are swept away by the media message; that is, you are drawn into the experience of the message so much that you lose track of time and place. For example, watching a movie in a theater, people can get so caught up in the action that they feel they are submerged in it. They experience the same intense emotions as the characters do. Their concentration level is so high that they lose touch with their real-world environment. They lose the sense that they are in a theater. They lose track of real time; instead they experience narrative time; that is, they feel time pass like the characters feel time pass.

The transported state is not simply the high end of the attentional state. Instead, the transported state is qualitatively different than the attentional state. While attention is very high in the transported state, the attention is also very narrow; that is, people have tunnel vision and focus on the media message in a way that eliminates the barrier between them and the message. People are swept away and "enter" the message. In this sense, it is the opposite of the automatic state where people stay grounded in their social worlds and are unaware of the media messages in their perceptual environment; in the transported exposure state, people enter the media message and lose track of their social worlds.

Self-Reflexive State. When you are in the self-reflexive state, you are hyperaware of the message *and of your own processing of the message.* It is as if you are sitting on your shoulder and monitoring your own reactions as you experience the message. This represents the fullest degree of awareness; that is, people are aware of the media message, their own social worlds, their positions in the social world while they process the media message. In the self-reflexive exposure state, the viewer exercises the greatest control over perceptions by reflecting on questions such as: Why am I exposing myself to this message?, What am I getting out of this exposure and why?, and Why am I making these interpretations of meaning? Not only is there analysis, but there is meta-analysis. This means that the person is not only analyzing the media message, he or she is also analyzing his or her analysis of the media message.

While the self-reflexive and transported states might appear similar in that they are characterized by high involvement of audience members, the two exposure states are very different. In the transported state, people are highly involved emotionally and they lose themselves in the action. In contrast, the self-reflexive state is characterized by people being highly involved cognitively and very much aware of themselves as they analytically process the exposure messages.

INFORMATION-PROCESSING TASKS

We engage in a series of three information-processing tasks as we encounter media messages. These tasks are filtering, meaning matching, and meaning construction. First, we encounter a message and are faced with the task of deciding whether to filter the message out (ignore it) or filter it in (process it). If we decide to filter it in, then we must make sense of it, that is, recognize the symbols and match our learned definitions to the symbols. Then we move on to constructing our own meanings for the message.

Sometimes we engage in this sequence of tasks in a very conscious manner, such that we are aware of and control our decisions. However, most of the time, we engage in this sequence of tasks unconsciously; that is, our minds are on automatic pilot wherein our mental code automatically makes filtering and meaning-matching decisions and thereby short-circuits the meaning construction process. Let's examine each of these three information processing tasks in more detail.

Summary of Three Tasks of Information Processing

Filtering Message

Task: To make decisions about which messages to filter out (ignore) and which to filter in (pay attention to)

Goal: To attend to only those messages that have some kind of usefulness for the person and ignore all other messages

Focus: Messages in the environment

Meaning Matching

Task: To use basic competencies to recognize referents and locate previously learned definitions for each

Goal: To access previously learned meanings efficiently

Focus: Referents in messages

Meaning Construction

Task: To use skills in order to move beyond meaning matching and to construct meaning for one's self in order to personalize and get more out of a message

Goal: To interpret messages from more than one perspective as a means of identifying the range of meaning options, then choose one or synthesize across several

Focus: One's own knowledge structures

Filtering

As we go through our day, we are continually flooded with information. In order to protect ourselves from being overwhelmed, we automatically filter that flood by ignoring most messages while paying attention to a small percentage of messages that gets through our filtering. Recall from the previous chapter that most of this filtering is accomplished when our minds are on automatic pilot. During this automatic process of filtering, our attention is governed by a mental code that tells our senses to avoid paying attention to all messages (filtering them out) until an element in a particular message trips a trigger code in our mind and we begin paying attention to the message.

Once we have filtered in a message (start paying attention to it), we need to determine its meaning. This determination of meaning is two—not one—tasks. First, we match meaning. Oftentimes, the information processing sequence stops with this task. But sometimes we move into the next task of constructing meaning.

Meaning Matching

With meaning matching, meaning is assumed to reside outside the person in an authority such as a teacher, an expert, a dictionary, a textbook, or the like. The task for the person is to find those meanings and memorize them. Parents and the institution of education are primarily responsible for passing this authoritative information along to each next generation. The media are also a major source of information, and for many people, the media have attained the status of an authoritative source, so people accept the meanings presented there and simply memorize those meanings.

Meaning matching is the process of recognizing elements (referents) in the message and accessing our memory to find the meanings we have memorized for those elements. This is a relatively automatic task. It may require a good deal of effort to learn to recognize symbols in media messages and to memorize their standard meanings, but once learned this process becomes routine. To illustrate, think back to when you first learned to read. You had to learn how to recognize words printed on a page. Then you had to memorize the meaning of each word. The first time you saw the sentence "Dick threw the ball to Jane" it required a good deal of work to divide the sentence into words, to recall the meaning of each word, and to put it all together. With practice, you were able to perform this process more quickly and more easily. Learning to read in elementary school is essentially the process of being able to recognize a longer list of referents and to memorize their meanings. Some referents in media messages were words, some were numbers, some were pictures, and some were sounds.

This type of learning develops competencies. By *competency,* I mean that either you are able to do something correctly or you are not. For example, when you see the phrase "2 + 2" you either recognize the "2" referents as particular quantities or you do not. You either recognize the "+" referent as addition or you do not. You can perform this mathematical operation and arrive at 4, or you cannot. Working with these referents does not require—or allow for—individual interpretation and creative meaning construction. Competencies are our abilities to recognize standard referents and recall the memorized denoted meanings for those referents. If we did not have a common set of referents and shared meanings for each of these referents, communication would not be possible. Education at the elementary level is the training of the next generation to develop the basic competencies of recognizing these referents and memorizing the designated meaning for each one.

Meaning Construction

While meaning matching is essentially a task that can be accomplished well automatically once we have acquired some basic competencies, meaning construction is a much more challenging task. Meaning construction is a process wherein we must do things to the messages in order to create meaning for ourselves. The things we do to messages require the skills of analysis and evaluation for screening messages consciously. Then, when information is screened in, we must use other skills such as induction, deduction, grouping, and synthesis to incorporate the new information with our existing knowledge structures to construct our own meaning.

Many meanings can be constructed from any media message; furthermore, there are many ways to go about constructing that meaning. Thus, we cannot learn a complete set of rules to accomplish this task; instead, we need to be guided by our own information goals, and we need to use well-developed skills creatively in order to construct a path to reach our goals. For these reasons, meaning construction rarely takes place in an automatic fashion. Instead, we need to make conscious decisions when we are constructing meaning for ourselves. Also, every meaning construction task is different, so we cannot program our minds to follow the same one procedure automatically when we are confronted with a range of meaning construction tasks.

While meaning matching relies on competencies, meaning construction relies on skills. This is one of the fundamental differences between the two tasks of meaning matching and meaning construction. Competencies are categorical; that is, either you have a competency or you do not. However, skill ability is not categorical; on any given skill, there is a wide range of ability. That is, some people have little ability, whereas other people have enormous ability. Also, skills are like muscles. Without practice, skills become weaker. With practice and exercise, they grow stronger.

To illustrate this distinction between competency and skills, let's return to the example of reading as it is taught in elementary school. Children learn to recognize referents that are words. This is a competency; that is, either a child knows how to recognize a given word or she or he does not. Also, in elementary school, children learn how to vocalize those words and how to fit those words together into sentences. Again, these are competencies; either they can do these tasks or they cannot. By the time people have completed elementary school, it is assumed that they have achieved a basic level of reading competency, yet they still practice reading. At these more advanced grades, however, reading is regarded less as a competency and more as a skill. Students focus on how to get more meaning out of paragraphs and stories. For example, when teachers ask students to read aloud in elementary school, it is to check students' competencies at word recognition and pronunciation. But when teachers ask students to read aloud in high school, it is to check students' skills at reading expression, which indicates how they are constructing their own meanings. Also, at higher grades, students are asked to write essays about stories they have read and express what that stories mean to them; thus the focus shifts from the competencies of meaning matching to the skills of meaning construction.

The two processes of meaning matching and meaning construction are not independent; they are intertwined. To construct meaning, we first have to recognize referents and understand the sense in which those referents are being used in the message. Thus, the meaning-matching process is more fundamental, because the product of the meaning-matching process then is imported into the meaning construction process.

ALGORITHMS

The key idea in explaining how people encounter media messages and process information from those messages is the algorithm. An *algorithm* is a set of mental codes that people use both consciously and unconsciously to make sense of media messages. Consciously, an algorithm is used as a guide in a thinking process to tell people where to start on a path of thinking; it lays out the steps in a process along with the options at each decision point; it provides direction down the path toward the goal; and it indicates when the path is completed, that is, a decision is reached. For example, you have an algorithm about accessing clips on YouTube. Your algorithm tells you how to turn on your Internet device, how to go to the YouTube website, and how to access a list of clips that you might like to watch. Your algorithm contains images from your past viewings that suggest which of the listed viewings today might be of interest to you. Your algorithm tells you how to play a clip, adjust its volume, adjust its size on the screen, and how to fast forward or replay parts of it. This algorithm was built by you through continual previous exposures with YouTube clips. If you've had a lot of YouTube sessions, your algorithm is likely to be very detailed and run very efficiently.

People construct these algorithms in order to make sense of their worlds, then continue to use them as they are constantly confronted with the challenge of achieving efficiency in this sense making. Algorithms are constructions that reside in a person's memory. These algorithms are composed of information of a cognitive, emotional, aesthetic, and moral nature; they include associations among facts, images, words, sounds, feelings, and judgments. And algorithms are organic; that is, they are continually in a state of change as people acquire new experiences and make adjustments to their existing algorithms to make them more useful and more efficient.

When a person uses a particular algorithm, it becomes more familiar to her. With more frequent use, the algorithm gets easier and easier to use; that is, over time it requires less and less mental effort to use. Humans like efficiency, so the path toward less mental effort is an attractive one. Eventually the use of an algorithm can become routine; that is, in a given situation the algorithm is loaded in a person's mind automatically and runs to completion without the person needing to expend any mental effort because all the decisions are habitually made in the same way. Thus when an algorithm is accessed in the same way repeatedly over a long period of time, it is what cognitive psychologists refer to as *chronically accessible* (Bargh, 1984).

Origin of Algorithms

People are not born with these information-processing algorithms; instead, people must either acquire them or build them as they experience life. Algorithms can be acquired from another person or the mass media, wherein someone else did the construction and passed it along to another individual, or they can be constructed by the person him- or herself.

Acquisition. The acquisition can be through a conscious or unconscious process. *Conscious acquisition* refers to when a person has an intention to learn something, usually the sender of the message has the intention to teach. People read a book, magazine, or newspaper or watch the evening news or a documentary with the intention of learning a particular fact or, more diffusely, picking up more information of a general nature about a topic in which they are interested.

Acquisition can also occur unconsciously. This is often referred to as *unintentional learning, incidental learning,* or *implicit learning.* When people expose themselves to entertainment messages, they are not trying to learn specific facts or social lessons; instead they simply want to be entertained or to escape their day-to-day lives. However, they can pick up facts and social lessons unintentionally, that is, incidental to their main purpose.

Construction. When a person constructs a new algorithm, the process is conscious and it requires an expenditure of mental energy; it is usually goal directed but it need not be. The construction process usually involves skills that the person uses to transform the media message information in some way to make it fit better into his or her existing set of algorithms.

Construction processes vary in terms of importance to the individual. When a construction process is of high importance, the person typically uses a *rational strategy.* With a rational strategy, the construction process has a clear goal, the mental energy expended is high, and the consequences of making a faulty construction are strong and negative. However, many construction processes are of low importance, so the person is governed by an ambiguous or emotionally felt but not clearly articulated goal, such as a drive to reduce uncertainty or dissonance. The degree of mental energy expended is small so that the person can achieve efficiency, that is, a quick resolution with minimal expenditure of resources. In these situations, a person typically does not use a rational strategy; instead she is likely to use a *shortcut strategy* in order to finish the task as quickly as possible, or he might use an *irrational strategy* in order to construct an algorithm that "feels" right even though it does not make a lot of logical sense.

Once an algorithm has been stored in memory, the person loses track of how it was created, that is, whether it was created using a rational strategy, a shortcut strategy, or an irrational strategy. The algorithm is a tool that is available for use in solving future problems. The more an algorithm is used, the more habitual it becomes, that is, the more likely it will continue to be used. The more an algorithm is used in an automatic or transported state, the less likely it is going to be examined or altered; instead the fact that it is used again is reinforcing. In the attentional state, the algorithm runs by taking a person from one decision point to the next. At each decision point, the algorithm presents the options but leaves the selections up to the person who is consciously making the decisions. In the self-reflexive state, the person confronts the algorithm as if it were a specimen on the dissecting table. The person is not using the algorithm online in a process of decision making; instead, the person is like a programmer analyzing the code. The person is not using the algorithm but instead examining it.

The algorithm is a construction of the individual him- or herself and also of conditioning by the media and other experiences over time. Thus the code in an algorithm is created and altered in conscious ways and unconscious ways. When people are in the attentional—and especially in the self-reflexive—exposure states, they are aware of their goals, the elements in the messages, and the processing of information; in this case they are largely in control of additions to and alterations of their codes. When people are in the automatic—and often in the transported—exposure states, they are largely unaware of the conditioning influence of the media, and therefore additions to and alterations of their codes are not under their control.

Use of Algorithms

Algorithms are accessed by individuals during media exposure situations and are used to guide decisions, regardless of whether those decisions are conscious or unconscious. Sometimes people will consciously access an appropriate algorithm to help them process

Structured Glossary of Terms About Media Effects

Algorithms   Templates (or sequences of mental codes) that people use to (a) guide their perceptions during exposures, and (b) interpret the meaning of messages in their exposures. Algorithms are constructions by individuals and are the product of their experiences filtered through their mental processes of sorting and meaning making; they are also programmed by the mass media. (*Note:* In the research literature, scholars use a variety of terms for these mental guides—*schema, mental models, cognitive maps*, and others. Each of these terms has a highly technical meaning, and those meanings often vary across scholars. For those reasons, I use the term *algorithm* as a kind of general umbrella term to refer to all of those meanings).

- The filtering task is governed by algorithms that are programmed by both the individual and the mass media.
- The algorithms used in the meaning-matching task are largely definitions that have been provided by authorities and internalized by the person so their use is automatic. They require basic competencies to perform well.
- The algorithms used in the meaning construction task are largely suggestive guides because meaning construction is always a partially specified problem. They require the use of higher-order skills to perform well.

Exposure states   The kind of experiences a person has when encountering media messages. There are four exposure states: attentional, automatic, transported, and self-reflexive. These are qualitatively different states that are separated by a liminal threshold (line of perception).

- In the attentional state, audience members process message elements consciously. They actively interact with the elements in the messages and can exercise some control over the processing, which can range from partial to quite extensive processing depending on the number of elements handled and the depth of analysis employed.
- In the automatic state, audience members are not consciously aware of the exposure. Messages are processed but not consciously or in the immediate control of the audience member.
- In the transported state, audience members experience tunnel vision with a very high level of concentration focused on the message to the point where the barrier between the message and the audience members disappears; all stimuli outside of this focus is ignored.

(Continued)

(Continued)

- In the self-reflexive state, audience members are not only consciously aware of the elements in the message, but they are also aware of their processing of those elements.

Information-processing tasks   Audiences for mass media messages are continually engaged in a series of three information-processing tasks of filtering, meaning matching, and meaning construction.

Media exposure   Occurs when a person meets the criteria for physical exposure, perceptual exposure, and psychological exposure. Media exposure does not require attention on the part of the audience member; that is, the person can be exposed in nonattentional states.

---

an unfolding narrative, such that when new characters appear, people can read a few cues in their appearance and use the algorithm to fill in other likely characteristics of the characters. Algorithms also provide guidance information about other message characteristics such as plot, setting, theme, and passage of time. However, at other times, algorithms will load automatically and "run in the background" as a person devotes mental energy to other tasks. Thus algorithms can activate automatically and run without requiring mental effort so that the person can navigate many exposure decisions very efficiently.

SUMMARY

This chapter laid the foundation for four ideas: nature of audience, media exposure, information-processing tasks, and algorithms. A definition was developed for each, and those definitions are used throughout this book.

As for nature of the audience, researchers have treated humans both as machine-like processors of information and as creative constructors of their own meanings. With media effects, there are times when we all respond the same way to a particular message and there are other times when we exhibit responses that are very different from those of other audience members.

Media exposure is not the same thing as attention to message; it is more involved. Media exposure requires physical presence of a message, the message being within a person's perceptual capabilities, and the recording of some psychological trace element. When exposure occurs, we experience the message in one of four exposure states: attentional, automatic, transported, and self-reflexive.

There are three information processing tasks of filtering, meaning matching, and meaning construction. Each of these tasks is governed by algorithms, which are automatic routines that guide our decision making about media messages.

Review Questions

1. Explain the two positions in the debate about how the human mind works.

2. What is the difference between exposure and attention?

3. What is the difference between subliminal and subconscious?

4. What are the four exposure states and how are they different from one another?

5. What are the three information-processing tasks and how are they different from one another?

6. What are the differences between competencies and skills?

7. What is an algorithm and how is it important to media effects?

8. Define *mass media*.

Further Thinking Questions

1. Think about your media exposure habits.
   - Can you remember any details about why you created those habits, that is, what initially attracted you to those types of messages?
   - Have any of your media exposure habits changed over time? If so, why?

2. Can you think of any media messages you have recently experienced in the transported state?

3. Can you think of any media messages you have recently experienced in the self-reflexive state?

4. Think about your favorite media messages.
   - With how much of that exposure are you engaged in meaning matching?
   - With how much of that exposure are you constructing your own specialized meanings?

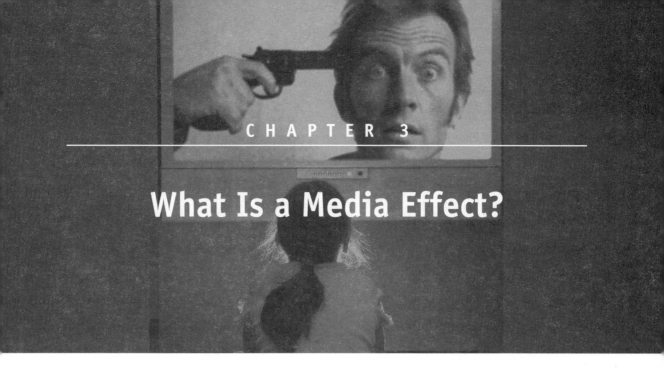

Source: ©iStockphoto.com/maica

CHAPTER 3

What Is a Media Effect?

CHAPTER 3

What Is a Media Effect?

This chapter focuses on the idea of media effect. The chapter begins with an analysis of the key elements that we must consider when thinking about media effects, then uses those elements to build to a broad definition. The chapter then presents two Media Effects Templates (METs) as a way of organizing the great variety of effects. These METs serve as the maps of media effects that will be used to structure all remaining chapters.

DEFINING MEDIA EFFECT

It is important to use a broad perspective on media effects in order to understand the incredibly wide range of influence the media exert and also to appreciate the truly wide range of effects research that has been produced by media scholars. However, when people in their everyday lives think about media effects, they typically limit their thinking to negative things that happen to other people after watching too much "bad" content. For example, people believe that exposure to media violence causes aggression; media stories with sexual depictions lead to risky sexual behaviors; and bad language leads to coarse expression in the population. These beliefs continually show up in public opinion polls. And these topics are popular among media effects researchers. This type of public opinion and this type of research are so prevalent that many people have come to think of media effects as primarily being negative behaviors that show up immediately after exposure to particular media messages. This perspective is a useful starting place for thinking about media effects, but then we need to move on to a broader perspective. To begin this movement toward a broader perspective, let's examine the key issues we need to deal with when considering a complete conceptualization of media effects.

Key Issues in Media Effects Definitions

When we look across all the ways that scholars write about media effects, we can see that there are eight issues that concern them. These issues are timing (immediate vs. long term), duration (temporary vs. permanent), valence (negative or positive), change (difference vs. no difference), intention (or non-intention), the level of effect (micro vs. macro), direct (or indirect), and manifestation (observable vs. latent). When you understand these issues, you can appreciate why we have such a wide variety of things that have been identified as media effects.

Timing. In everyday life, most people think that media effects are things that show up during a media exposure or immediately afterward. For example, if parents notice that their young children begin to wrestle aggressively when they watch Saturday morning cartoons, those parents are likely to see a connection between the TV shows and their children's aggressive behavior. Of course, the media exert immediate effects, but they also exert influences on people over the long term, when it takes a long time before we can see any evidence of an effect.

Duration. Some effects last a short time, then go away, while other effects are permanent. For example, Cindy may listen to the words of a new song on her iPod and remember those words the rest of her life, or she may not be able to remember them an hour later.

Valence. In everyday life, people typically think of media effects as being negative, such as exposure to violence leading to antisocial behavior. But the media also exert positive effects. We can learn all kinds of useful things by reading newspapers, magazines, books, and websites. We can use music and stories from all kinds of media to shape our moods and trigger pleasant emotions. We can use the media to interact with other people and make us feel part of interesting communities, both real and virtual.

There are times when a particular effect can be either negative or positive depending on the context. Let's take the desensitization effect as an example of an effect that can be either positive or negative. Desensitization can be positive when a therapist helps her patient overcome an irrational fear of flying in airplanes by showing her patient television shows about people happily boarding airplanes and enjoying air travel. But desensitization can be a negative effect when people lose their natural inclination to feel sympathy for other people after watching years of characters being victimized by violence.

Change. When we think of effects, we typically think of change, that is, a change in behavior or a change in attitude. If there is no change, some people argue that there is no effect. But some effects—perhaps the most important and powerful media effects—show up as no change. For example, most advertising has as its purpose the reinforcing of existing habits among consumers. Advertisers do not want their brand-loyal customers to change; instead they want to reinforce existing buying behaviors. If we ignore the reinforcement effect—where there is no change in behavior—then we will have too narrow a perspective on media effects.

Intention. When the media industries are criticized for negative effects, one of their defense strategies is to point out that they did not intend to create a negative effect. For example, when the media are criticized for presenting so much violence in Hollywood movies, producers of those movies will say that they are merely trying to entertain people, not teach them to behave violently. However, there are many effects that occur even though the producers of those media messages, as well as the consumers of those messages, did not intend them to occur.

Level. Most of the research on media effects looks at individuals as the targets of the effects. Scholars have produced a very large literature documenting a wide array of effects on individuals. But the media also exert influences on more macro-level entities such as the public, society, and institutions.

The research studies that examine individual-level effects differ fundamentally from the research studies that examine macro-level effects. These differences are not only in methods needed to measure the effects but also in the types of questions addressed and the types of conclusions presented. Typically, individual-level studies use an experiment or a survey as they focus on how individual people respond to different media messages. In contrast, macro-level studies gather aggregated data from institutions, such as the courts (rates of conviction and incarceration), education (rates of graduation, average scores on standardized achievement tests by school district, and such), religion (size of memberships, attendances at various services, and such), politics (voting rates, public opinion polls on various issues and support for candidates, and the like).

Direct and Indirect. Sometimes the media exert a direct effect on individuals, while other times the effect is more indirect, such as through institutions. For example, a direct effect occurs when a person watches a political ad and decides to vote for a particular candidate. An indirect effect occurs when the media continually raise the prices for political advertising, so that candidates must spend much more time raising money, which makes them more beholden to organizations that give them the most money, which influences the

Source: ©iStockphoto.com/sjlocke

policies they support most, which influences the services that governmental bodies provide, which influences us as individuals. Even people who are never exposed to political ads are affected by them indirectly.

Manifestation. Some effects are easy to observe, such as when someone changes her behavior soon after being exposed to a particular media message. For example, Heather might be watching TV and see an ad for a special offer for a pizza. She grabs her phone, dials the number on the screen, and orders a pizza. But other effects are very difficult to observe; this does not necessarily mean they are not occurring or that the media are not exerting an influence.

The Definition

Now that you have seen the list of issues that underlie the thinking about media effects, you are ready for the working definition that structures this book. That definition is, Media-influenced effects are those things that occur as a result—either in part or in whole—from media influence. They can occur immediately during exposure to a media message, or they can take a long time to occur after any particular exposure. They can last for a few seconds or an entire lifetime. They can be positive as well as negative. They can show up clearly as changes but they can also reinforce existing patterns, in which case the effect appears as no change. They can occur whether the media have an intention for them to occur or not. They can affect individual people or all people in the form of the public. They can also affect institutions and society. They can act directly on a target (a person, the public, an institution, or society) or they can act indirectly. And, finally, they can be easily observable or they can be latent and therefore much more difficult to observe.

This definition of media effect is, of course, very broad. As such, it includes many things. That is the point of the definition. Remember that media messages are so constant and so pervasive that we are continually being exposed to media information either directly from media exposures or indirectly by other people talking about media exposures. Therefore, we need to acknowledge that the media are continually exerting an influence on us. However, this does not mean that the media are constantly causing effects in us, because we are always able to reject the media influence and create our own effects. But in order to reject the media influence, we have to know what it is we are rejecting, that is, what effects will occur if we do not do something to head them off. For this reason, it is important that you learn what the full range of media effects are and how the media influence contributes to those many effects.

Need to Organize Media Effects

Because this definition is so broad as to capture the full range of media effects, it encompasses a great many such effects. See a partial list of those effects in Exhibit 3.1. With such a large number of effects, it is important that we organize them in some way to make the challenge of understanding the full set manageable. For Exhibit 3.1, I organized the effects alphabetically. But this alphabetical organization is not a useful one unless you already knew of an effect and wanted to see if it appeared on this list; then the alphabetical listing

Exhibit 3.1 Partial List of Media Effects

Advertising	Cultivation	Homogenization
Affluent society	Cultural imperialism	Imitation
Agenda building	Culture of narcissism	Indirect effects
Agenda setting	Decision making	Information flow
Aggression	Diffusion of innovations	Information seeking
Associative network building	Direct effects	Integrated response
Attitude construct creation	Disinhibition	Interpretation by social class
Audience as commodification	Disposition altering	Interpretive resistance
Audience construction by media	Distribution of knowledge	Knowledge gap
Audience flow	Double action gatekeeping	Double jeopardy
Audience polarization	Drench	Least objectionable programming
Automatic activation	Elaboration likelihood	Levels of processing
Availability-valence altering	Elite pluralism	Limited capacity information processing
Buffering	Empathy activation	Marketplace alteration
Capacity limits	Encoding-decoding	Mass audience
Catharsis	Excitation transfer	Media access
Channel repertoire reinforcement	Exemplification	Media as culture industries
Character affiliation	Expectancy value	Media culture
Civic engagement	Fraction of selection	Media enjoyment
Coalition building	Framing	Media enjoyment as attitude
Cognitive dissonance	Gatekeeping	Media entertainment
Cognitive response	Global village	Media flow
Conservative/moralist decision making	Gratification seeking	Media system dependency
Consumer culture creation and reinforcement	Gravitation	Medium as message
	Hegemony	Message construction
Cue activation	Heuristic processing	Mood management
	Hidden persuaders	

(Continued)

Exhibit 3.1 (Continued)

Motivated attention and motivated processing	Power elite	Social construction of meaning
Neo-associationistic thinking	Priming	Social construction of media technologies
Neo-mass audience	Principled reasoning	Social identity
Network political priming	Profit-driven logic of safety	Social learning
News content	Program choice	Social norms
News diffusion	Proteus effect	Sociology of news
News factory	Pseudo-events blur reality	Spiral of silence
News frame creation	Psychodynamics	Synapse priming
News selection	Psychological conditioning	Technological determinism
Newsworker socialization	Rally effect	Television trivialization of public life
One-dimensional man	Reasoned action	Third-person effect
Parasocial interaction	Reception	Transactional effects
Perception of hostile media	Resource dependency	Transmission of information
Persuasion	Revealed preferences	Transportation of audiences
Play	Ritual reinforcement	Two-step flow
Pluralistic ignorance	Selective exposure	Uses and dependency
Political socialization	Selective gatekeeping	Uses and gratifications
Political signification	Selective perception	Videomalaise
Polysemic interpretations	Semiotic interpretations	
	Social cognitions	

could be useful. However, this form of organization does not help us see the underlying structure revealing how the various effects are related to one another.

Another way to organize effects is by topic area, such as violence, news, persuasion, sex, new technologies, social groups (Blacks, Latinos, gays, Arabs, older adults, and so on), sports, religion, occupations of characters, and invasions of privacy. While these and other topics are certainly interesting and relevant to media effects, they hardly constitute a coherent set. That is, there are some effects that span across several topic areas. Also, there are many effects that do not fit into an organization by topic, and many media effects would be left out of such an organizational scheme. Therefore organizing media effects by topic leaves us with an organizational scheme that is incomplete.

In the following section of the chapter, I present a design that is broad enough to include the full range of media effects and that is organized such that it shows how the different effects are related to one another. This organizational scheme begins by making a distinction between individual-level effects and macro-level effects. This individual/aggregate distinction is concerned with whether the effect is focused primarily on the individual person or whether the effect is focused primarily on a group of people. Individual-level effects can be studied by looking at changes (or non-changes) in one person at a time. Each person is a unit. Researchers ask questions of each person or observe the behavior of each person. Results of these research studies are reported as how the media affect individuals either immediately or over time. In contrast, aggregate effects are those that act on large groups of people where the focus is on the group rather than on individual people. Aggregate units are typically the public, society, and institutions, such as the criminal justice system, the economy, the political system, and so on.

ORGANIZING INDIVIDUAL-LEVEL MEDIA EFFECTS

How can we organize all the media effects that researchers have discovered? With those effects on individuals, there are two dimensions that are particularly useful. One of these is the type of effect, such as whether the effect influenced a person's behavior, attitude, emotion, and so on. The second of these is how the media exert their influence on the individual. When we put these two dimensions together we construct a matrix that has enough categories to help organize all these effects.

Type of Effects on Individuals

There are six types of effects on individuals. These six differ in terms of the part of the person affected or the character of the experience of the effect within an individual. These six are cognition, belief, attitude, affect, physiology, and behavior. All individual-level media effects studies examine how the media exert an influence on one or more of these six types.

A *cognitive media effect* occurs when media exposure influences a person's mental processes or the product of those mental processes. The cognitive effect that is easiest to document is the acquisition of factual information from media messages, particularly from books, newspapers, television news stories, and informational websites. The human mind can absorb this information through the process of memorization. However, the human mind can do far more than memorize; it can transform information into knowledge. This transformation of information can take the form of inferring patterns across media messages. The human mind can also group media messages in different ways to create new meanings. It can generalize beyond media messages to generate principles about real life. All of these mental activities are cognitive effects on individuals.

Beliefs have been defined as cognitions about the probability that an object or event is associated with a given attribute (Fishbein & Ajzen, 1975). Simply stated, a belief is faith that something is real or is true. The media continually create and shape our beliefs by showing us more of the world than we are able to see directly for ourselves. None of us has ever met George Washington, but we all believe he existed and was one of the founders of the United States as a country, because we have read about him in history books and websites and seen films about him. Each of us holds beliefs about the existence of a great many things that we have never seen directly in our real lives; many of these beliefs have come from media messages.

Attitudes are judgments about something. For example, people see a character in a film and make judgments about that character's attractiveness, hero status, likeability, and so on. When the media also present stories about people, events, issues, and products in the real world, these stories often trigger the need for us to make our own judgments about controversial issues, political candidates, advertised products, and such.

Affect refers to the feelings that people experience. This includes emotions and moods. The media can trigger emotions, especially fear, lust, anger, and laughter. The media also provide people with lots of opportunities to manage their moods, such that when we are feeling stressed with all the problems in our real lives, we can chill by listening to music, forget our problems by watching television, or lose ourselves in the experience of playing games on the Internet.

A *physiological effect* is an automatic bodily response. The body response can be either purely automatic (such as pupil dilation, blood pressure, galvanic skin response) or quasi-automatic (heart rate, sexual responses). For example, when people watch an action/adventure movie, their heart rates and blood pressure typically increase. Their muscles tense and their palms sweat. They are experiencing a fight-or-flight response that has been hard wired into humans' brains. Threats trigger attention, and the body prepares itself to fight a predator or to flee. This fight-or-flight effect has enabled the human race to survive for thousands of years.

Behaviors are typically defined as the overt actions of an individual (Albarracin, Zanna, Johnson & Kumkale, 2005). Media effects researchers have conducted a lot of studies in which they observe people's media exposure behaviors to see which media they use and how they use those media. Researchers also expose people to particular media messages, then observe their subsequent behaviors for things like aggression, use of advertised products, and debating of political issues.

Media-Influenced Functions

When any of the six types of effects occur in an individual, we need to determine whether or not that occurrence was influenced by the media. If we conclude that the effect was influenced by the media, then we have a media effect. This does not mean that the media were the sole cause of the type of effect; instead we mean that the media played some sort of a role in bringing about that effect.

How do the media exert their influence? There are four possible ways. These four ways generally span across all six types of effects. They are functions in the sense that they refer to distinct actions that influence and shape the character of an effect differently in each of the six categories of type.

These four media-influenced functions are acquiring, triggering, altering, and reinforcing. The first two of these functions influence immediate effects that would show up either during the exposure or immediately after. The third—altering—has features that can show up immediately during exposure as an immediate effect, but it also has other features that may take a longer period of time to manifest themselves. And the fourth function is a long-term effect that would take a long time to manifest itself. Let's examine each of these functions in some detail, then we will use them to construct a map to organize the range of individual level effects.

Acquiring. Every media message is composed of elements, and during exposures to these messages individuals acquire and retain some of these elements. Message elements include things like facts, images, sounds, a pundit's attitude about something, the depiction of a sequence of events, and so on. During a media exposure, a person could pay attention to certain elements in a message and keep those elements in his or her memory. This is an immediate effect because the element is committed to memory during the exposure to the message. This memory might last a few seconds or a few years, but it is not how long the memory lasts that determines whether the effect is an immediate one or not—it is when the effect first occurs.

The acquiring function is applicable to all types of effects except for physiology, where media messages have no power to *create* a physiological element in an individual. Individuals acquire information and store it in their memory structures. People can also acquire beliefs, attitudes, affective information, and behavioral sequences in the same manner through the use of the skill of memorization. With all of these types of effects, the media are creating something in a person's mind that was not there before the exposure. It is possible to argue that all of these effects are essentially cognitive, because they all require the use of the cognitive skill of memorization and the retention of information in the individual's memory. And that is a valid point. However, while the process and the skill used may be the same across categories, the nature of what is retained is very different. Thus the function remains the same, but the effect itself is different and requires different categories of cognition, attitude, and belief.

Triggering. During media exposures, the media can activate something that already exists in the individual. The triggering effect is applicable for all six categories of effects. A media message could activate the recall of previously learned information, the recall of an existing attitude or belief, an emotion, a physiological reaction, or a previously learned behavioral sequence.

The media can also trigger a process that sets a person off on a task involving many steps. For example, when people read some news coverage about a political candidate that they have never heard about before, they have no existing attitude about that candidate. During exposure to this news coverage, people can take the information from the news story and compare it to their standards for political candidates and create an attitude. This is different than simple acquisition, because the person is not memorizing someone else's attitude presented in the media but instead going through a construction process in the creation of his or her own attitude; in this case the media message element of a new piece of information triggered in the person the construction of a new attitude.

The media can also trigger a reconstruction process. A media message might present information that does not conform to a person's existing knowledge structure, so the person must do something to incorporate the new information into his or her existing knowledge structure. For example, let's say that Mark has a very favorable attitude about a particular breakfast cereal but then is exposed to a media message that presents facts about the breakfast cereal using contaminated ingredients; this new information is likely to trigger a reevaluation of his previously positive attitude.

Altering. During an exposure, the media can alter something that is already present in the individual. The altering effect works with all types of effects. Media messages can alter a person's knowledge structures with the addition of new facts. A belief can be altered when the media present a fact revealing that an individual's existing belief was faulty. The media can alter individuals' standards for use in constructing attitudes. Individuals who continually expose themselves to arousing elements in stories of horror and violence will have their natural fight-or-flight responses worn down. By shifting content, the media can alter a person's mood. When individuals continually play interactive games, this practice serves to improve their hand–eye coordination and reduce reaction times to stimuli.

The alteration can show up immediately (that is, during an exposure or immediately after the exposure to the media message) or it can take a long time to show up. The alteration can be temporary (and disappear after a few seconds) or it can last a long time. Most of the research on long-term media effects is based on assumptions of long-term media influence as a gradual shaping process. This is a kind of a drip-drip-drip process of message after message slowly altering our knowledge structures. Greenberg (1988) reminds us that there are also "drench" influences. He says that not all media messages have the same impact and that not all characters in media stories are equally influential on our beliefs and attitudes. Some portrayals stand out because they "are deviant, are intense, and thus are more important viewing experiences" (p. 98).

Reinforcing. Through repeated exposures, the media gradually and continually add greater weight to something already existing in a person, thus making that something more fixed and harder to change. The reinforcement function is applicable to all six types of effects. When the media continually present the same people and events in the news over and over, individuals' knowledge structures about those people and events become more rigid and less likely to open to change later. When the media present the same beliefs and attitudes, individuals' comfort levels with those beliefs and attitudes become so strong that they are not able to change them. When the media present the same kinds of messages every week or every day, individuals' behavioral patterns of exposure become more fixed and harder to change.

The Media Effects Template for Individual-Level Effects

The Media Effects Template (MET) for individuals is displayed in Figure 3.1. Notice that the template contains 24 boxes—each representing a different kind of media effect on individuals. These 24 boxes are the result of crossing the six types of media effects with the four types of media influences. These 24 boxes indicate the fundamental building blocks of media-influenced effects. By building blocks, I mean the essential elements from which all media effects are composed. The template provides a useful device to help us think about the essential building blocks of effects on individuals and provides us with a common language from which to define those effects in a consistent manner and help clear up some of the definitional clutter.

The layout of the MET makes it look like the four functions are different from one another and the six types are different from one another. While there are important differences, there are also overlaps. For example, with functions, over the long term the altering function appears very much like a reinforcement function. Also, the six types are interrelated both in the sense that some scholars share definitions across types as well as that certain types are used as explanations or components for other types. To illustrate, some types of effects are strongly influenced by and are even dependent on another type:

- Cognitions influence belief formation (Tversky & Kahneman, 1973; Wyer & Albarracin, 2005), affect (Isen, 2000), as well as attitude formation and change (Chaiken, Liberman, & Eagly, 1989; Petty & Cacioppo, 1986; Wegener & Carlston, 2005).
- Beliefs influence attitudes (Fishbein & Ajzen, 1975; Kruglanski & Stroebe, 2005), and attitudes influence beliefs (Marsh & Wallace, 2005; McGuire, 1990).
- Behaviors influence attitudes (Festinger, 1957; Olson & Stone, 2005), and attitudes influence behavior (Ajzen & Fishbein, 1977, 2005), both consciously (Allport, 1935; Dulany, 1968) and unconsciously (Bargh, 1997).
- Affect influences attitudes (Clore & Schnall, 2005; Zajonc, 1980) as well as behaviors (Johnson-Laird & Oatley, 2000).

These overlaps create ambiguity and lead to confusion. So in this book, where my purpose is to achieve clarity in providing you with a strong, broad introduction of media influenced effects, I may err on the side of simplicity; that is, I will sharpen the differences between the rows and across the columns.

Figure 3.1   Media Effects Template: Individual-Level Effects

Type of Effect	Media Influence Functions			
	Acquiring	**Triggering**	**Altering**	**Reinforcing**
Cognitive	Memorize message element	Recall information	Change memory structure	Strengthen skills Construction of a pattern Reinforce connections
Belief	Accept belief	Recall belief	Change belief	Strengthen generalization Construction of a belief
Attitudes	Accept attitude	Recall attitude	Change attitude	Strengthen evaluation Construction of a new attitude Reinforce attitudes
Affects	Learn emotional information	Recall emotion	Change emotional sensitivity	Strengthen emotional connection
Physiology	Mood change	Reinforce mood	Automatic response	Reinforce reactions
Behavior	Learn behaviors	Recall of behavior	Behavioral change Imitation of behavior	Reinforce habits Performance of novel behavior

ORGANIZING MACRO-LEVEL MEDIA EFFECTS

Up to this point, this chapter has focused on media effects on individuals. We dealt with this topic first, because the literature on how the media have influenced individuals is much greater than the literature on larger aggregates such as the public, institutions, and the media themselves (Shoemaker & Reese, 1996). However, it is also important to understand how the media exert effects on aggregates.

Aggregates, at first, might seem to be the simple sum of effects on individuals. After all, isn't public opinion (which is an aggregate effect) really just the adding up of all individuals' attitudes? Mathematically that is correct. Public opinion is assessed in nationwide surveys of about a thousand or so individuals who are asked about their attitudes and beliefs, such as their approval of the way the president is doing his job. If in such a survey 600 individuals say they approve of the way the president is leading the country, while the other 400 individuals say they disapprove, then public opinion is 60% approval. But conceptually the idea of public opinion is more than the sum of individual attitudes. It is something else. To illustrate this, ask yourself if you are particularly interested in the opinion of a random individual halfway across the country. Your answer is likely to be no. Why should you care about his or her one opinion? Now think about some social issue that you care about—such as changing the age for drinking, driving, voting, or military service. Would you be interested in hearing about what the public in America thinks about the issue? The answer to this question is likely to be yes, because that information would provide context for your own opinion. That aggregate opinion would also be far more illuminating to you. For example, if you knew that a random guy in Nebraska was in favor of making military service mandatory for all males and females ages 18 to 22, it would not likely concern you. But what if you were told that public opinion was strongly in favor of mandatory military service for all citizens—male and female—ages 18 to 22? That would likely be of high interest to you. Also, other aggregates, such as institutions and society, seem to be entities that have a life of their own apart from individuals. Sociologists have known for a long time that studying aggregates is important (Mills, 1959).

The Media Effects Template that was developed for individual-level effects has been modified a bit to be useful in organizing macro-level effects (see Figure 3.2). The macro-level

Figure 3.2   Media Effects Template: Macro-Level Effects

Type of Effect	Media Influence On		
	The Public	**Institutions**	**Media Themselves**
Cognition	Public knowledge	Institutional knowledge	Media knowledge
Belief	Public beliefs	Institutional beliefs/norms	Media beliefs/norms
Attitudes	Public opinion	Institutional attitudes	Media attitudes
Affect	Public mood	Institutional mood	Media mood
Behavior	Public behavior	Institutional practices	Media practices

Structured Glossary of Terms About Media Effects

Media effects   The processes and products of media influence that act directly on targets (individuals and macro units of society and institutions) as well as indirectly on targets through other units. These effects can be intentional or nonintentional on the part of both the media senders as well as the target receivers. They can be manifested or hidden from natural observation. They are constant and ongoing. And they are shaped not just by the media influence but within a constellation of other factors that act in concert with the media influence.

- Individual-level effect: Effect on an individual person
- Macro-level effect: Effect on an aggregate, such as the public, institutions, society, or the media industries themselves

Type of effect   One of the six categories of effects: cognitive, belief, attitudinal, affective, physiological, and behavioral.

- Cognitive effect: Media exposure exercising an influence on an individual's mental processes or the product of those mental processes; typically involves the acquisition, processing, and storage of information
- Belief effect: Media exposure exercising an influence on an individual's perception that the probability that an object or event is associated with a given attribute
- Attitudinal effect: Media exposure exercising an influence on an individual's evaluative judgments; typically involves providing people with elements to evaluate or shaping standards of evaluation
- Affective effect: Media exposure exercising an influence on an individual's feelings such as emotions and moods
- Physiological effect: Media exposure exercising an influence on an individual's automatic bodily responses to stimuli
- Behavioral effect: Media exposure exercising an influence on an individual's doing something

Media-influenced functions   Generic ways the media can influence individuals. There are four in this conceptualization: acquiring, triggering, altering, and conditioning.

- Acquiring: The media influence the person to obtain something he/she did not have prior to a particular exposure

(Continued)

(Continued)

- Triggering: The media influences the person by activating something that already exists in the individual
- Altering: The media influence the person to change something that the person already had
- Reinforcing: The media influence the person by gradually making something in the person more difficult to change over time

Media Effects Template (MET)   A two-dimensional matrix that is used to categorize the media effects literatures. One MET is for individual-level effects and is structured by six types of effects with four media-influenced functions. The macro-level MET is structured by five types of effects with three macro structures.

MET is structured by five types of effects (behavior, cognitions, beliefs, attitudes, and affect) and three macro units (the public, institutions, and the media themselves).

Notice that the types of effects down the left side of that matrix are the same as in Figure 3.1, with the exception of physiological effects, which apply well to the human body but not to the public or other macro-level units. Also, the functions of acquiring, triggering, altering, and reinforcing were eliminated as column headings. These were important to classify the large literature of media effects on individuals; however, the literature of media effects on macro units is much smaller and at this time it would not be useful to classify it by functions. Instead, the columns represent the three major kinds of macro units that have been examined in the media effects literature: the public, institutions, and the media themselves.

SUMMARY

This chapter presents a broad definition of media effects that includes immediate as well as long-term changes and reinforcements. It includes positive as well as negative effects and the effects on individuals as well as larger aggregates, such as the public, institutions, and the media themselves.

In order to organize the many media effects included in this broad definition, the chapter develops an organizational scheme that is displayed by two Media Effects Templates— one for individual-level effects and the other for macro-level effects. Each of these is a two-dimensional matrix that categorizes the thinking and research of media effects.

The individual-level Media Effects Template (MET) is structured by type of media effects (cognitions, beliefs, attitudes, affects, physiology, and behavior) by media influence functions (acquiring, triggering, altering, and reinforcing). The macro-level MET is an alteration of the individual-level MET so that it can better organize the much smaller literature of media effects on larger aggregates.

Review Questions

1. Why is it important to have a broad definition of media effects?

2. What are the eight key issues that should be considered when defining media effects?

3. What is the definition of *media effects*?

4. What are the six types of effects on individuals?

5. What are the four media influence functions?

6. How is the MET for individual-level effects different from the MET for macro-level effects?

Further Thinking Questions

1. Now that you have read the introduction to the six types of media effects on individuals, which of the six do you think you experience most often?

2. For each of the six types of effects on individuals, can you list several examples of effects that have occurred in your life?

3. What institutions are most important to you?
   - Can you think of any ways the media have influenced those institutions?
   - Which of those institutions do you think has been most influenced by the media?

CHAPTER 4

Media Influence

Source: Ryan McVay/Digital Vision/Thinkstock

Media Influence

Now that you have broadened your perspective on media effects, it is time to shift your attention to media influence. In this chapter we examine the four general patterns of media influence. Then we introduce the factors about the media messages that have been found responsible for that media influence. The chapter concludes with a detailed example that shows how various factors work together to bring about patterns of media influence.

PATTERNS OF INFLUENCE

At the most fundamental level, the media exert four patterns of influence: gradual long-term change, long-term non-change (reinforcement), immediate shift, and short-term fluctuation change (see Figure 4.1). All media effects follow one of these four patterns. I know these terms may at first seem very strange and complicated, but once you understand what they are, you will see that these are simple patterns and the only patterns possible for media-influenced effects. To illustrate these patterns, I first clarify the distinction between baselines and fluctuations as well as between manifestations and processes.

Baselines and Fluctuations

With a long-term change type of effect, the messages from the media gradually alter a person's baseline. Figure 4.1a illustrates this pattern. To understand this pattern, first look at the axes in the figure. The horizontal axis represents time. The vertical axis represents the degree of an effect; this can be any effect—a cognition, a belief, an attitude, an affect, physiology, or a behavior. The line in the figure represents a person's baseline on a particular effect. Notice that in this example, the line ascends as it moves from left to right; this means that as time goes by the person is experiencing a slightly higher degree of this effect—whatever the effect is. Let's make this example a little more concrete by saying this is a cultivation effect. A *cultivation effect* is the gradual increase over time of a person's belief about the real world, such as that the world is a mean and violent place. Cultivation theory predicts that people who watch a great deal of television will gradually over time come to believe the real world is like the television world. Because the television world is a violent one, people who watch a lot of television will come to believe the real world is also a violent one. This cultivation effect can

Figure 4.1 Types of Media Influence Patterns

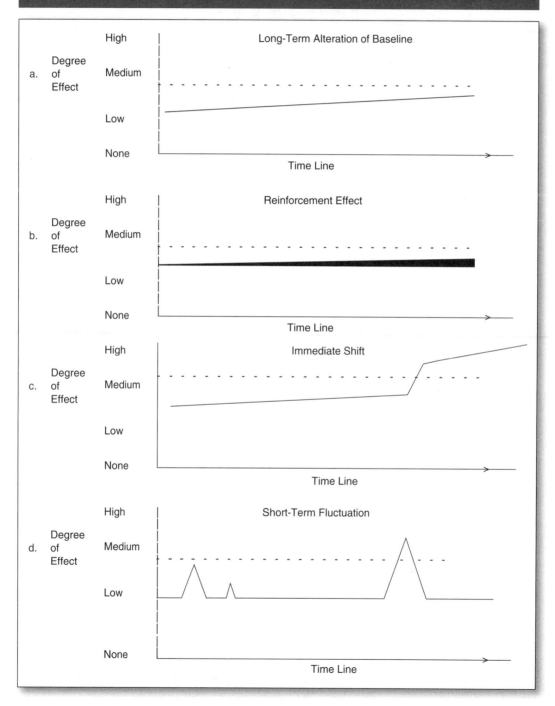

be illustrated graphically in Figure 4.1a by the very gradual upwardly sloping line. This line indicates that as time goes by, people show an increasing degree of cultivation; that is, they are more and more likely to believe the real world is like the television world.

Now let's consider a different type of effect: reinforcement. Let's say that over time a person's attitude about a political candidate gets stronger and stronger; that is, with more media exposure to campaign ads, news coverage, and expert pundits talking about political candidates, the person's existing attitude is reinforced. This is illustrated by Figure 4.1b, where the person's baseline stays flat over time; that is, it does not increase or decrease. However, the baseline grows thicker to indicate that it is weightier and thus harder to change over time.

With an immediate shift type of effect, the media influence serves to alter something in a person during an exposure or shortly after a particular exposure, and that alteration lasts for a long time (see Figure 4.1c). That alteration can be relatively minor or it can be large and dramatic. An example of a dramatic immediate change effect that lasts over the long term might be when a young person watches a movie about an attractive person in a particular career—say a heart surgeon—and the person decides she wants to be a heart surgeon, talks about this career choice continually, and alters her study habits to earn the grades necessary to go to college and medical school.

With a short-term fluctuation change type of effect, the media trigger a fluctuation off the baseline during the exposure or shortly after. The change is short lived and the person returns to the baseline level quickly (see Figure 4.1d). This is a fairly prevalent finding in a lot of studies of public information/attitude campaigns. Researchers find a spike up in knowledge, attitude change, or behavioral intention as a result of exposure to some media material, but this change is not observed in subsequent measurement periods beyond a few days after the exposure.

The baseline is the best estimate of a person's degree of effect at any given time. Baselines differ from one another in terms of slope and elasticity. *Slope* refers to angle (an upward slope indicates a generally increasing level of an effect, while a downward slope indicates a generally decreasing level of an effect) and degree (a sharp angle reflects a relatively large degree of change in effects level, while a flat slope reflects a continuing level in the baseline). *Elasticity* reflects how entrenched the baseline is. Over time, a baseline that has been reinforced continually by the same kind of media messages will become highly entrenched, making it less and less likely that there will be fluctuations off the baseline, and when there are fluctuation spikes, those fluctuation spikes are smaller and smaller over time.

Fluctuations have three characteristics: duration, magnitude, and direction. The *duration* refers to how long the fluctuation lasts before returning to the baseline. *Magnitude* refers to how far the fluctuation spike deviates from the baseline. And direction refers to whether the fluctuation spike moves upward (thus representing an increase in the level of effect) or downward (thus representing a decrease in the level of effect).

Manifestation and Process Effects

Notice the dotted line in all four graphs in Figure 4.1. These dotted lines represent the manifestation level. In the first graph (a), notice that the baseline stays below the manifestation level. This indicates that the degree of the effect has not reached a level where there are spontaneous observables. By *observables* I mean that people exhibit something that clearly indicates a change that can be attributed to media influence. In two of three graphics (4.1c and 4.1d), there are examples of the baseline breaking above the manifestation level; with those three patterns we can easily observe something that clearly indicates a media-influenced effect.

If we limited our thinking about effects to only those fluctuations that break through the manifestation level, we miss a good deal about how the media continually influence effects. We should also examine what occurs below the manifestation level. Returning to Figure 4.1a, notice that the baseline has an upward slope, which indicates a gradual long-term change. The line does not move above the manifestation level, so it is not observed; however, something is happening that indicates media influence. For example, let's say a young girl is exposed to lots of print messages on a particular topic. Over time these exposures gradually increase her reading skills and increase her interest in that topic as her knowledge base grows. Her baseline moves close to the manifestation level. Then one day she picks up an article on the topic and begins telling all her friends about what she has just learned (this activity takes place above the manifestation level because it is spontaneous and easy to observe her knowledge, attitudes, and emotions as she exhibits them to her friends). However, is it accurate to conclude that this manifestation was caused by the one exposure to the article alone? No, of course not. We must account for the long-term media influence that allowed her to practice her reading skills and grow her interest in this topic. The magnitude of the manifestation level is a combination of the initial level on the baseline and the magnitude of the fluctuation itself.

Contrast this with a young boy who did not have this pattern of practicing his reading skills or growing his interest on this topic; his baseline would be far below the manifestation level. If he were to read the same article, he would not be likely to manifest the same indicators as did the girl; however the boy could still have been influenced by his exposure to the article (change in level), although he did not manifest that effect.

Shaping the Patterns

What pushes baselines up or down, and what triggers fluctuations? The answer is that factors of influence are responsible for the shape of these patterns. The term *factors* is plural because almost never is there one factor that is responsible for an effect; instead, effects patterns are shaped by the continual influence of multiple factors acting in interaction over time.

Also, the factors that lead to media effects are not exclusively media factors. While characteristics in the media messages are of course important influencers of those effects, other factors—about the audience members and the exposure environment—are also important. They all work together.

With suddenly occurring fluctuation effects, it is easy to attribute these effects to the particular message the person is exposed to immediately before the manifestation. While that exposure is likely to be influential in creating the fluctuation, it is usually not solely responsible for that fluctuation. For example, let's say Hannah is listening to her car radio while driving home after work and she hears an ad for a fast food place. She decides to go to that place and buy some food for her dinner. The ad seemed to trigger a fluctuation effect, that is, the behavior of driving to the advertised restaurant and ordering the food featured in the ad. However, it is likely that factors about Hannah were also influential in triggering that fluctuation—factors such as Hannah's hunger, her being too tired to cook something for herself, her past experience in eating food from that restaurant, her desire for something fast and inexpensive, her proximity to the restaurant when she heard the ad, and so on. While factors in a media message are influential, they rarely act alone.

Because media influence is both constant and pervasive, some of the factors of influence come to us directly, but other factors work their influence indirectly. Indirect influence occurs when we interact with other people or with institutions, which are all themselves influenced by groups of media then pass that influence along to us. Also, once groups of media factors have exerted an influence on our algorithms, that influence continues whenever we access those algorithms. For example, when media factors shape our beliefs, they influence us later when we recall those beliefs. When media factors influence our standards, they influence our process of evaluation later when we use those standards. When media factors reinforce our behavior, they influence us each time we exhibit our habits. And when media factors shape how we think about things, they influence us each time we think.

FACTORS OF INFLUENCE

Now that you have seen what the patterns of media influence are, the next question is, What are the factors that are responsible for that influence? The answer to this question is that there are likely to be hundreds of factors, as you will see in upcoming chapters. For now, I simply introduce the idea of factors of influence by organizing them into three general families of factors. Then I highlight what have been found to be the most important four factors.

Families of Factors

Researchers have identified hundreds of factors that have been found to exert various degrees of influence on different kinds of media effects. To prepare you for all the detail on these factors that you will encounter in Chapter 6 through 11, I will focus your attention on three general families of factors. The first is an array of factors about the media messages. The second is a group of factors about the audience. And the third is a collection of factors about the exposure environment.

Factors About the Media Messages. Researchers have examined a great many things about the media messages to determine which are associated with which effects. These factors include fairly general characteristics such as the medium (for example, print vs. broadcast) and genre (for example, news vs. comedy). When researchers use a general characteristic such as genre, they are assuming that all messages presented in that genre are similar and that each genre presents messages that are very different from one another. For example, researchers might ask people how much television they watch in the genres of news and comedy to test the assumption that news messages present more information about current events than do comedy shows. The researchers then test audience members for their knowledge of current events to see if there is support for this assumption.

Other researchers are uncomfortable assuming that all messages within a genre are similar, so they examine more specific characteristics within those messages. Some of these characteristics concern the types of portrayals, such as violence, sexual activity, stereotyped characters, and so on. Others of these characteristics are more concerned with the context of portrayals, such as the motives characters attribute to their actions, the consequences of those actions, the use of humor, and so on.

Thus with media messages, there is a wide range of factors that differ primarily on their level of generality. Some researchers prefer to examine differences across broad classes of messages, while other researchers prefer to analyze media messages in more detail and thus focus their attention on particular characteristics within messages.

Source: © Image Source

Factors About the Audience. Researchers have also examined factors about the audience. These can be organized in three groups: demographics, traits, and states. *Demographic factors* are the relatively enduring surface characteristics about people, such as their genders, ages, ethnic backgrounds, and the like. Demographics make general categorical distinctions. By general, I mean that researchers assume all people in one category (such as preschoolers) are the same. By categorical, I mean that either you are a member of one group or you are not (for example, either you are female or you are not). Demographics are useful variables because they are easy to measure and test, but some researchers find them too superficial. For example, just because one male exhibits an effect does not mean that all males will exhibit the same effect. While biological sex is an important characteristic for medical doctors, media researchers are more interested in gender socialization, which is a continuous variable and one that recognizes that biological females are not all alike in gender role socialization and that these differences in role socialization are more strongly related to media exposure preferences and media effects than is their biological sex.

Researchers also like to measure audience traits and states, both of which are psychological characteristics, and then relate them to media effects. *Traits* are fairly stable psychological characteristics of an individual. Examples of traits are IQ, extroversion, compulsiveness, ambitiousness, and the like. Traits are continuous rather than categorical. For example, we do not say that some people have IQ while others have none; instead we say that there is a wide range of IQ among people.

States are temporary conditions that an individual experiences. These include drives for food, sex, information, entertainment, and so on. Once a drive is satisfied, the person no longer finds him- or herself in that state and is likely to experience a different state. Emotions are states. A person can experience the state of fear while watching a horror show or the state of anxiety right before a big test. States can be either categorical (either you feel fear or you do not) or continuous (your degree of fear).

Factors About the Exposure Environment. These are usually sociological factors that reveal things like whether people expose themselves to the media either alone or with others and whether they discuss their media experiences with others or not. Also, some researchers focus their examinations of influence on characteristics about the physical environment, such as how many TVs there are in a household, where those TVs are located, how far people sit from their TVs when viewing, and how many distractions occur during the exposures.

Most Influential Factors

Given the hundreds of factors that have been found to be related to media influence on the many effects on individuals, is there some way to whittle that list down to a small set of the factors that have been found to be most influential? In this section of the chapter, I direct your attention to four factors about media messages that have been found to be particularly influential in bring about media effects. These factors are the message's arousing nature, consequences of actions, point of view, and repetition. If you keep reminding yourself of these four factors, you will be better able to keep your focus on the big picture of media influence as you read through subsequent chapters.

Arousing Nature. Perhaps the most influential factor found in the media effects literature is the degree of arousal in audience members. Designers of media messages of all kinds know they must build elements into their messages to achieve this audience arousal. If a message is not arousing, it has little chance of attracting and/or holding audience attention. Media messages must first arouse us physiologically in order to trigger an orienting reflex that is needed to get our attention. Second, they must arouse our interest cognitively through suspense and curiosity to get us to keep paying attention to a message to find out what will happen next.

There are two arousal systems. One generates in a person's limbic system; this is autonomic in that is it is hard wired to respond to threats and get us ready to fight or flee. The other arousal system is cortical and energizes attention, alertness, and vigilance; thus it is more concerned with information-processing tasks of acquisition, processing, and retrieval. As for cortical arousal, media messages exploit the orienting reflex, that is, the capturing attention due to perceptual elements such as loud and unusual noises as well as fast-paced action, color bursts, and the like. Media messages can capture our attention through what has been called the *orienting response;* this is short-term attention. Stimuli that are novel, surprising, intense, or complex trigger the orienting response. The orienting response slows the heart rate down. Long-term changes in attention are called *tonic attention.* Tonic attention speeds up the heart rate. They are indications of concentration, vigilance, and thinking (Lang, 1994b).

The media are expert at generating arousal. Producers know how to trigger our innate physiological responses with the use of motion, sound, and images. Successful producers are also experts at pulling our interest into a story and taking us step by step through the action in a way that makes us feel we must continue. This is suspense. Zillmann (1991a) defines *suspense* as "an experience of uncertainty whose hedonic properties can vary from noxious to pleasant" (p. 281). Audiences enjoy suspense to the extent that they have empathy with characters and that this empathy distress is relieved. The more suspense distress, the more relief, and therefore the more enjoyment of the suspenseful story. In books, this is called a "page turner," meaning the reader could not put the book down until the story was completed. In film, producers must grab attention early and hold it for almost 2 hours—a major challenge. And television presents the greatest challenge to storytellers because those stories need to be interrupted every 10 minutes or so for commercial breaks; television producers must make the stories so compelling that viewers will not tune out during the relatively long breaks that repeatedly interrupt their stories.

Consequences of Actions. By the way the media tell their stories, they signal to us what is acceptable behavior and what is not. These social lessons are revealed to us by the way the storytellers treat the characters who perform actions as well as the characters who receive the action. As for the performers of the action, we can watch to see if they are rewarded or punished. Also, what do the performers feel about their actions, that is, are they portrayed as being happy or proud? Or are those performers portrayed as being sad and remorseful?

As for the receivers of the action, we need to watch to see if they are harmed by actions or not. If we expect characters to be harmed by certain actions but then they are portrayed as not being harmed, we tend to adjust our expectations of harm. Over time, we are desensitized to the suffering of others in the real world, because we do not expect them to be experiencing much harm.

Repetition. Repetition is a powerful force of influence for two reasons. First, the sheer volume of messages repeated over time is a constant reminder of certain things. Repetition defines the status quo. It is easier to go along with the mainstream flow of ideas and behaviors. When the media present the same messages over and over again, it wears down opposition and reinforces compliance.

A second reason for why repetition of media messages is such a powerful force is that the repetition is like a metronome that hypnotizes us into routines. We fall into rituals that are reinforced continually by the media, and these habitual patterns are performed without thinking, thus making them harder to alter. The longer we mindlessly follow a habit, the more it defines us, and the harder it is to perceive it—much less change it. Repetition reinforces our existing thoughts and behaviors.

Point of View. When the media tell their stories, they must present the action from a particular point of view. This is the case whether the story is a fictional one designed to entertain, a vignette designed to advertise a product, or a news story designed to inform. The point of view puts the audience member into the story by seeing the action through the eyes of one character. The audience members identify with that one character and tend to feel what that character feels.

Fictional stories are often told in the first person. This is especially the case with music. A singer tells a story about what happened to him or her and how that felt. The listener is meant to identify with the singer and experience the same feelings. With the visual media of film and television, the camera becomes the eyes of the audience member. As the camera moves through the action, the audience is shown certain things, while other things are left out. Thus there is a selection process that producers use to put the audience in a certain position, usually identifying with a particular character who is regarded as the protagonist. We as audience members come to care about what happens to this protagonist. When this character is happy, we feel joy; when this character is in danger, we feel the threat; when this character is unfairly harmed, we feel anger. This is the "good" character, because even when the character makes mistakes, we can justify that character's actions. That is, we do not hate the protagonist when she makes a mistake; instead we still like the character but feel sad that she made a mistake and root for her to overcome the situation that results from the mistake.

Advertising messages are told from the point of view of the target audience. Designers of these messages are saying that they know a need you have and they have just the product that would satisfy that need. The typical television ad presents a person with a need or problem; thus the point of view is you, the target audience member. The story then unfolds to show that you are bothered by this need or problem; then quickly there is a solution.

News messages are also told from a particular point of view. In their quest for objectivity, journalists try to present facts in a neutral manner. Also, when they cover controversies, journalists try to present at least two sides. However, journalists can never present all the facts about an event, nor can they cover all sides of complex issues. They must be selective, and what they select privileges one point of view over others. Also, journalists do not cover all possible stories; they make judgments about which events and people are worthy of being covered. This selection process is itself a point of view on the society. So in a given story, when journalists try to avoid slanting the coverage to show the event through only one participant's point of view, the journalists themselves bring a point of view to the task of selecting and writing their stories.

AN ILLUSTRATION OF MEDIA INFLUENCE

To illustrate these patterns, let's consider a disinhibition effect, which is a lowering of people's inhibitions that prevent them from behaving aggressively. Let's say Leo is a 12-year-old boy who has been raised to be highly aggressive and who has low degree of empathy for other people, while Julie is a 35-year-old mother who was raised by the golden rule and who has a high degree of empathy. Leo's disinhibition effect baseline is likely to be higher than Julie's. Let's say that Leo is continually exposed to many media messages of violence (in movies, television shows, and video games) that are high in arousal. Also, these violent stories are usually told through the hero's point of view, and heroes are likely to be as violent as the villains. But the heroes are rewarded for their violent actions while the villains are punished. Given the repeated viewing, the arousing nature of the messages with their positive consequence for violent action from the hero's point of view, Leo is likely to have an increasing baseline that is now close to the manifestation level, that is, likely to manifest a disinhibition effect. In contrast, Julie avoids violent messages as much as she can, and therefore her baseline is likely to be much lower and far below the manifestation level. Furthermore, over time Leo's baseline is likely to continue with an upward slope while Julie's baseline is likely to be flat or even have a downward slope.

Now let's say that Leo and Julie watch a *Dirty Harry* movie in which a great deal of violence is perpetrated by a rogue police officer who is glamorous, humorous, and successful in his use of violence. The movie is presented from Harry's point of view, wherein he repeatedly exhibits acts of aggression and feels rewarded for these actions. Leo is likely to show a sharp fluctuation increasing his level on a disinhibition effect; that is, during or after the exposure to this movie, Leo is likely to exhibit his own aggressive behavior. In contrast, Julie is horrified by Harry and finds his actions reprehensible and insulting to her. Julie is likely to show a sharp fluctuation decreasing her level on a disinhibition effect. Although the media message presented is the same for both Leo and Julie, the experience for each is very different because of what the two people bring to the exposure situation as reflected by their different baselines.

Let's say that later on Julie watches a lot of crime drama but with a very different point of view and very different consequences of the violent action. She watches shows such as the *Law & Order* TV series, in which criminals' violent acts are not glamorized or sanitized. Instead, the story is told from the point of view of law enforcement officials who usually avoid aggressive behavior, and when they do find themselves behaving aggressively, they are punished for it. Even though Julie continues to watch crime drama, the point of view of the story and the way the consequences are portrayed would tend to push Julie's disinhibition baseline even lower and serve to keep it far away from the manifestation level. If she were to see a violent portrayal in which the perpetrator was glamorized and the violence was sanitized, she would likely not experience much of a fluctuation effect, because her baseline has been so strongly reinforced. A reinforcement pattern is one where the position of the baseline is entrenched; that is, the baseline continues at its current level, and its elasticity is reduced, rendering fluctuations more rare. If the elasticity of the baseline is narrow, then the long-term stable factors (traits and typical story formula) are dominant; but if the elasticity is wide, then the immediate factors (dispositions and idiosyncratic factors in the portrayals) are dominant. Reinforcement narrows the elasticity and thus makes fluctuations smaller and rarer.

As you can see from this example, two people can be exposed to the same media message but have two very different reactions. This difference can be explained by a history of different factors that have been acting on both people. Not only do we need to take a broad perspective on media effects; we also need a broad perspective on factors of influence that include characteristics about the audience members as well as characteristics about the media messages themselves.

Structured Glossary of Terms About Media Influence

Media influence   The many ways the media work in a continuous ongoing manner within a constellation of many factors to shape micro and macro effects on baselines and fluctuations.

- Baseline pattern effect: The best estimate of a person's degree of effect at any given time. It is formed over the long term by the continual interaction of three types of factors: psychological traits of the person, sociological experiences of the person, and media exposure patterns.
- Reinforcement pattern effect: Through repeated exposures of the same type of messages, a person's baseline position is made more weighty; that is, it becomes over time much more resistant to change and it loses its elasticity, thus rendering fluctuations more minor and rarer.
- Fluctuation pattern effect: Observed in research studies in which there is a change between a person's pre-exposure and post-exposure effect level scores. The larger the difference, the larger the influence of the media exposure on the effect level. Fluctuation changes can be in the direction of increasing the level of an effect or decreasing the level. In either case, fluctuation changes are usually temporary. They are typically traceable to particular interpretations that the person made about the message.

Manifest effects   Spontaneous observables; evidence of an effect is easy to observe and to link to media exposures.

Process effects   Changes in the level of elasticity of a person's baseline; because these things occur below the manifestation level, they cannot be directly observed.

SUMMARY

This chapter focused on increasing your understanding of how the media exert their influence on you by making a distinction between baselines and fluctuations as well as a distinction between manifestation and process effects. Fluctuations are changes that occur during a media exposure or immediately afterward, while baselines take a long time to build. Baselines can indicate change, where that change can be a decrement to the baseline (such as with a gradual loss in intensity of emotional reactions to horror films over time), an increase in the baseline (such as gradually and constantly rewarding a person's exposure to a particular program thus increasing their habitual viewing of that program over time), or a reinforcement of the baseline (such as a steady stream of a particular kind of media message contributing greater and greater weight to a person's attitude about a political issue, thus making it much more difficult over time to convert that attitude to a different one).

Media influence is ongoing and constant. Sometimes we can observe evidence of this influence as with manifestation effects. Other times their influence is very difficult or impossible to observe, but this does not mean the media are not exerting an influence, only that their influence is shaping a process that cannot yet be observed.

The media exert their influence both directly on people as well as indirectly. Also, the media exert their influence through a constellation of factors. Some of these factors come from the media in the form of how they tell their stories, while other factors come from the person and the person's environment.

It is important to keep these ideas in mind when reading through the next 10 chapters as I lay out the many different media effects on individuals as well as on the more macro units. Think about where you are on these effects and see if you can answer the Further Thinking Questions at the end of this chapter.

Review Questions

1. What is the difference between a baseline and a fluctuation?

2. What is the difference between a manifestation and a process effect?

3. What are the three families of factors that researchers typically examine with media effects?

4. What are the four most influential factors?

Further Thinking Questions

1. Can you think of any effect that suddenly showed up as a fluctuation from your normal behavior and really surprised you?
   - For this effect, can you attribute it to media exposures?
   - What other factors about yourself and your environment were also likely to have been influential in bringing about this effect?

2. Think about the disinhibition effect illustrated in this chapter.
   - In what ways are you more like Leo and thus have a similar disinhibition baseline?
   - In what ways are you more like Julie and thus have a similar baseline?
   - Which effects have manifested and which have not been manifested in your life? Among the nonmanifested effects, where do you think your baseline is? Is your baseline close to the manifestation level or not? And what are the factors in your life that are suppressing the manifestation of some of these effects and which factors are pushing your baseline up to a manifestation level?

CHAPTER 5

Media Theories

Source: ©iStockphoto.com/JamesBrey

CHAPTER 5

Media Theories

Scholars have created a large number of theories to identify many effects of the media and to explain the processes behind those effects. Any book that deals with media effects must necessarily highlight the scholarly work that is encapsulated in theories. So this chapter begins with a brief analysis of the importance of theories, then poses the question: What are the most salient media effects theories? The chapter profiles the most salient dozen theories of media effects, then concludes with an argument for why it is so important to move beyond theories when examining the full range of what we know about media effects.

BEGINNING WITH THEORIES

Theories are essential tools for scholars. Theories help *organize* thinking about a phenomenon by highlighting key ideas and by providing carefully crafted definitions that can be shared by all scholars as they build knowledge about their phenomenon of interest. Theories can *predict* which effects will occur under certain situations. Theories can *explain* effects by revealing the factors that lead to those effects and showing how those factors work together. And theories can provide *critiques* of scholarly practices by pointing out shortcomings and suggesting alternative explanations, predictions, definitions, and structures.

Without theories, scholarly fields grow slowly and in a haphazard way. Scholars have few common sets of ideas or definitions for those ideas, so they spend a lot of time "reinventing the wheel," so to speak, as they waste their precious few resources struggling to construct a definition of a concept that someone else has already defined well. Scholars have few predictive statements to focus their work so they intuitively select factors that might or might not predict an effect. Scholars have few explanations for the "how" or "why" questions, and those explanations that do exist are shallow and not well developed. And with few critiques of their practices, they have little vision to correct faulty practices and make better use of their resources. Therefore theories are needed to help scholars develop understandings of their phenomena of interest in an efficient and effective manner. When a scholarly field has a few good theories, there is great efficiency because all scholars can share a common vision of which concepts are most important, how those concepts should be defined, how those concepts predict one another, and how those concepts work together in an effective system of explaining the phenomenon of interest to the field.

With the phenomenon of media effects, scholars have created a great many theories over the years. For a partial list of the more popular of these media effects theories, see Exhibit 5.1. While some of these are labeled as models, some as hypotheses, and some as effects, they all can be regarded as theories, because each one provides some sort of organization, prediction, explanation, or critique of some facet of the media effects phenomenon. Notice also that this list looks similar to Exhibit 3.1 in Chapter 3. You should not be surprised that the lists are similar, because the theories in Exhibit 5.1 are effects theories and they focus on organizing thinking, making predictions, and offering explanations about media effects as listed in Exhibit 3.1. However, the lists are not identical because some effects have stimulated the creation of more than one theory. Also, there are other effects that have been identified through exploratory research, and scholars have not yet presented conceptualizations to organize, predict, explain, or critique that effect.

The large number of theories is an indication of the vitality of the research field; that is, the topic of media effects has attracted a large number of scholars, each of whom has generated explanations about how the media effect people and society. However, the large number of theories is also an indication that scholars have not converged on a small set of theories that they agree are the best and most useful explanations of media effects. With such a large number of theories, it is difficult to see the big picture of media effects. We need to do something to sift through all these theories, some of which have accounted for only a study or two and which may deal with only a tiny fraction of the overall phenomenon of media effects. In order to keep the focus on the big picture in this chapter on theories, I highlight only those theories that have received the most attention by media effects scholars. These are the theories that have generated the most research activity and have been found to receive the strongest empirical support for their predictions and explanations. First, I identify these popular theories. Second, I offer a brief profile of each. Then I use the Media Effects Template (MET) to plot the theories and show where their attention has been directed and which parts of the overall media effects phenomenon have been relatively ignored.

WHAT ARE THE MOST PREVALENT MEDIA EFFECTS THEORIES?

The theories listed in Table 5.1 were gathered in a study I did with Karyn Riddle (Potter & Riddle, 2007). We analyzed a good deal of the media effects literature published in the major scholarly journals, and those theories were what we found. We also counted how often each theory appeared prominently in different articles. We reasoned that if our scholarly field had a dominant theory or two, those dominant theories would each appear in a relatively large percentage of articles. We found no such dominant theory. Among the 336 articles that we identified as theory driven, cultivation theory was mentioned in 27 articles, or about 8% of that literature. The top dozen mentioned theories are listed in Table 5.1. These 12 theories accounted for about half of all theory-driven articles. The rest of the theories on the list in Table 5.1 were mentioned only once or twice, so it is reasonable to conclude that they are not having much of an impact on the research field. Therefore the top 12 of these theories can be regarded as the most salient, that is, they have been found to be the most visible in the literature. They are profiled in the next section of the chapter.

Exhibit 5.1   Theories Explaining Some Aspect of the Media Effects Phenomenon

ABX balance model (Newcomb, 1953)
Advertising and social change (Berman, 1981)
Affective aggression model (Anderson, Collins, Schmitt, & Jacobvitz, 1996)
Affluent society (Galbraith, 1976)
Agenda building (Lang & Lang, 1981, 1991)
Agenda setting (McCombs & Shaw, 1972, 1993)
Associative network model (John Anderson, 1983)
Attitude construct approach (Fazio, 1990)
Audience as commodity (Jhally & Livant, 1986)
Audience flow (Eastman, 1993)
Audience polarization (Webster & Phalen, 1997)
Automatic activation Model (Fazio, 1990)
Availability heuristic (Tversky & Kahneman, 1973)
Availability-valence model (Kisielius & Sternthal, 1984)

Buffering Hypothesis (Davis & Kraus, 1989)

Capacity model (Fisch, 2000)
Catharsis (Feshbach, 1961)
Channel repertoire (Ferguson & Perse, 1993)
Channel theory of publication (Coser, Kadushin, & Powell, 1982)
Character affiliation theory (Raney, 2004)
Civic engagement (Putnam, 2000)
Coalition model of agenda building (Protess et al., 1991)
Cognitive dissonance (Festinger, 1957)
Cognitive flexibility theory (Lowrey & Kim, 2009)
Cognitive response theory (Greenwald, 1968)
Communication/persuasion matrix model (McGuire, 1985)
Consumer culture theory (Ewen, 1976)
Cue theory (Berkowitz, 1965)
Cultivation (Gerbner, 1969; Gerbner & Gross, 1976)
Cultural imperialism (Boyd-Barrett, 1977; Schiller, 1969)
Culture of narcissism (Lasch, 1978)

Decision-making models (Ryan & Peterson, 1982)
Diffusion of innovations (Rogers, 1995; Rogers & Shoemaker, 1971)
Direct effects model (Lasswell, 1927)
Disinhibition effect (Bandura, 1994)
Disposition theory (Zillmann & Cantor, 1976)
Distribution of knowledge (McQuail & Windahl, 1993)

(Continued)

Exhibit 5.1 (Continued)

Double action model of gatekeeping (Bass, 1969)
Drench hypothesis (Greenberg, 1988)

Elaboration likelihood model (Petty & Cacioppo, 1981)
Elite pluralism theory (Berelson, Lazarsfeld, & McPhee, 1954; Key, 1961)
Empathy theory (Zillmann, 1996)
Encoding-decoding model (Hall, 1980)
Exchange model of news (Sigal, 1973)
Exchange theory (Solomon, 1989)
Excitation transfer theory (Zillmann, 1983)
Exemplification theory (Zillmann, 1999; Zillmann & Brosius, 2000)
Expectancy value model (Palmgreen & Rayburn, 1982)

Fraction of selection (Schramm, 1954)
Frame analysis (Erving Goffman, 1974, 1979)
Framing (Cappella & Jamieson, 1997; Scheufele, 1999)
Free market model of media (DeFleur, 1970)

Gatekeeping (White, 1950)
Genre theory (Kaminsky, 1974)
Global village (McLuhan, 1964; McLuhan & Fiore, 1967)
Gratification seeking and audience activity model (Rubin & Perse, 1987)

Hegemony theory (Gramsci, 1971)
Heuristic processing model of cultivation effects (Shrum, 2002)
Hidden persuaders (Packard, 1957)
Homogenization hypothesis (Bagdikian, 1997)
Hostile media perception (Hwang, Pan, & Sun, 2008)

Imitation (Miller & Dollard, 1941)
Indirect effects model (Cartwright, 1949; Hyman & Sheatsley, 1947)
Information flow theory (Davis, 1990; Greenberg & Parker, 1965)
Information model of advertising (cited in Jeffres, 1994, pp. 279–281)
Information seeking (Donohew & Tipton, 1973)
Integrated model of media enjoyment (Vorderer, Klimmt, & Ritterfeld, 2004)
Integrated response model (Smith & Swinyard, 1982, 1988)
Interpretation by social class (Morley, 1980)
Interpretive resistance theory (Carragee, 1990)

Knowledge gap theory (Tichenor, Donohue, & Olien, 1970)

Law of double jeopardy (McPhee, 1963)
Least objectionable programming (Klein, 1971)

Levels of processing theory (Craik & Lockhart, 1972)
Limited-capacity model of mediated message processing (Lang, 2000)

Market power model of advertising (cited in Jeffres, 1994, pp. 279–281)
Marketplace model (Webster & Phalen, 1994)
Marxist theory (McQuail, 1987)
Mass audience (Blumer, 1946)
Media access (Westley & MacLean, 1957)
Media as culture industries (Jhally, 1987; Hay, 1989)
Media culture (Altheide & Snow, 1979, 1991)
Media enjoyment as attitude (Nabi & Krcmar, 2004)
Media entertainment theory (Mendelsohn, 1966)
Media flow theory (Csikszentmihalyi, 1988; Sherry, 2004)
Media-public relationships (McQuail & Windahl, 1981)
Media system dependency (DeFleur & Ball-Rokeach, 1975)
Medium is the message (McLuhan, 1962, 1964)
Medium theory (Meyrowitz, 1994)
Message construction (Shoemaker & Reese, 1991)
Mood management (Zillmann, 1988; Zillmann & Bryant, 1994)
Motivated attention and motivated processing (Nabi, 1999)

Neo-associationistic model (Berkowitz, 1984)
Neo-mass audience (Webster & Phalen, 1997)
Network model of political priming (Price & Tewksbury, 1997)
News content theory (Shoemaker & Reese, 1996)
News diffusion (Greenberg, 1964)
News factory (Bantz, McCorkle, & Baade, 1980)
News frame Theory (Tuchman, 1978)

One-dimensional man (Marcuse, 1964)

Parasocial interaction (Horton & Wohl, 1956; Rosengren & Windahl, 1989; Rubin,
    Perse, & Powell, 1990)
Play theory (Stephenson, 1967)
Pluralistic ignorance (Allport, 1924)
Political socialization theory (Graber, 1980)
Politics of signification (Hall, 1982)
Polysemy theory (Fiske, 1986)
Power elite theory (Mills, 1957)
Priming (Berkowitz, 1965; Roskos-Ewoldsen, Roskos-Ewoldsen, & Carpentier, 2002)
Principled reasoning theory (McLeod, Sotirovic, Voakes, Guo, & Huang, 1998)
Profit-driven logic of safety theory (Gitlin, 1985)
Program choice theory (Steiner, 1952)
Proteus effect (Peña, Hancock, & Merola, 2009)
Pseudo-events blur reality (Boorstin, 1961)

(Continued)

Exhibit 5.1 (Continued)

Psychodynamic model (DeFleur, 1970)
Psychological conditioning (Klapper, 1960; Skinner, 1974)

Rally effect (Coser, 1956)
Reasoned action theory (Fishbein & Ajzen, 1975)
Reception paradigm (Katz, 1987)
Reinforcing spirals model (Zhao, 2009)
Resource dependency theory (Turow, 1984)
Revealed preferences (Mansfield, 1970)
Riley & Riley sociological model of mass communication (Riley & Riley, 1959)
Ritual model of communication (Turner, 1977)

Selective exposure (Freedman & Sears, 1966; Lazarsfeld, Berelson, & Gaudet, 1944)
Self-perception theory (Bem, 1972)
Semiotic theory (Baudrillard, 1983)
Social cognitive theory of mass communication (Bandura, 2001)
Social construction of meaning (Berger & Luckmann, 1966; Lippmann, 1922; Mead, 1934)
Social identity (Meyrowitz, 1985)
Social learning theory (Bandura, 1977)
Social norms theory of enjoyment (Denham, 2004)
Social responses to computer technologies model (Nowak, Hamilton, & Hammond, 2009)
Sociology of news theory (Schudson, 2003)
Spiral of silence (Noelle-Neumann, 1974, 1991)
Star theory (Croteau & Hoynes, 2001)
Storage battery model (Fiske & Taylor, 1991)
Storage bin model (Fiske & Taylor, 1991)
Suspense theory (Knobloch-Westerwick, Hastall, & Rossmann, 2009)
Synapse model of priming (Fiske & Taylor, 1991)

Technological determinism (Fischer, 1992)
Technological drivers (Neuman, 1991)
Television trivialization of public life (Postman, 1985)
Third-person theory (Perloff, 2002)
Transactional model (Graber, 1988; McLeod & Becker, 1974)
Transmission model (Shannon & Weaver, 1949)
Transportation model (Carey, 1975)
Transportation theory (Green & Brock, 2000)
Two-step flow (Katz & Lazarsfeld, 1955)

Uses and dependency model (Rubin & Windahl, 1986)
Uses and gratifications (Katz, Blumler, & Gurevitch, 1974; Lasswell, 1948; Rosengren, 1974; Rosengren,
    Wenner, & Palmgreen, 1985; Wright, 1960)

Videomalaise (Robinson, 1976)

Theory	n	%
Cultivation	27	8.0
Third person	25	7.4
Agenda setting	24	7.1
Uses and gratifications	19	5.7
Priming	16	4.8
Cognitive capacity	14	4.2
Framing	12	3.6
Feminism	11	3.3
Social learning	7	2.1
Elaboration likelihood	7	2.1
Schema	6	1.8
Diffusion of innovations	4	1.2

Table 5.1 Twelve Most Salient Theories

Note: Percentages are based on 336 articles that mentioned a theory.

PROFILING MOST SALIENT MEDIA EFFECTS THEORIES

Each of the top dozen media effects theories is briefly profiled in this section. If you are interested in learning more about any one of these theories beyond the short descriptions provided here, you can read the citations that are provided.

1. Cultivation

Cultivation theory was created by George Gerbner in 1969 as a response to his criticism that media effects research had been focusing only on short-term laboratory effects and ignoring the long-term effects that were gradually taking place over the course of a person's everyday life. He argued that television, which he called the dominant storytelling of the time, presented messages with consistent themes and that people who were exposed to these stories over time came to believe that the themes and patterns in these television stories applied to the real world.

Gerbner (1969) argued that the media cultivate a "collective consciousness about elements of existence" (p. 138) and explained:

I use the term [cultivation] to indicate that my primary concern in this discussion is not with information, education, persuasion, etc., or with any kind of direct communication "effects." I am concerned with the collective context within which, and in response to which, different individual and group selections and interpretations of messages take place. (p. 139)

Key to cultivation is the focus on public information with an

awareness that a certain item of knowledge is publicly held (i.e., not only known to many, but *commonly known that it is known to many*) makes collective thought and action possible. Such knowledge gives individuals their awareness of collective strength (or weakness), and a feeling of social identification or alienation. (pp. 139–140)

The media have the ability to construct publics by making certain information available that shapes "collective thought and action quickly, continuously, and pervasively across previous boundaries of time, space, and culture" (p. 140). In creating cultivation theory, Gerbner was not interested in particular messages but broad patterns. Also he was not interested in individual interpretations of receivers but instead the beliefs that they shared.

2. Third Person

The third-person effect (TPE) was first observed in 1983 by W. Phillips Davison, a sociologist, who was examining patterns across the results of public opinion polls and noticed that typically people felt that the media exerted a strong effect on other people (third persons) but not on themselves (first person). He found consistent patterns that people overestimate the effect of media messages on other people and underestimate the effect of media messages on themselves.

This effect has been explained as a "self-serving" perception whereby people think the media exert powerful influences, but only on other people, not on themselves. This allows people to complain about the media and call for regulation of harmful content so as to control the media exposures of other people. At the same time, it excuses them from having to take responsibility for possible negative consequences of their own exposures as long as people tell themselves that the media have no influence on them personally. This effect has been widely cited in the research literature (Tal-Or, Tsfati, & Gunther, 2009), and it has been found to have strong empirical support (Paul, Salwen, & Dupagne, 2000).

3. Agenda Setting

Agenda-setting theory focuses its explanation on how news content in the media shapes the public's beliefs about what is important in society. The first clear empirical support of this agenda-setting effect was provided by McCombs and Shaw (1972) in their analysis of the 1968 campaign for president. They found that when the media presented certain issues more saliently than others, those salient issues became the focus of the campaign. Over time, this agenda-setting research has included findings that the media also tell us what to think about; this is called *second-level agenda setting*. This second-level agenda-setting research has found that media messages do not just emphasize issues but they present informational elements about those issues, and those informational elements tell us what to think about the issue.

Closely related to the agenda-setting theory is the spiral of silence theory, which also focuses on how the media influence public beliefs. However, the spiral of silence theory also moves into explaining how public beliefs influence public discourse. Noelle-Neumann (1974) created this theory after observing patterns of news coverage in Western Europe. In her theory, she explained that when the media avoid covering an issue, people typically will not express their beliefs on that issue even if those beliefs are very important to them. They will remain silent. Thinking that they are in the minority, they refrain from expressing their beliefs for fear of being ostracized. Then silence begets more silence, and the belief that the issue is not important gets reinforced over time.

4. Uses and Gratifications

Uses and gratifications is a very broad theory that is based on two assumptions about media audiences. One of these assumptions is that individuals are active in making choices about selecting media and messages. The other assumption is that individuals are aware of their motives for information and entertainment; people use these motives as guides as they actively seek out media messages to satisfy their needs.

The explanatory system of uses and gratifications theory makes five claims:

1. Communication behavior is goal directed, purposive, and motivated.

2. People initiate the selection and use of communication vehicles.

3. A host of social and psychological factors guide, filter, or mediate communication behavior.

4. The media compete with other forms of communication in the gratification of needs or wants.

5. People are typically more influential than the media in the effects process (Rubin, 2002).

Because uses and gratifications theory regards audience members as active, the effects of the media are not viewed as particularly powerful; that is, people can control the effects to a large extent. Rosengren (1974) argued that the key idea of uses and gratifications was that individual differences among audience members intervene between the media and any effects. This means that media effects are explained not just by the media content but also by audience characteristics, such as their motivations and involvement with the content.

These ideas can be traced back to Wilbur Schramm (1954), who argued that people make their selection of media exposures by comparing expectation of a reward with effort required. This idea was later elaborated by Palmgreen and Rayburn (1985), who contended that people compared gratifications sought (GS) with gratifications obtained (GO). Because media exposure is a process repeated over the course of a person's life, each person has a lot of experience with GOs from past exposures, and this helps in forming expectations for each decision in the present.

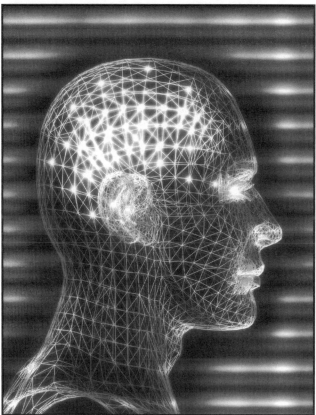

Source: Chad Baker/Photodisc/Thinkstock

5. Priming

Priming theory focuses on how one set of information or stimuli can affect the interpretation of a subsequent set in a person's memory. This theory conceptualizes the human mind as being organized in associative networks where each node in the network is a bit of information. When people think about a particular bit of information, that node is activated and the thinking proceeds from that node outward through associative networks to other nodes that are most closely related to the activated node. Thus when a node is activated, the next closest nodes in the associative network are primed; that is, they are most likely to be activated next (Jo & Berkowitz, 1994). The primed node is important because it sets up our expectations for our thought paths. Roskos-Ewoldsen, Roskos-Ewoldsen, and Carpentier (2002) say, "As applied to the media, priming refers to the effects of the content of the media on people's later behavior or judgments related to the content" (p. 97).

Originally referred to as cue theory, Leonard Berkowitz (1965) conducted early testing that showed that media portrayals contain particular symbols and when these symbols appear in a person's real life, those symbols cue the person to remember the media portrayal. Berkowitz conducted empirical research in the area of violent media content and how it affected viewers' behaviors. He found that when violent portrayals contained weapons, these weapons were powerful cues to people in real life. So when people saw a particular kind of weapon in real life, this real-life weapon triggered memories of the media portrayal and these memories were likely to lead to aggressive behavior.

Priming theory has undergone a good deal of testing with the topic of media violence. People shown a violent message in which characters are wronged will have the idea that violence is a good tool to use in getting revenge against one's aggressors. Later, in real life, when these people are victims of aggression, they will recall the use of violence as a successful tool to use in gaining vengeance and be more likely to behave in a vengeful manner.

6. Cognitive Capacity

Lang (2000) developed the cognitive capacity theory to provide a cognitive explanatory system for how people screen information then process it. She said that this process is structured by three tasks of encoding information, storage, and retrieval. The process begins with a person's sensory organs being stimulated; information then automatically enters a person's brain, where it spends up to a few seconds in a sensory storage area where most of it is wiped out, and only a small fraction moves on to short-term working memory. The person then selects certain bits of information to use in constructing what she called a "mental representation" of the outside event that stimulated the person's sensory organs. This selection is guided by a person's goals, existing knowledge, and the environment. Thus what is encoded is not an identical replica of the event; instead it is composed of a small fraction of the stimulus and is a highly idiosyncratic representation of the event. These representations are then stored in associative networks where ideas are linked together, making later retrieval possible. People undertake this processing in a parallel fashion; that is, there is more than one line of information being processed at the same time. Because processing resources are limited, people divide these resources across tasks at any given time. Those information-processing tasks that are given the most resources get processed in more detail and are therefore more likely to be remembered.

7. Framing

Framing regards meaning as residing primarily in the message, particularly news messages. The frame of news stories is constructed by journalists in the way they select certain bits of information while ignoring others and by how they structure their stories to direct attention toward certain facts. The frame is the way the story is presented; that is, it is the point of view from which the story is told. The frame is the news angle or the context for the story (Tuchman, 1978).

Source: Digital Vision/Photodisc/Thinkstock

The frame of a news story tells the audience members what the theme or meaning of the event is and therefore constrains and shapes the meaning of the event for the audience. The frame provides context in the way it defines a problem, diagnoses causes, makes moral judgments, and suggests remedies.

Framing theory is related to both the agenda-setting and priming theories. Framing explains how the agenda is set by the way the media frame their stories. Once a person is exposed to a media message, it is the framing of the message that determines which nodes get primed.

8. Feminism

Feminist theory contends that there is a sexist ideology permeating the media. This ideology presents a patriarchal world where there is a male-dominated social order that is assumed to be natural and just. In this ideology, women are weaker and less capable than are men, so women gain their identity through their association with male characters. Under feminist theory, the media continually present messages with paternalistic themes that foster a false belief system in their audiences (Rakow, 1992).

According to van Zoonen (1994), the focus of feminist theory is to provide answers to questions such as, How are discourses about gender encoded into media texts?, How do audiences use and interpret gendered media texts?, and How does audience reception contribute to the construction of gender at the level of individual identity? Some feminist scholars also contend that women can use the media to empower themselves by forming groups and creating their own meanings that reject the paternalistic themes (Radway, 1984).

9. Social Learning

This theory has its origin in the ideas of Miller and Dollard (1941), who found that people learned behaviors by observing the actions of others; they did not need to perform the behaviors themselves in order to learn those behaviors. Bandura (1977) took this idea and elaborated on it with the concepts of identification, vicarious reinforcement, and self-efficacy. Bandura showed that this observational-type learning was enhanced to the extent that observers identified with people who performed the behaviors (role models) as well as when those behaviors were rewarded or at least not punished. He also showed that the role models need not be people in real life but can be characters in fictional stories presented through the media. Bandura (1986) continued to elaborate this explanation by adding cognitive components. Bandura argued that is was not only characteristics about the environment that accounted for social learning but also characteristics about the person; that is, people think about what they experience and transform their experiences into cognitive models. This transformation is guided by four types of processes: attention, retention, production, and motivation.

10. Elaboration Likelihood

The elaboration likelihood model (ELM) was developed by Petty and Cacioppo (1981) to move scholarly thinking beyond the limited approach to opinion formation that assumed people paid attention to arguments and logically weighed the merits of those arguments when making up their own minds. Although the ELM is typically regarded as a theory of persuasion—not learning—fundamentally it is focused on how people encounter and process information. ELM acknowledges that there are times when people do carefully attend to information—what they call the "central route of information processing"—but that there are also times when people encounter information and arguments in an unconscious state or when they are not logical in their handling of the information—what they call the "peripheral route." The central route involves effortful cognitive activity whereby the person draws on prior experience and knowledge in order to scrutinize carefully all of the information relevant to determine the central merits of the position advocated (Petty, Priester, & Brinol, 2002, p. 165). Using this route, people actively think about the importance of claims, saliency of information, and the consequences of accepting the message claims. In contrast, the peripheral route requires low-effort processing of persuasive information; people react to simple cues in messages and act as cognitive misers, that is, allocate very little mental effort. With little mental effort, people are likely to select a peripheral reason and ignore more important reasons. Which route a person uses is really a decision about how much effort he or she is willing to expend in processing the information in a message. The key factors that affect the amount of thinking a person is willing to undertake are a person's cognitive trait of the general motivation to think, as well as a person's reaction to characteristics in the message—such as the perceived personal relevance of a message, trustworthiness of source, whether source is stigmatized or not, key arguments presented as questions or assertions, number of message sources, and expectedness of the position being argued.

11. Schema

Schema theory has attracted a wide range of scholars. George Herbert Mead (1934) is often credited with originating the idea of schema in his book *Mind, Self, and Society* in which he argued that symbols mediate and structure all our experience. Sets of symbols, called *schema,* are the templates that help us make sense of all the sensory stimuli we are exposed to constantly.

Cognitive psychologists built on this idea by conceptualizing schemas as associative networks that reside in a person's mind. A schema is "a cognitive structure that represents knowledge about a concept or type of stimulus, including its attributes and the relations among those attributes" (Fiske & Taylor, 1991, p. 98). Ideas are organized as nodes in associative networks. When we activate one idea, other ideas that are most closely related to the activated idea are also activated. Thus thinking proceeds from idea to idea according to how they are related together in these associative networks.

These schemas serve to organize an individual's memory for people and events. They are composed of linguistic and nonlinguistic information, images, words, sounds, and sequences of experiences (Graesser & Nakamura, 1982). Some schemas are sequences of events and are then referred to as *scripts*. They are culture specific, so they contain prejudices and beliefs embedded in the culture.

Schemas are used by individuals to help them comprehend events. Thus schemas are templates of expectations for people and events that have been developed and modified over the course of a person's lifetime. When we meet a new person, we read the salient cues about that person (for example, body type, obvious personality characteristics, and the like) and match these cues to our schema about people. When we find a schema that best matches the cues, we use that schema to set our expectations for that new person.

12. Diffusion of Innovations

In 1962 Everett Rogers conducted a major review and synthesis of the literature on how information gets disseminated in societies. He came up with the diffusion of information theory, in which he built on the ideas of Lazarsfeld and extended those ideas beyond the realm of political information and paid special attention to how information about innovations—especially about agriculture and health—was disseminated. Rogers argued that information about innovations was disseminated in a step-by-step fashion to different groups of people in a society. The first group to receive and use the information were people he labeled as "early adopters." These are people who liked to try new things and were continually monitoring the media to find out what those new things were. Rogers said that these early adopters passed their information along to the opinion leaders (à la Lazarsfeld), who then tested out the idea or innovation. If the opinion leaders found they liked the innovation, they passed it along to other people in their interpersonal networks (the opinion followers). Finally the information spread out to the "laggards" or later adopters.

THE BIG PICTURE WITH MEDIA EFFECTS THEORIES

The salient media theories are a good place to begin when learning about media effects. However, as you will soon see, they do not cover the entire phenomenon.

Take a look at Figure 5.1, which is a minor modification of the individual-level MET with its six types on the lines and the four functions in the columns. The three columns from the macro-level MET have been collapsed into one column at the right. This modified matrix has 30 cells.

Onto this matrix, I have plotted the dozen most salient theories profiled in the previous section of this chapter. Notice that there are theories plotted in only 10 of these 30 cells, which indicates that while these 12 theories are salient in the sense that they are the most tested theories, as a set they cover only about one third of the full media effects phenomenon.

We of course need to remember that there are many more theories than the 12 salient ones plotted on the MET in Figure 5.1, so this argument is not made to convince you that there is no theoretical activity in many cells. Instead, my argument is that the most well-known theories of media effects are concentrated into a few cells. First, learning a lot about what these 12 theories have to say about media effects is a good beginning, but this strategy will deliver only partial understanding of the full phenomenon of media effects. In order

Figure 5.1 Plotting Theories Onto the Media Effects Template

Type of Effect	Media Influence Functions				
	Acquiring	Triggering	Altering	Conditioning	Public
Behavior					Uses & Grats
Physiology	Cognitive Capacity	Priming	Schema	Schema	
Cognitive	Cognitive Capacity	Social Learning	ELM	Framing	
Belief	Third Person	Agenda Setting	Cultivation	Spiral of Silence	Feminism
Attitudes	ELM				
Affects					Uses & Grats

Note: Percentages are based on 336 articles that mentioned a theory. "Grats" is short for "Gratifications."

to get a more complete picture of the overall media effects phenomenon, we would have to learn about several hundred theories, and this makes for a rather inefficient approach.

There is also a second reason for why a theoretical approach is not a good strategy for learning about the big picture of media effects. This argument is based on the finding that much of the large literature concerned with media effects is not generated by theory. To illustrate this point, let's return to the content analysis study I mentioned earlier in this chapter (Potter & Riddle, 2007). This was a content analysis of the media effects literature published in the major scholarly journals. Recall that we found that 336 articles that were theory driven and that 144 theories were mentioned, with the top 12 most mentioned theories accounting for 168 of those articles or about 50% of the set of theory-driven articles. However, what I did not mention yet is that the total sample we analyzed was 962 media effects studies. Thus only about 35% (336 articles out of 962) of the total media effects literature featured a theory. The other 65% of the media effects literature was generated by no theory at all.

Other studies of the media literature also reported similar findings. This pattern of a low percentage of theory-driven studies has been found in the larger media literature percentages run as low as 8.1% (Potter, Cooper, & Dupagne, 1993) and as high as 27.6% (Riffe & Freitag, 1997) and 30.5% (Kamhawi & Weaver, 2003). In an analysis of published literature on mass communication from 1965 to 1989 in eight journals, Potter et al. (2003) found that only 8.1% of 1,326 articles were guided by a theory and provided a test of that theory; another 19.5% were tests of hypotheses but these hypotheses were not derived from a theory. Kamhawi and Weaver (2003) reported that only 30.5% of all articles published in 10 communication journals from 1980 to 1999 specifically mentioned a theory, which led them to argue that

> theoretical development is probably the main consideration in evaluating the disciplinary status of the field. As our field grows in scope and complexity the pressure for theoretical integration increases. It seems that scholars in the field should be developing and testing theories to explain the process and effects of mass communication. However, that was not widely evident in our sample. (p. 20)

While theories have been important to the development of the media effects scholarly field, we cannot conclude that our understanding of media effects is predominantly theory driven. Instead theory development is sporadic and thin. This clearly indicates that our research is not organized efficiently by a handful of theories that present scholars with a parsimonious set of conceptualizations and that direct long paths of programmatic research, much like what is done in other scholarly fields, particularly in the physical sciences. Returning to the Potter and Riddle (2006) analysis, there seem to be few examples of programmatic research guided by theory; among the 336 articles we found that did feature a theory, 144 theories were mentioned, and only 12 of those theories were mentioned in more than five studies. The remaining 132 theories were spread out over the remaining 168 articles that were theory driven. This indicates a pattern of rather thin theory development. This finding was also in evidence in the study by Kamhawi and Weaver (2003), who found that only three theories (information processing, uses and gratifications, and media construction of social reality) were mentioned in as many as 10% of their analyzed articles.

Less than one third of the very large media effects literature is guided by a theory of any kind. Therefore, in order to understand more than a relatively small segment of knowledge about media effects and how they work, we need to move beyond the theory-driven portion of the literature. That is the purpose of the next nine chapters.

SUMMARY

Theories are important to the development of any scholarly field. With the scholarly field of media effects, many theories have been developed. However, few of those theories account for more than a handful of research studies. And the most salient dozen theories as a set has generated only a small fraction (about 17%) of the total media effects research literature.

When trying to build your own understanding of media effects, the study of theories is a good place to begin. The most salient media effects theories orient us to the most popular effects. However, there is much more wisdom about media effects that is not conveyed by theories; that is, much of the vast literature of 10,000 research studies is not theory driven.

In Part II of this book, I take you through that literature. Of course, we will not visit each of the 10,000 studies—that would be too much detail! Just to list the citations of those studies would consume 650 typed pages. Instead of focusing on all the detail, I will try to direct your attention to the big picture patterns so that you develop an understanding of the overall phenomenon of media effects.

Review Questions

1. What is the purpose of theories?

2. List the most prevalent dozen media effects theories. What is the main idea of each one?

3. Why is it insufficient to limit our study of media effects to effects theories?

Further Thinking Questions

1. Figure 5.1 shows the most salient media effects theories mapped onto the Media Effects Template. Can you think of any reasons why certain areas of the map have multiple theories while other areas have none?

2. Pick an area on the Media Effects Template where there are no theories plotted. Can you create a theory to fill that gap?

PART II

Types of Mass Media Effects on Individuals

This second part of the book is composed of six chapters that focus on the range of media-influenced effects on individuals. The goal of this part of the book is to provide you with a structured overview of the full gamut of media effects on individuals. This is why there is a chapter on each type of media effect—physiological, cognitive, belief, attitude, affective, and behavioral—and why each chapter is organized by media influence function—acquiring, triggering, altering, and reinforcing.

Each chapter in this part of the book focuses on a different type of effect. Chapter 6 focuses on physiological effects, which are changes to bodily systems, such as heart rate, blood pressure, and other automatic responses that humans experience as they encounter messages. Chapter 7 illuminates cognitive effects, which are the processes of thinking. Chapter 8 deals with beliefs, which are the ideas we hold about ourselves and our world. Chapter 9 takes up attitudinal effects, which are the value judgments we make. Chapter 10 focuses on affects, which are primarily emotions and moods. And Chapter 11 is concerned with behaviors, which are the things we do in response to media influence.

Each chapter in Part II presents five important features: chapter outline, narrative, illustrations of effects, exhibits of research, and questions for review and thinking. The outline lists the major topics presented in the chapter. The narrative follows the outline and explains the *what* and *how* of the type of media effect that is the focus of the chapter. The *what* refers to the effects themselves, and the *how* refers to how the media exert their influence so that the effects can occur. In each chapter, the narrative begins with an examination of the general nature of the type effect that is the focus of the chapter, then it shows what the major effects are by media influence.

Each chapter includes anecdotes that make the effects more concrete and understandable. The anecdotes are designed to show what the effect looks like when it shows up in a person's everyday life. These examples, which are set off in boxes, are supplements to the narrative itself. If you feel you understand the effects from reading the narrative, you can skip over the examples. But if you feel that the narrative is a bit too abstract for you, then read the examples to help you understand the effects better.

Throughout each chapter there are exhibits that supplement the narrative. Most of these exhibits present an outline of the types of effect that are the topic of the chapter. Also, some of the exhibits display the sets of factors that have been found associated with particular effects. For each effect and each factor, there is at least one citation (sometimes many) that directs you to a research study. While many of the citations in those exhibits are mentioned in the narrative, others are not. These additional citations are included to give you a sense of the topics that have attracted the most research attention. Because the literature on media effects is so large, I have not cited every empirical study in that literature; the citation lists focus on more recently published studies as well as some older classic studies. After reading a chapter, it is a good idea to then read a few of the cited studies to get more detail about how various researchers have conceptualized a particular effect, gathered evidence of its occurrence, and explained the role of the media in shaping that effect.

At the end of each chapter, there is a list of questions for review and for further thinking. When you have finished reading a chapter, look at the Review Questions and see if you have absorbed enough information from your reading to be able to answer each question easily. Then look at the Further Thinking Questions to help you extend your knowledge about the particular media effects presented in that chapter.

Each of these five features is designed to help you keep your focus on the big picture on each chapter. After almost a century of research on media effects, there are so many empirical findings about effects and the factors of influence that bring about these effects that it is easy to get lost in all the details. I urge you to keep your focus on the big picture and do not let all the trees block out your sense of direction as you navigate through this fascinating forest.

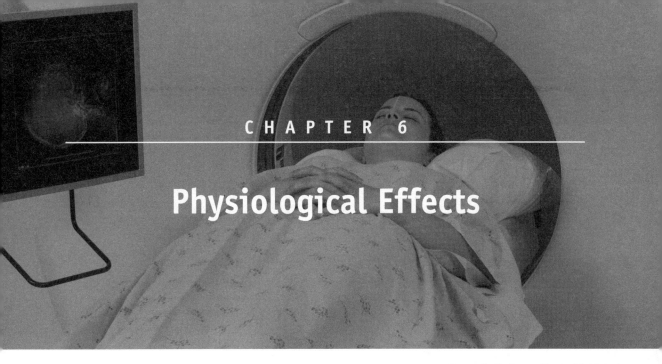

CHAPTER 6

Physiological Effects

Source: Jupiterimages/Creatas/Thinkstock

CHAPTER 6

Physiological Effects

These first two chapters on individual-level effects illuminate the brain/mind distinction that philosophers have explored for centuries. Some scholars regard the brain and the mind as the same thing, while others—called "dualists"—treat them as two separate entities. Simply put, this distinction is a debate between two approaches to studying human thinking: the physiological approach and the cognitive approach. In this book, you will be introduced to both approaches within the context of media influence. We deal with the physiological approach in this chapter, then move to the cognitive approach in Chapter 7.

The physiological approach regards the human brain as a physical organ of the body. Scholars using the physiological approach to studying humans believe that as the brain develops in a fetus, it is programmed to perform certain functions that ensure the survival of the person. When a person is born, the brain governs the person's growth and learning through a continual progression of chemical and electrical reactions that take place in that brain tissue (for example, see Campbell, 1973).

In contrast, scholars who focus on the cognitive approach believe human thinking is governed by the mind, which is located in the brain but is not the same thing as the physical brain. With the cognitive approach, scholars believe that thinking is more than chemical or electrical reactions; they believe that the complexity of human thinking cannot be explained adequately by brain chemistry alone. To clarify this distinction a bit more, let's consider a metaphor of a computer. When you take it out of the box and plug it in, the computer is already programmed to bring up images on your screen and to allow you to perform some basic functions. Also, there is a good deal of software programming that is always running in the background to ensure that the computer can perform its basic functions. This preprogrammed software, along with the architecture of the hardware, was designed to allow the computer to perform its basic, generic functions that are common to all computers. However, computers also allow us to program them; that is, we can change the look of our desktops, bookmark our favorite websites, create our own sets of folders for saving e-mail, alter the defaults on our word processing programs, and perform all sorts of changes to customize our computers to satisfy our particular needs.

Applying this computer metaphor to humans, we can see that people are a configuration of hardware (body parts) and software (automatic processes programmed before birth that run all the basic human systems, keep them running efficiently, and protect those systems from threats). Thus our brains are "hard wired" to perform certain functions, but they also include a lot of software that gives us the capability to think for ourselves. This basic hardware and software is a platform upon which we build our specialized needs, thoughts, and behaviors. Understanding the basic hardware and software requires a physiological approach, while understanding the specialized programming that we create as well as all the programming that is done by all kinds of influences on us throughout our lives requires a cognitive approach.

Both of these approaches have provided valuable insights into how people are influenced by media messages, so we must understand both approaches when studying media effects. Studying media effects from a physiological perspective gives us insights into how all humans are the same, that is, how the media affect our basic human programming. Studying media effects from a cognitive perspective (discussed more fully in Chapter 7) gives us insights into the many, many differences that exist across the array of humanity.

NATURE OF PHYSIOLOGICAL EFFECTS

The physiological approach regards the brain as a complex calculating machine that has been programmed to perform particular functions. All animal brains are hard wired with preprogrammed neural systems that perform a core set of basic routines automatically. These basic routines are drives that motivate the organism to eat, drink, protect itself from harm, reproduce, and care for its offspring. When humans are born, we are already able to do certain things automatically, like breathe and take in information through our five senses. We can perceive threats. We have a hard-wired drive of hunger and thirst that makes us seek nourishment to keep us alive. We don't have to think about these things. Our brains tell our bodies what to do whether we consciously think about it or not. Given certain stimuli, the human body reacts in certain prescribed ways. We do not have to learn these reactions; they are programmed into our systems. These things are fundamental to survival and to being human.

When it comes to media effects, two parts of the human brain are especially important to understand. One part is the brain stem, which is the *limbic system*. This part of the brain governs survival and the propagation of the species; these are functions that are essential for all organisms, and this part of the brain is shared by all animals. The limbic system is the oldest part of the brain; that is, it can be traced back through early species of humans, from vertebrae to early forms of fish that first appeared on earth about 500 million years ago (Campbell, 1973). This archaic brain tissue is still part of our heritage from lower creatures and has not changed much in all that time. The other part of the brain—the *cerebral cortex*—is much younger, occurring in the earliest mammals some 100 million years ago. This "younger" part of the brain is concerned with learning and memory, more so than automatic pre-programmed processes.

Notice that when we consider how the human brain has developed over time, we are talking about many millions of years. In contrast, the media are very, very new. Mass market newspapers, magazines, and books have been around for only about 150 years; film and radio have been around for about a century, and the rest of the media have been around for considerably less than a century. Therefore the human brain has not had nearly enough time to begin adapting physiologically to the new types of stimuli that these new media provide. The media—especially film, television, and computers—offer so many images that are interpreted as real-world stimuli by the basic hard wiring of our brains that was designed for an existence well before any of the media and well before even the advent of civilization.

Automatic and Quasi-Automatic

Many physiological processes are purely automatic; that is, they are hard wired into our brains and they run automatically with no need for us to think about them. For example, our hearts beat and lungs breathe whether we think about these functions or not. When we walk outside on a sunny day, the pupils of our eyes contract to prevent too much sunlight from burning our retinas. When we hear a sudden loud crash close by, our bodies quickly react to a possible threat of danger; a hormone is immediately secreted into the bloodstream to make the heart beat faster, thus giving us more physical energy to run away or to attack the threat. This fight/flight reaction is triggered automatically without us having the think about getting ready to deal with the threat. If it did not trigger automatically, we could be overwhelmed by the threat before we had a chance to flee or fight back. This automatic reaction is programmed into all humans—as well as all other animals—and is necessary for the survival of the species.

Some of these reactions are what we refer to as "quasi-automatic." A quasi-automatic reaction is one that is triggered automatically by a hard-wired program in our brain, but once the reaction occurs, we can become aware of it and take steps to enhance or reduce it. For example, pupil dilation, brain waves, sweat gland activity, and the orienting reflex are reactions generally believed as being outside the control of media audience members and are therefore regarded as purely automatic (Lang, 1995). But the fight/flight reflex is regarded as quasi-automatic. When the brain perceives a threat, it triggers a readiness to respond to the threat by making the heart beat more rapidly and our breathing becomes more rapid and shallow. But we can quickly assess the degree of threat, and if it is a false alarm, we can consciously force ourselves to breathe more deeply and thus calm ourselves down. Another example is with sexual arousal. When we see a physically attractive person who is a potential sexual partner, we can automatically become sexually aroused. At that point, we can think about the situation and either enhance or reduce this response. If we are on our honeymoon and we see our spouse, then we will consciously engage our imagination and feelings to enhance the sexual attraction. But if the attraction is triggered by a person other than our spouse, we will try to reduce the attraction by consciously thinking about something else.

Sometimes a person will think a physiological reaction is quasi-automatic when in fact it is not. For example, in movies we see portrayals of criminals trying to beat the lie detector, which is a device that monitors galvanic skin response. The brain automatically sends signals to the skin in times of stress. These electrodermal impulses are both subconscious and involuntary (Hopkins & Fletcher, 1994). Yet there are some people who believe they can feel the subtle degree of electrodermal impulses and modify them when they are given a lie detector test.

With quasi-automatic responses, what we try to do in essence is move the governing activity of the response from the limbic part of our brain that initially triggers the reflex to the cortical part of our brain, where we can gain awareness of the reflex then consciously try to alter that reaction. Thus we are trying to move away from a purely physiological reaction to a cognitively controlled reaction.

Four Types of Physiological Processes

While the human body engages in many physiological processes, four types are particularly important to us when we consider media influenced effects. These four types are perceptual processes, automatic survival mechanisms, sexual mechanisms, and neurophysiological processes. Let's examine each of these in a bit of detail.

Perceptual processes are hard wired into the human brain. These processes help people orient to their environments by selecting certain types of stimuli to attend to. Some of these stimuli are signals of threats and some are signals of pleasure. These processes are automatic; that is, they are programmed to tell us important things about our environment. These signals then can either trigger additional automatic processes or can trigger conscious attention through which we think about how to respond.

A second type of physiological process includes *automatic survival mechanisms*. When the human body perceives a threat, it automatically enters a fight/flight state. To prepare for fight/flight, the body produces hormones such as epinephrine, which causes the heart to beat more rapidly, breathing to quicken, muscles to tense, and palms to sweat. This produces a readiness to run away or to face the predator. Without this readiness, humans would not be able to deal successfully with threats, and their survival would be severely threatened.

A third type of physiological process includes *sexual mechanisms*. Humans need to reproduce in order for the ongoing survival of the human species. Therefore the human brain has been hard wired to monitor the environment for attractive sexual partners and to derive pleasure from sexual release. The media's continual stream of messages often presents visual images of highly attractive sexual objects, and these images generate attention as well as the expectation of pleasure.

Finally, there are *neurophysiological processes*. The human brain is a complex of chemical and electrical processes. The media can influence these processes with the repetition of its messages as well as their form (size, color, loudness, and content of its messages).

Now let's examine how the media influence these perceptual processes, automatic survival mechanisms, sexual mechanisms, and neurophysiological processes. The remainder of this chapter is structured to show how the media trigger, alter, and reinforce these processes.

TRIGGERING PHYSIOLOGICAL EFFECTS

Most of the research into physiological effects by the media has examined the triggering function. Within this function, two topics are dominant. First, there is the monitoring of the environment that often results in triggering something called the *orienting reflex*.

Second, there is the triggering of *arousal* that is required for attention, concentration, and information processing. This arousal is also important for the fight/flight reflex and for sexual attraction.

Source: ©iStockphoto.com/peeterv

Orienting Reflex

The human body automatically monitors its environment for meaningful information that comes to it through its five senses of sight, sound, touch, taste, and smell (Bryant & Miron, 2002). Our brains continually monitor all this incoming information automatically without us consciously considering it. We flow along in this automatic state of continual monitoring until our brain perceives a stimulus that is out of the ordinary and our orienting response is triggered. This orienting reflex causes us to pay attention to the stimulus (Anderson & Burns, 1991). For example, when you are driving your car down a highway, you are automatically and unconsciously monitoring all the sights and sounds from the road around you while your conscious attention perhaps is on the song playing on your car's sound system. Then suddenly a car whizzes past you and cuts right in front of you and your attention is immediately triggered by the car.

The Orienting Reflex

Jacob is wearing his iPod while he walks across campus. He is listening to a song where a guy is complaining about not being able to meet women. While Jacob is concentrating on the song, he is also unconsciously monitoring all the sights and sounds of campus as fellow classmates jam the sidewalks while they hurry between classes on bicycles, skateboards, and on foot. Although all this traffic is a potential threat to Jacob's safety, he is not concentrating on any of it; instead, his brain is processing all the stimuli unconsciously.

Suddenly Jacob notices Emily on the sidewalk about 50 feet up ahead of him. Emily is a girl in his next class. Jacob desperately wants to meet Emily, but he is too shy to approach her. He has made it a habit to sit several rows behind her in the large lecture hall so he can glance over at her and watch her take notes in the cute way she does. He realizes that he really has a thing for her and wishes there was some way to meet her. He watches as she arrives at their classroom building. As she is about to enter the door, she bumps into someone coming out of the building, causing her to drop the books she is carrying. Jacob sees this as his chance to help her, so he hurries toward her. But by the time he gets within 10 feet of Emily, another guy has started to help her. Jacob watches the other guy bend down to pick up her books and introduce himself to Emily. The guy and Emily walk into the building together as Jacob watches sadly.

When Emily disappears from his sight, Jacob's attention returns to the song. He finds himself humming along with the song about the guy who has such a hard time meeting women.

Analysis

Throughout the story, Jacob is in a stimuli rich environment with lots of activity. However, he is only paying conscious attention to the song. Then when he sees Emily, he experiences the first of two orienting reflexes. First his attention is triggered by Emily and he continues to concentrate on Emily while he stops paying attention to the song. But when Emily disappears into the classroom building, Jacob experiences a second orienting reflex when his attention is triggered back to the song, which has been playing on his iPod the whole time.

This orienting reflex is hard wired into our brains "and insures our safety since it makes certain that we will react suddenly and effectively to any major change that confronts us" (Singer, 1980, p. 37). The orienting reflex is accompanied by a general decrease in muscle activity, lowering of heart rate, and a pause in respiration followed by shorter, faster breathing (Ravaja, 2004a).

In today's world, media messages are a constant part of our environment. We monitor media messages, and while in that continual flow of experiences from both the media and the real world, we often are in a state of automaticity in which we do not consciously make distinctions between the two sources of stimuli. Therefore certain elements in media messages often act on us as if they were occurring in the real world. Remember that the hard wiring in the limbic part of our brain has been around for thousands of generations of humans, while media depictions of threats have been available for fewer than a half-dozen generations of humans. Thus the human brain has not had enough time to make much progress in its gradual adaptation over generations to make a clear distinction between real-world and mediated-world threats when we are *automatically* monitoring our environments. When we *consciously* monitor our environments, we easily make such distinctions; because we are now in an attentional state. It probably seems silly to you that I make a point about the difference between the real world and the media world. It seems so obvious! But remember that most of the time, we are not consciously monitoring our environment; instead the monitoring is done automatically and guided by some very, very old programming code that does not recognize a difference between a real-world threat and a mediated-world threat.

Although they are not experts in physiology, nor are they likely to use the technical term of "orienting reflex," producers of television and film stories know that we will orient toward threats on the screen. Intuitively, producers know that threats get our attention, so they use loud noises, strange sounds, sudden close-ups, fast cuts, and quick motions that make viewers sense that their personal space and safety are being invaded, and this triggers our attention (Reeves et al., 1985).

The orienting response is triggered not only by threats but by anything that suddenly appears as unusual in our environment. For example, in an experiment of ads on Web pages, Diar and Sundar (2004) found that pop-up ads triggered an orienting response as measured by heartbeats using an electrocardiogram (ECG). When we are on the Internet, we are monitoring our screens for certain types of images and information. Pop-up ads are not expected; they occur suddenly and invade our visual space, so they trigger the orienting reflex that shifts our attention to them and away from what we were thinking about before they popped up.

These perceptual tricks are especially prevalent in children's programming. In fact, a lot of children's programs (such as *Sesame Street*) were developed specifically to take advantage of this orienting reflex (Liebert & Sprafkin, 1988). When producers of media messages keep introducing unexpected noises, images, characters, plot developments, and the like, they repeatedly trigger the orienting reflex and thereby continually pull our attention from one thing to the next throughout the duration of their messages. This is especially important with programming for children, because producers believe that children have very short attention spans and therefore continually need triggers to capture their attention.

Arousal

The orienting reflex is not an isolated, discrete effect. Instead, when the orienting reflex is triggered, it usually leads to other effects, especially arousal. Media researchers have focused on four kinds of arousal subsequent to this orienting reflex. These four areas are generalized brain arousal, fight/flight reflex, sexual arousal, and excitation transfer.

Generalized Brain Arousal. The orienting reflex energizes our brains and stimulates brain activity. This activity usually is regarded as making the state of attention possible. This state of attention is needed for conscious learning, such as encoding of information and recall from memory. How do we know when the brain is aroused? Until recently, researchers were not able to observe the arousal of brain activity directly, so they relied on indirect indicators such as heart rate and blood pressure (Detenber, Simons, & Bennett, 1998; Detenber, Simons, & Reiss, 2000; Lang, Schwartz, Chung, & Lee, 2004; Lang, Zhou, Schwartz, Bolls, & Potter, 2000; Potter, 2000; Schneider, Lang, Shin, & Bradley, 2004; Suckfill, 2000) and skin conductance (Detenber et al., 2000; Sundar & Wagner, 2002). But now with MRI machines, we can scan the brain and look for more direct evidence of brain arousal and activity.

The arousal of brain activity gets our brains ready to perform other functions. This physiological arousal can be used to keep attention on a particular object such as a video screen. If the object is perceived as a threat, the arousal will trigger a fight/flight reflex (see next section of the chapter). If the object is perceived as sexually attractive, the arousal will trigger a sexual reflex. Sometimes this arousal energizes the brain to a point that we take on more difficult cognitive tasks and problems. Thus the arousal itself is a physiological effect, but it can lead to all sorts of emotional, behavioral, and cognitive effects.

Fast-paced media stories increase skin conductance—a measure of sympathetic nervous system activation (Detenber et al., 2000). Also, exciting content (compared to calm content) increases heart rate (Lang, Bolls, Potter, & Kawahara, 1999). A moving-face newscaster was associated with decreased respiratory sinus arrhythmia (RSA), an index of attention, and improved memory performance for positive messages (Ravaja, 2004b).

Media messages can trigger a psychological state of presence through triggering physiological responses such as electrodermal activity (EDA). It can also trigger emotions as measured by facial electromyography (EMG) and attentional engagement respiratory sinus arrhythmia, which is a function of the parasympathetic nervous system (Lombard, Reich, Grabe, Bracken, & Ditton, 2000; Ravaja, 2004a).

Television ads have been especially popular as a subject of study to see which techniques produce which physiological responses. Researchers have found that watching TV commercials can induce changes in the heart rate and orienting reflex (Lang, 1990, 1994a); electrodermal responses (Hopkins & Fletcher, 1994); facial electromyogaphy (Bolls, Lang, & Potter, 2001; Hazlett & Hazlett, 1999); and changes in brain alpha waves (Reeves et al., 1985; Simons, Detenber, Cuthbert, Schwartz, & Reiss, 2003; Smith & Gevins, 2004). Also, Lang et al. (2005) found that TV viewers experienced physiological arousal after changing channels; that is, the simple act of changing a TV channel could trigger the physiological effect of arousal.

When the brain is aroused, this arousal can spread to other parts of our bodies. Sometimes this arousal can lead to emotions. The arousal can be pleasant (such as love, lust, joy, and the like) and sometimes the arousal is unpleasant (such as anger, hate, frustration, and the like). Sometimes this arousal can lead to behaviors such as fighting or sexual actions.

Fight/Flight Reflex. One form of arousal is the fight/flight reflex. When we see a predator or other threat in our environment, we need to be ready to stand up to the threat or get away from it. And we need to be able to do this as quickly as possible, so this reflex is hard wired into the human brain. If this reflex were not automatic, our chances for survival would be considerably lower.

Arousal and Fight/Flight

A week has gone by since Jacob watched Emily drop her books, and he has had to endure watching the guy who helped her with her books sit next to her in class. He found out that the guy's name was Michael. Jacob hates Michael, whom Jacob regards as his competition for Emily.

Today as Jacob walks to class, he spots Emily up ahead walking alone into the classroom building. Jacob hurries to catch up with her so he can hold the door open for her and introduce himself. Suddenly he feels someone bump into him, knocking him off stride. Immediately his heart begins to race and his muscles tense as his body automatically gets him ready to respond to the threat. He spins around to confront the person who bumped into him and sees that it is Michael. His hatred boils over and he finds himself shouting, "Hey dude. Watch where you are going! Learn to walk!" Jacob feels a strong impulse to lunge forward and push Michael hard to the ground. Then Jacob notices that Michael is about a foot taller than he is and weighs about 50 pounds more—50 pounds of hard muscle. Jacob brushes himself off and adds, "And don't let it happen again," as he quickly moves away from Michael as fast as he can.

Analysis

When Jacob was bumped, his brain immediately triggered a fight/flight response. It released hormones into his bloodstream to make his heart pound faster and move oxygen to his muscles at a higher rate. At first, Jacob wanted to fight Michael but then he switched to flight when he quickly realized that avoiding a fight was the better alternative.

Many times when we are watching a movie or a TV show we find ourselves strongly identifying with the characters, and we begin experiencing what the characters must be experiencing. Oftentimes, these characters find themselves suddenly confronting serious threats to their survival. Producers show the character with eyes fixated on the threat, muscles tensing, and breathing rapidly as the character prepares to attack the threat or flee. Audience members watching this portrayal also experience the threat vicariously. We feel the fear. When we are in a theater watching the huge images on the screen and hearing the loud music, we tend to get transported away from the real world and into the film world of the characters; when this happens we can feel personally threatened and our arousal can be quite strong. The fictional threats depicted on the screen do more than merely trigger our attention; they also trigger our fight/flight reflex.

Sexual Arousal. Erotic material presented in media messages has been found to trigger different forms of sexual arousal in the human body, such as penile tumescence (Eccles, Marshall, & Barbaree, 1988; Malamuth & Check, 1980; Schaefer & Colgan, 1977), vaginal changes (Sintchak & Geer, 1975), and thermography (Abramson, Perry, Seeley, Seeley, & Rothblatt, 1981). People who view erotic images in magazines and on websites can become very sexually aroused. These people know that it is not possible to engage in sex with these images, yet they can become very aroused sexually.

Excitation Transfer. Once the body experiences physiological arousal of any kind, this arousal energy is often used to perform tasks that have nothing to do with the media messages that originally triggered the arousal. This effect has been labeled "excitation transfer" by Zillmann (1980). In several experiments, Zillmann found that certain media content (for example, suspenseful, violent, and sexual images) would trigger physiological arousal in his experimental participants. When the media exposure was over and Zillmann gave these participants some unrelated task to perform, those participants were still experiencing residual arousal left over from their media exposure. That is, it took some time for the arousal to dissipate. This dissipating arousal was still strong enough to energize those participants to exhibit higher levels of attention or a stronger affective reaction than they would have had they not been still experiencing arousal.

Oftentimes, the arousal is triggered by a media message, then transferred to a real-world task. For example, Zillmann (1980) observed that media portrayals that put favored characters in jeopardy create suspense, and this triggers an arousal jag, which is a surge of adrenaline into the bloodstream that increases attention. This arousal is physiological; that is, it is triggered by fight/flight or sexual attraction mechanisms. This arousal then leads to labeling as an emotion (more on this in Chapter 10).

ALTERING PHYSIOLOGICAL EFFECTS

The media can alter the natural hard-wired programming in our brains with repeated exposures over the long term. Media researchers have focused their attention on two altering effects: habituation and the altering of brain waves.

Habituation

When the media present the same pattern of stimuli over and over again, those stimuli begin to lose their power to elicit the same degree of reflex over time. This is the *habituation effect*. For example, people who experience a violent act in a TV show for the first time will likely exhibit a natural orienting reflex followed by a fight/flight reflex. Viewers will pay a great deal of attention to the threat cues, and the body will automatically increase heart rate and blood pressure. But if these people continually expose themselves to violence on television over time, these media messages lose some of their influence on triggering body changes.

The Habituation Effect

Tyler and David were watching *Slasher Summer Camp VIII* when Tyler hit the pause button on the DVD player and said, "So dude what do you think?"

"Pretty lame."

"Yeh, pretty lame. We're halfway through the flick and only . . . what, not even ten chicks have been slashed and killed so far?"

"Weak."

"You know what my favorite one was? *Slasher Summer Camp III.*"

"Yes! Was that the one where the slasher started using a chain saw?"

"No that was *II. Slasher Summer Camp III* was when he started using a Weed Wacker."

"Yes that was awesome. He really trimmed out the nerds that year. Then with *IV*, he started using machines like tree mulchers and those big farm harvesters. I didn't like none of that."

"Remember how scared we were when we watched the first one way back when we in the third grade?"

"Yes. I had nightmares for weeks."

"Me too, but you know what? I found a copy of that DVD and watched it a few weeks ago and it was no big deal. It didn't scare me at all."

"You lie."

"No. For real. I was actually bored by it, and I watched it alone at night. I can't believe I was so scared when I watched it for the first time with you years ago."

"We were only eight years old. We were dweebs. It didn't take much to scare us."

"I guess not. That slasher only killed three chicks and with each one you could see it coming a mile away."

"Which one was your favorite?"

Tyler carefully considered the question, then said, "I'd have to say my favorite was *VI* with the cannibalism. Especially when he popped out his victims' eyeballs and strung them together in a necklace."

"Yes. Then he started eating them like hard boiled eggs. I almost hurled."

"You hurled on that? That was nothing. Remember when he made half the kids eat raw broccoli and cauliflower, then killed them and made the other half eat their intestines? I hurled on that. I hate vegetables!"

Analysis

Horror films present a good topic to see habituation in action over time. Each year horror films need more suspense, gore, and maniacal behavior in order to keep attracting and

(Continued)

(Continued)

entertaining audiences—especially their target demographic audience of teenaged boys. Producers of horror films cannot present the same level of violence and grossness each year and expect to trigger the same reaction in their audiences because their audiences become habituated. In this example, Tyler and David were very scared when they viewed the first *Slasher Summer Camp* film when they were young boys. But as they watched more and more blood and gore, they became habituated so that it took more deaths and more violent forms of death to continue to evoke the same level of fear. It also took a higher level of grossness to make them feel nauseous.

Habituation is not necessarily a negative effect. In our everyday lives, it can be a positive effect. When we are very young, we are strongly stimulated by a wide variety of stimuli through our orienting reflex. But as we gain more experience, we learn that certain stimuli occur over and over, so we should not be too concerned about them. Thus we habituate to these common stimuli and avoid getting stimulated by them. If we did not habituate to these common, everyday stimuli we would continue to "freak out" each time we experienced them and could not live normal lives. This is the brain's natural protection against excessive stimulation from the environment. Through repeated exposures to a particular stimulus, the brain accommodates by requiring the stimulus to be stronger over time or different in order to evoke the same response. Singer (1980) reminds us that the orienting reflex requires the habituation process. "Just as we do respond by a quick orientation, we also quickly habituate once the situation can be assimilated into preestablished schema. This assures the fact that we will then be ready to respond to some new stimulus, should it occur" (p. 37).

However, habituation can also be a negative effect. There are people who seek out strong arousal experiences from media messages in order to experience an arousal jag; however, with repeated exposures, the messages gradually lose their ability to create that arousal jag, so those people seek out stronger and stronger forms of the message to achieve that same arousal jag.

Brain Processing

As mentioned previously, some of the human brain is hard wired. This means that at birth it is already programmed to carry out many of the basic routines of keeping ourselves alive, fed, and safe. These preprogrammed neural systems work without any conscious effort or awareness from us. But humans—more than any other organisms—also have large areas of uncommitted brain tissue that can be used to mold itself around the demands of a particular environment (Healy, 1990). This open circuitry is what we use to think consciously, make decisions, record information, store information, then retrieve information. It is shaped by our experiences. Healy argues that our culture, with the media, is altering the way this open circuitry is programmed. "The pace of our contemporary life, when many children are constantly being stimulated from outside so that they have little time to sit, think, reflect, and talk to themselves inside their own heads" (p. 55). There are natural processes that the brain uses to sort through stimuli and make sense of them; however, some media scholars point out that the media alter some of these natural processes. Healy says that infant brains need to learn to organize the confusing array of sensory stimuli. To do this they need time and reflection. As they get better at this they can take on more challenging tasks. But if they are overwhelmed by stimuli, they cannot engage in organizational tasks well; instead they go into a perceptual defense mode as a matter of "neural self-protection" (p. 229).

Another example of the media altering brain functioning has to deal with the balance between right and left brain activity. The right brain is holistic, global, and simultaneous; the left brain is linear, analytic, and sequential. Media scholars have found that TV viewing primarily stimulates the right brain, while reading stimulates the entire brain. Studies that monitor brain activity through an electroencephalogram (EEG) device show that the perception of images seems to activate more right brain activity, while the act of reading words on a page activates the linear functions in the left brain more (Mulholland, 1973). When people reflect on TV images and carefully analyze them, their left brains become active along with their right brains. However, television images are presented too quickly for the viewer to be analytical; viewers must accept the flow and go with it, so TV viewing is largely limited to stimulating right brain activity. In contrast with reading, people envision situations and characters, and this activates right brain activity. Thus, reading is much more likely to activate both sides of the brain while TV viewing activates mostly the right side. People who expose themselves to a great deal of TV and avoid reading are altering their brains by continually stimulating one side and ignoring the other side (Healy, 1990).

We live in a culture that is very high on stimulation, largely because the media are everywhere and are continually competing for our limited attention. This high degree of stimulation has a positive effect of growing our brains. By *growing* I do not mean merely providing more information to fill our brains; instead, I mean increasing the physical size of our brains. We know from research on the brains of rats that when rats live in enriched environments (more stimulation and activity) their brains are larger and heavier; those brains also have increased dendritic branching, which means that the nerve cells can communicate better with each other; there are also more support cells—the synapses. Thus the brain and nervous systems are altered by their environments (Diamond, 1988). Of course, these are the brains of rats, not humans. With rats, researchers are able to put them in highly controlled situations, then end their lives when it is convenient for their research and perform autopsies on them—a research process we cannot perform on humans. However, the evidence we do have indicates the same pattern for humans (Denenberg, 1987).

There is also a negative side to all this stimulation by media messages. Too much stimulation of the brain can lead to ADD (attention deficit disorder) or other learning disabilities. Some educators say that given the current definitions of learning disorders, upward of 80% of all schoolchildren could be diagnosed with learning disorders and that the number of children diagnosed with learning disorders more than doubled during the 1980s (Wang, 1988). Also by the late 1980s well over 4 million children had been diagnosed with hyper-activity disorder, another learning disability (Healy, 1990).

Television may be altering the brain in ways that nudges some children into a condition of a learning disability. Singer (1980) points out, "The TV set, and particularly commercial television with its clever use of constantly changing short sequences, holds our attention by a constant sensory bombardment that maximizes orienting responses" (p. 50). Producers of children's shows are especially fond of using perceptual tricks to get children's attention. This jerking children's attention around can lead to a shortening of children's attention spans. It is hard for people to concentrate on one thing when they are having their attention pulled away by an even more interesting or novel thing. Eventually children give in to the clamoring for attention and go with the flow. They become passive, thinking that it is useless to try to analyze any one thing because another thing will come along and replace the first thing.

People who have unmet emotional needs are poor learners because activity is focused on the emotional part of the brain, which is the limbic system or more primitive brain, and not the cerebral cortex where human learning is focused. Thus the emotional part of the brain is preoccupied with fears and anxieties, and it fails to activate the proper cortical switches for attention, memory, motivation, and learning. High levels of stress can also change the fine-tuned chemical balance that enables messages to pass through all these systems.

When Janet Healy was researching her book *Endangered Minds: Why Children Don't Think—and What We Can Do About It*, she remarked that while "scientists are acutely aware that large doses of any type of experience have shaping power over the growing brain" of children (p. 197), there is little research into how the viewing of television affects brain development. She said, "No sustained effort has been made to find out how TV might affect the basic neural foundations for learning" (p. 198). She points out that educational television programs for children such as *Sesame Street* are very good at getting and holding attention and entertaining children but that they foster passive learning; that is, educational television reduces vigilance, which is the sustained drive to learn and overcome obstacles in the way of solving problems.

Brain Waves

The human brain produces waves, particularly alpha waves and beta waves. *Alpha waves* are indications of the relaxation and peacefulness that come from a very low level of con-scious brain activity, whereas *beta waves* are indications of attentional states and a higher degree of brain activity. Healy (1990) says that when people are sitting peacefully doing nothing, brain waves are synchronized in a regular repeating patterns; this is the relaxed state of alpha waves in the brain. When people are "given a mental problem to solve, the brain's rhythm becomes 'desynchronized' because the rhythm is broken by being forced to think" (p. 175).

People can use the media to alter brain waves. Healy (1990) argues that people are con-tinually being overstimulated in our environment, so they seek out ways of achieving alpha states. Music on headphones with a regular beat can bring on alpha waves. Music with its steady beat can calm people down by acting like a metronome and put people into a meditative state high in alpha waves. Alpha waves are synchronized to a certain rhythm. However, a lot of music is arrhythmic, and this can cause irritation regardless of the volume. Healy concludes, "The brain needs time and quiet space in which to develop the ability to manage itself" and in order "to gain enough inner control to enjoy the quality of its own mental life" (p. 176).

Exposure to television can also alter brain waves. In everyday life we must concentrate on schoolwork and solving problems with finances, relationships, time scheduling, and so on. This mental concentration, especially during problem solving, is associated with brain rhythm that is desynchronized. It is also associated with beta waves in the brain. When people are presented with an unexpected stimulus, beta waves increase, and this is associated with greater concentration. When beta waves increase, there is an alpha wave block that reduces alpha wave activity. In contrast, during TV viewing there is an increase in regular rhythms of alpha waves. Thus, brain activity is altered when a person is watching TV; that is, there is a variation of alpha waves that varies inversely with mental concentration (Anderson & Burns, 1991). The experience of watching television alters brain functioning from beta waves that involve greater concentration and analytical functioning to alpha waves that involve a pleasant state of low consciousness as we float through exposure sessions.

REINFORCING PHYSIOLOGICAL EFFECTS

By providing physiological rewards, the media reinforce our exposures and gradually over time build habits. The media do this by first recognizing that there are hard-wired processes in our brains and that when some of these processes are stimulated they provide us with the experience of pleasure. Humans seek pleasure, so we are conditioned over time to go back to certain media experiences that we expect to provide us with pleasure. In this section, I present four examples of this: the orienting reflex, passivity, arousal, and narcoticization.

Orienting Reflex

The monitoring of our environments brings us pleasure. Campbell (1973) explains that a person's sense organs take in information that activates pleasure areas deep inside the brain. He says that humans are pleasure-seeking animals, so they look for experiences and messages that stimulate the senses in a way to trigger pleasurable sensations. Even when the orienting reflex reveals a dangerous threat, we feel pleasure; this pleasure is triggered not by the threat itself but by the satisfaction that we were able to perceive the threat in time to do something about it.

If it were not for this continual experience of pleasure in the monitoring, this function would eventually become extinguished. If instead it were punishing to monitor the environment or if it took a lot of hard work to do so, we would gradually do it less and less until we stopped monitoring altogether. This would put us in a very vulnerable state, as predators in our environment could take advantage of us before we were aware of their threat. Soon we would cease to survive. So the hard-wired pleasure reaction ensures that we are rewarded by the continual monitoring of our environment. This feeling of pleasure makes us want to continue the monitoring of our environment, and it thus conditions us to continue monitoring.

This conditioning also takes place when we experience messages from the media. We keep seeking out media messages to continue receiving this minor pleasure in the hopes that a message will be able to deliver a stronger sense of pleasure. This is how the media condition us to repeat exposures. Singer (1980) points out, "We are constantly drawn back to the set and to processing each new sequence of information as it is presented. . . . The set trains us to watch it" (pp. 50–51).

Passivity

Passivity can be conditioned by the media, particularly television. During television viewing there is a higher level of the more passive alpha waves. Alpha waves are associated with idleness of the prefrontal cortex of the brain (Walker, 1980). However, there is evidence that reading creates fast-wave beta activity, because reading requires more mental effort to do more interpretation and speculation. Reading—in contrast to television viewing—is likely to bump people into self-reflexive states in which they think about the strategies of interpretation they are using and try to adjust them to make those strategies continually work better (Healy, 1990).

Recall from the earlier section on triggering that producers of children's shows are especially fond of using perceptual tricks to get children's attention. This continual manipulation of children's attention can lead to a shortening of their attention spans. Children learn to avoid concentrating much on any one thing because another thing will come along very soon and replace it. This leads to passive learning, where people give up too easily on learning tasks. Researchers have found that that heavy television viewing reduces "vigilance," which is the ability to remain actively focused on a task.

Arousal

The media can arouse people, and this feeling of arousal is pleasurable. The connection between the story and the physiological arousal is conditioned (Zillmann, 1980, 1983). People develop media exposure habits to experience certain physiological reactions over time. When the media provide audiences with a certain reflex reaction in a pleasant way with each and every exposure, people come to depend on those media messages because they want to continue experiencing those pleasant reflexes.

Narcoticization

This is a long-term effect that builds up a dependency on exposure to certain kinds of media portrayals, especially portrayals of violence and sexual activity. Viewers begin this effect path by feeling an arousal jag with each exposure; that is, viewers experience heightened heart rates and blood pressure that they find pleasant. But over time, it takes stronger depictions and more of them in rapid succession for viewers to experience arousal jags. So viewers develop stronger and stronger drives to seek out these messages at the same time that these messages are exhibiting less and less power to deliver the desired arousal jag. Eventually these people get to a point when their lives are governed by the search for stronger and stronger depictions, and the messages act like a narcotic that drives exposure.

SUMMARY

People's brains are hard wired to be able to monitor their environments automatically and then quickly respond to threats as well as opportunities for pleasure. The media, of course, cannot influence this pre-birth programming, but they can trigger these hard-wired reactions, gradually alter that programming over time, and reinforce that programming by continually repeating certain rewards for some messages and continually withholding reward (or administering punishments) for other messages.

This chapter focused on the brain as a physical organ, especially the preprogrammed limbic portion of the human brain. In Chapter 7, we shift the focus away from the physical brain and its largely automatic processes in the physiological domain and toward the human mind with consciousness and attention in the cognitive domain.

Review Questions

1. What is a "physiological" effect?

2. How is the physiological approach to studying media effects different than the cognitive approach?

3. What is the orienting reflex? Can you list some examples of this?

4. With the triggering of arousal, how is the fight/flight reflex different from excitation transfer?

5. Compare and contrast the effects of passivity and narcoticization.

Further Thinking Questions

1. Are you primarily a right brain person or a left brain person? Can you think of ways that your exposure to media messages have altered the balance between your right brain and left brain?

2. Think about your favorite genre of media message (for example, comedy, action/adventure, romance, competitions, and so on) and all the exposures you have experienced with messages from that genre over the years.
   - What kinds of physiological reactions do those types of messages elicit?
   - Can you think of how your physiological responses to those types of media messages have changed over the years of exposure?
   - Do you think these changes are positive or negative?

3. From Exhibit 6.1, pick one of the physiological effects that you think may be an effect that you have experienced. Use the citation for a research study that has tested that effect and read that article, especially the abstract and the discussion section. Did the authors help you understand more about that effect and the role the media play in bringing about that effect?

Exhibit 6.1 Further Reading on Physiological Effects

Triggering

Orienting reflex triggered by:

- Production techniques, such as loud noises, sudden movement, and so on (Reeves et al., 1985)
- Production techniques on children's programming (Liebert & Sprafkin, 1988)
- Pop-up ads on websites (Diar & Sundar, 2004)

Arousal

- Generalized arousal in brain triggered by:
  - Fast-paced media stories (Detenber et al., 1998; Lang et al., 1999; Lombard et al., 2000; Ravaja, 2004b)
  - Ads (Bolls et al., 2001; Hazlett & Hazlett, 1999; Hopkins & Fletcher, 1994; Lang, 1990, 1994a; Reeves et al., 1985; Simons et al., 2003; Smith & Gevins, 2004)
  - News (Grabe & Kamhawi, 2006; Ravaja, 2004a)
  - Playing video games with self-selected avatars (Lim & Reeves, 2009)
- Fight/flight reflex (Reeves et al., 1985)
- Sexual arousal (Harris & Scott, 2002; Malamuth & Check, 1980)
- Excitation transfer (Zillmann, 1980)

Altering

- Habituation (Singer, 1980)
- Altering brain processing (Healy, 1990; Krugman, 1986; Mulholland, 1973; Singer, 1980)
- Altering brain waves (Anderson & Burns, 1991; Healy, 1990)

Reinforcing

- Orienting reflex (Campbell, 1973)
- Passivity (Healy, 1990; Walker, 1980)
- Arousal (Zillmann, 1980, 1983)
- Narcoticization (Horvath, 2004)

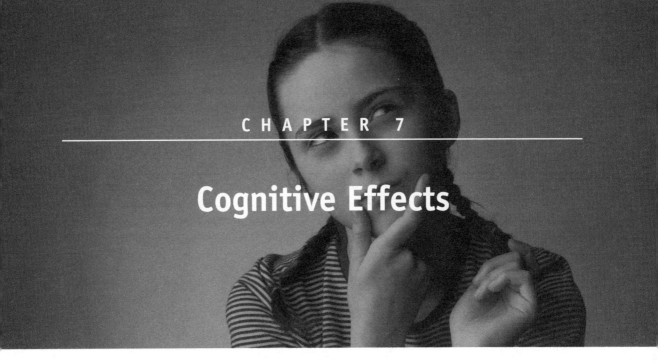

Source: Jupiterimages/Polka Dot/Thinkstock

CHAPTER 7

Cognitive Effects

Nature of Cognitive Effects
Kinds of Information
Types of Processes
Acquiring
Acquiring Information
Factors Influencing Acquiring Information
Triggering
Triggering Attention
Triggering Recall From Memory
Triggering Cognitive Processes
Altering
Altering Existing Knowledge Structures
Altering Cognitive Processing
Altering Cognitive Drives
Explaining Altering
Reinforcing
Reinforcing Attraction to Media
Reinforcing Existing Knowledge Structures
Reinforcing Existing Mental Processes
Process of Reinforcing
Summary

CHAPTER 7

Cognitive Effects

In Chapter 6, we discussed that *brain* refers to a physical organ in the body that is hard wired to perform certain tasks automatically. In contrast, *mind* refers to a nonphysical entity that we can program with our own thoughts and construct our own meaning as we encounter experiences. While Chapter 6 focused on the brain and the automatic processes of perception and survival, this chapter focuses on the mind and the processes of learning and thinking.

NATURE OF COGNITIVE EFFECTS

Cognitive effects essentially focus on how the human mind encounters media messages, how it filters those messages, how it processes information, and how it stores information for later use. Before we examine what the cognitive effects are, we first need to lay a foundation about kinds of information and types of processes.

Kinds of Information

The media present all kinds of information. To organize the major kinds of information from a cognitive point of view, Figure 7.1 illustrates a "core" surrounded by two donut-like bands. The core is labeled "Education" to indicate the condition in which senders have the intention to teach and audience members have the intention to learn. This includes news, public affairs, nonfiction books, and so on. This core is composed primarily of factual information. If we find some information useful to us, we will simply memorize it and thereby add it to our existing knowledge structure on a topic.

The donut-like band around the core is labeled "Instruction" to indicate the focus on the intention of the senders of these messages. That is, the message designers have a clear intention to convey some specific information, but audience members do not seek out these messages to learn. Instructional messages include ads for products, public service announcements (PSAs), public information campaigns, and program promos for TV shows and films. It would also include what is called "entertainment-education" (E-E), which refers to fictional programs in which the producers have written scenes to teach viewers

Figure 7.1 Types of Information Learned

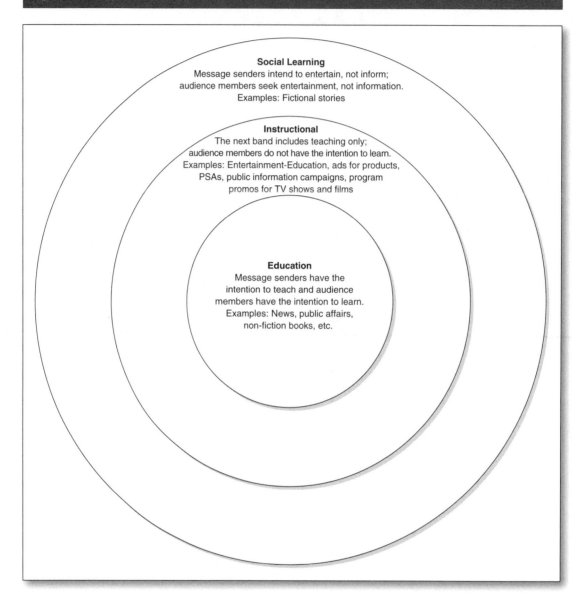

Social Learning
Message senders intend to entertain, not inform;
audience members seek entertainment, not information.
Examples: Fictional stories

Instructional
The next band includes teaching only;
audience members do not have the intention to learn.
Examples: Entertainment-Education, ads for products,
PSAs, public information campaigns, program
promos for TV shows and films

Education
Message senders have the
intention to teach and audience
members have the intention to learn.
Examples: News, public affairs,
non-fiction books, etc.

about the consequences of risky behaviors, such as drinking and driving, drug use, unprotected sex, and the like (see Comstock, Chaffee, Katzman, McCombs, & Roberts, 1978; Rice & Atkin, 1989).

The outer band ("Social Learning") includes messages designed purely for entertainment. Here the senders are not trying to teach, nor are the audience members intending to

Source: Digital Vision/Digital Vision/Thinkstock

learn; however, teaching and learning does take place. Most of what occurs in this outer band has been called "social learning"; that is, we learn social lessons from watching what other people (or characters) do in certain situations. While watching fictional movies and television shows as well as listening to the lyrics of recorded music, our exposure is not usually motivated by a desire to learn about how to make friends, impress romantic partners, or how to talk in a witty way. Producers of these media messages do not intend to teach you this information; their motive is to entertain you. However, you do acquire all kinds of ideas about relationships, how to dress, how to act, and what to say (and what not to say) in certain situations.

Types of Processes

The simplest way of absorbing information from media messages is through a process of memorization. This need not be a formal process that involves a lot of work and concentration, like when you cram for an exam. Instead, it often occurs effortlessly as you flow from one message exposure to another while certain facts and images stick in your memory. This information acquisition effect can be achieved in a relatively automatic way when you skim through a book, magazine, or newspaper and pick up a fact here and there.

While we can acquire information from media messages through memorization, a great deal of the information we have obtained from media messages required a skill more advanced than simple memorization; it required induction, which involves inferring patterns, then generalizing those patterns to a larger class of objects beyond what was originally observed.

To illustrate the two steps of induction (inferring patterns, then generalizing those patterns), let's say you go to the student health center and meet with Dr. Lavender for the first time. Dr. Lavender is a young female, and this is the first time you have gone to a female doctor. However, you have watched lots of television programs and movies about young female doctors, so you have a knowledge structure that sets up your expectations. Dr. Lavender meets some of those expectations but not others, so she does not fit the pattern that you have inferred (from only media exposures) about female doctors. You must alter your inferred pattern to accommodate the new information you just received about female doctors. You feel this new pattern is more accurate about female doctors and you use it to generalize to all female doctors. Then, later, as you continue to watch portrayals of female doctors in the media, you continue to alter your knowledge structure to accommodate the new information. Eventually, the pattern you perceived becomes stable (that is, further depictions of female doctors all conform to your inferred pattern that now resides in your elaborate knowledge structure), and further exposures to female doctors in the media serve to reinforce your inferred pattern. The media have provided information that you acquired about female doctors; the media have triggered the use of induction to infer more accurate and elaborate patterns; the media have altered existing knowledge structures over time; and the media have reinforced an existing pattern when the messages continue to conform to the pattern.

The use of the induction process is especially prevalent with messages in the outer two bands of Figure 7.1. When we watch a fictional program we often are less concerned about what a particular character does in a particular situation. Instead what we take away from many fictional stories are social lessons. Humans are "storytelling animals, and for thousands of years our myths and religions have sustained us with stories of meaningful patterns—of gods and God, of supernatural beings and mystical forces, of the relationship between humans with other humans and their creators, and of our place in the cosmos" (Shermer, 2002, p. xxii). While we may be attracted to fictional stories in the media primarily to be entertained, we also value the monitoring of our culture and the comfort that comes from seeing social lessons reinforced. And because fictional stories emphasize showing over telling, we must use induction to infer the social lessons illustrated by the sequence of actions and their consequences throughout the story. "Humans are pattern-seeking animals. We search for meaning in a complex, quirky, and contingent world" (Shermer, 2002, p. xxii).

In order to perform induction well, we often need to expend considerable mental effort in order to infer patterns and then generalize those patterns in a reasonable manner. Induction can be performed in a careful, logical manner with much mental effort when we seek out many media messages before feeling comfortable enough to infer a pattern. Also, when we finally do infer a pattern, we want to test it repeatedly with more specially selected media messages before generalizing to a larger class of objects. However, there are times when people use induction in a very "quick-and-dirty" manner; that is, they infer a pattern and generalize it with almost no mental effort. A person might experience only two or three media messages on a topic and immediately make an inference about a pattern, then generalize to the full set of elements on that topic. The results of these inductions are typically faulty.

ACQUIRING

The claim that people acquire a great deal of information from the media is so obvious that it might appear silly to make a big point about it. However, we *must* make a big point about it, not take it for granted. If we overlook this information acquisition effect, we will greatly underestimate the enormous number of positive things the media provide and leave us to focus primarily on the smaller number of negative things.

Acquiring Information

Research has documented a lot of kinds of information that people acquire from the media about both the real world and the media world. There is a long history of researchers documenting people getting information about current events, political information, and features of advertised brands. See Exhibit 7.1 for illustrations about different types of information that have been documented as learned from media exposure.

Exhibit 7.1 Further Reading on Acquiring Information

Acquiring Specific Facts About the Real World

Current events (Brosius, Donsbach, & Birk, 1996; Chang, 1998; Eveland, Marton, & Seo, 2004; Fox, Lang, Chung, Lee, Schwartz, & Potter 2004; Grabe & Kamhawi, 2006; Greenberg & Brand, 1993; Lang, Newhagen, & Reeves, 1996; Lang et al., 2005; Lucas & Schmitz, 1988; Maurer & Reinemann, 2006; Moy, Torres, Tanaka, & McCluskey, 2005; Newhagen, 1998; Price & Czilli, 1996; Ravaja, 2004b; van der Molen & Klijn, 2004)

Political candidates and campaigns (Baek & Wojcieszak, 2009; Bennett, 1989; Benoit & Hansen, 2004; Brewer & Cao, 2006; Garramone & Atkin, 1986; Graber, 1988; Kim, Scheufele, & Sanahan, 2005; Kim & Vishak, 2008; Shen, 2004; Valentino, Hutchings, & Williams, 2004)

Information about advertised brands and products (Austin, Pinkleton, & Funabiki, 2007; Baker, Honea, & Russell, 2004; Cline & Kellaris, 2007; Diar & Sundar, 2004; Hitchon & Thorson, 1995; Lowrey, 2006; Moorman, Neijens, & Smit, 2007; Sundar, Narayan, Obregon, & Uppal, 1999)

Health and nutrition (Juanillo & Scherer, 1991; Morgan, Movius, & Cody, 2009; Niederdeppe, Davis, Farrelly, & Yarsevich, 2007; Sandman, 1994; Singer & Endreny, 1994)

Science (Pifer, 1991; Ressmeyer & Wallen, 1991)

Acquiring Specific Facts About the Media World

Information about fictional narratives and characters (Bandura, 2002)

Information about TV production (Tidhar & Lemish, 2003)

While acquiring information from media messages is generally a positive effect, it can also be a negative effect—when the information acquired is faulty. There are many examples of people acquiring wrong information from media messages (Maurer & Reinemann, 2006; Segovia & Bailenson, 2009). For example, Maurer and Reinemann tested German voters' knowledge about economic facts after they watched a televised debate among presidential candidates. The researchers found a substantial learning effect among debate viewers; that is, those viewers acquired a lot of new information as a result of exposure to the debate. However, the researchers found that most of the information that viewers acquired during the debate was wrong. Viewers were misled by candidates' selective presentation of facts, so while viewers acquired information, that information was faulty and did not improve their knowledge structures. The authors of this study pointed out that

Acquiring Information

"So Jennifer, how much do you weigh?"

"Kyle! I'm not going to tell you how much I weigh. You're not even my boyfriend!"

"I'm a boy and I'm your friend. So how much do you weigh?"

"You know what I mean. That's private. Why do you want to know anyway?"

"I read somewhere that the average weight of women in college is now 95 pounds."

"What!?! Where did you read that?"

Kyle scratched his beard and thought, "I'm not sure. I think it was in a magazine. Or maybe it was a website. Could have been a TV show."

"I wish I knew where you read that. It can't be right."

"Yes, it sounded off to me too. That's why I'm asking you."

"Because I'm average?"

"Yes, you look about average. Not too thin and not to big."

"Gee, thanks."

"So how much do you weigh?"

"Not 95 pounds!"

Analysis

Oftentimes we acquire facts from media messages and forget the sources. When the information is inaccurate we cannot go back and check it. Yet the fact often remains in a knowledge structure, and when we later access the fact from our knowledge structure, we assume it is accurate. Unless someone challenges us on our claim that something is accurate, we continue to keep the faulty piece of information in our knowledge structure. And even when someone does challenge us, we often argue that our facts are correct—surely we would not put an inaccurate fact into our memory!

Source: Stephen Colbert in Iraq/The US Army/Wikimedia.org

candidates running for election are not interested in educating voters; rather they are primarily interested in gaining votes, so they only present information to support their positions. This selective presentation of information is misleading to voters and often includes faulty facts. So voters who watch the debates in order to become better informed do not achieve their goal. While they may acquire additional information on an important topic, much of that information may be faulty.

There has been concern about the way people use comedy programs as the source of their political information. Baek and Wojcieszak (2009) found that exposure to late night comedy increases political knowledge, but primarily on simpler ideas and mainly among the inattentive citizens. Also, Baumgartner and Morris (2008) conducted a study to examine the effect of *The Colbert Report*, which is intended as a satire of conservative politicians and commentators; however the study found that when young adults were exposed to *The Colbert Report's* humor, they were *not* led to be more critical of the far right. Instead, the opposite happened, and there was an increased affinity for President George W. Bush, Republicans in Congress, and Republican policies. Ironically, Colbert's attempts to poke fun at conservative commentators may be helping those same commentators spread their message. Research has found that when political messages are presented in a humorous fashion, audience members' level of critical viewing is reduced, and the presented information is more likely to be accepted at face value (Young, 2008).

Factors Influencing Acquiring Information

Source: Hemera Technologies/AbleStock.com/Thinkstock

Under what conditions do people best acquire information from the media? There has been a lot of research conducted to answer this question, and the findings of that research can be organized into four categories: factors about the mass media, message factors, audience factors, and environmental factors.

Factors About the Medium. We have a long history of research that has examined whether people learn more from news in print or from television. In reviewing this literature, Roberts and Maccoby (1985) arrived at the rather equivocal conclusion that in general no one medium is superior to the others in providing information for learning. That is, all media can be good teachers or bad teachers. The medium itself is less a predictor of learning facts than are factors about how the message is presented and factors about the learner. More recently, it has been popular to compare the medium of the computer (Rice, 1994) or, more specifically, hypermedia (for a review see Eveland & Dunwoody, 2001) to other media and determine which is the best teacher. The research on this topic over the past several decades supports this equivocal conclusion; that is, no one medium is superior to others for generating learning effects.

The research is more clear about particular kinds of information and particular kinds of learning. Each medium has its own special features that make it a better teacher than other media *for certain tasks*. When the topic is complex, print media are generally better than electronic media, because print can present more detailed information per story, offers the opportunity for readers to progress at their own pace, and allows readers to return to any part of the story again and again until they understand it (Robinson & Davis, 1990). Print media (including print on computer screens) allow people to wander around in the information, and this leads to serendipitously stumbling onto new information (Eveland & Dunwoody, 2002). Radio and recorded music offer the appeal to the imagination more than do other electronic media. Television, with its visual motion, allows for the demonstration of processes better than print. And computers allow for interactivity better than other media. For example, Bracken and Lombard (2004) found that children learn more from computers when they engage in social interactions with them, that is, treat their computers as social actors and behave as if there is a conversation taking place.

Selecting the right medium to teach or learn is not enough to be successful in information acquisition. How you use the medium is even more important. That is, the message must be designed well. To illustrate this point, van der Molen and Klijn (2004) conducted an experiment and found that the recall advantage of either television or print depends on the level of overlap between verbal and visual information in the television presentation. Thus if an instructional message is designed to present the information both verbally and visually, people will be more likely to learn it than if the message presents the information in only one format—either verbally or visually. Thus television can be a better teacher than print, but the information must be presented in both audio and visual modes in order for this superiority to be achieved.

Factors About the Message. There are many factors that can increase the probability that people will learn information. For learning to be achieved efficiently, the message should be short and simple. Learning is reduced when the complexity of the information increases (Bradley & Shapiro, 2004), when atypical elements are presented (Shapiro & Fox, 2002), and when cognitive overload is not reached (Fox, Park, & Lang, 2007). Also, Lowrey (2006) found that acquiring information from TV commercials is related to narrative complexity and audience involvement with the advertised product. When involvement is low, narrative complexity needs to be simple if learning is to occur.

Emotional appeals have been found to enhance the learning of messages (Hitchon & Thorson, 1995), and news images that evoke anger are likely to be remembered better than images that evoke fear or disgust (Newhagen, 1998). In general, negative video (graphic images of death, maiming, and injury) in news stories increases attention, increases the amount of capacity required to process the message, increases the ability to retrieve the story, facilitates recognition of information presented during the negative video, and inhibits recognition for information presented before the negative video (Lang, Newhagen, & Reeves, 1996). And arousing elements increase learning (Bolls, Lang, & Potter, 2001; Zhou, 2005). Memory for media messages is highest when messages are arousing and when they are positive. Thus people allocate the most cognitive capacity to messages that are both arousing and positive (Lang, Dhillon, & Dong, 1995).

The style of the information is also important. For example, movement on screens is generally good, except when it distracts from learning (Diar & Sundar, 2004). Fast pace and arousing content increase the allocation of processing resources to messages, but the combination of the two overloads the processing system, and this results in less recognition and cued recall for specific content of the message (Lang et al., 1999). Redundancy is good; that is, the more overlap between verbal and visual information in the message, the better for learning (Fox, 2004). People remember information in ads better when the humor is strong and related to the message (Cline & Kellaris, 2007).

Messages are also successful when they have interesting visual and sound elements as long as those elements are all on point and support the main facts. Visual intensity of the information adds to the learning (Bolls & Lang, 2003; Zhou, 2004). The use of graphics can enhance learning, especially when the message is complex (Fox et al., 2004). For example, Ravaja (2004a) found that facial motion was associated with improved memory performance for positive messages. A talking facial image on a small screen increases attention and knowledge acquisition. Pictures in television newscasts need to fit the information in the story in order for learning to take place efficiently (Brosius, Donsbach, & Birk, 1996).

The structure of the information is also important, such as how it is physically laid out (Eveland, Cortese, Park, & Dunwoody, 2004; Grabe, Zhou, Lang, & Bolls, 2000) and how it is conceptually framed (Shah, Kwak, Schmierbach, & Zubric, 2004; Shen, 2004; Valentino, Buhr, & Beckmann, 2001). Information gaps in structure create drive for continuity and closure (Levin & Simons, 2000; Metzger, 2000). Brand names are remembered better when they are placed at the beginning rather than at the end of TV ads (Baker, Honea, & Russell, 2004).

The genre of media message has also been found to be related to differences in learning. Brewer and Cao (2006) examined the relationship between exposure to candidate appearances on soft news programs and knowledge about the 2004 Democratic primary campaign. Seeing a candidate on a late-night or political comedy show was positively related to knowledge. Hollander (2005) found a similar effect of learning political information related to differences in comedy and late-night programs. However, entertainment messages were less effective than news messages in acquiring factual information, particularly in retaining issue and procedure knowledge (Kim & Vishak, 2008).

Online news, particularly by young Americans, can lead to learning, but the use of in-text hyperlinks may discourage learning for inexperienced Web users (Eveland et al., 2004). News teasers, especially teasers that feature the program reference, enhance viewer recall and comprehension of TV news stories (Chang, 1998).

Audience Factors. Some people are in better positions to acquire information from the media than are other people. That is, their baseline is closer to the manifestation level. What elevates a person's baseline so he or she is in a position to acquire more information from media exposures? Looking at Exhibit 7.2, we can see there are three important factors: a person's existing knowledge on a topic, cognitive styles, and skills/abilities.

Exhibit 7.2   Further Reading on Acquisition of Information Effect

Factors About the Mass Medium

In general, no one medium is better than others for conveying information (Eveland & Dunwoody, 2001; Rice, 1994; Roberts & Maccoby, 1985; van der Molen & Klijn, 2004)

- Print media are sometimes superior (Robinson & Davis, 1990; Sundar, Narayan, Obregon, & Uppal, 1998)

Message Factors

Amount of information (Lang, 1995)
Type of information

- Complexity of information (Armstrong, 2002; Bradley & Shapiro, 2004; Lang, 1995; Lowrey, 2006, Yaros, 2006)
- Cognitive overload (Fox et al., 2007)
- Atypical information (Shapiro & Fox, 2002)
- Emotional appeals (Hitchon & Thorson, 1995; Newhagen, 1998)

- Negative video (Lang et al., 1996)
- Arousing elements (Bolls et al., 2001; Zhou, 2005; Lang et al., 1995)

Style of Information

- Redundancy (Fox, 2004; Fox et al., 2004; Lang, 1995; van der Molen & van der Voort, 2000; Van der Molen & Klijn, 2004; Zhou, 2004, 2005)
- Production techniques (Bolls & Lang, 2003; Diar & Sundar, 2004; Lang et al., 1999; Lang et al., 2005; Niederdeppe et al., 2007; Zhou, 2004)
- Humor (Cline & Kellaris, 2007)
- Graphics (Fox et al., 2004)
- Pictures (Brosius et al., 1996)
- Facial motions (Ravaja, 2004b)

Structure of Information

- Layout of information (Eveland et al., 2004; Grabe et al., 2000)
- Framing of the information (Shah et al., 2004; Shen, 2004; Valentino et al., 2001)
- Information gaps (Levin & Simons, 2000; Metzger, 2000)
- Position of information within a message (Baker et al., 2004)

Genre of Message

- Online news (Eveland et al., 2004)
- Entertainment messages (Kim & Vishak, 2008)
- Comedy programs (Brewer & Cao, 2006; Hollander, 2005)
- News teasers (Chang, 1998)

Audience Factors

Prior knowledge (Bird, 1999; Huang, 2000; Price & Czilli, 1996; Shen, 2004; Valentino et al., 2004)

- Reasons for message exposures (Eveland, 2001, 2002)
- Selective exposure (Zillmann et al., 2004)
- High interest in a topic (Carpentier, 2009; Graber, 1988)
- Greater attention to the messages (Morgan, Palmgreen, Stephenson, Hoyle, & Lorch, 2003)
- High motivation for retaining information (David, 2009; Huang, 2000)
- More cognitive elaboration of messages (Eveland, 2001; Eveland & Dunwoody, 2002)
- Ability to disconfirm information (Bird, 1999)

Skills and abilities (Fisch, 2000; Kim et al., 2005)

- Ability to process fast-paced message (Lang et al., 2004)
- Cognitive styles (Mendelson & Thorson, 2004)
- Arithmetic aptitude (Zillmann, Callison, & Gibson 2009)
- Involvement with messages (Hitchon & Thorson, 1995; Newhagen, 1998; Moorman et al., 2007)
- Gender (Grabe & Kamhawi, 2006)
- Ethnicity (Fujioka, 2005)

The Environment

Distractions (Pool, Koolstra, & van der Voort, 2003)

Existing Knowledge. The key audience factor is the set of existing knowledge structures. The reason this is key is that a person's set of knowledge structures determines the topics one is interested in, the motivation to learn more, and the willingness to expend cognitive energy to learn more. When people have high interest in a particular topic, they will seek out more information on that topic (Morgan et al., 2003; Zillmann, Chen, Knobloch, & Callison, 2004), be more emotionally involved with those messages (Hitchon & Thorson, 1995; Moorman et al., 2007), be more likely to expend more effort processing those messages (Eveland, 2001; Eveland & Dunwoody, 2002), and therefore be more likely to retain that information (Eveland, 2001, 2002; Graber, 1988; Huang, 2000). It is easier for a person to learn a new bit of information about a topic already familiar than to have to expend the mental energy to figure out what to do with a bit of information that does not fit with an existing knowledge structure or for which the person does not already have a knowledge structure (Shen, 2004).

Acquiring information from stories requires that we can follow the narrative. In order to follow the narrative, we use story schemas that tell us how stories are structured and thus what to expect at any given time in the story (Kintsch, 1977).

Skills/Abilities. Some people have a higher ability to process messages than do others. This skill is related to developmental level, so young children generally have less ability than older children, who have less ability than adolescents (Fisch, 2000). However, there are skills that are better developed in younger people than in older people. For example, Lang et al. (2004) found that adolescents are better able to process fast-paced messages than are college-aged viewers. Also, older viewers engage in more controlled processing of television news stories, whereas college students process television in a more automatic fashion (Fox et al., 2004).

Ability is also related to intelligence and skills and attentional patterns (Kim et al., 2005). People who are high verbalizers learn more from news stories than do low verbalizers (Mendelson & Thorson, 2004). High verbalizing is associated with being more word oriented, showing high fluency with words, preferring to read about ideas, and enjoying word games. Recall of numeric quantities embedded in printed news reports is better for people with higher arithmetic aptitude (Zillmann, Callison, & Gibson, 2009). And cognitive styles are related to learning information (Mendelson & Thorson, 2004).

Emotional involvement is an important factor in learning (Newhagen, 1998). For example, researchers have found that learning from TV advertising is better when people have higher emotional commitment with the advertised products (Hitchon & Thorson, 1995) and when viewers are more highly involved with the action in the program in which the ads appear (Moorman et al., 2007).

For some time we have known that learning is best when learners are aroused—not too much or too little but a medium amount (Berlyne, 1960). This cognitive arousal leads to a higher degree of attention to messages, which results in more psychic energy and a higher degree of comprehension and memory encoding so that it can be recalled later.

The acquisition of information elements effect can take place in higher states of exposure, such as the attentional state wherein a greater proportion of the information is likely to be catalogued into long-term memory. In the self-reflexive state of exposure, the audience member is very active in pursuing a goal for a particular kind of information, so he or she is likely to catalogue the useful information found and quickly purge the rest.

Finally, a person's demographic characteristics have been found to be important, not because of those characteristics per se, but because how those demographic characteristics interact with other more active factors. For example, considering gender, the way males learn from TV news stories differs from how females learn from news stories. In one research study, Grabe and Kamhawi (2006) found male viewers to be more likely to have a negativity bias for all news, so they tend to like negative stories and learn more from them. In contrast, female viewers are less likely to like negative news stories, so they tend to avoid those stories; they find positively valenced stories as more arousing. So females learn more from positive stories, while males learn more from negative stories. As for ethnicity, Fujioka (2005) compared the learning of Mexican American and White American participants in an experiment. He found that Mexican American participants rated Mexican American news stories more favorably and as more arousing, recalled the news more, and evaluated recalled news more positively than did their White American counterparts. Consistent with the principles of self-schema and social identity theory, these findings demonstrate that people process and evaluate self-referencing information differently than they process non-self-referencing information.

Environmental Factors. The key factor of the environment that determines the amount of learning is distractions. Sometimes media exposure can interfere with learning. Students who were doing homework during soap operas experienced interference with their learning. However, music playing in the background did not interfere with learning (Pool et al., 2003).

TRIGGERING

Media messages can trigger attention, trigger recall from a person's memory, and trigger all sorts of cognitive processes (see Exhibit 7.3).

Triggering Attention

If the media did not trigger attention, there would be little reason for their existence. Therefore it should be no surprise to see that the media are successful at triggering our attention for all sorts of messages. Being a successful producer of media messages requires the ability to know how to trigger the attention of audiences.

In our everyday lives, however, we typically filter out almost all of the messages clamoring for our attention; there are just too many of them to be able to pay attention to more than a small fraction of them. So the important question arises: Why do some messages trigger attention much better than other messages? Scholars have generated a good deal of research to answer this question, and their many findings cluster in two groups: message factors and audience factors (see Exhibit 7.4).

Exhibit 7.3   Further Reading on Triggering Cognitive Effects

Triggering Attention

To stories (Cohen, 2002; Knobloch et al., 2005; Valkenburg & Janssen, 1999; Valkenburg & Vroone, 2004)

To news and information content (Bergen et al., 2005; Ravaja, 2004a; Dutta-Bergman, 2004; Eveland et al., 2004; Fox et al., 2007; Fujioka, 2005; Tewksbury, 2005; van der Molen & Klijn, 2004; Zhou, 2005; Zillmann et al., 2004)

To video games (Eastin, 2006; Schneider et al., 2004)

To ads (Escalas, 2004; Neely & Schumann, 2004)

To PSAs (Lang et al., 2004)

Triggering Recall From Memory

Activation of associative networks in memory (Shrum, 2002)

Triggering Mental Processes

Needs for cognitive resources (Wise, Bolls, Myers, & Sternadori 2009)

Cognitive involvement (Hall, 2009; Wise, Bolls, & Schaefer, 2008)

Cognitive disengagement (Potter, 2009)

Thought processes (Shermer, 2002; Zhou, 2005)

Daydreaming (Valkenburg & Van der Voort, 1995)

Interpretation of meaning (Anderson, 1983; Berkowitz, 1984; Givens & Monahan, 2005; Gorham, 2006; Krcmar, 1998; Potter & Tomasello, 2003; Roskos-Ewoldsen, Roskos-Ewoldsen, & Carpentier, 2002; Zillmann, 2002)

Priming sexual thoughts (Paul & Linz, 2008)

Hostile thoughts (Eastin, Appiah, & Cicchirillo, 2009)

Flow state (Weber, Tamborini, Westcott-Baker, & Kantor, 2009)

State of transportation (Green et al., 2008)

As for message factors, producers need to build in lots of elements to make them interesting. Rapid pacing and frequent scene changes can be engaging up to a point, because they involve audiences in the messages and require a frequent redirection of visual attention. Also, manipulations of semantic content such as the inclusion of humorous or anomalous elements can elicit cognitive engagement (Smith & Gevins, 2004). But if messages include too many elements or too many scene changes, they can appear too

Exhibit 7.4   Further Reading on Triggering of Attention

Message Factors

Number of elements (Bergen et al., 2005)

Pacing (Smith & Gevins, 2004)

Type of character (Gorham, 2006; Neely & Schumann, 2004)

Type of programming element
- TV program promos (Eastman & Newton, 1998)
- TV ratings and advisories (Krcmar & Cantor, 1997)

Audience Factors

Thoughts primed in memory (Roskos-Ewoldsen et al., 2002)

Information-seeking strategy (Dutta-Bergman, 2004)

Exposure state (Escalas, 2004)

Family communication patterns (Krcmar, 1998)

Channel loyalty and genre loyalty (Cohen, 2002)

Daydreaming style (Valkenburg & Van der Voort, 1995)

Demographics
- Gender (Eastin, 2006; Knobloch et al., 2005)
- Age (Valkenburg & Janssen, 1999; Valkenburg & Vroone, 2004)

complex and thus repel audiences. In a study examining how people pay attention to all the information in CNN headline news, Bergen, Grimes, & Potter (2005) found that when the visuals in a message were complex, viewers typically shifted more attention to auditory cues that were simpler.

The type of character on the TV screen has an effect on triggering as well as the type of content (Eastman & Newton, 1998; Krcmar & Cantor, 1997). For example, ads that use animated characters trigger children's attention to ads; they also increase character and product recognition (Neely & Schumann, 2004).

Television programs use program promos and ratings as a way of triggering attention. Eastman and Newton (1998) found that the more salient TV program promos are, the more successful those shows are in attracting viewers. *Salience* is defined in terms of maximal prominence of structural (placement within an advertising pod of small size and good positioning within the pod, frequency) and content elements. Krcmar and Cantor (1997) report that television exposure choices are affected by TV advisories and ratings for children and parents. Parents typically avoid programs with the more restrictive ratings, and they speak more negatively about these programs; however older children made more positive comments about shows with more restrictive ratings.

Certain audience factors are also associated with more success in triggering. When particular thoughts are primed in people's minds, those people will be more likely to have their attention triggered when the media message appeals to those particular thoughts (Roskos-Ewoldsen et al., 2002). Related to this is the person's strategy for seeing information (Dutta-Bergman, 2004) and even his or her daydreaming style. For example, Valkenburg and Van der Voort (1995) found that a positive-intense daydreaming style is stimulated by watching nonviolent children's programs, while an aggressive-heroic daydreaming style was stimulated by watching violent dramatic programs.

Exposure state is also important. Ads can trigger mental stimulation of hypothetical scenarios, especially when people are in transported states (Escalas, 2004). In addition, family communication patterns (Krcmar, 1998), channel loyalty, and genre loyalty (Cohen, 2002) have been found to predict the triggering of attention to messages.

Demographic characteristics of people—particularly age and gender—have also been found to be associated with the media's success in triggering attention. As for age, children's attention is triggered by TV that has comprehensible plots and lots of action (Valkenburg & Janssen, 1999; Valkenburg & Vroone, 2004).

There are very few studies of infants' and toddlers' preferences of television content. One study on this topic (Valkenburg & Vroone, 2004) investigated how young children's attention to television is determined by auditory, visual, and content features of the program and by program difficulty. Fifty 6- to 58-month-olds were presented with a videotape consisting of segments of the news, *Sesame Street, Teletubbies,* and *Lion King II.* The study found that young children pay most attention to television content that is only moderately discrepant from their existing knowledge and capabilities. Among infants, salient auditory and visual features (for example, applause, visual surprises) particularly attracted their attention. These features also attracted older children's attention, but older children predominantly allocated their attention to television content on the basis of nonsalient (for example, moderate character action) and content features (for example, letters and numbers, meaningful dialogue, and the like). The attentional shift from salient to nonsalient and content features started between 1.5 and 2.5 years of age.

As for gender, a cross-cultural study of Chinese, German, and American children found that boys show a strong preference for aggressive stories while girls prefer peaceful, nurturing stories. Both sexes favored stories featuring protagonists of their own gender (Knobloch et al., 2005). Also, Eastin (2006) found that when playing violent video games, females experience greater presence and more aggressive thoughts from game play when a gender match between self and game character exists (Eastin, 2006).

Triggering Recall From Memory

The media trigger mental connections. Recall that many scholars conceptualize the human mind as being composed of associative networks (Schrum, 2002). When we see an image of a familiar public figure, it activates a particular network of information nodes that radiate out from the image that is stored in our minds. We are triggered to think about where we have seen that public figure before, what her name is, why she is famous, and so on.

We are motivated to access information we have stored in our minds and make the connections between symbols we encounter and meanings we have learned. With meaning matching, we both learn connections in the acquiring function and then use those learned connections when the media trigger such need.

Triggering Cognitive Processes

The media trigger all sorts of cognitive processes. Fundamentally, media messages trigger a *need* for cognitive processing; that is, people quickly assess the story structure and use that as a way of determining how much mental effort they will need to process the story. Wise et al. (2009) found that news stories structured by an inverted pyramid (the placement of the most important information first then tapering down to information of lesser importance) triggered the need for more cognitive resources to process than did stories structured by story narratives. This determination of resource requirements leads to either cognitive involvement (Hall, 2009; Wise, Bolls, & Schaefer, 2008) and subsequently to particular thought processes (Shermer, 2002; Zhou, 2005) or to cognitive disengagement (Potter, 2009) such as daydreaming (Valkenburg & Van der Voort, 1995).

Arguably the most primary of all these mental processes is the triggering of the construction of meaning. For example, there has been considerable research documenting that the viewing of violence triggers interpretations of the meaning of that violence (Anderson, 1983; Berkowitz, 1984; Gorham, 2006; Krcmar, 1998; Potter & Tomasello, 2003; Roskos-Ewoldsen et al., 2002). Also, video presentations of African Americans on TV can prime viewers to real-life attributions about African Americans (Givens & Monahan, 2005). Also, Gorham found that when TV news presents crime stories of racial minority suspects in a crime, audience members are more likely to use abstract language when talking about the suspects, that is, talk about their race.

The media trigger interpretive cognitive processes that are needed to transform information into knowledge. That is, a person acquires another fact on a topic and is motivated to organize all the facts into a pattern that is easier to remember. This organizing function is essential to human thinking. If I were to give you a list of 10 random numbers, that would be relatively difficult to memorize. But if I told you that these 10 numbers were a phone number, it would be easier for you to memorize it because the numbers can be organized into fewer units (that is, the three-digit area code, the three-digit exchange, and the four-digit number). When we recognize patterns, it is easier for us to navigate through the individual elements and to remember them. The facts are the elements and the knowledge structures are the patterns. When the media provide us with lots of elements, they motivate us to look for patterns and thus create knowledge structures; they trigger the use of the mental skills of grouping, induction, and deduction.

The media trigger the process of us making our own interpretations. When we encounter a new bit of information in a media message, we check to see how that new bit of information fits into an existing knowledge structure. Sometimes this new information fits neatly into an existing knowledge structure, but sometimes it does not. When it does not fit well, we must adapt our existing knowledge structure to accommodate the new information. Thus, as the media continually present new information, they are continually triggering us to modify our knowledge structures with new information.

The media have been found to often trigger exposure states, particularly the transported state. Green et al. (2008) conducted two studies investigating whether transportation was affected by the medium of story presentation, especially when the narrative was experienced for a second time (for example, watching the movie version of a previously read story). Their first study found that people who read a novel before viewing the film version were more transported into the film compared to nonreaders. In their second study, participants came to the lab on two separate occasions either to read a passage or to watch a movie clip. Reading followed by watching provided the greatest transportation. Furthermore, high-need-for-cognition individuals were more transported when reading, whereas low-need-for-cognition individuals were more transported when watching a narrative.

Related to the transported state is the flow state, which is like a transported state with the addition of a goal. When people are in a transported state, they are typically passive as the message transports them into a different world and they lose track of time and place. However, in flow, people are active in trying to reach a goal, such as getting to the next level in a video game. While in this state of flow, players lose track of real time and place (Tamborini et al., 2004; Weber et al., 2009).

There has been considerable research illuminating the process of meaning construction (see Exhibit 7.5). The factors that explain meaning construction can be grouped into message factors and audience factors. As for message factors, redundancy is important. That is, when messages are consistent across media and over time, people have an easier time processing those messages because that processing is done automatically and requires few cognitive resources (Gerbner et al., 1978; Hawkins & Pingree, 1982; Liebert et al., 1973; Nisbet et al, 2002; Potter, 1994; Tan, 1982; Zillmann & Weaver, 1997). Messages are easier to process when they conform to story formulas with which audiences are familiar. People who expose themselves to one type of portrayal more than others will be influenced more by that type of information in constructing patterns (Fan et al., 2001; Segrin & Nabi, 2002; Sotirovic, 2001).

Redundancy of visual elements within a story is also important for the triggering of cognitive processes. For example, Zhou (2005) examined the effects of arousing visuals and audiovisual redundancy on viewers' cognitive assessment of television news stories. Four dimensions of thoughts—salience, polarity, originality, and emotionality—were analyzed. Results showed that redundancy had main effects on all four dimensions, whereas arousing visuals affected two.

Exemplars are also an important feature of media messages. Zillmann (2002) explains that people pull up a memory of examples of something. These memories of events share attributes with others to a degree that makes them classifiable as members of the same population of events. In this way people do not need to remember all events in the population but can rely on a few exemplars. Exemplars exert a powerful influence on inferring patterns because they are easier to remember and comprehend than are abstract principles. What exemplars are most likely to be remembered and used? Zillmann answers that events that are more consequential (compared to those less relevant), more concrete (compared to abstract ones), and those that arouse emotions are most likely to be recalled. He explains, "Research on the effects of news reports in which arrays of exemplars are supplemented or juxtaposed by base-rate information shows with great consistency that

Exhibit 7.5   Further Reading on Triggering of Meaning Construction

Message Factors

Redundancy of messages

- Across messages (Gerbner et al., 1978; Hawkins & Pingree, 1982; Liebert, Neale, & Davison, 1973; Nisbet, Gross, Jackson-Beeck, Jeffries-Fox, & Signorelli, 2002; Potter, 1994; Tan, 1982; Zillmann & Weaver, 1997)
- Familiar portrayals (Fan, Wyatt, & Keltner, 2001; Segrin & Nabi, 2002; Sotirovic, 2001)
- Of message elements within a message (Zhou, 2005)

Exposure to particular content (Kirsh & Olczak, 2000; Rossler & Brosius, 2001)

Exemplars in messages (Zillmann, 2002)

Audience Factors

Existing schema (Potter et al., 2002; Potter & Tomasello, 2003)

Existing beliefs (Scott, 2003)

Thoughts primed in memory (Roskos-Ewoldsen et al., 2002)

Personality characteristics

- Level of intelligence (Perloff, 2002)
- Self-perceptions of knowledge (Salwen & Dupagne, 2001)
- Trait hostility (Kirsh & Olczak, 2000)
- Degree of societal awareness (Valentino et al., 2004)

Processing strategy (Greene, Krcmar, Rubin, Walters, & Hale, 2002; Shrum, 2002)

Ego involvement with an issue (Perloff, 2002)

Typical exposure patterns (Chory-Assad & Tamborini, 2003; Davis & Mares, 1998; Ex, Janssens, & Korzilius, 2002; Romer, Jamieson, & Aday, 2003)

Demographics

- Gender (Kwak, Zinkhan, & Dominick, 2002)
- Age and developmental level (Collins, 1973; Collins, Berndt, & Hess, 1974)
- Race and culture (Appiah, 2002; Oliver, 1999; Oliver & Fonash, 2002)
- Level of education (Peiser & Peter, 2000, 2001; Scharrer, 2002)

recipients form their assessments of the presented issues on the basis of the exemplar sets rather than on abstract, quantitative information" (p. 31).

Audience factors are also important in explaining the media triggering of meaning construction. The key factors here are a person's existing schema (Potter et al., 2002; Potter & Tomasello, 2003) and beliefs (Scott, 2003) as well as their personality characteristics (Kirsh & Olczak, 2000; Perloff, 2002; Salwen & Dupagne, 2001; Valentino et al., 2004).

ALTERING

With the cognitive altering function, researchers have concentrated their work in three areas: altering existing knowledge structures over time, altering how we process information over time, and altering our cognitive drives. This section displays the findings in these three areas, then examine explanations for the altering function.

Altering Existing Knowledge Structures

The media can alter a person's existing knowledge structures over time (see Exhibit 7. 6). Some of these knowledge structures contain factual information, such as current events,

Exhibit 7.6   Further Reading on Altering Cognitive Effects

Altering Knowledge Structures

Factual knowledge

- Current events (Vincent & Basil, 1997)
- Politics (Cho & McLeod, 2007)
- Environmental issues (Ostman & Parker, 1987)
- Advertised products (Shapiro & Krishnan, 2001; Yang, Roskos-Ewoldsen, Dinu, & Arpan, 2006)

Social knowledge (Bandura, 2002)

- Norms about violence reducing inhibitions to behave aggressively (Andison, 1977; Baker & Ball, 1969; Bandura, 2002; Carlson, Marcus-Newhall, & Miller, 1990; Chaffee, 1972; Comstock, Chaffee, Katzman, McCombs, & Roberts, 1978; Goranson, 1969; Grimes, Bergen, Nicholes, Vernberg, & Fonagy, 2004; Liebert & Baron, 1972, 1973; Liebert, Neale, & Davidson, 1973; Liebert & Schwartzberg, 1977; Lovaas, 1961; Maccoby, 1964; Paik & Comstock, 1994; Scharrer, 2002; Sherry, 2001; Slater, 2003; Stein & Friedrich, 1975; Tannenbaum & Zillmann, 1975; Wood, Wong, & Chachere, 1991)
- Norms about sex (Peter & Valkenburg, 2008a, 2008b)
- Expectations about gender roles (Harris et al., 2004)

Altering Cognitive Processing

Cognitive strategies (Healy, 1990)

Limits intellectual growth (Morgan & Gross, 1982)

Limits imagination and creativity (Harrison & Williams, 1977)

Promotes mindlessness (Langer & Piper, 1988)

Altering Cognitive Drives

Cognitive dissonance (Festinger, 1957)

Drive for thinness (Park, 2005)

politics environmental issues, and advertised products. Other knowledge structures are composed primarily of social information, such as norms about violence and sex. For example, the continual exposure to violent messages in the media has been found to wear down a person's inhibitions about aggression, thus making it more likely that when people are presented with an opportunity to behave aggressively themselves, their inhibitions are no longer strong enough to prevent them. Also, continual exposure to sexually explicit material on the Internet has been found to alter people's norms about sex issues (Peter & Valkenburg, 2008b) as well as their expectations about gender roles (Harris et al., 2004).

Even though we may have a well-developed knowledge structure on a topic, this does not mean that new information on that topic does not exert an altering influence on that knowledge structure. We continually experience flow of new facts, images, sounds, and portrayed behaviors from media messages. When a new bit of information does not quite fit with our existing knowledge structure, we make some alterations to that knowledge structure in order to accommodate that new bit of information. This can occur in a conscious manner when we feel dissonance over the knowledge structure not quite working and we expend the mental effort to undertake the needed renovation. In such a situation, we might rearrange our categories or we might perceive new patterns to explain the information better. Alterations can also occur in an unconscious manner when we accept new information and allow it to coexist in an existing knowledge structure without accommodating the new information; that is, the new information might contradict the old information in the knowledge structure but we are not consciously aware of it. This lays the basis for faulty beliefs or attitudes.

Altering Cognitive Processing

The alteration of cognitive processing effect focuses on how exposure to media messages can change patterns of thinking; it is concerned with the structure of thinking rather than the content of those thoughts. Critics speculate that television in particular alters the human mind subtly over time in negative ways. While research on this effect is sparse, there is some support for this. For example, television has been found to limit intellectual growth, because it "spoon feeds" viewers and therefore provides them with little challenge to think carefully (Morgan & Gross, 1982). Television limits imagination and creativity (Harrison & Williams, 1977). And television viewing habitually has been found to promote mindlessness (Langer & Piper, 1988).

Janet Healy, in her book *Endangered Minds: Why Children Don't Think and What We Can Do About It* (1990), argues that intense video or computer game playing shifts cognitive strategies from sequential to parallel. Thus children raised in today's media environment get much more practice at developing their parallel thinking than their sequential thinking processes. Parallel thinking is required with multitasking. Children who watch TV while listening to music and reading textbooks for homework are multitasking with media messages. They learn how to apportion their cognitive effort across several parallel tasks and continue to make progress on all of them. Video games also require parallel processing strategies. In contrast, reading and logical thinking require sequential processing in which you address one task at a time and you move systematically from one task to the next.

Healy and others worry that the focus on parallel processing will leave little time for or interest in practicing sequential processing. Because traditional education focuses on sequential processes, such as reading and arithmetic, academic performance will suffer without continual practice of the sequential processing tasks.

Altering Cognitive Drives

The media can alter people's cognitive drives over time. Cognitive drives are different from physiological drives (refer to Chapter 6). Physiological drives are typically hard wired into the human brain and manifest themselves in physical changes, such as the drive for food, water, sex, and fighting for survival. In contrast, cognitive drives are experienced as something that does not make sense so we are driven to get more information or figure something out. A well-documented cognitive drive is called "cognitive dissonance," in which something in our set of information is out of balance and we experience a desire to sort through the information to get it back in balance. To illustrate, let's say you have a strongly positive set of information about a political candidate and another strongly positive set of information supporting a controversial issue. But then you find out that the political candidate does not support that issue and in fact opposes it. You feel dissonance, and you have a drive to reduce that uncomfortable dissonance by either reducing your support for the political candidate (by looking for negative information) or by switching your position on the controversial issue (by looking for counter-information).

The media can also increase cognitive drives. For example, Park (2005) conducted a study to investigate the effect of magazine use on the desire to be thin within the theoretical framework of presumed influence. The research concluded that reading beauty and fashion magazines increased the drive for thinness in a double-barreled manner. One way the media exercised its influence was to present attractive images of thin people, thus influencing readers of magazines to think that attractiveness and thinness were linked. The other way the media exercised its influence was to make readers of magazines think that other people defined attractiveness in terms of thinness. So if readers wanted to feel attractive to other people, they must become and stay very thin. Thus the media were altering cognitive drives to be thin in order to feel better about oneself and in order to be attractive to other people.

Explaining Altering

The altering function takes place typically through induction. The media provide new information to a person, who then must fit that new piece of information into an existing knowledge structure; this often requires altering that structure. The altering influence on cognitions is explained by factors about the media messages, the medium used, and audience factors (see Exhibit 7.7).

As for message factors, the framing of the information is especially important. Framing refers to how the information is selected and sequenced in a media message.

Exhibit 7.7 *Further Reading on Altering Effect*

Message Factors

Media framing of messages altering knowledge structures

- Election campaign coverage (Rhee, 1997)
- Advertised products (Braun-LaTour & LaTour, 2005; Braun-LaTour et al., 2004)
- Television news (Corner, 1999)

Repetition (Huntemann & Morgan, 2001)

Message factors by medium (Sicilia, Ruiz, & Munuera, 2005; Valkenburg & Beentjes, 1997)

Audience Factors

Existing knowledge structures (Kepplinger & Daschmann, 1997)

Thoughts chronically primed in memory (Roskos-Ewoldsen et al., 2002)

Information processing skills (Abelman, 1995; Harrison, 2006; Oliver, 1999; Park & Kosicki, 1995; Weiss & Wilson, 1998; Wicks, 1992)

Mental energy (Shrum, 2002)

Emotional reactions (Hale, Lemieux, & Mongeau, 1995)

Thus if information about X is typically included in a story on a given topic, and information about Y is typically ignored, then people's knowledge structures will grow with X information but not include any Y information. Every media message has a frame. For example, Rhee (1997) found the way election campaign coverage is framed in TV and newspaper stories influences how people receive the information in those stories. The framing helps audiences make their interpretations of the stories. Also, advertising can frame a person's experience with the product—before the product usage and even after the product usage. If a person uses a product, then sees an ad for it afterward, the memory of that experience can be framed by the post-usage ad (Braun-LaTour & LaTour, 2005; Braun-LaTour, LaTour, Pickrell, & Loftus, 2004).

Repetition of messages is also essential. Huntemann and Morgan (2001) say the "quantity and redundancy of media images accumulate as part of the overall childhood experience" and serves to contribute "to the cultivation of a child's values, beliefs, dreams, and expectations, which shape the adult identity a child will carry and modify throughout his or her life" (p. 311). This influence by the media is not simple. Instead, "the media play a reciprocal and multifaceted role in the ongoing process of identity development among young people" (p. 312).

In addition to the way the media frame stories, they present other characteristics that can lead to faulty inductions. For example, the news on television oversimplifies what are typically complex issues. The emphasis on the concrete visualizations of particulars, especially in nonfiction, diverts attention away from the abstract principles (Corner, 1999). Thus viewers of TV news are given only one type of information about complex issues. No matter how careful and logical viewers induce a pattern from this information, their inductions will be faulty because the sample of information they construct the pattern from is so superficial.

Messages in some media have a greater influence in altering people's knowledge structures. For example, Valkenburg and Beentjes (1997) found that people have more novel responses to a story when listening to stories on the radio than watching stories on TV. This is not due to people learning more with TV stories; instead it appears that TV provides both audio and video information, and this serves to fix the story more in audience members' minds and results in less novel interpretations. Also, in another study interactive websites were found to be better than noninteractive ones because they lead to more information processing (Sicilia et al., 2005).

Audience factors are also important in the process of altering knowledge structures. Certain factors about audience members can reduce (or enhance) the media influence. Key is a person's existing knowledge structures. Viewers of TV news interpret information about new events in the context of past events (Kepplinger & Daschmann, 1997). Also important is a person's information-processing skills. People who are more sophisticated about a news topic use reasoning processes that are more complex and consistent (Park & Kosicki, 1995). Younger children are less likely to keep action in subplots on sitcoms separated; that is, what happens in a subplot can confuse them and reduce their comprehension about what happens in the major story line (Weiss & Wilson, 1998). Learning temporal sequencing in television is influenced by a child's skill level (with learning disabled children having a lot of trouble with this task) and amount of television viewing (Abelman, 1995). Over time, with heavier TV viewers (above 20 hours of viewing per week) there is a reduction in self-complexity, which is the number of dimensions of self-concepts. Greater self-complexity is associated with greater psychological resilience, such that people with multidimensional self-concepts appear to suffer fewer emotional and physical health problems in response to stress (Harrison, 2006). As people think about the images they see in the media, their mental processes and biases can alter the memory of those images. Oliver (1999) found that when viewers watched a news story about a murder that featured a wanted poster of the alleged perpetrator, people often altered the race of the presumed perpetrator when they were asked to recall it later. Hale et al. (1995) found that when people read a message that elicited a high degree of fear, message information was processed peripherally, whereas low-fear messages were processed centrally.

How often do audience members expend mental energy to conduct an induction well? Not very often, according to cognitive psychologists who have studied this. For example, Shrum (2002) points out that people typically use the "heuristic/sufficiency principle" that states that

> when people construct judgments, they typically do not search memory for all
> information that is relevant to the judgment, but instead retrieve only a small

subset of the information available. Moreover, the criterion for what is retrieved is "sufficiency." That is, only the information that is sufficient to construct the judgment is retrieved, and the determinants of sufficient are related concepts such as motivation and ability to process information. (p. 71)

Shrum (2002) adds that people also use what is called the "accessibility principle," which states that "the information that comes most readily to mind will be the information that comprises the 'small subset' of available information that is retrieved and, in turn, is the information that is most likely to be used in constructing a judgment" (p. 72). Shrum also points out that the determinants of what will be accessible are the frequency and recency of activation, vividness, and relations with accessible constructs.

REINFORCING

Reinforcing, like altering, is a long-term influence the media exert on individuals. When the continual flow of messages on a topic generally conforms to one of our existing knowledge structures, that structure is continually confirmed. That knowledge structure gets weightier and more stable, thus making it more difficult to change.

Reinforced knowledge structures have some important advantages as well as disadvantages. They become more valuable over time because they can be used more efficiently. When we are familiar with the elements in a knowledge structure, we become more comfortable relying on it. If we are presented with some information that does not fit into our structure, we can quickly reject that new bit of information as being irrelevant or faulty because we trust our reinforced structures over anything new. And this points up the negative side of a reinforced knowledge structure; that is, they are inflexible. This is especially a problem in areas where the world is changing, and it is essential to accommodate new information in order to keep up with the world. People who reject new information in these areas will gradually over time lose the ability to function well in society.

The research on cognitive reinforcement is focused in three areas: reinforcing attraction to media, reinforcing existing knowledge structures, and reinforcing existing mental processes. The most popular of these three areas has been examining how the media reinforce attraction to certain types of content and fictional characters (see Exhibit 7.8).

Reinforcing Attraction to Media

Recall from the definition of the mass media that they are organizations that attract and maintain audiences. The maintaining of audiences requires the reinforcement of attraction. Producers of media messages continually tinker with their formulas to increase the attractiveness of those messages and at the same time reduce cognitive costs. When the rewards of a message go up while the costs go down, the value of the exposure increases. When exposures continue with high value, audience exposures are reinforced.

Researchers have largely stayed away from the challenge of conducting direct empirical tests of this effect, preferring instead to offer indirect tests. For example, some researchers argue that the reason people continue to expose themselves to a particular newspaper,

Exhibit 7.8 Further Reading on Reinforcing Cognitive Effect

Reinforcing Attraction to Media

Particular kinds of content

- Crime drama (Reith, 1999)
  - ○ Violence (Cantor & Nathanson, 1997)
  - ○ Health and nutrition (Juanillo & Scherer, 1991)
  - ○ Political knowledge (Bennett, 1989; Garramone & Atkin, 1986)
- Political candidates and campaigns (Valentino et al., 2004)
  - ○ Current events (Greenberg & Brand, 1993; Lucas & Schmitz, 1988)
  - ○ General scientific knowledge (Pifer, 1991; Ressmeyer & Wallen, 1991)

Particular kinds of characters (Harrison, 1997; Harwood, 1997)

Reinforcing Existing Knowledge Structures

Advertised products (Braun-LaTour & LaTour, 2004; Shapiro & Krishnan, 2001; Yang, Roskos-Ewoldsen, Dinu, & Arpan, 2006)

Reinforcing Existing Mental Processes

Mindless exposure (Langer & Piper, 1988)

magazine, or television show is that those people have their expectations gratified. Researchers design questionnaires that ask people to specify how much time they spend with various media, vehicles, and messages; then they ask the same people how much gratification they received from this time. They usually find that the messages with the greatest amount of exposure time are associated with the highest ratings of gratifications. This type of research has been labeled "uses and gratification." But there is something unsatisfying about this research. On the surface, the findings make sense, but when we examine them more closely, one feels uneasy about the evidence. Think about the experience of filling out a questionnaire that asks you how much time you spend on each type of message, then asks you how much enjoyment you got from each type of message. Are you likely to say you spent a huge amount of time with a particular kind of media message yet received no enjoyment from it? Even if this were the case, you would not be likely to admit it to a researcher that you are such a loser. So we must be skeptical of the validity of such data. The problem lies in how to measure cognitive costs and message rewards. Audience members do not think at this level of precision during everyday mundane exposures, and social scientists are not likely to be able to develop questions that will be able to measure levels of gratification at an acceptable level of precision.

However, just because researchers have problems in measuring a reinforcement effect does not mean the effect is not taking place. It is logical to conclude from reasoning alone (even if we do not have strong empirical findings at the present time) that many people are being reinforced by exposures to certain media messages to become habitual, loyal users of those messages.

We do have a literature that indicates that people over time develop preferences for certain kinds of content and particular kinds of characters and that the media, by providing messages that fulfill those preferences, serve to reinforce those preferences over time. For example, most people demonstrate a preference for characters their own age (Harwood, 1997), and many people are conditioned over time to prefer models that fit the thin body ideal presented so often in magazines, films, and television programs (Harrison, 1997).

Reinforcing Existing Knowledge Structures

Some designers of media messages are trying to get us to reinforce our existing knowledge structures so that these structures do not change. This is especially the case with advertisers. It has been estimated that 80% of all advertising has a reinforcement goal; that is, most advertisers are primarily interested in repeatedly putting reminders of their products and services in front of their existing customers. They want to reinforce brand loyalty and thus inoculate their customers against the advertising claims of all their competitors. For example, Braun-LaTour and LaTour (2004) found that companies that consistently use the same advertising theme from consumers' early lives have an advantage of strongly reinforcing people about that message and avoiding claims of other companies that might confuse people later. Also, exposure to advertising often results in implicit rather than explicit memory for the advertised brands. This indicates that learning is subconscious rather than fully conscious, when people remember the exposure experience and the information they learned in that exposure. When people see ads in video games, the memory of brands is implicit, not explicit (Yang et al., 2006). This means that people are not conscious of the exposures themselves nor of the reinforcing influence.

Advertisers are not the only senders of media messages that want to reinforce the audience's existing knowledge structures. News producers also want to reinforce their audiences' knowledge structures about the stories they cover, because then it will be easier for their audiences to continue following their stories in the future. Also, producers of entertainment programming know that their audiences will have an easier time following their continuing stories when they are thoroughly familiar with the characters and what has happened to them in the past.

Reinforcing Existing Mental Processes

Because of our continual exposure to media messages, certain mental processes that are activated in those exposures get reinforced over time. The one process that has received the most attention and criticism is the mental state of mindlessness. Some critics claim that television viewing habitually promotes mindlessness (Langer & Piper, 1988). This can be harmful to individuals because the more they live in the habitual environment that is determined for them and relieves them of needing to make decisions, the less feeling of control they experience. They say this is harmful because "choice plays a part in stress reduction, in improving task performance, and in health and longevity" (pp. 247–248). They continue that active involvement in any task increases a person's confidence. They say this is especially a problem among the elderly adults who

Reinforcing Attraction to Media Messages

Zachary and John were leaving their psychology class where they had filled out a media usage questionnaire in order to earn some extra credit in the course.

"Hey, Zac. Did you fill out all the questions?"

"Mostly. Didn't you?"

"I skipped some. They asked some questions and I didn't have a clue."

"Yes, like all those pages of TV shows and websites and magazines. I couldn't remember how many minutes a week I spent which each of those."

"Me neither. I put a zero for most of them, especially for the *World Wrestling Federation*."

"What? You love that show and never miss one of those cheesy matches!"

"I know it. But I don't want my professor to know I watch that kind of show, especially after how she trashed shows like that in class! I didn't want her to think I was a moron, so I put a zero. But then later on when they asked how much I liked wrestling, I couldn't lie so I gave it the maximum score. I do love wrestling; it's the best entertainment on the tube!"

"Dude, now I don't feel so bad. But I did the opposite on *Jersey Shore*. I admitted that I watch it like 5 hours each week. It's my favorite show. But when it came to the Gratifications section on the questionnaire, I couldn't admit that I liked it, so I gave it a zero."

"What do you think the professor is going to do with all that bogus data?"

Analysis

The quality of research findings is dependent on the quality of data used to generate those findings. If people are asked about their everyday mundane thoughts and actions, they are not likely to be able to recall them accurately. And when people are asked about sensitive topics (in this case the liking of TV shows that the professor trashes), respondents are likely to "bend the truth" so as to make themselves look better.

When you read about the findings of research studies, think about how the researchers gathered their data and about how you would have acted had you been a participant in that study. While most research studies achieve high standards and go through a rigorous review process to ensure quality, sometimes faulty data slip through and distort findings. Be skeptical when you read research findings.

are too often asked to live in environments that have already been mastered. Thus they are robbed of the opportunity to experience control. All obstacles are removed to make life easier, decisions are made by others to save them from stress and the possibility of deciding poorly, and work becomes a thing of the past to make life struggle-free. With nothing to master, it is difficult to feel masterful. (p. 248)

Process of Reinforcing

The media condition people through reinforcing certain knowledge structures. These knowledge structures become the most familiar to people; this makes them more efficient to use and people become less likely over time to seek out information that conflicts with their existing knowledge structures (Lazarsfeld, Berelson, & Gaudet, 1944; Freedman & Sears, 1966), which in turn further reinforces those knowledge structures. This is called "selective exposure." When people do encounter conflicting information, they tend to interpret it more in line with their existing knowledge structures so that it more easily fits. This is called "selective perception" (Klapper, 1949).

There are characteristics about audience members that make it easier (or more difficult) to condition them to repeat exposures of a particular kind of message. As an example, let's take violent content as an example. Attraction to violence and crime drama on TV has been found to be related to an authoritarian aggression structure in the minds of some audience members (Reith, 1999). People with this high need for authority and a high trait of aggressiveness are easier to condition to repeat exposures to violence. In contrast, it has been found that attraction to violence in cartoons declined with age throughout childhood and was higher with boys than with girls (Cantor & Nathanson, 1997).

The media are influential in reinforcing people's existing knowledge structures for a combination of three reasons. First, the media present a wide array of information. With relatively little effort (searching the Internet, scanning magazines at a bookstore, checking the TV guide) people can usually find messages on any topic. And if the topic is even the least bit controversial, people can also easily find a body of facts supporting any side of a debate. Second, people are usually selective in their searching for facts in the media. This means that they look for facts on a particular topic and filter out all other messages. Or if the topic is controversial, most people will search for facts on only one side of the debate and filter out all other facts. Thus their set of facts for their side of the debate grows and the other side withers away in their mind. And third, the media continue to present similar information in those particular vehicles (because the media are conditioning people for repeat exposures), so people's knowledge structures get reinforced. It is easier on an individual to experience reinforcement and therefore feel that he or she is already expert and correct on an issue than to deal with the dissonance of having to alter his or her knowledge structure.

SUMMARY

This chapter focused on the four functions—acquiring, triggering, altering, and reinforcing—the media perform with cognitive effects on individuals. These cognitive effects are essentially about learning. The media provide a rich resource from which to acquire all kinds of information both factual as well as social. The media messages also trigger recall of previously learned information. Media alter our existing knowledge structures when they present new information. And finally, the media reinforce our existing knowledge structures and attentional processes.

Cognitive effects along with physiological effects are the most fundamental of all types of media effects. Some scholars argue that beliefs and attitudes are really only subsets of cognitive effects, that emotions require cognitive labeling or they do not exist, and that behaviors are cognition driven. So the effects displayed in Chapters 8 through 11 stem directly from the processes outlined in Chapters 6 and 7. Thus the human brain/mind is key to understanding almost all media effects; that is, the more you understand the human brain/mind, the more you will understand the nature of media effects and how they occur.

Review Questions

1. Compare and contrast the advantages and disadvantages of conscious and automatic processing of information from media messages.

2. Compare and contrast the learning of factual information with the learning of social information.

3. In what ways is the using of comedy programs as a source of political information a good thing and a bad thing?

Further Thinking Questions

1. Think about where you acquire your information on important issues about politics and the economy.
   - What is it about those sources that have made them so influential as a place for you to acquire information? (You may want to refer to Exhibit 7.2.)
   - Is it possible that those sources have provided you with inaccurate information that is now firmly entrenched in one of your knowledge structures so that you use it to construct faulty beliefs and attitudes?
     - If not, how can you be so sure?
     - If so, how will you go about identifying which information is faulty?

2. Think about what kinds of media and what kinds of messages have had the most success with triggering cognitive processes in you.
   - What is it about those kinds of messages that have made them so influential as a trigger of your attention? (You may want to refer to Exhibit 7.4.)
   - What is it about those kinds of messages that have made them so influential as a trigger of your construction of meaning? (You may want to refer to Exhibit 7.5.)

3. Can you think of any knowledge structure that you have altered a lot over time? What role did the media play in this alteration? That is, did particular media or messages supply you with information that altered your knowledge structure?

4. Can you think of one of your knowledge structures that has not changed much over time? Did you use the media to reinforce your knowledge structure so that it would not change?

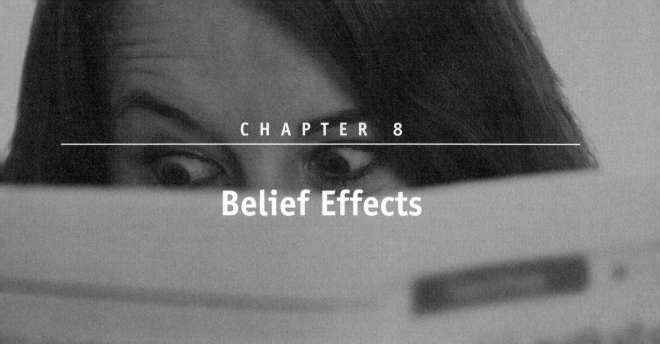

Source: ©iStockphoto.com/diego_cervo

CHAPTER 8

Belief Effects

Belief Effects

This chapter focuses on how the media influence our beliefs. First I formally define beliefs. Then I show you the variety of ways the media have been found to influence the acquiring, triggering, altering, and reinforcing of beliefs. The chapter concludes with a discussion about the process of media influence on beliefs.

NATURE OF BELIEFS

Beliefs are a type of cognition; that is, they require cognitive processes to construct, and they reside in human memory. They are mental constructions about the probability that an object or event is associated with a given attribute (Fishbein & Ajzen, 1975). For example, many people hold a belief in a god. This means these people have faith that there is a very high probability (some say an absolute certainty) that a supreme being exists. Most children believe that their parents love them. These children have faith in a very high probability that their parents are associated with the characteristic of love. Many beliefs—like these two examples—are deeply held and fundamental to a person's personality. However, beliefs can range in importance. Some beliefs are less important and less central to a person's being. For example, you may believe that it will rain tomorrow. This means that you think there is a high probability that tomorrow it will rain. Not only do beliefs vary in importance to the person, beliefs also vary in intensity. Many sports fans have a relatively weak belief that their favorite team will win its next game.

Beliefs require the use of the inductive skill to make the judgment of probability. Recall that induction is the process of inferring a pattern from a set of observations, then generalizing that pattern to a larger set. In these steps of inferring a pattern, then generalizing, people assess probabilities that the pattern they perceive is accurate and that it is okay to generalize this pattern to a larger set. While engaging in these processes, some people have strong confidence in their inferences and generalizations and thus associate a high probability in their beliefs. For example, let's say Harry follows the sport of college basketball very closely. He has analyzed the talent level of his team at every position and compared this to the talent level at every position of next week's opponent. He infers a pattern that in almost every position, his team has superior talent compared to next week's opponent. Because he has analyzed every position, he has high confidence in this pattern. He has based his analysis on how all the players on both teams have performed so far up to this point in the season. Of course, he has no information on next week's game because it has not been played yet. So he must generalize the pattern he inferred from the set of past information to a new set—that is, next week's game. Because Harry perceives a lot of consistency in players' past performances over time, he has a high level of confidence that those players will perform at the same levels they have in the past. So Harry's belief that his team will win next week's game is very high.

Typically, the more information a person has about something, the more confident that person will be about the object's existence or the probability of something occurring. When we are considering a belief that is very important to us, we will be motivated to gather a lot of information and carefully work through our inference and generalization processes. However, there are many times when we need to construct beliefs that are of relatively minor importance to us, such as whether it will rain this afternoon. In this case, we hastily construct a belief without putting much effort into it.

Most beliefs—but not all—are open to tests of verification. This means that beliefs can be tested to see if they are correct or false. Beliefs can be verified or falsified with objective criteria external to the person (Eagly & Chaiken, 1998). There are people who believe the Earth is flat and not a sphere. Because we have objective evidence that the Earth is in fact a sphere, the flat Earth belief can be shown to be false. Also, the belief that it will rain tomorrow can be tested for truth by waiting until tomorrow and seeing whether it rains or not. However, some types of beliefs cannot be tested for truth because we cannot get external evidence in our lifetimes (such as a belief that the Earth will stop spinning on its axis by the year 9999 or that there is life on a planet 100-million light-years away). Also, metaphysical beliefs (such as the existence and nature of a god) present considerable challenges in generating evidence that everyone is willing to use as a truth criterion.

When we look at belief formation, it is useful to make a distinction between two types of beliefs: descriptive and inferential (Fishbein & Ajzen, 1975). Descriptive beliefs come from direct experience with an object. We use our own senses to observe the object and use this information to construct a belief. When we touch a stove's red glowing coils and burn our hand, we construct a belief that red coils on a stove are very hot and dangerous. These descriptive beliefs are held with maximum certainty, because we have had direct experience in verifying them.

But we also form beliefs that go beyond direct observation; that is, they must be inferred. For example, when we observe a person lying and cheating, we will typically form the belief that he is dishonest. We cannot observe the personality characteristic of honesty directly; instead we must infer such a personality characteristic from what we can observe, which are individual actions of the person. This holds for many other personality characteristics, such as intelligence, trustworthiness, sweetness, and so on. Some of these inferences are made inductively; that is, we make observations, then hypothesize a pattern that explains the individual observations. Or we could reason in a more deductive manner, such as illustrated in the following three sentences:

Andre is taller than Joe.

Joe is taller than Sally.

Therefore we reason that Andre must be taller than Sally, although we never saw Sally standing next to Andre.

Now it's time to focus on the beliefs that have been attributed to media influence. There are times when the media present messages that contain beliefs that people acquire or that trigger people's own beliefs. As you will see in the following sections of this chapter, researchers have paid less attention to immediate belief effects compared to the longer-term belief effects in which the media exert their influence over time in altering and reinforcing people's existing beliefs.

ACQUIRING BELIEFS

People can acquire a belief immediately from exposure to one media message. An example of this acquisition of belief is with the Y2K scare. The media presented stories about how computers and other electronic devices running on time codes were likely to crash and cause havoc when the year 2000 rolled around. As a result of this coverage, many people simply accepted this belief (Salwen & Dupagne, 2003; Tewksbury, Moy, & Weis, 2004). Also, Meirick (2005) found that the media exert an influence on how people acquire beliefs about health, particularly smoking. For more examples of research on acquiring beliefs, see Exhibit 8.1.

Exhibit 8.1   Further Reading on Acquiring Beliefs

Beliefs About the Real World

Beliefs about Y2K (Salwen & Dupagne, 2003; Tewksbury, Moy, & Weis, 2004)

Beliefs about health (Meirick, 2005)

Beliefs about jobs and careers (Hoffner, Levine, & Toohey, 2008)

Beliefs About Media Influence

General influence of the media on beliefs (Gunther & Chia, 2001; Gunther & Storey, 2003; McLeod, Detenber, & Eveland, 2001; Peiser & Peter, 2000, 2001)

Beliefs about effectiveness of:

- Direct-to-consumer prescription drug advertising (Huh, Delorme, & Reed 2004)
- Political ads (Meirick, 2004)
- Public service announcements (Andsager, Austin, & Pinkleton, 2001)
- Beliefs about violence on television (Hoffner et al., 2001; Hoffner & Buchanan, 2002; Salwen & Dupagne, 2001; Scharrer, 2002)
- Beliefs about influence of Internet pornography (Lo & Wei, 2002)

Acquiring Beliefs

Luke and Mason were super bored after surfing through 200 cable channels during the past hour. Then Luke found a program on unidentified flying objects that caught their attention.

"Do you think that UFOs really exist?" asked Luke.

"Of course. Look at all those examples in this show. They are flying objects and they are unidentified."

"Yes, but do you think they came from outer space. Like from different planets?"

"Naw," Mason quickly answered. "They are stuff that the producers of this show could not identify. But I bet the government knows what all those things are."

"How can you be sure?"

"Do you know how many satellites and airplanes, and weather balloons and other things that are flying around up there at any given time? I bet it's thousands! The guy who produced this show doesn't have a clue about how to identify all that stuff. He just wants to scare us." Mason was exasperated. "Look at those images. They are too fuzzy to tell what they are and this is a 50-inch high-def TV! They could be searchlights hitting clouds."

"Or they could be space ships from other planets. Look how they move in such jerky motions. Airplanes and weather balloons don't move like that."

"That jerky movement is from the guy holding the camera. He has the shakes—probably laughing so hard about fools like you who would believe anything!"

"Fool? You think I'm a fool? Just because I have an open mind?" Luke was getting angry. "Do you know how many stars and planets there are out there? Billions! Don't you think that there is life anywhere but here?"

"So you're telling me that you believe there are planets out there with intelligent life and that one of them has sent down a space craft that we can't identify?"

"Yes, I guess I do believe that," admitted Luke.

"From watching this cheesy documentary?"

"Okay, I agree this documentary is weak, but doesn't it make you at least think about the possibilities?"

"No, not at all." Mason was exasperated.

Analysis

Two people can be exposed to the same media message and react in two different ways. In this story, Luke and Mason both watch the same TV documentary on UFOs and both agree the documentary is not very good. However Luke accepts the belief that UFOs exist and that they are space ships from outer space, while Mason rejects that belief.

Media effects are often explained by the message and how it is presented. But we usually have to consider what audiences bring to the exposure situation in terms of their personality characteristics, motivations, and history in order to provide a more complete explanation about why a particular media message does not exert the same influence on the beliefs of everyone who is exposed to it.

People acquire the belief that the media are powerful and exert many effects on individuals (Gunther & Storey, 2003; McLeod et al., 2001; Peiser & Peter, 2000, 2001). More specifically, people generally believe that the media influence public opinion (Gunther & Chia, 2001), that political ads influence political opinions (Meirick, 2004), that public service announcements (PSAs) work (Andsager et al., 2001), and that drug advertising works (Huh et al., 2004). They also believe that television violence (Hoffner et al., 2001; Hoffner & Buchanan, 2002; Salwen & Dupagne, 2001; Scharrer, 2002) and Internet pornography (Lo & Wei, 2002) exert strong negative effects on other people. Often these beliefs are simply accepted, because people hear these beliefs expressed by someone in the media.

TRIGGERING BELIEFS

Once beliefs are formed or acquired, we use those beliefs to make sense out of our experiences both in the media world and in the real world. Thus certain elements in media messages trigger our recall of our existing beliefs. Let's examine how researchers have documented this triggering of existing beliefs in three areas: beliefs about the media, beliefs about the real world, and generalizing from the media world to the real world. For more examples of research on triggering beliefs, see Exhibt 8.2.

Exhibit 8.2 Further Reading on Triggering Beliefs

Beliefs About the Media

About media texts in general (Hall, 2003)

Beliefs about the realism of media content (Shapiro & Chock, 2004; Weiss & Wilson, 1998)

Beliefs about stories on television (Dorr, 1980; Shapiro & Chock, 2003)

Beliefs About the Real World

False beliefs about the elderly (Bramlett-Solomon & Wilson, 1989; Gantz, Gartenberg, & Rainbow, 1980; Schramm, 1969)

Triggering Beliefs About the Media

We all hold beliefs about the realism of various types of media messages (Dorr, 1980; Hall, 2003; Hawkins & Pingree, 1981; Potter, 1988; Shapiro & Chock, 2004). When one of these messages is presented to us, it triggers our recall of this belief. For example, we all know that horror movies are fiction. However, there are times when we are swept away by the movie and we become unpleasantly aroused by extreme fear as we strongly identify with a character who is in mortal danger from a superhuman monster. The intensity of the experience triggers our recall that this is just a movie. We remind ourselves of our belief that monsters do not exist in real life. This is a strategy that parents can use with their children to get them to calm down as they process fearful content in media messages (Cantor, 2002).

Another example of triggering was found in two studies by Shapiro and Chock (2004) who examined the beliefs about the reality of news and entertainment stories. They found that when news stories took place in people's home countries, those stories triggered a higher belief in the reality of those stories than if the stories took place in foreign countries. This difference in reality belief did not hold for entertainment programming.

Triggering Beliefs About the Real World

As people encounter media content, they continually have their existing beliefs triggered so that they can make sense of that content. For example, when people watch a documentary on UFOs (unidentified flying objects), their existing beliefs about the existence (or not) or UFOs is triggered. People who do not believe UFOs exist will think the claims in the documentary are bogus, and they are likely either to stop watching it or to laugh at it. In contrast, people who believe in the existence of UFOs will continue to watch carefully in order to gather more information to reinforce their beliefs and to be able to use that additional information in arguments with skeptics later.

Generalizing From Media World to Real World

As we watch portrayal after portrayal of fictional stories on TV, we of course infer patterns about the nature of characters and what will happen to them in their fictional narratives. By creating expectations for characters and plots, we are better able to follow the stories and get more involved in the unfolding action. But we often do more than infer patterns within stories; often the stories trigger us to generalize those patterns to our real lives. Often stories trigger us to think about what it would be like to have these characters interacting with us in our own lives or what it would be like for us to behave like those characters. We often see characters deliver clever lines that impress other characters, and we develop the belief that we could deliver such lines in our lives and impress our friends in a similar manner. The development of such a belief was triggered by the media message and accomplished through generalizing from the media world to the real world.

One example of this is that people see portrayals of the elderly on fictional television shows and construct patterns that the elderly are quirky, spry, and sarcastic. Many people are then triggered by these portrayals to generalize to the elderly in the real world, especially those audience members who do not have much direct contact with the elderly in their lives. Thus they generalize highly stereotyped portrayals as beliefs (Bramlett-Solomon & Wilson, 1989; Gantz et al., 1980; Schramm, 1969).

Let's consider another example. *Friends* was one of the most popular shows on television for nine seasons from the fall of 1994 to the spring of 2003. It was a half-hour situation comedy that featured three male and three female friends in their twenties living in downtown Manhattan. Two of the characters, Rachel and Monica, shared a spacious, two-bedroom apartment where much of the action took place. For most of the

Source: Getty/Getty Images Entertainment/Getty Images

series, Rachel was a waitress and Monica was a part-time cook; however, their near minimum wage incomes were portrayed as being enough to support a lifestyle of stylish clothes, costly entertainment events, and of course the apartment. Viewers of *Friends* believed the show was fairly realistic in setting, lifestyle, and relationships. This belief that it was possible for these characters to live their lifestyle on their low income was triggered each time fans watched the show, and this allowed them to get involved in the action. But something else is often triggered in the minds of those fans, and that something else is a belief that they too could live an exciting comfortable life with lots of friends and lots of free time in a big city with little income.

ALTERING BELIEFS

With continual media exposure, we encounter new bits of information that influence our existing beliefs over time. When those additional bits of information on a particular topic conform to our existing belief, that belief is reinforced, but when those additional bits of information go against our existing belief or go beyond the scope of that belief, the altering function is activated.

In our everyday lives we encounter new bits of information that either conform to our existing beliefs or challenge them. These bits of information come from many sources, such as parents, siblings, friends, and institutions. The media are also a major source of information that influence our beliefs because of two factors: (1) we have so much exposure to media messages every day throughout our entire lives, and (2) the media can present us with all kinds of information that we cannot get from other sources. For example, consider how your beliefs were shaped over time about your choice of a future career. Perhaps you had a parent, sibling, family member, or friend give you lots of valuable information about your chosen career because they have worked in that career. But more likely you have gotten a good deal of information about that career from watching movies and television programs about fictional characters leading exciting lives in that career (Hoffner et al., 2008). However, the media do not present an accurate picture of any career because their stories leave out the day-to-day minor frustrations and boring elements that make up so much of any profession and instead the media focus on the most dramatic highs and lows. This leads to the shaping of beliefs about professions as being more intense, exciting, and fast paced than they are in everyday life.

Exposure to media messages present us with new observations about people and events. This new information can gradually alter our perceptions of patterns and thus alter our existing beliefs about all kinds of things in the real world, about 'ourselves, about social norms, about what is important in the world, and about the media.

Altering Beliefs About the Real World

Throughout our lives we are continually altering our beliefs about all kinds of things in the real world. The media influence this alteration process by continually presenting messages that either depict the real world directly (as with news and information type content) or indirectly (as with fictional stories). As Exhibit 8.3 reveals, we are continually altering our beliefs about crime and violence in society, beliefs about people in society, beliefs about behaviors in society, and other real-world beliefs.

The two dominant theories that have been advanced to explain the alteration of real-world beliefs have been cultivation and third person. *Cultivation* asserts that the media continually present a world to us that has unrealistic elements, and that over time we come to believe the real world is like the world presented to us through the media, particularly television (Gerbner, 1969; Gerbner & Gross, 1976). Cultivation researchers have shown repeatedly that people who watch the most TV are most likely to hold beliefs that the world is a mean and violent place; that is, the crime rate is high and their risk of being victims of crime and violence is high. For example, Williams (2006a) found a cultivation effect among his experimental participants who played online video games for one month. People in the game-playing condition were significantly more likely to believe they would experience a robbery with weapons in real life.

This cultivation effect has also been found with other topics (see Exhibit 8.3). For example, heavy viewers of television are more apprehensive about the state of the environment

Exhibit 8.3   Further Reading on Altering and Reinforcing Beliefs

Beliefs About the Real World

Crime and violence in society (Appel, 2008; Gerbner et al., 1978; Goidel, Freeman, & Procopio, 2006; Grabe & Drew, 2007; Hawkins & Pingree, 1982; Hetsroni & Tukachinsky, 2006; Nabi & Sullivan, 2001; Potter, 1994; Romer, Jamieson, & Aday, 2003) and the use of violence as an effective solution to conflict (Liebert, Neale, & Davidson, 1973; Tan, 1981; Zillmann & Weaver, 1997)

- Use of violence as an effective solution to conflict (Liebert et al., 1973; Tan, 1981; Zillmann & Weaver, 1997)
- Race of criminal suspects in news stories (Appiah, 2002; Dixon, 2008; Dixon & Azocar, 2006; Oliver, 1999; Oliver & Fonash, 2002)
- About personal risk (Gibson & Zillmann, 2000; Griffin, Neuwirth, Dunwoody, & Giese, 2004; Nabi & Riddle, 2008; Rimal & Real, 2003; Williams, 2006a)
- Frequency of deviant behaviors (Davis & Mares, 1998; McLeod, 1995)

Beliefs about people in society

- Medical doctors (Chory-Assad & Tamborini, 2003; Pfau, Mullen, Deidrich, & Garrow, 1995; Quick, 2009)
- Attorneys (Pfau et al., 1995)
- Public relations practitioners (Sallot, 2002)
- Welfare recipients (Sotirovic, 2001)
- Body image (Botta, 1999, 2000; David, Morrison, Johnson, & Ross, 2002; Holmstrom, 2004; Thomsen, McCoy, Gustafson, & Williams 2002)
- Men's attractiveness to women (Aubrey & Taylor, 2009)
- Women as sex objects (Peter & Valkenburg, 2009b)

Beliefs about behaviors in society

- Drinking (Zwarun, Linz, Metzger, & Kunkel, 2006)
- Sexual behaviors of others (Chia, 2006; Peter & Valkenburg, 2006)
- Lesbian or gay male relationships (Rossler & Brosius, 2001)
- Civic engagement of other people (Putnam, 2000)
- Socialization to work (Hoffner et al., 2008)

Other real world beliefs

- Beliefs about paranormal phenomena, such as UFOs (Sparks, Nelson, & Campbell, 1997; Sparks, Sparks, & Gray, 1995)
- Beliefs about global warming (Zhao, 2009)
- Beliefs about science (Hwang & Southwell, 2009)

(Continued)

Exhibit 8.3 (Continued)

- Third-Person Effect: Acquiring faulty beliefs about one's own risk of being affected in comparison with risk of other people being affected (Davison, 1983; Perloff, 2002)
- Influence of television violence on self and others (Hoffner et al., 2001; Hoffner & Buchanan, 2002; Salwen & Dupagne, 2001; Scharrer, 2002)
- Beliefs about how self and others would prepare for Y2K (Salwen & Dupagne, 2003; Tewksbury et al., 2004)
- Influence of the media on self and others (Gunther & Storey, 2003; McLeod, Detenber, & Eveland, 2001; Peiser & Peter, 2000, 2001; Sun, Shen, & Pan, 2008)
- Body image effects on self and others (David et al., 2002)
- Influence of direct-to-consumer prescription drug advertising (Huh et al., 2004)
- Political ads (Meirick, 2004)
- Internet pornography (Lee & Tamborini, 2005; Lo & Wei, 2002)
- Of Holocaust-Denial advertisement in campus newspapers (Price, Tewksbury, & Huang, 1998)
- On perceptions of body images (David & Johnson, 1998)
- On perceptions of support of press restrictions in the O. J. Simpson trial (Salwen & Driscoll, 1997)
- Frequency of deviant behaviors (Davis & Mares, 1998)
- Environmental issues (Jensen & Hurley, 2005)
- Media influence of unreal TV programs (Leone, Peek, & Bissell, 2006)
- Beliefs about neighborhoods (Tsfati & Cohen, 2003)
- Beliefs about support for funding anti-drug campaigns (Meirick, 2008)
- Beliefs about optimistic bias (Li, 2008)
- Beliefs about the effectiveness of anti-drug ads (Cho & Boster, 2008)

Beliefs About What Is Important

Agenda Setting (Althaus & Tewksbury, 2002; Davis & Mares, 1998; Golan & Wanta, 2001; Gross & Aday, 2003; Iyenger, 1991; Iyenger & Kinder, 1987; Kim, Scheufele, & Shanahan, 2002; Kiousis & McCombs, 2004; Kiousis & McDevitt, 2008; Ku, Kaid, & Pfau, 2003; McCombs & Shaw, 1972, 1993; Noelle-Neuman, 1974, 1991; Ostman & Parker, 1987; Roberts, Wanta, & Dzwo, 2002; Shehata, 2010; Tewksbury, Jones, Peske, Raymond, & Vig, 2000; Tsfati, 2003)

Spiral of silence effect (Matthes, Morrison, & Schemer, 2010; Noelle-Neuman, 1974, 1991)

Beliefs About Social Norms

Beliefs about sanctions to violence and aggression or disinhibition (Andison, 1977; Baker & Ball, 1969; Carlson, Marcus-Newhall, & Miller, 1990; Chaffee, 1972; Comstock, Chaffee, Katzman, McCombs, & Roberts, 1978; Grimes, Bergen, Nicholes, Vernberg, & Fonagy, 2004; Hapkiewicz, 1979; Hearold, 1986; Liebert & Baron, 1972, 1973; Liebert, Neale, & Davidson, 1973; Liebert & Poulos, 1975; Liebert & Schwartzberg, 1977; Lovaas, 1961; Maccoby, 1964; Paik & Comstock, 1994; Scharrer, 2001; Sherry, 2001; Shirley, 1973; Slater, 2003; Stein & Friedrich, 1975; Tannenbaum & Zillmann, 1975; Wood, Wong, & Chachere, 1991)

Beliefs About Values in Society

- Beliefs about social norms (Bandura, 1977, 1994)
- Beliefs about social secrets and backstage behaviors (Meyrowitz, 1985)
- Beliefs about values in a culture (Zhang & Harwood, 2002)
- Beliefs about sexual norms (Chia, 2006)
- Beliefs about rape norms (Check, 1985; Malamuth, 1984)
- Beliefs about smoking norms (Gunther, Bolt, Borzekowski, Liebhart, & Dillard, 2006)
- Degree of materialism in society (Kwak, Zinkhan, & Dominick, 2002)
- Beliefs about environmental concern (Shanahan, Morgan, & Stenbjerre, 1997)
- Beliefs about motherhood (Ex, Janssens, & Korzilius, 2002)
- Beliefs about social responsibility of businesses (Lind & Rockler, 2001)

Beliefs About Oneself

Political knowledge (Moy, McCluskey, McCoy, & Spratt, 2004)

Political participation (Austin & Pinkleton, 1995)

Beliefs about body image (Botta, 1999, 2000; David, Morrison, Johnson, & Ross, 2002; Harrison & Fredrickson, 2003; Holmstrom, 2004; Thomsen et al., 2002)

Beliefs About Mass Media

Belief that media news coverage is biased (Lee, 2005)

Hostile media effect (Coe et al., 2008; Gunther, Miller, & Liebhart, 2009)

Beliefs in reality of television portrayals (Weiss & Wilson, 1998)

Presumed media influence (Cohen & Tsfati, 2009; Cohen & Weimann, 2008)

and are less willing to make sacrifices for environmental reasons (Shanahan et al., 1997). People who watch more primetime network programs featuring physicians perceive doctors as more likely to be female and young and as having an interpersonal communication style, physical attractiveness, and power but less moral character (Pfau et al., 1995). Chia (2006) found that adolescents use the media to infer what their friends believe about sexual norms and behavior; their perceptions of media influence on peer norms regarding sexual issues are positively related to adolescents' own sexual permissiveness. Dixon and Azocar (2006) ran two experiments to test how the media influence participants' beliefs about Blacks. They found that news stories about Black criminals can lead people to believe that Blacks who were reported in news stories being arrested for crimes were guilty; participants in this study also were found to generalize their beliefs about Black crime to beliefs that Blacks face structural limitations to success. People who watch programs that regularly depict paranormal activity have an increased tendency to endorse paranormal beliefs, especially those people who have no prior experience with paranormal phenomena (Sparks, Nelson, & Campbell, 1997). Zwarun, Linz, Metzger, and Kunkel (2006) conducted an experiment that assessed the effects of exposing college students to beer commercials with images of activities that would be dangerous to undertake while drinking. Those exposed to the ads were more likely to believe in the social benefits of drinking than those not exposed, particularly among males. The findings suggest that the imagery in beer commercials can contribute to beliefs about alcohol that predict drinking and to an increased acceptance of dangerous drinking behavior.

The other dominant theory that explains the alteration of real-world beliefs is the *third-person effect* (TPE), which was first observed in 1983 by W. Phillips Davison, a sociologist who was examining patterns across the results of public opinion polls and noticed that typically people felt the mass media exerted a strong effect on other people (third persons) but not on themselves (first person). He found consistent patterns that people overestimate the effect of media messages on other people and underestimate the effect of media messages on themselves.

The third-person effect has received a great deal of research. Through repeated media exposure people gradually form faulty beliefs about their own risk of being affected in comparison with risk of other people being affected (Davison, 1983; Perloff, 2002). For example, by watching a great deal of crime news and entertainment programming about crime, people come to believe that there is an increasing risk for people to be victimized by criminals in this society. However, because most people are not victimized by criminals, they feel that their personal risk is low. Thus they fear for third persons but not for themselves. TV news has been found to alter a person's perception of public opinion as well as viewers' own opinion (Leone et al., 2006; Perry & Gonzenbach, 1997).

The third-person effect has also been found in the area of health. For example, Meirick (2005) examined beliefs about media effects in the area of health. This study found that beliefs were affected by perceptions of social distance; that is, groups that are more socially distant from oneself (like the public in general) are perceived to be more affected by cigarette ads than are close groups, such as friends. However, individual measures of respondents' social distance from any given comparison group generally are unrelated to perceived effects on the group. The research of Paek, Pan, Sun, Abisaid, and Houden (2005) also supports this finding.

In a test of whether the third-person effect could be attributed to an optimistic bias, Wei, Lo, and Lu (2007) found that it was not. They concluded that although both optimistic bias and third-person effect are psychological perceptual judgments that can be attributed to self-serving motivation, the third-person perception is a biased interpretation of media influence, while biased optimistic perceptions are a social psychological mechanism of bolstering self-esteem in self-other comparisons regarding a risk. (Cultivation and third-person effect are discussed further later in the chapter in the "Process of Media Influence on Beliefs" section.)

Altering Beliefs About What Is Important

The media gradually alter people's beliefs about what is important in society. This has been labeled the "agenda-setting" effect. The agenda-setting effect says that people learn what is most important in a society by following the topics that the media present (McCombs &

Shaw, 1972, 1993). This effect has been well studied especially in the area of social and political issues (see Exhibit 8.3). People develop ideas about what is important from talking with people in real life. Also, real-life institutions exert their influences on getting people focused on what is important. The media also play a role in setting the agenda because of the repetition of certain images and ideas.

There has been a great deal of research to support the agenda-setting effect. To illustrate, Kiousis and McCombs (2004) conducted a study to examine the consequences of

Source: ©iStockphoto.com/labsas

agenda-setting effects for attitudes toward political figures during the 1996 presidential election. This study tested the relationships among media coverage, public salience, and the strength of public attitudes regarding a set of 11 political figures. The findings indicated that increased media attention to political figures was correlated with higher levels of public perception of the salience of issues. In another study, Tsfati (2003) examined whether skepticism toward the media had an influence on the agenda-setting effect. He found that the agenda-setting effect was weaker for skeptics compared to nonskeptics.

This agenda-setting effect has been found to be especially strong on people who expose themselves to media messages more often and when that exposure is to the same kind of media messages (Iyengar, 1991; McCombs & Shaw, 1972, 1993). For example, people who see a lot of news coverage about environmental issues will come to believe that the environment is an important issue (Ostman & Parker, 1987). Also, people who regularly follow the mainstream news in major newspapers and network television programs are likely to hold the same beliefs about what is important. This is because all of these news outlets socialize their journalists with the same news values and use the same news services; therefore most news vehicles in the media cover the same stories and present those stories in the same ways.

The news stories themselves change over time, so all these media outlets might cover a murder trial of a celebrity, then shift into covering the devastation from a major weather event such as a hurricane or earthquake, then shift into covering the candidates running for president, then shift into yet something else. Thus there are changes in news focus over time, but the pack mentality of the major news outlets ensures that the same stories get covered by all major news outlets at any given time. Thus most audiences of news share the same beliefs about what is important at any given time. And from week to week, these beliefs about what is important are altered to keep up with the changes in coverage of current events.

Related to the belief of what is important is the belief about what is *not* important. Beliefs about what is not important is explained as the "spiral of silence effect" (Noelle-Neuman, 1974, 1991). This spiral of silence effect states that when an issue, person, or event is not covered in the media, people do not talk about it or think about it even if they know about it. Because people do not talk about it, people come to think that it is not important, which leads to more silence about it. Thus, the longer something is ignored, the more difficult it is for that thing to be regarded as important.

Altering Beliefs About Social Norms

As we go through life, we learn social norms, which are beliefs about how the world works. At a very early age, our parents teach us how to behave around other people. These social lessons are called "social norms"; that is, these are beliefs about how you should be treated by others and also how you should treat others in return.

The media exert a gradual and continual influence on us that slowly over time alters our social norms. Media socialization is strongest when children have a high degree of media exposure, when they have few alternatives for social information, when the content is realistic, and when the purpose of viewing is diversion; thus there is little critical thinking (Van Evra, 1997).

Let's take a look at some types of norms that have been found to be altered by the constant influence of the media. I present the research on norms of preventing aggressive behavior, sexual behavior, rape, and smoking.

Norms Preventing Aggressive Behavior. An important norm that people learn is that when we become angry, we need to hold our tempers in check and not physically assault other people. Thus we are socialized to avoid behaving aggressively in a physical manner, and this belief inhibits us from behaving aggressively (Bandura, 1994). However, the media present a continual stream of messages where violence is used successfully to solve problems. More often than not, it is the "good" characters or heroes who use violence in a rewarded manner. This stream of media messages in which violence and physical aggression is portrayed as a good thing gradually alters our belief that violence is bad; that is, our socialized inhibitions gradually erode. This gradual wearing down of a person's socialized beliefs that the use of violence and aggression is socially unacceptable has been labeled the "disinhibition effect" (Bandura, 1994). We are socialized in a way to inhibit aggressive behavior, so when the media show that when our favorite characters behave aggressively and that this results in them getting what they want, we have our inhibitions eroded—that is, disinhibited.

We have a long history of research studies that have documented the media's influence on this disinhibition effect (see Exhibit 8.3). Meta-analytical studies that have reexamined the data quantitatively across sets of studies have also consistently concluded that viewing of aggression is likely to lead to antisocial behavior (Andison, 1977; Carlson et al., 1990; Hearold, 1986; Paik & Comstock, 1994; Wood et al., 1991). Disinhibition typically happens from exposure to violent portrayals on television (Grimes et al., Scharrer, 2001) but it also occurs from playing violent video games (Sherry, 2001; Slater, 2003). This effect has been found with children (Liebert & Baron, 1972, 1973; Lovaas, 1961), especially with boys (Liebert & Schwartzberg, 1977), and it has also been found with adults (see Hearold, 1986).

Beliefs About Sexual Norms. Chia (2006) found that adolescents use the media to infer what their friends believe about sexual norms and behavior; their perceptions of media influence on peer norms regarding sexual issues are positively related to their own sexual permissiveness.

Beliefs About Rape Norms. Exposure to pornography over time serves to disinhibit sanctions against rape (Check, 1985; Malamuth, 1984). Heavy viewers of pornographic material gradually over time have their beliefs altered so that they come to believe that many women like to be dominated sexually and that the psychological consequences to rape victims are less serious than they are in real life.

Beliefs About Smoking Norms. Gunther et al. (2006) found that smoking-related media content has an indirect influence on adolescent smoking behavior via its effect on perceived peer norms. That is, adolescents who believe that smoking-related messages in the media will influence the attitudes and behaviors of their peers will use this belief to guide their own smoking behaviors. This effect is called the "presumed influence hypothesis."

Altering Beliefs About Oneself

The media have been found to alter how people think about themselves. Research has focused primarily on three areas that demonstrate this.

Source: Pixland/Pixland/Thinkstock

One of these areas is the *belief about how much knowledge one has*. Researchers have found that people who expose themselves a great deal to political stories in local news develop greater belief that they have a lot of knowledge on the topic (Moy et al., 2004). Some of these people have acquired a great deal of knowledge by gradually adding accurate information to their knowledge structures over time and by continuing to allow the new information to alter their existing knowledge structures. However, other people have acquired inaccurate information and have failed to check this information for accuracy; so over time their knowledge structures and beliefs have become more faulty.

There are also people who have a narrow perspective on information acquisition, so they are very selective in their exposures. Thus they expose themselves only to messages that tend to support their existing knowledge structures, so over time, these knowledge structures do not grow and develop; instead, they stay the same. However, these people believe they are keeping up with changes in the world and think they are increasing their knowledge. Thus people who devote greater attention to political stories in local news come to believe that they have a lot of knowledge on the topic, even though some do not (Moy et al., 2004). Also, voters who think they can see through what they perceive as lies by candidates in media messages are more likely to believe that their political participation can make a difference (Austin & Pinkleton, 1995).

The second of these areas of altering beliefs about one's self is the *belief in one's own body size*. Most people depicted in magazines, films, and television shows are physically fit and model a thin body ideal. Over time, audiences come to think of most people as being thin. These thin body images then make people, especially women, believe they are overweight. To illustrate, one half of fourth-grade girls are on a diet, and 51% of 9- and 10-year-old girls stated they felt better about themselves when they were adhering to a diet. By high school, 1 out of 10 girls is overweight, however, 9 out of 10 high school juniors and seniors diet. Media present images that lead to these beliefs. Over the past three decades, fashion models, Miss America contestants, and *Playboy* centerfolds have grown steadily thinner, while the average woman's weight has risen. Now, the average U.S. woman is 5 feet 4 inches tall and weighs 140 pounds; in contrast the average U.S. model is 5 feet 11 inches and weighs 117 pounds. This disparity is growing. In 1980, the average model weighed 8% less than the average American woman; but by 2000, the average model weighed 23% less than the average American woman (Media and Eating Disorders, n.d.).

This negative body image belief has been found to be especially strong with females, particularly younger females. For example, Botta (1999) found that adolescent girls process body images from the media, and these images alter their beliefs about their own body image. There is also a great deal of other research on this topic (Botta, 2000; David et al.,

2002; Harrison & Fredrickson, 2003; Holmstrom, 2004; Thomsen et al., 2002). Also, watching sports has been found to lead to self-objectification, which leads to mental health risks such as body shame, disordered eating, and depression (Harrison & Fredrickson, 2003).

A third area includes *beliefs about oneself in romantic relationships*. Eggermont (2004) conducted a study aimed to explore the relationships between overall and romantically themed television viewing and adolescents' expectations of a romantic partner. A sample of 428 15- and 16-year-olds from Belgium rated the importance of physical attractiveness and a pleasant personality in a romantic partner. Results show moderate but significant associations for overall television viewing after background variables and the quality of other relationships were accounted for.

Altering Beliefs About the Media

The media alter people's beliefs about the media themselves over time. Typically those beliefs are negative ones. For example, despite research to the contrary, the general public and a significant number of politicians are convinced the U.S. news media have a liberal and pro-Democratic bias. To understand why many people believe the media have such biases, Lee (2005) conducted a study to examine whether such a perception is related to an observer's own partisan and ideological positions. Findings based on two large national surveys suggest that audiences' ideologies and partisanships affect how they view the media. Strong conservatives and Republicans are more likely to distrust the news media, whereas the best predictor of a media bias perception is political cynicism.

Perhaps the most researched negative belief about the media has been called the "hostile media effect," which is the tendency for partisans of an issue to judge media coverage as unfavorable to their own points of view. An interesting test of this was conducted by Gunther and Liebhart (2006), who ran an experiment on people who had strong opinions about genetically modified organisms (GMOs). Participants completed an online questionnaire then were asked to read an article about GMOs. Some of these people were told that the article was written by a college student for a class in environmental science, and others were told the article was written by a journalist in the environmental science class. Participants were then asked to rate how biased the article was. The participants who thought the article was written by the journalist rated the article as significantly more biased than did the participants who thought the article was written by a student. In another feature of the study, some participants were told that the article was simply a class paper, while other participants were told that the paper was published as an article in *USA Today*. Again there was a difference in the ratings of bias, with more bias being perceived in the published article. But the most interesting finding of this study was that people on both sides of the issue thought the article was biased in favor of the other side of the issue. For example, people who favored GMOs thought that the writer of the article did not favor GMOs, especially when they thought the writer was a journalist and when they thought the article was published in *USA Today*. However, people who were against GMOs thought the writer was in favor of GMOs, especially when they thought the writer was a journalist and when they thought the article was published in *USA Today*. This shows that people on both sides of an issue believe that journalists and newspapers are biased.

Partisan groups, highly important actors in public discourse and the democratic process, appear to see media content as biased against their own points of view. Although this hostile media effect has been well documented in recent research, little is understood about the mechanisms that might explain it. Three processes have been proposed: (1) selective recall, in which partisans preferentially remember aspects of content hostile to their own sides; (2) selective categorization, in which opposing partisans assign different valences to the same content; and (3) different standards, in which opposing partisans agree on content but see information favoring the other side as invalid or irrelevant. Given these three possible explanations for the hostile media effect, the selective categorization explanation appears to be the most useful one (Schmitt, Gunther, & Liebhart, 2004). The hostile media effect is the tendency for individuals highly involved in a controversial issue to see media coverage of that issue as hostile to their own points of view. Coe et al. (2008) found evidence of a relative hostile media phenomenon, in which partisans perceive more bias in programs that do not align with their own political perspectives. Furthermore, the results indicate that partisanship informs viewers' perceptions of news content as interesting and informative.

This effect is in direct contrast to what has been called the "assimilation effect," which says that people expose themselves only to information that supports their positions. Researchers have also found support for this effect (Gunther & Christen, 2002; Gunther & Schmitt, 2004).

REINFORCING BELIEFS

Like altering beliefs, reinforcing beliefs is a gradual long-term effect. With reinforcement, the media present messages that conform to a person's existing beliefs. Thus by repeatedly confirming an existing belief, the media make that belief weightier, that is, more firmly fixed and harder to change.

We resist changing our beliefs. Snelson (1993) calls this the "ideological immune system" and explains "educated, intelligent, and successful adults rarely change their most fundamental presuppositions (p. 54). The more knowledge individuals have accumulated, the greater the confidence they have in their beliefs. Intelligent people are continually looking for more information, but this information we seek is almost always confirmatory, not information that challenges our beliefs. So the higher the IQ, the more chance there is of ideological immunity. History is filled with examples of thinkers who were ignored or hated for new ideas: Galileo, Copernicus, Darwin, and Freud to name a few.

The research literature on beliefs does not make much of a distinction between alteration influences and reinforcement influences. This is because very few of the research studies on this topic use a longitudinal design; that is, few studies measure a person's beliefs at multiple points over time to be able to plot where changes take place and where a reinforcement effect takes over. There are, however, a few longitudinal studies in this literature examining long-term media influence on beliefs, and these typically show both an alteration as well as a reinforcement influence by the media. One example is by Peter and Valkenburg (2009b), who conducted a longitudinal panel survey among 962 Dutch adolescents in order to see if there was a link between adolescents' exposure to sexually explicit Internet material (SEIM) and beliefs of women as sex objects. Their results indicate that exposure to SEIM and notions of women as sex objects had a reciprocal direct influence on each other. This means that over time, adolescents who expose themselves to a lot of sexual material on Internet sites have their beliefs altered to regard women more as sexual objects. And with continued exposure, these beliefs are reinforced.

Because of the confounding of alteration influences (which are manifested by gradual changes over time) and reinforcement influences (which are manifested by a greater weight for existing beliefs over time), this large body of literature on long-term belief effects needs to be regarded as evidencing both types of influences.

Reinforcing Attraction to Media Messages

"Jason, are you looking at *Playboy* nudes on the Internet again?"

Jason quickly switched to another window. "Geez Maria, don't sneak up on me like that. You scared me."

"You mean I caught you." Maria wagged her finger at her boyfriend like he was being naughty and should be punished. "I know you surf a lot of porn websites."

"Okay, but so what? It's fun."

"Jason, it's bad for you. Don't you realize that it distorts your idea about women—about me."

"Naw. It might affect other guys. I'll give you that. There are a lot of people out there who spend too much time with Internet porn. But not me. I just surf a few sites when I take a break from studying. It distracts me."

"You think it distracts you but it also gives you the wrong idea about women."

"What wrong ideas?"

"Ideas about how we should all look. And ideas that we want all kinds of kinky sex all the time."

"I don't believe that! Other guys may be affected that way by porn surfing but not me."

"How do you know that?"

"I just know. Let me ask you, in all the time we've been dating have you ever seen me act like I've been affected by it?"

"No, I guess I can't think of any examples."

"Then see. My porn surfing has not affected me at all!"

"But we've only been dating one month."

(Continued)

(Continued)

Analysis

This story illustrated the third-person effect on Jason. He has developed the belief that exposure to pornography on Internet sites is harmful to society, but only to other people. He does not believe it has been harmful to him.

Also, notice that when Jason asks Marie for examples that he has been harmed, she could think of no examples. But this lack of memory for examples is misleading and does not necessarily mean that Jason's beliefs about women and sex have not changed. Belief alteration is a long-term effect, and Marie has not known Jason very long, so she is not in a position to observe any gradual changes over a long period of time.

PROCESS OF MEDIA INFLUENCE ON BELIEFS

There are two general patterns about how the media influence beliefs. One of these is that the media exert a relatively weak but persistent influence over long periods of time through the repetition of certain messages and that this gradual influence leads to changes in beliefs. The other explanation is that the media exert a very strong influence that creates a sudden or immediate change in a person's belief. Let's examine each in some detail.

Gradual Change

Media exposure has been found to gradually alter individuals' existing belief structures over time (Cappella & Jamieson, 1997; Cartwright, 1949; Hyman & Sheatsley, 1947; Katz & Lazarsfeld, 1955; Lasswell, 1927; Scheufele, 1999). Beliefs are usually formed over the long term, so the media exert their greatest influence on beliefs by altering and reinforcing them with a constant flow of messages over the years. This process begins when a media message presents a new bit of information that the person needs to incorporate into his/her existing belief structure, but where the new bit of information does not nicely fit into an existing category. Thus the person needs to create a new category or change the arrangement of categories.

There has been a great deal of research about how the media alter and reinforce beliefs over time. Here I focus on two of these—cultivation and third-person effect, introduced in the "Altering Beliefs" section of the chapter—to show the explanations that have been developed for these two long-term altering and reinforcing effects.

Cultivation. What are the explanations for the cultivation effect? Three types of explanations have been offered for this very important effect. One explanation is based on *logical induction;* that is, people take in so much information on a topic that they begin to look for patterns across all those bits of information. Once they see a pattern, they tend to generalize that pattern from the media world to the real world. Thus when media messages continually present the same types of examples and people expose themselves repeatedly to these same messages (Gerbner, 1969; Gerbner & Gross, 1976; Gerbner et al, 1978), it is easy to construct a pattern. However, tests of this have found that people are not so systematic or logical with many of their beliefs.

An alternative explanation is the *heuristic processing model* of cultivation (Shrum, 1995, 2002). Shrum has shown that people will take quick and dirty shortcuts in their mental reasoning process. When people take shortcuts, they are motivated by efficiency over accuracy. Thus a single vivid example is often enough to motivate an alteration of a belief. For example, Sparks, Sparks, and Gray (1995) found that vividness of mental imagery influenced the beliefs about UFOs after exposure to a television show about UFOs.

A third explanation is *faulty memory*; that is, people often confuse information from fictional messages with real-world information later when asked to recall information. Thus people acquire information from exposure to fictional stories and use it to apply to their beliefs about the real world (Mares, 1996). An example of this explanation comes from the research of Goidel et al. (2006), who conducted a study to explain beliefs about juvenile crime rates and the effectiveness of the juvenile justice system. Special attention was devoted to viewers of television news and shows like *Cops* and *America's Most Wanted*, wherein researchers expected a greater misperception of crime rates and the effectiveness of the criminal justice system. The study found that as viewers watched more crime-related television, they were more likely to misperceive realities of juvenile crime and juvenile justice.

The construction of cultivated beliefs has also been found to be influenced by the person's perception of experiential closeness and mediated closeness (narrative experience) (Bilandzic, 2006).

Third-Person Effect. There are several explanations for this TPE (Perloff, 2002). One explanation is a human drive to preserve self-efficacy. So people can believe the mass media exert powerful effects, but this influence only works on other people (third persons), while we (first persons) are very effective at controlling the mass media effects on ourselves. Another explanation uses Freud's idea of projection; that is, people are influenced by the media but cannot accept this fact as a personal weakness, so they project this weakness onto other people rather than acknowledging it in themselves. A third explanation is that individuals attribute failings in their own actions to situational factors that are outside their control while at the same time attributing the failings of other people to personality characteristics that are inside their control (Gunther, 1991). Thus individuals feel they are more responsible in their own lives for avoiding negative influences where possible but that other people are not as responsible and are therefore influenced by both failings in personality characteristics as well as situational influences.

What are the factors that enhance the TPE? Because the TPE is an example of the more general socialization process, the factors presented in Exhibit 8.4 generally apply, but there are also additional factors (see Exhibit 8.5).

Some of the explanations for the third-person effect attribute influence to particular elements of the way the media present messages, such as pacing. For example, one study found that increasing the pacing of anti-substance radio public service announcements increased perceived effects on self and diminished perceived differences between effects on self and on others (Chock, Fox, Angelini, Lee, & Lang, 2007). This was more evident for messages with arousing content than for those with calm content. The impact of increased pacing was greater for those who made third-person judgments (others more affected than self) than by those who made first-person judgments (self more affected than others). In addition to message features, behavior also influenced perceived message effects. Analysis of a subset of PSAs using antismoking messages found that smokers were more likely to make third-person judgments and nonsmokers first-person judgments about message effects.

Most of the explanations for the third-person effect are traced to some aspect of the person rather than to the message. Perhaps the most interesting of these explanations is the in-group/out-group explanation (Lambe & McLeod, 2005; Meirick, 2004). For example, Lambe and McLeod explain that the third-person effect is also explained by people's feelings about who is with them in an in-group and who is in the out-group. Reid and Hogg (2005) found a third-person effect on the influence of newspapers and the TV show *Friends*. But this effect was reduced to the extent that respondents felt that other third persons were members of their own groups. And Meirick (2004) showed 2000 presidential primary ads from Al Gore and George W. Bush to a combined sample of student and

---

Exhibit 8.4   Further Reading on Media Influence on Beliefs

Message Factors

Constancy of messages

- Coverage of same issues across media
- Same portrayals across media, vehicles, and messages (Gerbner, 1969; Gerbner et al., 1978)

Characteristics of messages

- Exposure to media messages in which violence and aggression are used successfully by attractive characters who are unpunished for these antisocial actions (Bandura, 1977, 2001)
- Vividness (Sparks, Sparks, & Gray, 1995)
- Ability of message to transport audiences (Bilandzic & Busselle, 2008)

Audience Factors

- High exposure to media messages (Gerbner & Gross, 1976)
- Continual exposure to particular genres or shows (Grabe & Drew, 2007; Hawkins & Pingree, 1980; Potter, 1991)
- Greater attention to stories (Moy et al., 2004)
- Belief in the reality of those messages (Potter, 1988; Weiss & Wilson, 1998)
- People have developed multiple dimensions for making assessments of realism in media messages. These dimensions are typicality, factuality, emotional involvement, narrative consistency, and perceptual persuasiveness (Hall, 2003)

Construction of cultivated beliefs influenced by the person's perception of experiential closeness and mediated closeness (narrative experience) (Bilandzic, 2006)

Faulty memory (Mares, 1996)

Personality: low trait-anxious individuals, and to a lesser extent high sensation seekers, are more susceptible to cultivation regarding personal vulnerability to crime, whereas those low in psychoticism are susceptible to cultivation regarding societal violence perceptions (Nabi & Riddle, 2008)

Exhibit 8.5   Further Reading on Media Influence on Third-Person Beliefs

Message Factors

Pacing of messages (Chock et al., 2007)

Audience Factors

In-group/out-group (Lambe & McLeod, 2005; Meirick, 2004; Reid & Hogg, 2005)

Uncertainty reduction (David et al., 2004; Paek et al., 2005)

Need for self-enhancement (Perloff, 2002)

Social distance (Tsfati & Cohen, 2004)

Belief in collectivism (Lee & Tamborini, 2005)

Helpfulness of messages (Jensen & Hurley, 2005)

Perceptions about the reality of the messages (Leone, Peek, & Bissell, 2006)

Gender (Lo & Wei, 2002)

nonstudent partisans. Participants perceived greater effects on the out-group and on the general public then on themselves for ads from the out-group candidate.

Another explanation is uncertainty reduction. For example, Paek and colleagues (2005) designed a study of the third-person effect in which they conceived of message perceptions as a form of social judgment under varying degrees of uncertainty. They collected data from both a survey as well as an experiment and found that credible information on overall message ineffectiveness leads to reductions in estimated effects of the messages on both self and various others and in self/other perceptual gaps when the other is most distant from self. Consistent with the uncertainty reduction argument, the self/other perceptual gaps are related to perceived similarity of the others and vary in response to labels of the others that cue different degrees of similarity with self. Also, David, Liu, and Myser (2004) tested for differences in perceived influences of positive and negative media messages that were examined in a series of three experiments. Their findings indicate that the third-person phenomenon is not merely a methodological artifact but a persistent social judgment bias that cannot be easily neutralized.

Factors about audience perceptions and personality characteristics have been found to influence the third-person effect. Perloff (2002) found that people do not want to admit they are affected by media messages that reflect negatively on the self. Tsfati and Cohen (2004) found that the third-person effect is influenced by social distance perceptions, that is, how close the others are perceived to be to the person making the judgments. Lee and Tamborini (2005) found that beliefs in collectivism were influential such that the TPE was less when people had a stronger belief in collectivism. Jensen and Hurley (2005) tested a helpfulness-of-messages explanation and found a third-person effect on environmental issues; that is, respondents thought others were more susceptible to media influence than they themselves were. However, people who felt environmental messages were helpful to them personally admitted to a greater media influence. And Leone et al. (2006) tested perceptions about the reality of the messages explanation and found a third-person effect was found to be more influenced by the reality of the media messages than the amount or type of exposure.

Finally, gender was also found to be a factor in the third-person effect. Lo and Wei (2002) examined the role of gender in the third-person effect in the context of Internet pornography. The results indicate that most respondents believe Internet pornography has a greater negative influence on others than on themselves. Female respondents tend to perceive greater negative effects of Internet pornography on other males than on other females, and they are readier to support restrictions of Internet pornography. Finally, the magnitude of perceptual bias appears an unreliable predictor of support for media restriction, which may help explain the mixed results in previous studies. This novel gender-differential approach strengthens the growing literature on the third-person effect.

It is likely that all of these factors are useful and that none is the one and only influence. Media influence is complex, especially when we take a long-term view on effects. Therefore, it is likely that there are many factors that exert an influence and explanations for why it occurs.

Sudden Change

There are times when people can acquire a belief immediately from exposure to one media message. Greenberg (1988) proposed a "drench hypothesis" to contrast it with the "drip-drip-drip" perspective that underlies most media effects research. This "drip-drip-drip" perspective regards the influence of media messages as a steady drip that builds up a residue of meaning in a person's mind—kind of like the formation of a stalagmite in a cave. It takes a long time for a stalagmite to form as it builds up with the addition of one grain of mineral at a time dripped in the same place until enough grains accumulate to become a rock formation. In contrast, the drench hypothesis explains that there are times when a person can suddenly alter a belief because of the influence of a single media message. To illustrate this drench, let's say you watch a political pundit predict that a particular candidate will win an election. You are so impressed with that pundit's confidence and reasoning that you accept her belief and make it your own—that is, you too believe that candidate will win the election. An example of acquiring of a more substantial belief occurs when a person watches a religious service on TV and experiences a sudden religious conversion, or when a person watches a political debate and experiences a sudden conversion to a political candidate or party. This type of a conversion to a new belief is relatively rare; however, such an effect can have a profound influence on a person's life.

SUMMARY

Beliefs are a type of cognition. They are mental constructions about the probability that an object or event is associated with a given attribute. Most, but not all, beliefs are subject to verification. They vary in intensity according to how much confidence people have in the belief being accurate.

The media present many beliefs in their messages. Audience members can acquire these beliefs by simply accepting them. The media also trigger people to recall their existing beliefs. However, with belief effects the media exert their most prevalent effect over the long term. That is, the media through their continual stream of messages gradually alter people's beliefs, then reinforce them.

Review Questions

1. In what sense are beliefs a type of cognition?

2. How is the skill of induction related to beliefs?

3. Compare and contrast descriptive and inferential beliefs.

Further Thinking Questions

1. Think about where you have acquired your beliefs on important issues, such as beliefs about politics and the economy.
   - Which media and which messages have been the most influential in providing you with those beliefs?
   - Is it possible that those messages have provided you with inaccurate beliefs, that is, beliefs that do not hold when you try to confirm them?

2. Can you think of being exposed to a media message on a controversial topic that triggered one of your existing beliefs such that you started arguing against the belief presented in that media message?

3. Can you think of any of your beliefs that have been altered a lot over time?
   - What factors influenced that alteration? Was it parents, siblings, friends, or social institutions? Or was it a series of media messages?
   - If it was the media, what made those messages so influential?

4. Can you think of any of your beliefs that are so strong that nothing will ever alter them?
   - What factors influenced the reinforcement of those beliefs so that they have grown so strong? Was it parents, siblings, friends, or social institutions? Or was it a series of media messages?
   - If it was the media, what made those messages so influential?

5. Do you think you have any beliefs that other people may consider strange? To answer this question, you might want to take a look at a book like *Why People Believe Weird Things: Pseudoscience, Superstition, and Other Confusions of Our Time* (2nd edition) by Michael Shermer or check out his website (www.skeptic.com).

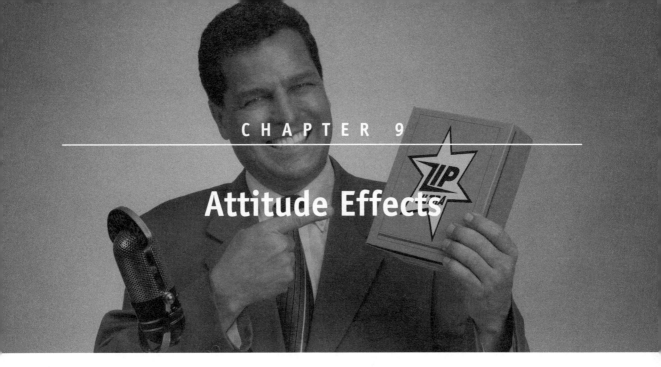

CHAPTER 9

Attitude Effects

Source: ©iStockphoto.com/jgroup

CHAPTER 9

Effects on Attitudes

The study of how the mass media shape attitudes has been a very important part of mass media effects research throughout its history. An important reason for this is that much of this research has been conducted from a social psychological perspective, and social psychology has been dominated by the study of attitudes. In fact, Gordon Allport (1935) claimed that the concept of attitudes is the essence of all of social psychology. Allport's claim has held up over the decades of social science research, as indicated from the results of a recent search of the American Psychological Association's comprehensive index to psychological and related literature (PsycINFO), which yielded 180,910 references for the use of the term *attitude* (cited in Albarracin, Johnson, & Zanna, 2005). And using Google Scholar in a search of articles published in the social sciences with the keyword *attitude* resulted in more than 2 million hits in March 2011.

Despite the common use of the term *attitude,* there is some confusion among scholars and the general public regarding what an attitude is. In this chapter, we first examine the nature of attitudes to arrive at a clear delineation of what they are. Then we look at how the mass media influence the acquiring, triggering, altering, and reinforcing of attitudes.

NATURE OF ATTITUDES

There are times where people—and even scholars—use the terms beliefs and attitudes as synonyms. Granted, beliefs and attitudes can be highly interrelated (Albarracin, Zanna, Johnson, & Kumkale, 2005). They both require mental constructions by individuals, and they both vary in intensity; that is, both beliefs and attitudes can be strong, weak, or non-existent. But this does not mean they are the same thing. It is important to make a clear distinction between the two ideas.

As you saw in Chapter 8, beliefs are estimates of the likelihood that the knowledge one has acquired about something is correct or that something will occur (Eagly & Chaiken, 1998; Wyer & Albarracin, 2005). The key difference between an attitude and a belief is that an attitude is clearly an evaluation; thus it is the comparison of something against a standard. With attitudes the judgment is about something's worth or value, such as a news story's credibility, an advertised product's usefulness, an actor's attractiveness, or the degree of a song's "awesomeness."

These evaluative judgments have valence and intensity (Fabrigar, MacDonald, & Wegener, 2005). *Valence* refers to whether the object of the attitude meets (satisfactory), exceeds (positive), or falls short of the standard (negative). *Intensity* refers to how far from the standard the object is perceived to be. Thus attitudes require the skill of evaluation wherein some element in a media message is compared to the person's standard on the relevant element. Thus standards are essential to the evaluation; that is, there needs to be a standard in play or there cannot be an evaluation. The standard can be explicit (obvious and consciously applied by the person) or implicit (unconsciously applied).

Verification is another distinction between beliefs and attitudes. Most beliefs—but not all—are open to tests of verification. This means that beliefs can be tested to see if they are correct or false. In contrast, attitudes can never be verified. There is no objective truth standard that can be used for attitudes. Instead, each individual has personal standards for his or her preferences. These standards grow out of a person's experience, so they differ widely across individuals. If Harry evaluates political candidate X as being the best for an elective office while Julie evaluates political candidate Y as being best for the same elective office, this does not mean that either Harry or Julie is right and the other is wrong. It means that they each have a different set of standards for what makes a candidate good for a particular elective office. Not only are standards personal, they are often inexplicable; that is, people have a difficult or impossible time trying to tell others what their standards are. To illustrate this, consider a conversation you might have with your sister after you find out she has a very positive attitude about a boy named Buster. You point out that Buster has tattoos covering almost all parts of his visible body and that your sister has never liked guys with tattoos; your sister agrees. You point out that Buster is short, bald, and runty, while your sister usually prefers guys who are tall, blonde, and athletic; your sister agrees. You point out that Buster dresses like he is in prison, while your sister usually prefers guys who are preppy and neat; your sister agrees. In frustration you plead, "Then why do you like Buster so much?" and your sister replies, "I don't know, but he is so cool." Your sister clearly has a positive attitude about Buster, but she cannot articulate her standard or the process she used in arriving at her evaluation. Therefore your attempt to get her to analyze her attitude and show her its faulty nature falls woefully short of being convincing.

We use many different standards in evaluating mass media messages. One of the most prevalent standards is usefulness. Whenever we search out a certain kind of experience from the media, we continually evaluate whether or not a message meets our standard of usefulness. If a message does not meet our standard, we likely tune it out and keep searching for a message that does meet or exceed our standard. As we scan through messages, we are developing attitudes about different kinds of media messages as being useless or useful.

When we watch fictional stories on TV, in a theater, or on the Internet, we develop attitudes about characters in those stories. Each of us has a set of standards for what makes a character interesting, attractive, believable, or fun to watch. We apply these standards in our evaluations of characters and in so doing develop attitudes about which characters we like and which we do not like. The same procedure is used to develop attitudes about real people and events covered in nonfictional messages in the media. For example, we have our own personal standards about what makes a good political leader. When we read the news on a website or watch a political debate on television, we apply these standards and develop attitudes about the people seeking elective office.

Where do we get our standards? Some standards we develop for ourselves. But many of our standards have been taught to us by others, such as our parents and institutions through "socialization." Socialization is a process through which representatives of society (such as education, religion, criminal justice system, and the like) continually teach us about how we should think and behave in order to function well in society. These lessons are called "social norms," which are the rules that have been developed by a society to structure our expectations for how people should treat one another. Institutions tell us what these rules are, and we learn these rules by observing how people interact in real life. These social norms are standards for how we should behave and how we should regard the behavior of other people. When we watch a movie, we continually compare the characters' actions against our social norms and thereby create our attitudes about whether the characters' actions are justified.

The mass media play a big role in transmitting these social norms. Institutions rely on books, pictures, films, recorded music, and Internet sites to convey information about these norms. For example, you probably have learned a good deal about the criminal justice system even though you have never been arrested, convicted of a crime, and served time in prison. There are many TV shows, films, and books about criminal behavior, solving crimes, trials, and prison life. Even though you do not have any direct real-world experience in this area, you likely still have standards about what constitutes criminal behavior, what makes a good attorney, and so on.

People can memorize the attitudes of other people, thus making those memorized attitudes their own. Or they can construct their own attitudes. For example, a person reads a review of a new song and simply accepts that reviewer's attitude about the song. Or the person can listen to the song and formulate her own attitude, which might be the same or different from the reviewer.

Attitudes can be stable or flexible. They can be learned in one exposure and stored to be accessed later (Fazio, 1986). Or they can be continually changed as people are exposed to more information or as their standards for evaluation change over time.

The mass media play a role in both the creation and shaping of attitudes over time. The mass media present information about social norms that we can learn and accept as our own standards. Also, the mass media present a great many elements in messages that trigger a demand for evaluation. When we hear a new song, watch a TV show, or visit an Internet site, we are motivated to make judgments about its value. These judgments are attitudes. Over the long term, the continual flow of media messages gradually alters some of our standards and attitudes as well as reinforcing other standards and attitudes (Schwarz & Bohner, 2001).

Now let's take a look at the range of attitudinal effects organized in four categories of acquiring, triggering existing attitudes, altering, and reinforcing attitudes over time. Within each of these four categories, I first lay out the effects found by researchers, then display the various factors that have been found to bring about these effects.

ACQUIRING ATTITUDES

The mass media exert two kinds of influences with the acquiring of attitudes. One influence is to get us to accept the attitudes presented in the mass media messages; that is, we acquire the attitudes as they are presented. A second influence is to get us to accept the standards presented in the messages. We then use these acquired standards to construct our own attitudes.

Acquiring Attitudes

Researchers have found that we can acquire many different kinds of attitudes from exposure to media messages (see Exhibit 9.1). Some of these acquired attitudes were planned by the senders of the media messages. For example, advertisers of commercial products and political candidates want us to simply accept the evaluations of their products and candidates without question, and oftentimes we do just that.

Audiences have also been found to acquire certain attitudes from media messages when the senders of those messages were not trying to convey those attitudes. Journalists intend to inform us by presenting the events of the day in as objective manner as possible. But embedded in those "objective" stories are attitudes expressed by different people, and often we hear attitudes expressed there that we like, so we accept those attitudes as our own. For example, people can hear a "talking head" in a news program present a negative or a positive attitude about presidential behavior (Bucy & Newhagen, 1999b), about government in general (Becker & Whitney, 1980), about foreign countries (Perry, 1990), about racial policy and equality (Richardson, 2005), about women's rights (Holbert, Shah, & Kwak, 2003), about the conduct of the police (Moy, Pfau, & Kahlor, 1999), and about defendants in rape trials (Mullin, Imrich, & Linz, 1995), then people acquire the attitudes they hear expressed in those news messages.

People have also been found to acquire certain attitudes that are expressed in fictional messages. Even after only one exposure to a dramatic TV program, people can accept the attitudes presented there on controversial issues, such as support for the death penalty (Slater, Rouner, & Long, 2006). We learn attitudes about political matters, social issues, and institutions such as the criminal justice system. For example, Whites who are exposed to negative, stereotypic depictions of Blacks reported higher levels of negative evaluations of Blacks (Ford, 1997).

Acquiring Standards

Standards are essential in the construction of attitudes. When we create an attitude we make a judgment about something, that evaluative judgment is our attitude. We cannot make an evaluative judgment without comparing something to a standard. In the case of the mass media, we compare information from media messages to our standards. Where do we get our standards? Many of them come from our parents, friends, and other institutions, such as religion, education, the criminal justice system, and so on. And some of our standards come from the mass media.

Exhibit 9.1   Further Reading on Acquiring Attitudes

Acquiring Attitudes

About advertised products (Andsager, Austin, & Pinkleton, 2002; Basil, 1996; Berney-Reddish & Areni, 2006; Buijzen & Valkenburg, 2000; Hitchon & Thorson, 1995; Kim & Morris, 2007; Nabi, 2003; Pfau et al., 2001; Pfau et al., 2004; Russell & Stern, 2006; Pfau, Holbert, Zubric, Pasha, & Lin, 2000)

- Especially with familiar brands (Homer, 2006)

About political matters

- Candidates and campaigns (Cwalina, Falkowski, & Kaid, 2000; Kim, Scheufele, & Shanahan, 2005; Valentino, Hutchings, & Williams, 2004)
- Presidential behavior (Bucy & Newhagen, 1999a and b)
- Foreign countries (Perry, 1990)
- Government (Becker & Whitney, 1980)
- Reduce voting preferences (Pinkleton, 1998)

About social issues

- Women's rights (Holbert et al., 2003)
- Social trust (Moy & Scheufele, 2000)
- Support for the death penalty (Slater et al., 2006)
- Racial policy and equality (Pan & Kosicki, 1996; Richardson, 2005)

About institutions

- Public schools (Moy et al., 1999)
- Police (Moy et al., 1999)
- Criminal court system (Moy et al., 1999)
- Defendants in rape trials (Mullin et al., 1995)

Acquiring Criteria for Judgments About:

Standards for health and body image (Harrison & Fredrickson, 2003)

Expectations for romantic partners (Eggermont, 2004)

Expectations for marriage (Segrin & Nabi, 2002)

Standards for what constitutes an important current event (Iyengar & Kinder, 1987)

Standards for socially responsible business practices (Lind & Rockler, 2001)

Researchers have documented several areas in which people acquire standards from the mass media. For example, people have been found to acquire standards about current events (Iyengar & Kinder, 1987) and for health and body image (Harrison & Fredrickson, 2003) from the mass media. Also, people learn expectations for marriage

(Segrin & Nabi, 2002) and romantic partners (Eggermont, 2004) from the mass media. And people learn standards about social responsibility for businesses from watching news programs (Lind & Rockler, 2001).

Acquiring Standards About Body Image

Anna threw her book across the room, "I am so depressed I can't study. I can't concentrate."

Grace picked up the book and tried to give it back to her roommate. "Anna, you have to study. You don't want to flunk out, do you?"

Anna ignored her textbook and picked up a fashion magazine instead. "What's the use? I hate college. I thought college was going to be fun. But I'm not having any fun."

"How can you say that? We went to parties the last three nights! That was fun!"

"Fun for you. You had lots of guys talk to you. One guy even called you tonight and asked you out. Not me. No guys called me! I haven't had a date in over a month."

"Guys will call you. Give it time."

"I have given it time. No guys are calling me. I'm too fat!"

"What? You are not. You've got a great figure."

"It's getting better. I lost 5 pounds these last few weeks. So why am I not more popular? It makes no sense!"

"Are you kidding me?"

"It's true. I'm too fat. When you're fat, cute clothes don't fit right. And if you can't look hot in cute clothes there is no point in going to parties. No guy is going to talk to you. It's true." Anna grabbed two handfuls of her fashion magazines and tossed them into the air. "Show me one fat girl who is popular."

"You just need more confidence."

"I need to lose 5 more pounds to feel more confident."

Analysis

Anna has evaluated her body and judged it to be too fat. Where did she get her standard for body weight that she used in judging her own body? It is likely that after reading fashion magazines with the ultra-thin, air-brushed models, Anna accepted the standard that women need to be ultra-thin to be popular.

Process of Acquiring Attitudes

The acquiring of attitudes is explained by a combination of message and audience factors along with environmental factors (see Exhibit 9.2). One of the most influential message factors is how the media message is framed. For example, in an experiment to investigate

Exhibit 9.2 Further Reading on Attitude Acquisition Effect

Message Factors

How message is framed (Richardson, 2005)

Product spokesperson (Mehta & Davis, 1990; Whipple & Courtney, 1980; Berscheid & Walster, 1974; Wilcox, Murphy, & Sheldon, 1985), especially celebrity endorsers (Basil, 1996)

Humor (Duncan & Nelson, 1985; Wu, Crocker, & Rogers, 1989)

Visuals (Edell, 1988; Lee & Barnes, 1990)

Nonverbal elements (Hallahan, 1994)

Music (Gorn, 1982; Park & Young, 1986)

Techniques of persuasiveness (Nabi, 2003; Pfau et al., 2000; Pfau et al., 2001; Pfau et al., 2004; Sopory & Dillard, 2002; Sotirovic, 2001; Tal-Or, Boninger, Poran, & Gleicher, 2004)

Emotional appeals (Hitchon & Thorson, 1995)

Audience Factors

Existing attitudes (Dolich, 1969; Homer, 2006; Russell & Stern, 2006; Slater & Rouner, 1996)

Frequency of exposure to a particular attitude (Naples, 1981; Sutherland & Galloway, 1981)

Prior knowledge (Sujan, 1985)

Perceived credibility of source of message (Groenendyk & Valentino, 2002)

Experience with product (Kolter, 1988; Thompson, Locander, & Pollio, 1989)

Processing strategy (Chang, 2002; Slater & Rounder, 2002)

Perceived realism (Andsager, Austin, & Pinkleton, 2001)

Sensation seeking (Stephenson, 2003)

Degree of societal awareness (Valentino et al., 2004)

Involvement

- Degree of involvement with message (Nabi & Hendriks, 2003)
- Involvement with purchase decision (Park & Young, 1986)

Positive affective reactions to ad and product (Burke & Edell, 1989; Holbrook & Westwood, 1989; Kim & Morris, 2007; Stout & Leckenby, 1986)

(Continued)

Exhibit 9.2 (Continued)

Mood (Gardner & Hill, 1988)

Demographics

- Age (Buijzen & Valkenburg, 2000)
- Gender (Berney-Reddish & Areni, 2006; Mullin et al., 1995)

Gender role socialization (Andsager et al., 2002)

Environmental Factors

Degree of clutter (Keller, 1991; Kent & Machleit, 1992)

Influence from program in which TV ad appeared (Goldberg & Gorn, 1987; Hsia, 1977; Kim, 1994)

the impact of editorial framing on readers' political attitudes toward different racial groups, Richardson (2005) asked participants to read newspaper editorials about a U.S. Supreme Court decision upholding affirmative action in higher education. The results indicated that the way the stories were framed had an influence on the participants' attitudes about Blacks and Whites in the news stories.

With audience factors, existing attitudes are especially important in explaining the acquisition of new attitudes. For example, when persuasive messages are congruent with people's own values and when those messages are supported with statistical evidence, they were found to be more persuasive (Slater & Rouner, 1996).

Persuasiveness of messages is also related to amount of cognitive effort required to process those messages. When people are presented with new brands in ads, they are less likely to use cognitive processes in acquiring attitudes than when they see familiar brands; familiar brands involve the use of existing information in the attitude and therefore require more cognitive processing (Homer, 2006). Also, when messages are automatically processed, those messages enter people's minds subconsciously, what cognitive psychologists call the "peripheral route," as opposed to the "central route," by which messages are encountered consciously. Peripheral processing requires much less mental effort, because people do not analyze the message and argue against it, so it is more likely to be accepted (Chang, 2002).

A person's demographics have also been found to be associated with attitude acquisition. With age, advertising has been found to have a stronger effect on younger children (Buijzen & Valkenburg, 2000). With gender, women are more likely to accept advertising claims than are men (Berney-Reddish & Areni, 2006). And men exposed to predatory rape publicity are more likely to favor defendants in rape trials; in contrast, men who saw messages of rape framed as a miscommunication did not exhibit such an attitude. Women were unaffected by the framing of such information (Mullin et al., 1995).

Source: ©iStockphoto.com/ozgurdonmaz

TRIGGERING ATTITUDES

The mass media trigger attitudes about the content they present, such as the reality of stories, attractiveness of characters, and the credibility of news stories (see Exhibit 9.3). The media also get us thinking about the real world by presenting images of real-world people and real-world events in their news stories. This often triggers the recall or construction of attitudes about real-world events and issues.

Exhibit 9.3 Further Reading on Triggering Attitudes

Triggering the Construction of Attitudes About the Media

Evaluations about the media in general (Edy & Meirick, 2007; Gunther & Christen, 2002; Gunther & Schmitt, 2004)

Evaluations about media credibility (Flanagin & Metzger, 2000; Johnson & Kaye, 1998; Kim, Weaver, & Willnat, 2000), news stories (Arpan & Peterson, 2008; Grabe, Zhou, Lang, & Bolls, 2000; Melican & Dixon, 2008; Sundar & Nass, 2001), and of advertising (Groenendyk & Valentino, 2002)

- Credibility of news sources (Bracken, 2006)

Evaluations of PSA message effectiveness (Lang & Yegiyan, 2008)

Evaluations of persuasive messages

- Advertising in general (Magee & Kalyanaraman, 2009)
- Radio ads (Potter, 2009)
- PSAs (Andsager et al., 2001)

Evaluations of reality

- Stories on television (Dorr, 1980; Shapiro & Chock, 2003)
- Media texts (Hall, 2003)

Evaluations of characters in stories (Kirsh & Olczak, 2000; Mastro, Lapinski, Kopacz, & Behm-Morawitz, 2009; Mastro, Tamborini, & Hullett, 2005)

- Moral judgments about characters (Krcmar & Vieira, 2005; Lachlan & Tamborini, 2008; Raney, 2004)
- Avatars in video games (Chandler, Konrath, & Schwarz, 2009; Nowak, Hamilton, & Hammond, 2009)

Evaluations of usefulness of search engines (Kalyanaraman & Ivory, 2009)

Judging degree of media violence in show (Riddle, Eyal, Mahood, & Potter, 2006)

Triggering the Construction of Attitudes About the Real World

News media trigger attitudes about the content they present, especially on social issues and controversial topics

- Importance of social issues (Sheafer, 2007)
- Social protest (McLeod & Detenber, 1999)
- Political candidates (Bucy & Newhagen, 1999a; Carpentier, Roskos-Ewoldsen, & Roskos-Ewoldsen, 2008; Hwang, Gotlieb, Nah, & McLeod, 2007; Meffert, Chung, Joiner, Waks, & Garst, 2006)
- Support for public policies (gay marriage, death penalty) (Slater, Rouner, & Long, 2006)
- Attitudes about homosexuality (Calzo & Ward, 2009)
- Partial birth abortion controversy (Simon & Jerit, 2007)

- The degree of punishment of violent actions (Krcmar & Cooke, 2001)
- Attitudes toward Blacks (Pan & Kosicki, 1995)
- Immigration (Igartua & Cheng, 2009)
- Organ donation (Morgan, Movius, & Cody, 2009)
- Genetically modified organisms (Gunther & Liebhart, 2006)

Advertising messages trigger evaluations about products (Chang, 2007; Coulter & Punj, 2004; McQuarrie & Phillips, 2005)

Entertainment messages trigger evaluations about satisfaction with one's own body (Harrison & Fredrickson, 2003)

Triggering Construction of Attitudes About the Media

As we expose ourselves to media messages, this experience often triggers the need to construct an attitude about the media in general (Gunther & Schmitt, 2004) or about some element in a media message, such as about the characters in stories (Kirsh & Olczak, 2000) or the degree of violence in the story (Riddle et al., 2006).

One very popular topic for researchers is how media exposures trigger the construction of attitudes about content credibility (Flanagin & Metzger, 2000), particularly of news stories (Bracken, 2006) and of advertising (Groenendyk & Valentino, 2002). Another popular topic for researchers has been how media exposures trigger the construction of judgments about the reality of stories on television (Shapiro & Chock, 2003), the reality about media texts (Hall, 2003), and the reality of PSAs (public service announcements) (Andsager et al., 2001).

When people watch entertainment messages that contain acts of violence, they are usually triggered to form an evaluation about the degree of violence in the overall message. Most people would think that the evaluation of how violent a movie was would be related to the number of acts of violence in the movie, but this is not the case. That is, the standard people use to judge the degree of violence in a media message is not the number of violent acts in the message but rather the degree of graphicness of the violence (Riddle et al., 2006). Thus a show with two acts of highly graphic violence will be judged as more violent than another show with dozens of acts of violence that are shown in a sanitized manner. Thus when we are trying to understand how people form their attitudes about media messages, it is not sufficient to examine only the elements in the media message; we must also examine the standards they use to make their judgments.

Triggering Construction of Attitudes About the Real World

News stories on controversial topics have been found to trigger the formation of new attitudes about these topics. For example, news stories have been found to trigger the creation of attitudes about partial birth abortions (Simon & Jerit, 2006), degree of punishment for violent actions (Krcmar & Cooke, 2001), gay marriage, the death penalty (Slater et al., 2006), genetically modified organisms (Gunther & Liebhart, 2006), and acts of social protest (McLeod & Detenber, 1999). Advertising messages have been found to trigger the formation of attitudes about products (Chang, 2007) and political candidates (Bucy & Newhagen, 1999a). The media can trigger the formation of attitudes about people such as toward Blacks (Pan & Kosicki, 1996) and about one's own self. For example, media messages trigger the formation of attitudes about satisfaction with one's own body (Harrison & Fredrickson, 2003).

The media trigger attitudes about how important various issues are. For example, Sheafer (2007) found that the public's evaluation of issue importance is influenced by the issue saliency in the news and by the evaluative tone of media coverage. The media also trigger attitudes about candidates, which lead to later voting behaviors.

The media trigger the formation of sexual attitudes. In a study of exposure to Internet pornography by adolescents in Taiwan, Lo and Wei (2005) found that this exposure was associated with attitudes about sexual permissiveness.

Process of Triggering Attitudes

Researchers have found that the triggering of attitudes has been enhanced by a large number of factors (see Exhibit 9.4). These factors generally fall into two categories: message characteristics and audience characteristics.

Exhibit 9.4 Further Reading on Attitude Triggering Effect

Message Factors

Framing of story (Goffman, 1979; McLeod & Detenber, 1999; Simon & Jerit, 2006)

Production techniques (Bucy & Newhagen, 1999b)

Metaphors (McQuarrie & Phillips, 2005)

Audience Factors

Thinking skills

- Ability to engage in reflection (Hwang, Gotlieb, Nah, & McLeod, 2007)
- Matching the appropriate cognitive resources required to the demands of this task (Coulter & Punj, 2004)
- Information processing strategies (Chang, 2007)
- Moral reasoning (Krcmar & Vieira, 2005)

Perceptions of issue saliency (Sheafer, 2007)

Perceptions of in-group and out-groups (Mastro et al., 2005)

Emotional appropriateness heuristic (Bucy & Newhagen, 1999b)

Message Characteristics. Among message factors, framing is very important. *Framing* refers to the way the story is presented, that is, what is emphasized, what is left out, and how ideas are labeled. For example, the way words are used can trigger different attitudes on controversial issues. Simon and Jerit (2006) found that with the partial birth abortion controversy the use of the word *baby* or *fetus* made a difference in people's opinions and thus either increased or decreased support for banning partial birth abortion. Also, McQuarrie and Phillips (2005) found that metaphors and metaphorical pictures used in magazine advertisements can trigger positive inferences about the advertised brand; that is, people spontaneously generate positive inferences. While the way controversial issues are framed in the media is important, framing does not always determine how attitudes are triggered. For example, Edy and Meirick (2007) found that while evaluations of events covered in the media were triggered by media coverage, people did not automatically accept the frames used by the media, such as war frames or crime frames. Instead people constructed their own attitudes from a combination of frames and information.

Production techniques are also important. The length of shots, graphics, staging factors all go into a person's evaluation of political candidates. Close-ups helped viewers identify more with candidates, as did town hall meetings with extended shots of the candidates (Bucy & Newhagen, 1999a).

Audience Characteristics. There are many characteristics about the audience that explain triggering of attitudes. These include thinking skills, existing attitudes, demographics, and family communication patterns.

Among thinking skills, certain characteristics about the audience members are associated with the triggering of attitudes. These include the amount of cognitive resources people devote to the task (Coulter & Punj, 2004), the use of heuristics (Bucy & Newgagen, 1999a), and perceptions of issue saliency (Sheafer, 2007). For example, Hwang et al. (2007) ran an experiment and found that people who had a higher propensity to engage in reflection and watched a presidential candidate debate had that exposure exert a stronger effect on their judgments of candidates than did people with a lower propensity to engage in reflection. Also, when triggering evaluations about candidates in televised presidential debates, people have been found to use an emotional appropriateness heuristic; that is, people compare the nonverbal behavior of the televised candidates to a standard of emotional appropriateness (Bucy & Newhagen, 1999a). Thus if a candidate exhibits emotions that people regard as appropriate for a leader (that is, toughness and grace under pressure), then the candidate is evaluated as being good. But when candidates lose their tempers or break down and cry, then they are evaluated as weak.

Existing attitudes are important. When people have existing attitudes about political candidates, they approve political information with a bias that triggers what they think about different facts presented in news stories (Meffert et al., 2006). Also, when people have strong attitudes about ethnic groups, they process news information differently about racial inequality (Pan & Kosicki, 1995).

Triggering of attitudes can sometimes be explained by demographic characteristics of audiences. For example, there is a gender difference in information-processing strategies. Comparative ads encouraged greater levels of brand evaluation involvement with men; this triggered more favorable brand evaluations. For women, the comparative ads were regarded as manipulative, and this led to negative brand evaluation (Chang, 2007). There are also age differences. With television news, the most favorable ratings of news credibility are triggered in elderly viewers (Folkerts & Lacy, 2001).

Family communication patterns are also important to explaining the triggering of mental processes involved with attitudes. For example, children's judgments of the meaning of violence in stories are influenced by their family communication patterns. Children raised in high-control households (parents are authorities who make rules) were likely to judge punished violence as less justified. But children raised in communication households (ideas are openly expressed and the child's ideas are often valued) were more likely to judge motivated violence as more justified (Krcmar, 1998).

Moral reasoning is also important. Krcmar and Vieira (2005) conducted a study in which parent–child dyads responded to a questionnaire investigating the relative impact of exposure to television violence, family communication patterns, and parents' moral reasoning on the moral reasoning of children. The results of this study indicated that exposure to television violence had a negative effect on children's moral reasoning, but when children where able to take the perspective of victims of violence they were able to make better moral judgments about violence.

Interactions. There are interactions between message elements and audience elements. For example, Chang (2004) found that when product information in ads is ambiguous, consumers are more likely to engage in heuristic processing and make quick, intuitive evaluations of the product. However, when information is unambiguous, consumers are likely to engage in systematic processing and evaluate the product based on their assessment of the actual attributes of the product.

ALTERING ATTITUDES

As you saw in the previous sections, people can acquire attitudes they see in media messages as well as have those messages trigger the construction of a new attitude. These are immediate effects because they occur during the media exposure or immediately after the exposure. Now we shift our focus to longer-term effects, beginning with altering. The media can alter both existing attitudes as well as a person's standards (see Exhibit 9.5).

Altering Existing Attitudes

One of the most researched topics about attitudes is the way media messages can change and shape people's attitudes over time (Festinger, 1957; Fishbein & Ajzen, 1975; Peter & Valkenburg, 2006; Petty & Cacioppo, 1981). Studies have documented a long-term shaping of attitudes about sex (Peter & Valkenburg, 2006), opinions about political issues (Meffert et al., 2006), opinions concerning women's rights (Holbert et al., 2003), attitudes about journalists (Lee, 2005), and attitudes about body image (Aubrey, 2006).

One of the most documented long-term altering effects on attitudes is the "sleeper effect." This is when people acquire information from the media but later forget what the source of that information was (Hovland, Lumsdaine, & Sheffield, 1949). An example of this was found by Yegiyan and Grabe (2007), who presented their research participants with

Exhibit 9.5   Further Reading on Altering Attitudes

Altering Attitudes

General attitudes (Festinger, 1957; Fishbein & Ajzen, 1975; Goffman, 1974, 1979; Kisielius & Sternthal, 1984; Newcomb, 1953; Perry & Gonzenbach, 1997; Peter & Valkenburg, 2006; Petty & Cacioppo, 1981; Solomon, 1989)

Long-term shaping of attitudes about:

- Sex (Brown & L'Engle, 2009; Eyal & Kunkel, 2008; Peter & Valkenburg, 2006, 2008a; Zhang, Miller, & Harrison, 2008)
- Political positions (Meffert et al., 2006)
- Sociopolitical opinions concerning women's rights (Holbert et al., 2003)
- Attitudes about body image (Aubrey, 2006)
- Attitudes about journalists (Lee, 2005)

Third-person effect (Leone, Peek, & Bissell, 2006; Perry & Gonzenbach, 1997)

Sleeper effect (Hovland et al., 1949)

- Political attitudes (Yegiyan & Grabe, 2007)

Mere exposure effect (Zajonc, 1980)

Altering Standards

For ideal body image (Harrison & Cantor, 1997)

For relationships (Eggermont, 2004)

For political campaigns (Pinkleton, Austin, & Fortman, 1998)

For political leaders (Cho, 2005)

political messages in three types of formats: conventional political ads, news-like political ads, and news stories. Memory for the source of information was measured immediately after exposure and again a week later. The results of this experiment indicate that format and time had a significant effect on memory for the source. Participants identified the source of information with about the same level of accuracy across formats right after their exposure. A week later, participants were significantly more inept at attributing information contained in news-like ads to its source than doing so for conventional ads and news stories. At that point, information presented in news-like ads was incorrectly attributed to news about 70% of the time.

Media exposure over a long period of time can also alter attitudes about sex. In a study of Dutch adolescents, Peter and Valkenburg (2008a) found that the more frequent exposure to sexually explicit Internet material was associated with more positive attitudes toward

Source: ©iStockphoto.com/youliya

uncommitted sexual exploration (that is, sexual relations with casual partners or friends or with sexual partners in one-night stands). Zhang et al. (2008) found that exposure to more sexually explicit music videos was associated with more permissive attitudes toward premarital sex and stronger endorsement of the sexual double standard, regardless of gender, overall television viewing, and previous sexual experience. However, Eyal and Kunkel (2008) found that exposure to shows that portrayed negative consequences of sex led to more negative attitudes toward premarital intercourse and to more negative moral judgments of characters engaged in this behavior. Results were observed immediately after the viewing and persisted two weeks later.

Finally there is something called the "mere exposure effect" (Zajonc, 1980), which states that when people are in nonconscious states and are exposed repeatedly to an object, then later are presented with the object when they are in aware states, those people will have a more favorable evaluation of the object than if they had not been exposed to the object repeatedly. Usually people do not recall the previous exposures in the nonconscious state; that is, people have a positive feeling about the object but they do not know why.

Altering Existing Standards

Over time, the media alter our standards for all sorts of things. We use these standards to shape our attitudes. One example of the altering of standards concerns what has been labeled as the "ideal body image." Models in magazines and role models in television shows are typically thin. Thus we develop a standard of body shape and size. When we compare our own bodies to this unrealistic standard, we usually fail to measure up to the standard. Harrison and Cantor (1997) conducted research on this topic and found that for women, media use predicted a negative attitude about their own bodies. For men, media use predicted attitudes in favor of thinness for women. Also, numerous studies have shown that exposure to pornography, with its highly attractive models and supercharged sexual activity, alters people's standards, and people's real-life partners are judged as less attractive and exciting (Harris & Scott, 2002).

Researchers have also found that the way the media tell their stories about dating and partner seeking gradually alter our standards over time. For example, Eggermont (2004) conducted a study with Belgian teenagers and found that those who watched the most television had their standards about dating altered the most concerning the importance of physical attractiveness and a pleasant personality in a romantic partner. Furthermore, these alterations were not related to the teenagers' direct experience with dating relationships.

Researchers have also found that media exposure alters a person's standards for political campaigns and candidates. For example, Pinkleton et al. (1998) found that negative coverage of political campaigns increases cynicism and reduces beliefs in political efficacy. Thus voter expectations are lowered.

Process of Altering Attitudes

Attitudes are altered over the long run by a combination of message factors acting along with audience factors (see Exhibit 9.6). With message factors, the repetition of certain messages can alter a person's standards. This has been found to be the case with body image. Aubrey (2006) found that the media's practice of objectifying bodies socializes individuals to take an outsider's perspective on the physical self (that is, self objectifying). She also found that exposure to these images led to males increasing their self-monitoring of their bodies.

Research has found both that television news emphasizes candidates' character rather than policy issues and that political discussion is usually between people who hold similar

Exhibit 9.6   Further Reading on Attitude Altering Effect

Message Factors

Repetition of messages (Aubrey, 2006; Gibbons, Lukowski, & Walker, 2005)

Use of concrete exemplars (Perry & Gonzenbach, 1997)

Type of genre of the messages (Holbert et al., 2003)

Audience Factors

Amount and type of exposure (Cho, 2005; Glynn, Huge, Reineke, Hardy, & Shanahan, 2007; Peter & Valkenburg, 2006)

General liking for the media message (Nan, 2008)

Identification with fictional characters (Moyer-Gusé & Nabi, 2010)

Personal bias (Meffert et al., 2006)

Media literacy training (Austin et al., 2007; Buijzen & Valkenburg, 2005)

political beliefs. Cho (2005) conducted a study that hypothesized that frequent television news viewers are more likely to rely on their perception of candidate image to make an electoral choice, whereas voters who frequently talk to others about politics are more likely to vote on the basis of party identification. Also, Glynn and colleagues (2007) examined the influence of daytime talk shows on opinion formation. Using agenda-setting and cultivation perspectives (see Chapter 8), they hypothesized that both exposure to daytime talk shows and the apparent reality of these shows would be positively related to support for government involvement in social issues. In addition to exposure and apparent reality being positively related to levels of support, it was found that both talk show exposure and respondent's reported perception of the apparent reality of television played a moderating role in the relationship between political ideology and support for government involvement in family issues. This study demonstrated that daytime talk shows can play a significant role in public opinion formation.

As for audience factors, long-term shaping of attitudes about sex have been found to be influenced by long-term exposure to sexually explicit messages on the Internet (Peter & Valkenburg, 2006). Also, Meffert et al. (2006) found that two biases (negativity and congruency) influence how voters selected information from the media and processed that information about political candidates.

Media literacy instruction has also been found to alter attitudes. Austin et al. (2007) conducted a study examining the effects of media literacy training on adolescents' attitudes about tobacco use. Media literacy training altered individuals' attitudes about the desirability of certain portrayals in the media. Also, Buijzen and Valkenburg (2005) conducted a study to investigate the effectiveness of various types of parental mediation of three potentially undesired effects of television advertising. In a survey among 360 parent–child dyads with children in the 8 to 12 years age range, they investigated how different styles of advertising mediation (active vs. restrictive) and family consumer communication (concept oriented vs. socio oriented) moderated the relations between the children's advertising exposure and their materialism, purchase requests, and conflicts with their parents. Their results showed that active advertising mediation and concept-oriented consumer communication were most effective in reducing the effects of advertising. In another study, interactive websites were found to be better than noninteractive ones because they led to higher favorability to the advertised product and a greater flow state (Sicilia, Ruiz, & Munuera, 2005).

REINFORCING ATTITUDES

Researchers have known for a long time that one of the most consistent and powerful effects of exposure to media messages is to reinforce people's existing attitudes over time (Klapper, 1960). People typically think the media have a reinforcement effect on existing attitudes rather than assume that media content necessarily creates or changes attitudes (Oliver, Yang, Ramasubramanian, Kim, and Lee, 2008). Researchers have also found evidence of a reinforcement effect on attitudes across a wide range of topics (see Exhibit 9.7).

Exhibit 9.7   Further Reading on Reinforcing Attitudes

Reinforcing Attitudes (Klapper, 1960)

Existing attitudes of credibility

- Of information across media (Flanagin & Metzger, 2000; Johnson & Kaye, 1998; Kim et al., 2000)
- Of news stories (Grabe, Zhou, Lang, Bolls, 2000; Oliver et al., 2008; Sundar & Nass, 2001)
- Of advertising (Groenendyk & Valentino (2002)
- Of sponsor's credibility (Burgoon, Pfau, & Birk, 1995)

Existing partisan political attitudes (Holbert, 2005; Knobloch-Westerwick, & Meng, 2009)

Authoritarian aggressive attitudes (Reith, 1999)

Of political issues, such as affirmative action (Oliver et al., 2008)

Reinforcing Standards

For presidential candidates (Benoit & Hansen, 2004)

This wide range of topics for attitude reinforcement is examined in three groups: attitudes about credibility of information, attitudes about dating and sex, and attitudes about political matters.

Reinforcing Attitudes About Credibility of Information

One of the most researched areas of attitude reinforcement over time has focused on attitudes about credibility of the media for reporting information. Differences have been found across media (Kim, Weaver, & Willnat, 2000) as well as genre, especially with news stories (Grabe, et al., 2000; Sundar & Nass, 2001) and advertising (Groenendyk & Valentino, 2002).

Reinforcing Attitudes About Dating and Sex

Another popular area for research has been the reinforcement of attitudes about dating and sex. Attitudes about dating are reinforced by watching TV dating shows, especially when viewers hold higher perceptions of reality of the shows (Ferris, Smith, Greenberg, & Smith, 2007). These dating attitudes are also reinforced by watching prime-time comedy and drama (Ward & Rivadenrya, 1999). Exposure to sexually explicit material online reinforces adolescents' attitudes about recreational sex (Peter & Valkenburg, 2006).

Reinforcing Attitudes About Political Issues

A third area of research deals with political issues. Viewing presidential debates on TV reinforces a person's partisan attitudes (Holbert, 2005). When watching televised presidential debates, voters are likely to have their existing attitudes reinforced (Benoit & Hansen, 2004). Issue advocacy ads have less of an effect of changing attitudes than a reinforcement effect of enhancing the sponsor's credibility among people who already favor a corporation's position (Burgoon, Pfau, & Birk, 1995). And authoritarian aggression attitudes (such as the favoring of strict punishment for those who break the law) have been found to be reinforced by viewing crime drama (Reith, 1999).

Arguably, the strongest reason for this effect of reinforcing people's existing attitudes is the selective exposure explanation. The selective exposure argument says that people typically seek out messages that conform to their existing attitudes, so that over time, they are only exposed to information that supports those attitudes and therefore those existing attitudes get reinforced. There has been a good deal of research to test this selective exposure explanation, and it has generally been found to be a good explanation. For example, Knobloch-Westerwick and Meng (2009) found that people spend more time reading political news that conforms to their existing attitudes. There are people who do seek out a wider range of information, including information that does not support their existing attitudes, but these people are typically higher educated and more interested in politics in general. People with lower interest in politics have more habitual voting behavior, so they want to avoid information that challenges their existing attitudes.

Reinforcing Attitudes About Politics

"Grandpa, who are you going to vote for in the coming election?"

"All the Democrats. You know I always vote Democrat, Hannah."

"Why Democrats?"

"I've always voted for the Democrats. Always. Just like what they stand for and besides I hate the Republicans."

"Why?"

"Just do. That's all there is to it!"

"So you know who is running for president and congress?"

"I know about the Democratic candidates. That's all I need to know. I read the newspaper every day and know what my candidates stand for."

"Do you read about the Republican candidates too?"

"No, why would I? I don't plan to vote for any of them. Don't need to know what they stand for."

"How about the election for mayor of our town. Are you going to vote for Chris Taylor?"

"Is he the Democrat?"

"She. Chris Taylor is a woman. And yes, she is the Democratic candidate for mayor."

At this point the old man scratched his head and pursed his lips. "Hmm, I don't know about that. Don't think a woman could handle the job of mayor. That's a pretty tough job."

"Chris Taylor is a Democrat. I thought you always voted for the Democrats."

"Always do. But I don't know about a woman. All the women I heard about that are in political office aren't that good. Not tough enough."

"What about Nancy Pelosi? She was speaker of the House of Representatives. That is a very tough job and she did it well. She got a lot of legislation passed."

"Didn't like the job she did."

"Grandpa, what did you not like about the job she did?"

"Just didn't like it. Can't say anything specific."

Analysis

The grandpa in this story has a strong positive attitude about Democrats and strong negative attitude about Republican and woman politicians. It appears that he only reads stories about Democrats, so the information he gets from those stories does not challenge or extend his existing information base. Instead all the new information he sees serves to reinforce his already existing attitudes, and his existing attitudes serve to filter out all information that would challenge those attitudes. Therefore all the information he sees is positive about Democrats (except Democratic woman) and negative toward Republicans. Because he is unwilling to expand his media exposures to messages that are favorable toward Republicans or women candidates, it is unlikely that his existing attitudes will ever change.

SUMMARY

This chapter focused on the attitude effect, that is, how the media influence attitudes of individuals. An attitude is an evaluative judgment, and this judgment process involves comparing an object to a standard. With media effects, the objects are elements in media messages, such as news sources, political leaders, actors, singers, and any other element in a media message. The standards are the values a person holds for things like credibility, trustworthiness, acting quality, singing talent, and the like.

The media present people with lots of attitudes that can simply be accepted by individuals; thus people often acquire the attitudes they hear expressed in media messages. The media also trigger evaluative processes where people make their own judgments of the value of things, such as advertised products, political candidates, and the media messages themselves. And over time, the media alter and reinforce existing attitudes held by individuals.

Review Questions

1. Why is the study of attitudes so important?

2. Why is it faulty to use the terms *attitudes* and *beliefs* as synonyms?

3. What does it mean when we say that attitudes are evaluative judgments?

4. Why are standards so important?

Further Thinking Questions

1. Think about your own attitudes about social issues and political matters and try to list as many as you can. You might want to refer to Exhibit 9.1.
   - For each attitude you have listed, where do you think you acquired it? From parents, siblings, friends, institutions, or the media?
   - For those attitudes you acquired from the media, which types of messages were likely to have been the most influential?

2. Can you recall instances when you had a particular attitude of yours triggered by a media message? If so, what was it about the message that triggered your attitude?

3. Think about your favorite genre of media message (for example, action/adventure, romance, comedy, games, reality, and so on) and all the exposures you have experienced with messages from that genre over the years.
   - What kinds of physiological reactions do those type of messages typically elicit?
   - Can you think of how your physiological responses to that type of media message have changed over the years of exposure?
   - Do you think these changes are positive or negative?

4. Think about an attitude you have held for a long time, such as about political parties, body image, sex, or support for a sports team. Do you typically avoid media messages that would challenge your attitude?

Affective Effects

Source: ©iStockphoto.com/Airyelf

CHAPTER 10

Affective Effects

This chapter deals with how the media influence our feelings. The term *affect* is used rather than the more common term *feelings,* because it is more precise and includes some things that are not usually regarded as feelings.

One thing you should notice in this chapter is that the research literature on affective effects is narrower and deeper than the research literatures you encountered in Chapters 7, 8, and 9. Media researchers have documented fewer affective effects compared to the wide range of cognitive, belief, and attitudinal effects. This can be traced to the fact that humans can experience virtually an unlimited range of cognitions, beliefs, and attitudes; however, the number of emotions is rather limited. To compensate for a relatively narrow scope, this literature is fairly deep; that is, once media effects researchers examine an emotional effect (especially fear and desensitization), they concentrate on a greater number of factors that work with the media in bringing about that effect.

NATURE OF AFFECT

Affect refers to both emotions and moods. We need to make a distinction between these two types of affective experiences. Emotions are typically triggered by a particular person, object, or event, while moods are more generalized feelings and are often not triggered by any one thing (Albarracin, Zanna, Johnson, & Kumkale, 2005; Berkowitz, 2000). For example, when someone insults you, the emotions of anger and embarrassment are likely to flare up, and it is easy to attribute those emotions directly to the insult. In contrast, you may be in a grouchy mood all day, and nothing in particular happened to create that annoying mood.

Affect can be conscious, when people are aware of their feelings, or it can be unconscious, when people are not aware how they are feeling (Schimmack & Crites, 2005). When emotions are generated unconsciously, they usually start with some form of physiological change (LeDoux, 1996). For example, fear is triggered automatically by a perception of a threat; the body responds with all kinds of physiological changes as the person gets ready to fight or flee. We don't have to consciously tell our hearts to beat faster; this reaction happens automatically and unconsciously.

Emotions usually require some form of labeling, and this requires conscious processing. For example, if you are experiencing "butterflies in your stomach," you need to think about what this reaction means: Is it love? Is it nervousness? Or is it nausea, meaning you now have the flu? Some feelings are easy to label, such as anger, frustration, and laughter. But other, more complex, feelings are more subtle and require more conscious effort to label (Reeves, Newhagen, Maibach, Basil, & Kurz, 1991). For example, a new character might appear in a television show, and that character triggers an uneasy feeling in you but you are not sure what that feeling is. Perhaps it is wariness that this character might pose a dangerous threat. Or perhaps it is a new kind of attraction that puzzles you. You know you feel something, but you aren't sure what it is until you label it.

As with attitudes, affect has valence (positive and negative) and intensity. But unlike attitudes, the characteristics of frequency and duration are also important. Affect is often a powerful basis for attitudes, but affects are not attitudes themselves (Wyer & Srull, 1989). For something to be an attitude, there needs to be an evaluation of an object; emotion can be a part of the evaluation but it is not the evaluation itself. For example, a person might watch a trashy love story in a film and feel lust, which is an affect generated by the characters and the story. But the person might form the attitude that the film is bad, because it does not come up to his standard of what he should be watching.

Now let's take a closer look at emotions and moods. We need to see how they are different. We also need to see what they have in common such that they can be put in the same category of affect.

Emotions

Emotions are typically intense affects that are directed at objects and have a known cause. Examples of emotions are hate, jealousy, love, pity, terror, outrage, disgust, and anger.

Emotions have long been considered to have a physiological component. Our current conceptualizations of emotion go back to William James (1894), who argued that emotional stimuli trigger bodily responses and that we must notice them in order to have an emotional experience. He argued that each emotion was different physiologically and that humans needed to learn how to recognize these physiological differences in order to know what each emotion feels like. Thus when we are angry we have a different physiological reaction than when we experience the emotion of fear.

However, after a century of research testing this theory, scholars have been able to find very little evidence of physiological differences across emotions (Eagly & Chaiken, 1993). Now it is believed that emotions are composed of a combination of physiological and cognitive components (for example, see Frijda & Zeelenberg, 2001). This point is emphasized in Schachter and Singer's (1962) two-factor theory of emotions, which says that the physiological arousal is responsible for the intensity of the emotion, and cognitions are responsible for the labeling of the feeling into qualitatively different states. For example, the physiological reaction of hate and anger can "feel" the same physiologically (an unpleasantly high state of arousal that makes us want to lash out), but when we think of the context of the situation, we are able to label that feeling as either hatred or as anger.

Moods

Moods are generalized states of feeling. Moods are usually not associated with a particular object, as emotions are. Moods have lower intensity than emotions. Examples of moods are optimism, nostalgia, indifference, restlessness, grouchiness, boredom, fatigue, alertness, relaxation, and tension. Moods require bodily monitoring; that is, we need to think about our levels of mental and physical energy. They are often related to neurological states, such as the case with depression or anxiety.

Affect—whether an emotion or a mood—can be influenced by exposure to media messages. There are four fundamental ways in which media messages can influence the affect of audience members. Media messages can provide people with emotional information that they can acquire. Media messages trigger affective reactions in the short term. Over the long term, media messages can alter and reinforce people's affective responses (see Exhibit 10.1).

ACQUIRING AFFECT

The media provide a continual flow of stories that can be used by audiences to observe emotions of all kinds of characters in all kinds of situations. Thus people can learn how to label these feelings as different emotions. Because the media provide people with a wider range of emotional experiences than they typically encounter in their everyday lives, people find these messages valuable as a source of information about how different emotions are expressed.

People often search out fictional narratives to learn social lessons about how to use and control their emotions. By watching how characters in those stories are rewarded or punished, viewers can learn a good deal of social information. The media are a valuable source of this social information, because people can learn the lessons at low risk to themselves. By vicariously watching characters deal with their emotions, viewers can learn the social lessons without having to experience negative consequences (such as embarrassment or frustration) that would have occurred to them had they tried to experiment in their real lives.

One of the most important factors that explain how people process emotional information from media messages is their emotional IQ. In his book *Emotional Intelligence*, Goleman (1995) argues that there are variations among humans in emotional intelligence in addition to the more commonly understood intellectual intelligence. People high in emotional intelligence are able to read the emotions of others and to control their own emotions better than are people who are lower on emotional intelligence. Therefore people with higher emotional intelligence will be able to perceive more emotional information in media messages and be able to process that information better. In contrast, people with lower emotional intelligence may often not understand the emotions that characters in the media are feeling, or they may misinterpret the emotions of characters.

Exhibit 10.1 Further Reading on Affective Effects

Acquiring

Learning appropriate emotional responses (Goleman, 1995)

Triggering

Triggering of general emotional reactions

- Emotional arousal (Lee & Lang, 2009; Vettehen, Nuijten, & Peeters, 2008)
- Enjoyment of media messages (Green, Brock, & Kaufman, 2004; Hall, 2009; Knobloch, Patzig, Mende, & Hastall, 2004; Oliver & Bartsch, 2010; Oliver, Weaver, & Sargent, 2000; Raney, 2004; Sherry, 2004; Vorderer, Knobloch, & Schramm, 2001; Weaver & Wilson, 2009; Zillmann, Taylor, & Lewis, 1998)
- Favorable dispositions (Zillmann & Cantor, 1972; Zillmann et al., 1998)
- Positive emotional responses from video game playing (Ravaja, 2009)
- Negative emotions (Mares, Oliver, & Cantor, 2008)

Triggering specific emotions

- Fear (Berger, 2000; Bryant, Carveth, & Brown, 1981; Cantor, 1994, 2002; Cantor & Hoffner, 1990; Cantor & Nathanson, 1996; Cantor & Sparks, 1984; Cantor & Wilson, 1988; Comisky & Bryant, 1982; Feshbach & Roe, 1968; Geen & Rokosky, 1973; Groebel & Krebs, 1983; Gunter & Furnham, 1984; Hare & Blevings, 1975; Himmelweit, Oppenheim, & Vince, 1958; Mares & Acosta, 2008; Ogles & Hoffner, 1987; Osborn & Endsley, 1971; Sapolsky & Zillmann, 1978; Smith & Wilson, 2002; Surbeck, 1975; Tannenbaum & Gaer, 1965; von Feilitzen, 1975; Zillmann, 1980, 1991b; Zillmann & Cantor, 1977)
- Hostility (Cicchirillo & Chory-Assad, 2005; Farrar, Krcmar, & Nowak, 2006; Geen, 1975; Geen & Berkowitz, 1967; Kirsh, Olczak, & Mounts, 2005; Schneider, Lang, Shin, & Bradley, 2004; Tamborini et al., 2004; Zillmann, Bryant, Comisky, & Medoff, 1981; Zillmann & Sapolsky, 1977)
- Anger (Holbert & Hansen, 2008)
- Indignation (Hwang, Pan, & Sun, 2008)
- Apprehension (Berger, 2005)
- Suspense (Knobloch-Westerwick, David, Eastin, Tamborini, & Greenwood, 2009; Peterson & Raney, 2008)
- Humor (King, 2000)

Triggering other feelings

- Feeling of presence (Bracken, 2005; Lee & Nass, 2005).
- Feeling of identification with characters in media messages (Chory-Assad & Yanen, 2005; Cohen, 1997; Eyal & Cohen, 2006; Harwood, 1999)
- Feeling of empathy (Zillmann, 1996)
- Feeling of pride in country (Pfau et al., 2008)

Altering

Altering emotions (Cline, Croft, & Courrier, 1973; Gunter, 1985; Hoffner, 1995, 1997; Lazarus, Speisman, Mordkoff, & Davison, 1962; Mullin & Linz, 1995; Sander, 1995; Speisman, Lazarus, Mordkoff, & Davison, 1964; Thomas, 1982; Thomas, Horton, Lippencott, & Drabman, 1977; Van der Voort, 1986)

Altering existing moods (Anderson, Collins, Schmitt, & Jacobvitz, 1996; Chang, 2006; Davis & Kraus, 1989; Knobloch, 2003; Knobloch-Westerwick, 2007; Knobloch-Westerwick & Alter, 2006; Mares & Cantor, 1992; Nabi, Finnerty, Domschke, & Hull, 2006; Roe & Minnebo, 2007; Zillmann, 1988; Zillmann & Bryant, 1994)

Enhancing existing moods (Csikszentmihalyi, 1988; Denham, 2004; Green & Brock, 2000; Knobloch, Patzig, Mende, & Hastall, 2004; Oliver, Weaver, & Sargent, 2000; Raney, 2002, 2004; Raney & Bryant, 2002; Sherry, 2004; Vorderer, Klimmt, & Ritterfield, 2004; Vorderer, Knobloch, & Schramm, 2001; Zillmann & Cantor, 1972; Zillmann, Taylor, & Lewis, 1998)

Altering sexual satisfaction (Peter & Valkenburg, 2009a, b)

Enjoyment of soap operas over time (Weber, Tamborini, Lee, & Stipp, 2008)

Desensitization and loss of empathy (Cline et al., 1973; Gunter, 1985; Lazarus et al., 1962; Mullin & Linz, 1995; Sander, 1995; Speisman et al., 1964; Thomas, 1982; Thomas et al., 1977; Zillmann, 1996)

Reinforcing Affective Effects

Emotional habituation to television violence (Thomas et al., 1977; Van der Voort, 1986)

TRIGGERING AFFECT

Media messages can trigger specific emotions, especially the strong and simple emotions of fear, lust, and laughter. Within the topic of media's influence on affect, researchers focus much more on triggering than on the other three functions combined. This is because there are a great number of experiments in which researchers show their participants a particular kind of media message, then measure their emotional reactions during those exposures or immediately after those exposures.

Triggering Specific Emotional Reactions

The most studied emotional reaction triggered by the media is fear (see Exhibit 10.1). Some of these studies have used an experiment in which researchers have shown their participants acts of violence in a horror, suspense, or crime drama, then observed the participants' emotional reactions. Others of these studies have used surveys, which asked

Acquiring Learning About Emotions

Sue was very angry with her 4-year-old son Bobby. She looked over at him sitting next to her as she drove him home from preschool in the middle of the day. This was the second time this week she had been called by the preschool to come pick Bobby up early and take him home. One more incident like today and Bobby would be expelled. Then Sue would have to find another preschool that would take him.

Sue didn't like putting Bobby in a preschool, but she had no choice. She was recently divorced and she needed to take a job and could not spend all day at home taking care of her son. At first Bobby seemed to be making the adjustment, although he was unusually quiet, but then this week he started acting out aggressively with other children.

Sue was becoming frustrated because nothing she was doing seemed to help their situation. She had tried reasoning with Bobby. That did not work. She tried punishing him. That did not work. She tried rewarding him with trips to get ice cream when he was good, but that did not seem to work either. She was so frustrated that she felt like yelling at him to scare him into behaving better. But she knew that would not work.

That night after she calmed down, she went online and did a search for videos about young boys with behavioral problems. She downloaded several of those videos and watched their stories that depicted boys Bobby's age dealing with problems at school, such as being bullied, being lonely, and being embarrassed. The stories were heartbreaking, but each story did show their characters dealing with their problems and making their situations better.

The next morning was Saturday, and Sue made Bobby his favorite breakfast. "Bobby, today we are going to have a special day together. Today is TV and playground day!" That got Bobby's attention, although he pretended like he did not hear his mom.

After breakfast, Sue snuggled with Bobby on her lap and played the first story. She frequently paused the story, asking Bobby how he felt and how he thought the character felt. She pointed out how the characters acted when they solved their problems. And they cheered when the characters ended up happy. After the videos were over she discussed with Bobby how people can control their emotions and how they can do things to make other people and themselves happy.

That afternoon, while Sue drove them to a playground, she said, "Let's do two kinds of play this afternoon. We'll play with the playground stuff that you like—the swings, the seesaw, and the monkey bars! That is one kind of play. The other kind of play is with the people there. Let's try to make some new friends." She could tell Bobby was skeptical, but Sue remained excited and eventually Bobby got excited too, especially when he got to play on the monkey bars. Sue made some new friends with a few of the mothers at the playground and nudged Bobby into making friends with some of the kids. She reminded him about how the boys on the DVDs made friends and how they became happier when they made other people happy.

Analysis

Sue used media messages to illustrate how children can have problems with their emotions. She showed her son that he was not the only person with problems. Then she used the stories to show her son how he could use emotions well.

In this story, the media messages did not act alone. The mother was a very important part of the learning process for Bobby. Sue needed to work hard to get Bobby invested in the learning, then she had to carefully point out the social lessons being illustrated from the media stories. And finally she had to guide her son through the practicing of the social lessons in his real life. Of course, the media stories were an integral part of this process, but they did not act alone.

people to recall their emotional reactions from past media exposures. In surveys over the years, between 75% and 93% of all children say they have been frightened or horrified by a motion picture (Cantor, 2002).

Another emotional reaction studied frequently by researchers has been hostility (Zillmann & Sapolsky, 1977). A popular research topic has been to examine the effects of exposure to violence in film and TV shows. Researchers will show their participants a violent program, then give those participants a chance to aggress against a real-world target. In addition to the behavioral measure of aggression, researchers will measure the degree of hostile emotions that have been triggered in the participants.

Triggering More Generalized Feelings

The media have also been found to trigger more generalized feelings in addition to specific emotions. These include the triggering of enjoyment of media messages (Knobloch et al., 2004), the triggering of favorable dispositions (Zillmann et al., 1998), the triggering of a feeling of presence (Green & Brock, 2000), and the triggering of a feeling of identification with characters (Eyal & Cohen, 2006), and just generally enhancing of existing moods (Csikszentmihalyi, 1988; Raney & Bryant, 2002).

Process of Triggering Affect

What is it about media content that triggers emotional reactions? There are many factors about the message and the person that influence emotions (see Exhibit 10.2). These can be grouped into two categories: factors about the messages and factors about the audiences.

Exhibit 10.2 Further Reading on the Triggering of Emotional Effects in General

Message Factors

How the message is framed (Richardson, 2005)

Presentation attributes of TV messages affect viewers' emotions

- Size of image (Detenber & Reeves, 1996; Lombard, 1995)
- Picture motion (Detenber, Simons, & Bennett, 1998)
- Quality of the picture (Bracken, 2005)

By medium (Chaudhuri & Buck, 1995)

Audience Factors

Thinking style (Berger, 2005)

Exposure motivations (Cacioppo, Gerdner, & Bernston, 1999; Johnston, 1995; Schneider et al., 2004)

Degree of transportation (Green et al., 2004; Schneider et al., 2004; Lee & Nass, 2005; Sherry, 2004; Tamborini et al., 2004)

Greater involvement with television shows is associated with greater enjoyment (Hall, 2009; Pfau et al. (2008)

Traits

- Hostility (Farrar et al., 2006; Kirsh et al., 2005)
- Sensation seeking (Cacioppo et al., 1999)

Control over experience (Jansz, 2005)

Moral judgments (Raney, 2005)

Feeling of relationship with fictional characters (Konijn & Hoorn, 2005)

Intensity of the parasocial relationship with the favorite character (Chory-Assad & Yanen, 2005; Eyal & Cohen, 2006)

Demographics

- Gender differences (Hitchon & Chang, 1995; Petrevu, 2004)

Message Factors. Certain message elements can increase audience arousal; these factors include the size of image, motion, and quality of the picture. The bigger the size of television images and the more rapid replacement of shots on television, the greater the audience arousal (Detenber & Reeves, 1996; Lombard, 1995). Also, watching TV programming on high-definition television triggers a higher degree of presence than watching messages on a non-high-definition television (Bracken, 2005).

There are also differences across media in their abilities to trigger emotions. For example, emotional responses from advertising are generated more strongly with electronic media than with print media. Print media engenders more rational, analytical involvement than do electronic media that offer pictures, motion, and sound (Chaudhuri & Buck, 1995).

Triggering of affect is influenced by how the message is framed. For example, Richardson (2005) conducted an experiment to investigate the impact of editorial framing on readers' affect toward racial groups. Participants read mock newspaper editorials endorsing a U.S. Supreme Court decision upholding affirmative action in higher education. The editorials were systematically manipulated to present different frames in four randomly assigned versions: remedial action, diversity, combined (both frames), and control (neither frame). The diversity frame induced White participants to score higher on a measure of pro-Black affect.

Why do people sometimes seek out negative emotions from the media? Mares and colleagues (2008) conducted a survey of people from three age groups (younger adults, ages 18–25; middle adults, 26–49; and older adults, 50 and over. They found that younger adults expressed the greatest interest in experiencing negative emotions in their everyday lives, in viewing dark, creepy, or violent content, and in viewing media to escape boredom and for amusement; older adults were most interested in experiencing emotional stability and in viewing films with uplifting, heartwarming content. Results suggest that lifespan differences may help explain the allure of programming that triggers negative emotions among some groups.

People also seek out positive affect. For example, exposure to sexual material in various media can lead to pleasant feelings of arousal. In a review of this literature, Harris and Scott (2002) report that this has been found to be the case in numerous media effects studies.

Mood states can be triggered by particular elements within media messages. Research has found that news stories presenting people enjoying good fortune were better able to trigger enjoyment compared to news stories where people experienced bad fortune (Zillmann et al., 1998). Also, enjoyment of crime dramas is enhanced when fictional characters are punished for their bad actions (Raney, 2005). However, enjoyment is also keyed to moral judgments about the appropriateness of the degree of punishment depicted. Thus if a bad character is punished too lightly or too harshly, viewers' enjoyment diminishes.

Enjoyment of media messages has been found to have several dimensions. For example, Oliver and Bartsch (2010) conducted a series of studies to examine the multidimensionality of viewers' entertainment gratifications with more serious, poignant, and pensive media messages, which are typically associated with the genres of drama, history, documentary, and art films. They found three dimensions of enjoyment: fun and suspense, emotionally moving, and thought provoking.

Violence in a story often leads to enjoyment, but not necessarily. In an experiment, Weaver and Wilson (2009) found that the nonviolent version of a show was significantly more enjoyable than two alternative violent versions of that show. This finding held regardless of participants' sex, level of trait aggression, and sensation-seeking tendencies. Thus, the widely held belief that violence increases enjoyment was not supported. It appears that violent actions in a show typically lead to arousal, which most viewers find enjoyable. However, it is the feeling of arousal instead of the violence itself that is most associated with enjoyment.

When it comes to emotions, television is regarded as a paradox. Zillmann (1991b) points out that television is used by many people as both an "unwinder" that reduces emotional drives as well as a stimulator that increases emotional feelings. How is it possible to use television both to chill and to get excited? The answer is that some programming allows us to float along without thinking, thus generating alpha waves that calm us and make us forget our problems. Other programming stimulates us and thus increases our drive energy. This is why it is so important *not* to treat all content in a medium as the same. With television, for example, there is a very wide range of content, and people can find some kind of content to increase or decrease just about any conceivable emotional feeling.

Audience Factors. Audience factors, such as motivation, are also important. For example, Johnston (1995) examined the reasons why people expose themselves to graphic horror films and how they were affected by those exposures. He found four types of people as distinguished by motivations: gore watching, thrill watching, independent watching, and problem watching. Each type of person had a different emotional reaction during their exposures.

Emotional reactions are also influenced by moral judgments about the characters in narratives. Characters whose moral judgments match the expectations of viewers are liked more, and viewers are more prone to enjoy these narratives (Raney, 2004).

Source: ©iStockphoto.com/nycshooter

Reactions are influenced by a person's control over the experience. Violent video games provide players with many different emotions. Because players are largely in control of the game, they can seek out emotions they want, including emotions that are not sanctioned in real life (Jansz, 2005).

Emotional triggering is enhanced when people are transported into the narrative world (Green et al., 2004; Schneider et al., 2004; Lee & Nass, 2005). *Transportation* is the condition of being swept away with the action and feeling that you are in the story itself, as you lose the sense that you are a part of the audience rather than part of the action inside the story. This sense of transportation is what all fictional storytellers hope to achieve, but only the most talented ones are able to do this consistently.

Related to transportation is the idea of flow. Like transportation, *flow* is a state in which audience members lose track of real time and place and instead are swept into the media message. However, flow applies more to people actively engaged in tasks, such as playing games, rather than passively viewing. Flow occurs when an individual's abilities match the demands from the message exposure (Sherry, 2004). When people play computer games in which they are continually challenged but able to meet each challenge step by step, flow occurs. As each challenge gets more difficult, players get more skilled and thus are pulled more and more into the experience of the game.

The degree to which a person identifies with characters in narratives is influential. For example, Cohen (1997) found that males increased their parasocial relationships with the favorite TV characters as they were more anxious about their current dating partners, while females increased their parasocial relationships with TV characters as they were more secure in their current dating relationships (Cohen, 1997). Also, Eyal & Cohen (2006) conducted a study to examine TV viewers' reactions to parasocial breakup with mediated characters. Following the airing of the last episode of the television show *Friends*, 279 students completed surveys assessing their viewing habits, their attitudes toward the show and their favorite characters, and their loneliness. The intensity of the parasocial relationship with the favorite character is the strongest predictor of breakup distress. Other predictors include commitment and affinity to the show, the character's perceived popularity, and the participant's loneliness. In another study examining parasocial feelings of TV viewers with characters, Chory-Assad and Yanen (2005) examined viewer involvement by investigating the relationships among parasocial interaction, wishful identification, and emotions (hopelessness and loneliness) among older participants. Results indicate that loneliness predicted wishful identification.

Konijn and Hoorn (2005) developed a model to explain how spectators of motion pictures establish affective relationships with fictional characters. They found that positive appraisals of fictional characters enhanced involvement and appreciation, whereas negative appraisals enhanced distance. They reasoned that character appreciation is a baseline from which involvement and distance pull in different directions. Because many characters have both negative and positive characteristics, there is a conflict in the viewer's mind, and this conflict creates evaluative tension or attitudinal ambivalence. The authors argued that while this type of conflict causes discomfort in a person's real life, this conflict in media stories increases pleasure.

Triggering of apprehension has been found to be influenced by a person's thinking style. Berger (2005) conducted several experiments that examined the interactive effects of rational thinking style on emotions. Participants who were highly rational demonstrated less apprehension than low rationals after reading news stories containing graphical depictions of increasing rates of campus theft.

Triggering of hostility is related to degree of a feeling of telepresence. Tamborini et al. (2004) examined how playing a violent virtual reality (VR) video game triggered feelings of hostility. Five weeks before a lab experiment, participants completed a questionnaire measuring prior violent video game use and trait aggression. Participants were randomly assigned to play a violent video game, play a standard violent video game, observe a violent video game, or observe a nonviolent video game. Following exposure, measures of telepresence experienced, hostile thoughts, and aggressive acts were obtained. The researchers found that personal variables (prior video game use) and situational variables (violent media exposure) influence participants' feelings of telepresence, which in turn led to increases in hostile thoughts.

As for demographics, there are gender differences in emotional reactions. For example, women's affect is higher with ads that are verbal, harmonious, and complex. In contrast, men's affect is higher with ads that are comparative and simple (Petrevu, 2004).

To examine the triggering process in more detail, refer to Exhibit 10.3, which abstracts the considerable research on how the media trigger a fear effect. This line of research has been stimulated mainly by violence, crime, and horror in media messages.

ALTERING AFFECT

The altering function with affects can be conscious or unconscious. When it is conscious, people typically are feeling emotions or moods that they do not like so they use the media to alter those feelings. When it is unconscious, the media are gradually altering the way people feel about something, usually in a negative direction, such as desensitization or habituation. The conscious altering usually has a relatively short time frame of hours, while the unconscious altering takes much longer, such as months or years.

Conscious Altering

Audience members know they can use the media to alter their emotional reactions, so they actively expose themselves to particular kinds of content in order to generate the emotions they want to experience (Hoffner, 1995, 1997). For example, people who are sad will seek out comedy shows or listen to some uplifting music.

Media messages are used by individuals to manage their mood states (Nabi et al., 2006). Audience members seek out certain messages to arouse and excite them, then seek out other types of messages to calm them down and reduce their stress. Shaping mood states is different than triggering emotions in two ways. First, shaping allows for more control by the audience. Of course, triggering emotions is often under audience control (such as

Exhibit 10.3   Further Reading on Profiling the Triggering of Fear

Baseline Factors

Message Factors

Individual differences in vividness of mental imagery influence the emotional impact of frightening images of UFOs in television shows (Sparks, Sparks, & Gray, 1995)

Triggering of emotions such as apprehension of victimization can be reduced when news stories present more quantitative data that contextualize the rates of crime (Berger, 1998)

Negative video (graphic images of death, maiming, and injury) increases the self-reported negative emotional impact of the story, thus making it more arousing and more negative (Lang, Newhagen, & Reeves, 1996)

Audience Factors

Prior experience with fearful events in real life (Hare & Blevings, 1975; Himmelweit et al., 1958; Sapolsky & Zillmann, 1978)

Information-processing styles, mathematical problem-solving skills, and sex role responses sets (Berger, 2000)

Understanding of narrative flow increases feelings of suspense and fear in children (Smith & Wilson, 2002)

Fright reactions are influenced by characteristics of the viewer: gender, motivations for the exposure, trait emotionality, developmental differences cognitively and emotionally (such as perceptual dependence, difficulty in distinguishing fantasy from reality, responses to abstract threats, and ability to use cognitive as well as noncognitive strategies to reduce the fear) (Cantor, 2002)

Developmental differences (Cantor & Sparks, 1984; Cantor & Wilson, 1988; Cantor, Wilson, & Hoffner, 1986)

Ability to perceive the reality of the portrayals (Dorr, 1980)

In a meta-analysis of mediated violence triggering fright reactions, Hoffner and Levine (2005) found that male viewers, individuals lower in empathy, and those higher in sensation-seeking aggressiveness reported more enjoyment of fright and violence.

Fluctuation Factors

Message Factors

Narrative structure (linear, reversal, or inverted type) influences feelings of suspense, curiosity, and reading enjoyment (Knobloch et al., 2004).

(Continued)

Exhibit 10.3 (Continued)

Fright reactions are increased by certain elements in the messages, such as dangers and injuries to characters; distortions of natural forms, such as monsters and freaks; the experience of endangerment and fear by others—vicarious emotion; and the similarity of depicted stimuli to real-life fear evokers (Cantor, 2002).

An effect increases when "bad" characters are shown committing a great deal of unjustified violence and when they are shown as successful and never stopped. Also, fear is increased when the violence is shown graphically and the victims are shown suffering. Finally, realistic portrayals also increase a fear effect.

Type of stimuli: Cantor (1994) says that the fright effect is triggered by three categories of stimuli that usually are found in combination with many portrayals of violence in the media. First, there is the category of dangers and injuries, which are stimuli that depict events that threaten great harm. This includes natural disasters, attacks by vicious animals, large-scale accidents, and violent encounters that can be interpersonal or range in scale to the intergalactic. Second, there is the category of distortions of natural forms. This includes familiar organisms that are shown as being deformed or unnatural through mutilation, accidents of birth, or conditioning. And third, there is the category of experience of endangerment and fear by others. This type of stimuli evokes empathy for particular characters, and the viewer then feels the fear that the characters in the narrative are portraying.

Unjustified violence: When violence is portrayed as being unjustified, viewers become more fearful (Bryant et al., 1981).

Graphicness: Higher explicitness and graphicness leads to more viewer fear (Ogles & Hoffner, 1987).

Rewards: When violence goes unpunished, viewers become more fearful (Bryant et al., 1981).

Realism: Live action violence provokes more intense fear than cartoon violence (Cantor, 1994; Cantor & Hoffner, 1990; Cantor & Sparks, 1984; Geen, 1975; Geen & Rokosky, 1973; Groebel & Krebs, 1983; Gunter & Furnham, 1984; Lazarus, Opton, Nomikos, & Rankin, 1965; Osborn & Endsley, 1971; Sparks, 1986; Surbeck, 1975; von Feilitzen, 1975). For example, Lazarus and colleagues found that showing gory accidents to adults served to arouse them physiologically less when the participants were told that the accidents were fake. This effect has also been found with children (Cantor & Hoffner, 1990; Cantor & Sparks, 1984; Sparks, 1986). Also, fear is enhanced when there is a similarity between the elements in a portrayal and the characteristics in a person's own life (Cantor, 1994).

Attractiveness of characters (Zillmann, 1980, 1991b)

- Heroic (Comisky & Bryant, 1982; Zillmann & Cantor, 1977)
- Similar to viewers (Feshbach & Roe, 1968; Tannenbaum & Gaer, 1965)

Audience Factors

Viewer states

- Degree of physiological arousal and identification with characters can increase the probability of an immediate fear effect. Physiological arousal (increased heart rate and blood pressure) are essential for a strong fear effect. When people are in this state, they tend to feel strong emotions and seek to label them. Some people who feel this strong arousal while watching media violence label it as fear, but others could label it as anger, frustration, and so on (Cantor, 2002).
- The more a person, especially a child, identifies with a character in danger, the more likely the person will experience an immediate fear effect. Identification sets up a vicarious experience such that when the character is in danger, the viewer who identifies with that character also feels the danger (Comisky & Bryant, 1982; Feshbach & Roe, 1968; Tannenbaum & Gaer, 1965; Zillmann, 1980, 1991; Zillmann & Cantor, 1977).

Belief that the depicted violent action depicted could happen to the viewer (Cantor & Hoffner, 1990).

Motivations for exposure (Dysinger & Ruckmick, 1933; Zillmann, 1978, 1982). If a person's motivation to view violence is for entertainment, he or she can employ a discounting procedure to lessen the effects of fear (Cantor, 1994).

Level of arousal (Cantor, Zillmann, & Bryant, 1975; Cantor, Ziemke, & Sparks, 1984; Hoffner & Cantor, 1990; Nomikos, Opton, Averill, & Lazarus, 1968; Zillmann, 1978)

Ability to use coping strategies (Koriat, Melkman, Averill, & Lazarus, 1972; Lazarus & Alfert, 1964; Speisman, Lazarus, Mordkoff, & Davison, 1964; Cantor & Wilson, 1984)

deciding to go to a horror movie to feel fear and become aroused), but the role of the audience is a much more reactive one. With mood management, the audience is more proactive in making choices. Another difference is the longer-term nature of moods compared to triggered emotions.

Use of Television to Manage Moods. Roe & Minnebo (2007) found that adolescents who exerted little effort in their school studies had much more tension at home and were therefore more likely to use television to manage their moods. This was especially the case with younger adolescents.

Drive to Maintain Positive Moods. In a meta-analysis of the mood state literature, Hullett (2005) found that people are often goal directed with their media use and seek particular media exposures to attain and maintain positive moods. She offered something called the "hedonic contingency model," which states that people monitor their moods in relation to media exposures. When they find content that enhances the positive mood they are seeking, they continue with the exposure for as long as it enhances the positive mood.

Unconscious Altering

Even when people are not consciously using the media to change emotions or shape moods, the media can still exert an altering influence. When people watch particular kinds of media messages that arouse them, they will typically find the arousal pleasant and want to repeatedly expose themselves to such messages. However, over time, the messages lose their ability to arouse or even please audiences. That is, audiences will "habituate" to the messages; their repeated exposures have become habits, but the habits lose their ability to deliver the positive or strong feelings over time. If people continually expose themselves to the same kind of violent or sexual messages over time, those messages will gradually lose their ability to generate the same degree of emotional response. With habituation, media messages can erode away audience members' natural emotional responses to certain images. This has been found to be the case with violent media content. When people watch a good deal of violent content over time, they are likely to experience emotional habituation (van der Voort, 1986) and become emotionally desensitized to the acts of violence and the harm that they do to victims (Mullin & Linz, 1995). Also, Peter and Valkenburg (2009a) found that adolescents' use of sexually explicit Internet material was negatively related to sexual satisfaction over time for both male and female adolescents.

While habituation is often regarded as a negative effect, it can also be used in a positive manner. For example, therapists can repeatedly show patients images of something they fear (such as dogs, spiders, snakes, and so on), and gradually over time the patients will experience less and less fear of those stimuli. By repeated exposures to fearful events that are depicted with consequences that are safe and peaceful, sometimes people can reduce their fear of these stimuli, then transfer this reduction in fear to stimuli presented in their real lives.

Process of Altering Affect

Sometimes, this alteration of emotional responses does not occur within the person's control and sometimes it does. For example, desensitization is a long-term alteration in a person's emotions that occurs largely outside of his or her control. Because so many messages in the average person's TV and film exposure contain violence, people typically lose empathy for those who are victimized by violence. This is the "desensitization effect." This long-term affective effect has received a good deal of research study (see Exhibit 10.4).

There are also long-term alterations of emotions that are within the control of the person. Over time, people have developed strategies to use the media to manage their moods. They learn how to do this by trial and error, so that when they are in a mood they do not like they know what media and which messages to search out. For example,

---

Exhibit 10.4   Further Reading on Profiling the Altering of Desensitization

---

Baseline Factors

Message Factors

Heavy viewing of television over a long period of time will cause audience members to come to be more accepting of violence and less likely to feel sympathy for victims. While this attitude is learned from media exposure, then reinforced through repeated viewing, the attitude can be generalized beyond the media world to apply also to real-world instances (Cline et al., 1973; Thomas, 1982; Thomas et al., 1977; Van der Voort, 1986).

Audience Factors

Some viewers are socialized to have empathetic value systems. These people start from a stronger position and it takes more counter-conditioning to reduce this disposition for empathy. When viewing media violence, these people will be more likely to identify with the victims or at least feel their pain.

Fluctuation Factors

Message Factors

A desensitization effect increases when violence is shown graphically and humorously. For example, cartoons are highly desensitizing when they continuously show victims being blown to bits followed by the bits reassembling themselves and thus restoring the character. This leads us to laugh away the horror until gradually we lose sympathy for victims of violence.

Justification and attractiveness are also an important content factor in this process. When attractive characters are repeatedly shown as being justified in committing violence on unattractive victims, viewers come to believe that violence is deserved by victims.

Graphicness of violence (Cline et al., 1973; Lazarus & Alfert, 1964; Lazarus, Mordkoff, & Davison, 1962; Speisman, Lazarus, Mordkoff, & Davison, 1964).

Humor contributes to the desensitization effect (Gunter, 1985; Sander, 1995).

Audience Factors

Children and adults can become desensitized to violence upon multiple exposures through a process of temporary habituation. But it appears that the habituation is relatively short term (Mullin & Linz, 1995).

Source: Jupiterimages/Goodshoot/Thinkstock

people use TV to manage moods, with stress being related to viewing of more comedy and less news. Also, people who have been unfaithful in romantic relationships will seek out different storylines than those who have not been unfaithful. Both types of people are looking for ways to enhance their moods by experiencing fictional story-lines (Nabi et al., 2006).

There are gender differences in mood management (Knobloch-Westerwick & Alter, 2006). Before reacting to antagonism, females are likely to prevent aggression by dissolving aversive states through media consumption. When anticipating a retaliation opportunity, females spent more time reading positive news to dissipate their anger. In contrast, males expecting a retaliation opportunity spent more time on negative news to sustain their anger. In a subsequent study, Knobloch-Westerwick (2007) found that after a mood-affecting experience, men tended to distract themselves with absorbing messages, whereas women tended to ruminate about the experience and thus preferred messages with low absorption potential. When anticipating a mood-affecting activity, men tended to distract themselves right before it by selecting absorbing content, whereas women focused on it and preferred less-absorbing messages. Also, stressed women watch more game and variety programming, as well as more TV overall. Stressed men watch more action and violent programming (Anderson, Collins, Schmitt, & Jacobvitz, 1996).

People develop strategies to help themselves and others to cope with the effect of negative emotions when they are triggered by media messages. For example, Hoffner (1995) has shown that people have developed effective coping strategies to scary films, such as blunting (distraction or reinterpretation of scary events) and monitoring (attention to threat cues) that enhance empathetic viewers' enjoyment of the films. Children choose to identify with various characters in television programs. Boys nearly always select male characters and value the qualities of intelligence and strength; about half the girls will pick male characters, and those girls especially value the qualities of humor and attractiveness (Hoffner, 1996). Coping style influences children's emotional reactions to scary films; negative emotions of fear and worry are reduced in blunters when they have prior knowledge of the happy outcome (Hoffner, 1997).

REINFORCING AFFECT

Media messages can reinforce affective reactions (see Exhibit 10.1). In the long term, the reinforcement function works along with the altering function such that at times it is hard to tell the two apart. This is especially the case with a lot of the research on long-term shaping of affects, such as with emotional habituation. When you read many of the studies in this research literature, you will notice that researchers make claims of their research participants being habituated to violence in media messages (Thomas et al., 1977; Van der Voort, 1986) as well as desensitization to the suffering of victims in real life (Cline et al., 1973; Gunter, 1985; Lazarus et al., 1962; Mullin & Linz, 1995; Sander, 1995; Speisman et al., 1964; Thomas, 1982; Thomas et al., 1977). Although most often the researchers only measure their participants at one point in time, they make claims that their participants have had their emotions altered or reinforced over time. Thus these researchers assume that their participants had normal emotional reactions to violence at some point in time but that because of frequent exposure to violent messages over time, their emotional reactions have been blunted. Also, there is the assumption that because of all the exposure to violence, these blunted emotional reactions have been reinforced, thus making it more and more difficult for their heavy violence-viewing participants to recover their initial sensitivity to violence.

Reinforcing Habituation of Emotions

"Dylan, do you know why your parents brought you here to see me?"

"Yes, they think I play computer games too much?"

"Do you think you play computer games too much?"

"No. I think I play them just the right amount."

"And how much is the right amount?"

Dylan squirmed in his chair, feeling he was about to be ambushed by this creepy counselor. He squared his shoulders and responded in a defiant voice, "About 12 hours."

"A week?"

"No. A day."

"Every day?"

"Maybe more on the weekends."

"How is that possible? Aren't you in school?"

"Big deal. It's only the seventh grade. Teachers don't care. I sit in the back of the room and play on my phone."

"What kinds of games do you play?"

"All kinds. Cards, board games, action/adventure games."

"Competitions against others?"

"Yes, when I have access to wi-fi, I find players online. When I have no connection I play against the computer. Doesn't matter."

"Why games?"

"Like what else is there?"

"You could text friends, post tweets, watch YouTube. There are lots of things you could do besides games."

"Those are all boring."

"So you like the competition."

"Duh. I guess."

"Why?

"It's fun."

"In what way is it fun?"

"The challenge. It keeps me going. It's easy to see when I'm getting better at playing. And it makes the time go faster in my boring life."

"So you don't feel challenged in your real life?"

"No way. School is boring."

"Do you have homework?"

"Of course, but it's a joke. Takes me five minutes to do it . . . when it's even worth doing."

"Are you good at the games?"

"Very good. Now it's getting hard to find players who are not morons."

"So you are starting to lose enjoyment with the games."

"Yes. It used to be exciting. Players were really good and I would lose most of the time. But now I almost always win. The world is getting dumber out there."

"Maybe you should try something else besides games."

"No. I keep playing because I know I'll eventually find a good player or two to challenge me."

"But if you try something else, you might get even more challenged and excited about that."

"Naw, I'll stick with computer games."

"But you said it's getting boring."

"I just have to keep looking harder for better players to challenge me."

"But they are hard to find. Why not try something else?"

"They're out there. I just have to find them."

"Isn't it boring looking for them? By the time you know someone is not a challenge, you have already played some games with him and wasted that time."

"Yes. But I know it will be exciting again when I eventually find a good player."

Analysis

Dylan is clearly addicted to playing computer games. Part of this addiction is emotional habituation; that is, game playing was once able to trigger emotions that he liked. He was transported into the competition of playing the games and experienced flow states in which he lost track of time and place. But eventually as he got more experienced, his emotional reactions gradually eroded. Now he is bored with game playing, like he is with his real life. Yet he continues to play the computer games in the hope of recapturing his early experiences before he was habituated and could feel emotions strongly from his game playing.

The game-playing messages have altered his emotional reactions over time until those reactions were stamped out. Now, continued game playing reinforces the habituation. His memory of earlier successes and strong emotions haunts him. He desperately tries to recapture those feelings, but his continued game playing only reinforces his habituation.

SUMMARY

This chapter focuses on affect, which includes emotions as well as more generalized feelings such as moods and dispositions. People can acquire emotional information through social learning by watching characters experience emotions. Media messages also have the power to trigger emotional reactions. This is especially the case with entertainment messages, with their goals of eliciting maximum emotional impact, as well as with advertising messages with their goals of triggering good feelings about their advertised products. There are also long-term affective alterations as well as reinforcements, especially with the effects of emotional habituation and desensitization.

Some of these affective effects occur suddenly and are outside of the person's control; these are typically emotions that are triggered by media content. Other affective effects, such as the alteration of moods, occur within the person's control. People have been found to search out specific kinds of media content to attain and maintain positive moods.

Review Questions

1. What is the difference between emotions and moods?

2. Compare and contrast affects and attitudes.

3. How are cognitions important to emotions?

Further Thinking Questions

1. Watch a movie and monitor how well you are able to perceive the emotions and moods of each character.
   - How much of the time were the emotions and moods obvious, that is, the actors provided clear clues as to how they were feeling and even labeled their own emotions?
   - How much of the time did you really have to analyze the context of the action to infer what the characters were feeling?
   - Given how you answered these two questions, what does this tell you about the movie and the ability of the actors? What does this tell you about your ability to read emotions and moods?

2. Think about how emotions are triggered in you by the media. Focus on the emotion of fear and plot where your baseline is on that emotion.
   - Refer back to Chapter 4 where the ideas of baselines and fluctuations were introduced.
   - Refer to Exhibit 10.3 to look at all the factors that researchers have found to influence a fear effect.
   - Think about what factors can trigger a fluctuation off your baseline on fear. How strong would those factors have to be in order for you to experience a fear effect from a media message?

3. Think about another emotion besides fear.
   - Think about the kinds of factors that would shape your baseline on that emotion, then see if you could plot your baseline on that emotion.
   - Think about what factors can trigger a fluctuation off your baseline on that emotion. How strong would those factors have to be in order for you to experience that kind of an effect from a media message?

4. Think about your favorite genre of media message (for example, action/adventure, romance, comedy, games, reality, and so on) and all the exposures you have experienced with messages from that genre over the years.
   - What kinds of affective reactions do those types of messages typically elicit?
   - Can you think of how your affective responses to that type of media message have changed over the years of exposure?
   - Do you think these changes are positive or negative?

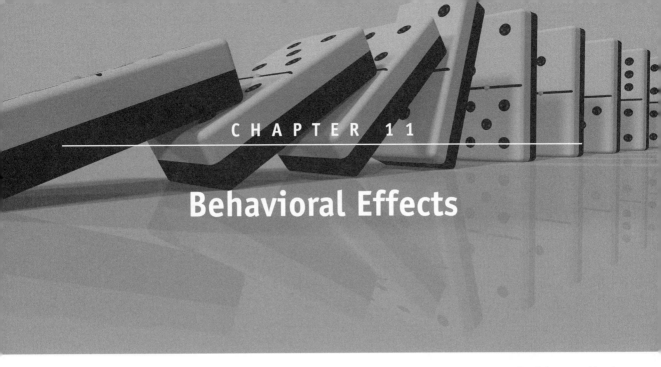

CHAPTER 11

Behavioral Effects

Source: ©iStockphoto.com/theasis

Behavioral Effects

This chapter deals with the last of the six types of individual level effects. Here the focus is on behavior, that is, what people do. We begin with an examination of the nature of human behavior, then we look at the research on how the media have been found to lead people to acquire behavioral patterns, have behaviors triggered, altered, and reinforced.

NATURE OF BEHAVIOR

Behaviors are typically defined as the overt actions of an individual (Albarracin, Zanna, Johnson, & Kumkale, 2005). Therefore behaviors can be observed as people perform them. A media-influenced behavioral effect is one in which people can be observed doing something in response to a media message. While *behavior* is a term that is used often in media effects research, we must be careful to make a distinction between actual behavior and a person's self-reported intentions for behavior. Actual behavior is that which can be observed; it must be performed.

Self-reported behavior is often very different from actual behavior; there are two reasons for this difference. One reason is that intentions are often too ambitious and we end up performing at a lower level than we intended. For example, most of us have the best intentions to perform all sorts of healthy behaviors (such as eating less junk food, exercising regularly, and avoiding risky behaviors), but the actual behaviors we perform are often less than our intentions. A second reason for the difference between self-reported behaviors and actual behaviors is that we are often unaware of what our actual behavior is, especially when we are asked about trivial behaviors or everyday mundane behaviors we perform as habits. Because many of our media use behaviors are so automatic and habitual that we have no memory to draw from, our self-reports of media behaviors are often nothing more than wild guesses. For example, Ferguson (1992) conducted a study in which he allowed people to watch TV with remote control devices in their hands while they purportedly waited to begin their participation in a research study in another room. He recorded how often the participants changed channels with the remote control devices. Then later, after the "other" study was completed, he asked participants how many times they changed channels during the previous TV viewing session. He found a zero correlation, that is, everyone was making wild guesses, and participants were as likely to underestimate their channel changes as they were to overestimate them.

Acquiring Behavior

People rely on the media as a source of information about all kinds of behaviors. When people expose themselves to a media message, they typically see a behavioral sequence described (as with print media) or performed (as with motion media). The *acquisition* of a behavioral sequence can be primarily a cognitive process or primarily a behavioral practice process. When the acquisition is primarily a cognitive process, people learn the steps in a behavioral sequence by watching the portrayal of that sequence in the media message. An example of this is watching a podcast that shows people how to download apps to their smartphones. This is a relatively simple procedure, and viewers of the podcast can learn the behavioral sequence in one viewing. Furthermore, they do not have to perform the sequence in order to learn how to do it. In contrast, the acquisition of other behavioral sequences requires the actual behavior performance in order to learn it. An example of this is watching a video showing how to ride a bicycle. When viewing such a video, people can learn about the steps involved, but they cannot learn how to ride a bicycle until they use those behaviors themselves and practice them. In either case—with the cognitive process or behavioral process of acquisition—we cannot be sure people have learned a behavioral sequence until they perform the required behaviors in that sequence; for this reason, both types are included here in the chapter because in both cases people need to perform the behaviors in order to convince observers that they have acquired the behaviors.

Another important distinction to make about the acquisition of behavior is concerned with the type of behavior portrayed in the media message. One type of behavior can be regarded as factual in nature, while a second type of behavior is more social in nature. Let's example each type in some detail.

Factual Behavioral Process

The media present a good deal of messages that teach people about factual behavioral processes. Within book publishing, a huge market is textbooks, which typically present factual behavioral processes (for example, how to perform science experiments). The two most popular sections in bookstores are cooking and self-help. Cookbooks teach people the behavioral sequences of assembling, then mixing ingredients, heating the mixture, and serving the food. Self-help books show people how to change their behaviors to improve their financial habits, their golf games, their performance at work, and thousands of other things. There are also manuals that show people how to fix their homes, their furniture, their cars, and their computers. These books and manuals are now also available online and presented in the form of radio and television shows. There are many other instructional resources available in the media that will show you step by step how to take a good picture, how to play the guitar, how to perform yoga exercises, and so on.

It is likely that the media are so successful at helping people acquire all kinds of behavioral sequences that this is one of the most widespread media effects. However, there is an irony that researchers have almost totally ignored this effect. Perhaps researchers feel that this effect is so obvious that there is no need to document it with research evidence.

Social Behavioral Process

Social behavior is what we perform in our everyday lives as we interact with other people. We learn these behavioral sequences by watching how people behave around us. When we are young we watch our siblings and friends perform all sorts of behaviors to see if those behaviors are good things or bad things. If the person who performs a behavior is punished for it, we learn that it is bad and we are not likely to perform it ourselves. If instead the person is rewarded—or at least not punished—for performing a particular behavior, we learn that the behavior is okay. We continually monitor the social behaviors of ourselves and other people in order to learn about the rules of society that underlie these behaviors.

The media present a great deal of social behavior. We watch the news of people who are reported as performing good or bad deeds. We watch fictional programming that tells us stories in which we observe the behaviors of fictional characters as the plot unfolds and reveals to us the consequences of those characters' actions. This is vicarious learning; that is, we do not have to perform the behaviors ourselves in order to learn whether the performance of those behaviors is likely to lead to happiness or to a negative outcome (Bandura, 1977).

TRIGGERING BEHAVIOR

The media present messages that have the effect of triggering behaviors (see Exhibit 11.1). Research has focused on three types of triggering behavior: media exposure behavior, imitative behavior, and suggested behavior.

Triggering Exposure Behaviors

One of the most often conducted media research studies is the examination into media exposure behaviors (Hall, 2005; Himmelweit, Swift, & Jaeger, 1980; McIntosh, Schwegler, & Terry-Murray, 2000; Shah, McLeod, & Yoon, 2001; Sherry, 2001; Slater, 2003). These studies typically examine where people spend their time; that is, do they spend more time with television, radio, print, or the computer? Other studies focus on one medium, such as television (Lang et al., 2005; Riggs, 1996), or video and computer games (Funk & Buchman, 1996).

Some studies focus on types of content of messages within a medium, such as TV news (Tsfati & Cappella, 2005), reality TV programming (Reiss & Wiltz, 2004), TV violence (Krcmar & Greene, 1999; Krcmar & Kean, 2005; Slater, 2003; Vandewater, Lee, & Shim, 2005); sports (Gantz, Wang, Paul, & Potter, 2006), or public affairs news on the Internet (Tewksbury, 2003). And some research focuses on a specific topic, such as the death of Princess Diana (Basil, Brown, & Bocarnea, 2002).

Exhibit 11.1 Further Reading on Triggering Behaviors

Triggering Exposure Behaviors

Exposure to the media in general (Hall, 2005; Himmelweit et al., 1980; McIntosh et al., 2000; Shah et al., 2001; Sherry, 2001; Slater, 2003)

- Television (Eastman, Newton, & Pack, 1996; Kaye & Sapolsky, 1997; Lang et al., 2005; Riggs, 1996)
- TVs in public places (Krotz & Eastman, 1999)
- Video and computer games (Funk & Buchman, 1996)

Exposure to particular kinds of content

- Violent content (Krcmar & Greene, 1999; Krcmar & Kean, 2005; Slater, 2003; Vandewater et al., 2005)
- TV news (Tsfati & Cappella, 2005)
- Public affairs news on the Internet (Tewksbury, 2003)
- Health information (Rains, 2008)
- Reality TV programming (Reiss & Wiltz, 2004)
- Sports (Gantz et al., 2006; Knobloch-Westerwick, David, Eastin, Tamborini, & Greenwood, 2009)
- Coverage of the death of Princess Diana (Basil et al., 2002)
- Companionship seeking through parasocial interactions (Greenwood & Long, 2009)
- Sad films (Oliver, 2008)

Triggering Imitative Behavior

Imitation of aggression (Miller & Dollard, 1941; Rosekrans & Hartup, 1967)

Signing up for organ donation (Morgan, Movius, & Cody, 2009)

Physical exercise (Fox & Bailenson, 2009)

Voter turnout (Kiousis & McDevitt, 2008)

Triggering Message-Suggested Behavior

Aggressive behavior (Byrne, Linz & Potter, 2009; Krcmar & Lachlan, 2009; Tamborini et al., 2004)

Shopping and buying products

- Online shopping activity (LaRose & Eastin, 2002)
- Purchasing products (Hitchon & Thorson, 1995; Perry & Gonzenbach, 1997)

Political participation and civic engagement (De Vreese & Semetko, 2002; Hardy & Scheufele, 2005; Mastin, 2000; Moy, Torres, Tanaka, & McCluskey, 2005; Newhagen, 1994; Pinkleton, 1998; Pinkleton, Austin, & Fortman, 1998; Scheufele, 2002; Scheufele, Shanahan, & Kim, 2002; Shah, Cho, Eveland, & Kwak, 2005; Wilkins, 2000)

Triggering prosocial behaviors (Mares & Woodard, 2005)

- Healthy behaviors (Harrison, Taylor, & Marske, 2007; Kennedy, O'Leary, Beck, Pollard, & Simpson, 2004)
- Exercising after exposure to models in magazines (Aubrey & Taylor, 2009)

This large body of research has given us a good idea about how particular media content and particular experiences with various media trigger exposure behaviors. The media then try to reinforce these initial exposures (see the later section of the chapter on reinforcing behavior).

Triggering Imitative Behavior

Exposure to media messages has been found to trigger viewer behavior that imitates the behaviors in the media messages. Positive examples of imitative behavior include performing physical exercises (Fox & Bailenson, 2009), signing up for organ donation (Morgan et al., 2009), and voting (Kiousis & McDevitt, 2008).

However, there are also negative examples of media exposure triggering antisocial behaviors. Critics of negative content (such as violence) argue that when people, especially children, are exposed to media content, they often imitate those behaviors. There are a few research studies that support this criticism (Miller & Dollard, 1941; Rosekrans & Hartup, 1967). For example, Rosekrans and Hartup ran an experiment to test the role of reward and punishment on triggering imitative behavior. They found that children who watched role models behave aggressively and were rewarded for such behavior were most likely to behave aggressively themselves. In contrast, children who watched role models get punished when they behaved aggressively were least likely to imitate that aggressive behavior.

Source: ©iStockphoto.com/nycshooter

Triggering Message-Suggested Behavior

From the previous section, you can see that there is evidence of imitative behavior. However, imitative behavior is a rare effect. Although media messages present specific behaviors, viewers of those behaviors do not typically imitate them; instead, people learn about a type of behavior, then generalize to similar types of behaviors. For example, Tamborini et al. (2004) conducted an experiment in which their participants played violent video games and were later more likely to behave aggressively. That is, these participants were not literally imitating the violent behaviors they—or their avatars—performed in the video games. Instead, the participants learned to perform a more general class of behaviors (aggression) and behaved more aggressively after the game playing. A similar finding was reported by Cicchirillo and Chory-Assad (2005), who also found that people who played a violent video game for only 10 minutes were more likely to exhibit novel aggressive behaviors.

Another example of how the media can trigger message-suggested behavior is with eating disorders. Harrison et al. (2007) showed women slides that depicted slender female models. The women who perceived a discrepancy between their own bodies and the depicted models were found to eat *less* later when they were with their female peers.

Researchers have also found that the media can influence people toward prosocial behaviors (Mares & Woodard, 2005). For example, the media have been found to influence political participation and civic engagement (De Vreese & Semetko, 2002; Hardy & Scheufele, 2005; Mastin, 2000; Newhagen, 1994; Pinkleton, 1998; Pinkleton et al., 1998; Scheufele, 2002; Scheufele et al., 2002; Wilkins, 2000). Also, calls to an AIDS hotline increased dramatically the hour after a soap opera portrayed a subplot that delivered HIV prevention messages (Kennedy et al., 2004).

A single media message can have the potential to trigger both positive and negative behaviors. For example, advertising content has been found to lead to positive or negative purchasing behaviors (LaRose & Eastin, 2002).

Triggering Message-Suggested Behavior

Ryan had just finished watching several sporting events on television. It seemed that every few minutes the coverage of the game was interrupted by commercials, and that most of the commercials were for pizzas. He marveled at how all those pizza companies could make their pizzas sound like they were so much different from their competitors' pizzas. And they made them all look so good! Chewy, cheesy crusts. The deep red tomato sauce. And the meat toppings glistening among the colorful morsels of peppers and mushrooms. He grabbed his phone and started dialing when his mother walked through the den where he was watching television.

"Ryan, you are not calling a takeout place are you?"

"Mom, I'm really hungry."

"I'm making a good dinner and it'll be ready in about two hours."

"But I'm hungry now!"

"You are so suggestible. I saw you watching all those pizza commercials. Can't you resist the media manipulation? Don't order a pizza!"

"I'm not. You don't know me at all." Ryan heard his phone call being answered and he spoke into his phone loud enough so his mom could hear, "Hello, Cantonese Palace. I'd like to place an order for delivery. I want an order of egg rolls, orange peel chicken, and steamed rice." He looked over at his mom and said to her, "See, no pizza. I am not being manipulated by all those commercials. The media have no effect on me. I'm just hungry."

Analysis

Ryan clearly had his hunger triggered by media messages. However, he did not respond with imitative behavior; that is, he did not imitate the portrayals of people ordering and eating pizzas. The media messages triggered his hunger. And while Ryan did not order a pizza, he did follow the suggestion provided by those commercials, which was to avoid cooking something himself and instead order fast food.

Process of Triggering Behavior

There are many factors that influence the triggering of behavior. For example, Exhibits 11.2 and 11.3 display some of the factors that explain the triggering of media use behaviors. Exhibit 11.2 displays the factors that have been shown to be the general predictors of media use. These factors are predominately concerned with characteristics of the audience members. Then Exhibit 11.3 shows the factors that account for the triggering of exposure behaviors to particular kinds of media channels and program content. These factors are keyed predominately to particular kinds of content.

Message Factors. In general, promos for prime-time series placed in TV coverage of sporting events by the major broadcast networks had a mixed and modest impact on program shares and ratings (Eastman et al., 1996).

Exposure to political sites online was found to trigger political conversation and online texting. Shah et al. (2005) conducted a study that examined the role of the Internet as a sphere for public expression. They used a two-wave national panel survey data and found that online media complement traditional media to foster political discussion and civic messaging. These two forms of political expression, in turn, trigger participation behaviors in civic functions.

In a meta-analysis of effects of exposure to pornography that leads to subsequent aggressive behavior, the type of pornography was found to be a key factor. Exposure to pictorial nudity reduces subsequent aggressive behavior; exposure of material depicting

Exhibit 11.2 Further Reading on Triggering of Media Use Behaviors in General

Audience Factors

Motives are important (Krotz & Eastman, 1999; Mendelson, 2001; Reiss & Wiltz, 2004)

Involvement with certain stories (Basil et al., 2002; Morgan et al., 2009; Reagan, 1996)

Existing knowledge on topics presented in media (Moy et al., 2005; Shah et al., 2005)

Existing attitudes about elements in the messages (Cho, 2005; Lo & Wei, 2005)

Appeal of and ability to identify with people in the messages (Basil, 1996; Knobloch-Westerwick & Hastall, 2006)

Personality traits (Grimes, Bergen, Nicholes, Vernberg, & Fonagy, 2004)

- Sensation seeking (Slater, Henry, Swaim, & Cardador, 2004)
- Lower self-esteem: Playing video and computer games among girls is predicted by lower self-esteem (Funk & Buchman, 1996)

Expectations

- That media messages will give people information they can use to talk with others (Riggs, 1996)
- Of relatively low cognitive effort (Lang et al., 2005)

Situational variables (Shen, 2009; Slater et al., 2004)

Exhibit 11.3 Further Reading on Triggering of Particular Behaviors

Message Factors

Program promos trigger exposure to programs (Eastman et al., 1996)

Attraction to violent content is related to:

- Gender: Adolescents who are most attracted are males, those who are alienated, and those who are high on trait aggression and sensation seeking (Slater, 2003)
- Sensation seeking (Krcmar & Greene, 1999)
- Personality characteristics (Hall, 2005; Krcmar & Kean, 2005)

Attraction to news: People have a high need for cognition; that is, they like to listen to diverse points of view, like to deliberate about problems, and like to engage in thinking per se (Tsfati & Cappella, 2005)

Attraction to reality television series is predicted by:

- Need for companionship and voyeurism (Papacharissi & Mendelson, 2007)
- External locus of control, low mobility, and low interpersonal interaction (Papacharissi & Mendelson, 2007)

Advertising can trigger behavior with:

- Humor (Perry & Gonzenbach, 1997)
- Emotional appeals (Hitchon & Thorson, 1995)

Political messages trigger political participation and civic engagement (De Vreese & Semetko, 2002; Hardy & Scheufele, 2005; Mastin, 2000; Newhagen, 1994; Scheufele, 2002; Scheufele et al., 2002; Wilkins, 2000)

- Print ads that make comparative claims of political candidates increase election involvement (Pinkleton, 1998)
- Negative coverage of political campaigns reduces media use and voting behavior (Pinkleton et al., 1998)

Triggering aggressive behavior from exposure to media violence

- Arousal due to psychopathologies (Grimes et al., 2004)
- Personality (Slater et al., 2004)
- Pornography (Allen, D'Alessio, & Brezgel, 1995)
- Game players' similarity to avatars (Yee & Bailenson, 2009)

Audience Factors

Involvement with certain stories

- The death of Princess Diana (Basil et al., 2002)
- As a personal interest in a topic increases, the number of media sources audience members use increases (Reagan, 1996)
- Health stories (Morgan et al., 2009)
- High involvement with product in ads (Hitchon & Thorson, 1995)

Need to belong stimulates searching for companionship through parasocial interactions in:

- Fictional television (Greenwood & Long, 2009)
- Reality television programs (Papacharissi & Mendelson, 2007)

nonviolent sexual activity increases aggressive behavior; and that media depictions of violent sexual activity generate more aggression than those of nonviolent sexual activity (Allen et al., 1995).

Audience Factors. In explaining why people are attracted to media messages, motives are important. Many of these behavior-triggering studies ask respondents about their reasons or motivations behind these behavioral patterns. For example, Papacharissi and Mendelson (2007) report that watching reality television series is predicted by a need for companionship and voyeurism. They also reported that viewers who have external loci of control, low mobility, and low interpersonal interaction were more likely to have behavioral habits of viewing reality series. In another study, Reiss and Wiltz (2004) conducted a survey in which adults rated themselves on 16 motives to watch reality TV. They found that people who watched reality TV had above-average trait motivation to feel self-important; they also scored high on need to feel vindicated, friendly, free of morality, secure, and romantic as compared with others. The authors conclude that people prefer TV shows that stimulate the feelings they intrinsically value the most, and these feelings are individually determined.

Political behavior is more strongly associated with trust in political organizations than in political knowledge. Moy et al. (2005) conducted a study that explored the process of media effects on participation, focusing on knowledge and trust in the organization as intervening variables between attention to World Trade Organization (WTO) news and anticipated behaviors related to the WTO. Survey data were collected from 277 adults from the greater Seattle area prior to the WTO meeting. The results indicated that people who trusted the newspaper and television coverage were more likely to have their political behavior triggered.

Triggering aggressive behavior from exposure to media violence has been found to be related to certain psychological problems. Children with diagnosed psychopathologies may experience aggravation of those illnesses with their exposure to media violence. Children with the most common, often undiagnosed, form of psychopathology—disruptive behavior disorders (DBDs)—manifested changes in heart rate, heart vagal heart tone, and other psychophysiological reactions to media violence. Children without such a diagnosis did not manifest these same psychophysiological responses. These reactions, or the absence of them, made determining the effect of violent media on children a more reliable measure than did acted-out behavior, which can be more susceptible to experimenter interpretation and, thus, experimenter bias (Grimes et al., 2004). Also, the relationship between teen use of violent media and aggressiveness is contingent on personality, such as degree of alienation, need for sensation seeking, and sense of victimization by peers (Slater et al., 2004).

ALTERING BEHAVIOR

The media present messages that influence alterations in our behavioral patterns (see Exhibit 11.4). Some of these altered behaviors are concerned with media use and others are personal behaviors.

Altering Exposure Behaviors Over Time

The media have been found to shape people's media habits over time. This has been found to be the case particularly with television (Eggermont, 2006), the Internet (Hardy & Scheufele, 2005; Parks & Floyd, 1996), and video game playing (Lucas & Sherry, 2004). For example, Parks and Floyd (1996) found that people, especially females, use the Internet to develop personal relationships and that the longer a person uses it, the more personal relationships they will develop with those people they meet online, and they will continually increase the amount of time they spend online.

Exhibit 11.4   Further Reading on Altering Behaviors

Altering Exposure Behaviors Over Time

Television

- Viewing television is inertial (Hawkins, Tapper, Bruce, & Pingree, 1995).
- Repeat viewing rates of television programs are relatively low (Zubayr, 1999).
- People often expose themselves to more than one media message at the same time (Schmitt, Woolf, & Anderson, 2003).
- Increased TV viewing beyond a certain point displaces other media use (Koolstra & Van der Voort, 1996).
- Teens generally decline in TV use throughout adolescence except for an increase in late night viewing (Eggermont, 2006).

Video games

- Time playing games (Lucas & Sherry, 2004)
- Video game addiction (Lemmens, Valkenburg, & Peter, 2009)

Internet

- Developing personal relationships with people online (Parks & Floyd, 1996)
- Internet use to access hard news alters people's self-reported participatory behavior in political process (Hardy & Scheufele, 2005)

Violence (Vandewater, Lee & Shim, 2005)

Sports (Gantz et al., 2006; Harrison & Fredrickson, 2003)

Altering Personal Behaviors Over Time

Harmful behaviors

- Risk-taking behaviors (Krcmar & Greene, 2000)
- Risky health behaviors (Nabi & Clark, 2008)
- Smoking (Gunther, Bolt, Borzekowski, Liebhart, & Dillard, 2006)
- Eating disorders (Bissell & Zhou, 2004; Botta, 1999; Harrison, 2000; Harrison & Cantor, 1997; Moriarty & Harrison, 2008)

Aggressive behavior from exposure to media violence (Grimes et al., 2004; Slater et al., 2004)

Sexual behaviors (Bleakley, Hennessy, Fishbein, & Jordan, 2008; Fisher et al., 2009)

Prosocial behaviors (Mares & Woodard, 2005)

- Proenvironmental behavior (Holbert, Kwak, & Shah, 2003; Ostman & Parker, 1987)

Civic participation (Hoffman & Thomson, 2009)

As for alterations in television usage, Eggermont (2006) conducted a study to look at the trajectories of television viewing throughout adolescence. Results indicated that changes in viewing habits are different when daytime, prime-time, and late-night television viewing are examined separately. Although daytime and prime-time viewing showed a decline, viewing during later waking hours increased. Teenagers who have access to television sets in their rooms watch more; male viewers tend to avoid the "family hour" and "female contents."

Other scholars have studied online video game behavior. Williams (2006a, 2006b) conducted a one-month panel study of an immersive online video game in order to examine its social and civic impact. The data revealed mixed effects. Although the game led to an improved global outlook and some online community improvements, some kinds of existing friendships eroded, and the most social players became more insulated from one another. Family interactions were unaffected. News media use was unaffected, but entertainment media were displaced. A decline in face-to-face interactions was detected and described as "cocooning." Lucas and Sherry (2004) conducted a large-scale survey of young adults' reasons for video game use, preferred game genres, and amount of game play. Female respondents report less frequent play, less motivation to play in social situations, and less orientation to game genres featuring competition than did males.

Other scholars have examined habitual patterns of exposure to particular kinds of content, especially violent content. Vandewater et al. (2005) conducted a national survey of children ages 6 to 12 to determine the best explanation for differences in the amount to which children expose themselves to violence on television and in video games. They found the best explanation was family conflict; that is, when people in a family fight a lot, the family tensions increase interest in violent media content; children raised in other types of homes do not expose themselves to as much violence.

Sports fans become more ritualistic in their behavior over time. Compared to viewers of other types of TV programs, sports fans are highly ritualistic. Many sports fans engage in a variety of previewing activities as well as follow-up activities (Gantz et al., 2006).

There are also characteristics about the media messages that influence this altering of behavior effect. Lang et al. (2005) found that characteristics of news stories altered TV viewing behaviors. They investigated whether news story length and production pacing affect channel-changing behavior in younger and older adults. Viewers used remote control devices to choose among four local news programs that varied systematically by story length and pacing. In general, pacing and length have greater effects on younger viewers. Fast pacing increased viewers' favorable evaluations of the newscasts, but when combined with long stories, decreased younger viewers' time spent on channel. Viewers' cognitive effort, physiological arousal, and recognition all decreased before and increased after a channel change. Frequent channel changing was associated with lower cognitive effort and recognition.

The way the media alter people's exposure patterns over time is a complicated procedure involving many factors. To illustrate, Cooper and Tang (2009) conducted a study to determine the factors that are most influential in habitual television exposure; their findings suggested that there was no single factor that explained exposure to television. It takes many variables to explain people's media use habits. Their top seven factors (ritualistic motivations, use of the Internet, audience availability, the cost of multichannel service, age, instrumental motivations, and gender) in combination explained only about 30% of viewing behaviors.

Altering Other Behaviors Over Time

Source: ©iStockphoto.com/sedmak

The media have been found to influence personal behaviors, both harmful and helpful, over time. Among harmful behaviors, risk-taking behaviors, such as problem drinking and driving, delinquency (vandalizing, trespassing, truancy), reckless driving, and drug use, are related to exposure to violent television in the form of violent drama, realistic crime shows, and contact sports among adolescents (Krcmar & Greene, 2000). The media have also been found to increase aggressive behavior over time from repeated exposure to media violence (Grimes et al., 2004; Slater et al., 2004). Other researchers have examined the harmful behavior of smoking. Gunther et al. (2006) found that pro-smoking-related media content has an influence on adolescents' smoking behavior. The influence is indirect via its effect on perceived peer norms; that is, adolescents assume that smoking-related messages in the media will influence the attitudes and behaviors of their peers, and these beliefs in turn influence adolescents' own smoking behaviors. This effect is called the "presumed influence hypothesis." Using a longitudinal Web-based survey of adolescents 14–16 years of age, Bleakley and colleagues (2008) found that sexually active adolescents are more likely to expose themselves to sex in the media, and those exposed to sex in the media are more likely to progress in their sexual activity.

The media have been shown to be an influence in increasing eating disorders (Bissell & Zhou, 2004; Botta, 1999; Harrison, 2000; Harrison & Cantor, 1997). College females eating patterns have been found to be altered by exposure to programs in which people are portrayed with an ideal body of thinness; females who expose themselves to a lot of these images are more likely to develop eating disorders (Bissell & Zhou, 2004). Watching sports can lead to self-objectification, which leads to mental health risks such as body shame, disordered eating, and depression (Harrison & Fredrickson, 2003).

The media have also been found to influence prosocial behaviors over time (Mares & Woodard, 2005). One example of this is proenvironmental behavior (Holbert et al., 2003; Ostman & Parker, 1987).

Over time, the media have been found to alter civic participation. For example, Hoffman and Thomson (2009) found that while civic participation has been declining among adults, it appears to be growing among adolescents. This study assessed the effects of television viewing on high school students' civic participation. Results demonstrate that viewing late night TV and local TV news had a positive, significant effect on civic participation.

Explaining Altering Behaviors

There are many factors that influence the alteration of behavior over time. In the area of health communication, Fishbein and Cappella (2006) developed a model for using the media to create effective health communication campaigns. In this model, exposure to the media interacts with other factors such as a person's past behavior; demographics and culture; attitudes toward targets (stereotypes and stigma); personality, moods, and emotions; and other individual difference variables such as perceived risk. This set of factors influences a person's beliefs, which influence attitudes, which then influence intentions and eventually predict health behaviors.

REINFORCING BEHAVIOR

The media present information that has the effect of reinforcing existing behavioral patterns (see Exhibit 11.5). The research on reinforcing behaviors has focused primary on three topics: reinforcing habits with all media in general, habits with a particular medium, and habits with particular messages.

Exhibit 11.5 Further Reading on Reinforcing Behaviors

Habits With All Media

Reinforcing media exposure habits (Freedman & Sears, 1966; Himmelweit et al., 1980; LaRose & Eastin, 2002; Lazarsfeld, Berelson, & Gaudet, 1944; McIntosh et al., 2000; Shah et al., 2001; Sherry, 2001; Slater, 2003

Reinforcing dependency on media (Ball-Rokeach & DeFleur, 1976)

Reinforcing media addiction (Himmelweit, Oppenheim, & Vince, 1958; Jhally, 1987; Kaplan, 1972; LaRose et al., 2003; Levy, 2007; Maccoby, 1954; Mander, 1978; McLeod, Ward, & Tancill, 1965; Winn, 1977)

Habits With Particular Medium

Television viewing (Hawkins et al., 1995; Krcmar, 1996; Mares & Woodard, 2006; Rosenstein & Grant, 1997; Zubayr, 1999)

Television addiction (Horvath, 2004; Jhally, 1987; Kaplan, 1972; Mander, 1978; McIlwraith, 1998; Winn, 1977)

Books (Koolstra & Van der Voort, 1996)

Internet (LaRose & Eastin, 2004)

Habits With Particular Messages

Pornography (Allen et al., 1995)

PBS (Sherman, 1995)

Habits With All Media

Researchers have been concerned with whether long-term media exposure can reinforce people to become addicted to those exposures over time. While most people do not show signs of media addiction over time, there are many people who do develop a dependency on the media (Ball-Rokeach & DeFleur, 1976). This dependency shows up in the reinforcement of media exposure habits (Freedman & Sears, 1966; Himmelweit et al., 1980; LaRose & Eastin, 2002; Lazarsfeld et al., 1944; McIntosh et al., 2000; Shah et al., 2001; Sherry, 2001; Slater, 2003). Some researchers have gone so far as to characterize this dependency on the media as an addiction (Himmelweit et al., 1958; Horvath, 2004; Jhally, 1987; Kaplan, 1972; LaRose et al., 2003; Maccoby, 1954; Mander, 1978; McLeod et al., 1965; Winn, 1977). For example, Jhally (1987) says there is "significant evidence that this watching activity is less than free, that it is somehow out of our control. Further, it is not as if there were no recognition of the harmful effects of this watching—people know what is happening to them." He says that people overindulge, and this gives them a sense that their viewing is "beyond their control," and that it "affords them no real sense of satisfaction. The activity seems almost to stand in a hostile relationship to the individual's self-perceived preferences. The activity seems to be alienated from the watchers themselves" (p. 181). Habitual behavior and deficient self-regulation are determinants of media behavior (LaRose & Eastin, 2004). Also, Horvath (2004) used principles developed by psychiatrists to develop a measure of problem television viewing and found that many people do exhibit an addiction problem with the media. The measure contains four factors measuring distinct components of addictive behavior: heavy viewing, problem viewing, craving for viewing, and withdrawal. These factors were positively related to an alcoholism screening instrument adapted to television use.

People who are addicted to TV are more likely to be easily bored and to score high on the neurotic and introverted dimensions of the Eysenck Personality Test, a general test of personality that is based on five factors of openness to experience, conscientiousness, extroversion, agreeableness, and neuroticism. Addicts are more likely to use TV to distract themselves from unpleasant thoughts, regulate moods, and to fill time (McIlwraith, 1998). In a *Newsweek* article, Levy (2007) described people getting on Facebook and quickly becoming addicted to it. People would feel compelled to check the site many times a day to visit their friends' sites and see what was new with them; some people had hundreds of friends linked to their sites.

Habits With a Particular Medium

Researchers have examined the reinforcement of exposure habits with particular media over time, such as books (Koolstra & Van der Voort, 1996) and the Internet (LaRose & Eastin, 2004). However, the most examined medium in this regard has been television habits (Hawkins et al., 1995; Krcmar, 1996; Mares & Woodard, 2006; Rosenstein & Grant, 1997; Zubayr, 1999) and television addiction (Horvath, 2004; Jhally, 1987; Kaplan, 1972; Mander, 1978; McIlwraith, 1998; Winn, 1977).

Researchers have found that viewing television is inertial. The longer a person looks at the screen, the greater likelihood that the looking will continue even across content boundaries. People use both strategic and nonstrategic means for viewing. Nonstrategic viewing is explained by attentional inertia (Hawkins et al., 1995). Habit plays a significant role in television viewing behavior (Rosenstein & Grant, 1997). Older adults do watch more television on average than other age groups (Mares & Woodard, 2006). Repeat viewing rates of television programs are relatively low; that is, only about one third of viewers of one episode of a TV show will watch the next episode. However, rates of repeat viewing are higher with continuing story lines such as soap operas (Zubayr, 1999). Media use was observed in real households; researchers found that 46% of the time people had the TV on they were doing some other activity, such as talking, eating, or doing household chores. These extra exposure behaviors were more typical during daytime hours and during ad breaks (Schmitt et al., 2003). Increased TV viewing beyond a certain point decreases book reading among elementary schoolchildren. Television displaces book reading through two mechanisms: It deteriorates attitudes supporting book reading, and it deteriorates children's ability to concentrate on reading (Koolstra & Van der Voort, 1996).

Habits With Particular Messages

Researchers have examined how behavior is reinforced over time by particular kinds of media messages, such as pornography (Allen et al., 1995), violence (Rosengren, Johnsson-Smaragdi, & Sonesson, 1994), and even PBS (public television) (Sherman, 1995). For example, repeat viewing of a program on public television is predicted by the presence of a continuing dramatic story line, household cable status, and habitual scheduling (Sherman, 1995).

Reinforcing Behavior

"Brianna, please turn off that computer and go to sleep," said Liz, Brianna's roommate. "It's 2 o'clock and I'm trying to sleep. You can study tomorrow."

"I'm not studying."

"Oh no, you're not on Facebook again!?"

"Don't get on my case. I love Facebook."

"I do too but give it a rest. You were on it all day. Turn it off!"

"Okay, just a few more minutes. I need to text two more friends."

"How many friends do you have?"

"327."

"What? That's 20 more than last night?"

"21 more. This is so cool." Brianna's fingers were flying over her keyboard. "Wait, there's another one. 328!"

"How many friends do you need?"

"Can't have too many." Brianna continued texting.

Liz dragged herself wearily from bed and pulled on her jeans and sweatshirt, "Cm'on, I've got to get you out of here for a break. We're going to the student union to hang out with some real people. Let's go."

"Okay, okay but just let me finish two more texts."

"No. Stop now. Let's go!" Liz pulled Brianna up from her desk and pushed her away from her computer and toward the door.

Brianna grabbed her iPhone on the way out the door. "Okay. Let's go."

Liz stared at Brianna holding her phone and said, "You're not taking that with us."

"But I have to."

"No! Say good night to your friends. They need to sleep too."

"What makes you think that all my friends live in this time zone?"

"Where are these friends?"

"All over the world. Isn't that cool?"

"Brianna, how many of these friends have you actually met?"

"All of them, silly."

"No I mean in person."

"In person? What does that have to do with friendship?"

Analysis

This story asks us to think about the line between habits and addiction. Habits are behaviors we perform regularly. While habitual behavioral patterns are often performed automatically, we do choose to perform those behaviors and we can stop performing them if we so choose, such as when they stop being useful or pleasurable. With addiction, we perform behaviors over and over again but we cannot stop ourselves, that is, we lose control over those behaviors and those behaviors then control us. Also, with addiction those behaviors lose their power to make us happy, yet we continue to perform them in a compulsion to get back the good feelings that those behaviors once provided.

In this story, Brianna is addicted to Facebook. It is cutting into her sleep and study time. She appears unable to stop texting her Facebook friends, even when her real-life friend tries to help her.

Even when people have a large number of television channels available, they typically have a relatively small viewing repertoire, which is the set of channels they typically watch. For example, Chinese viewers were found to have a viewing repertoire of about 13 channels, which is around one third of the channels available (Yuan & Webster, 2006). Americans typically have a larger choice of channels and a smaller repertoire (Webster & Phalen, 1997).

Finally, habitual viewing of television can reinforce behavioral patterns over time. For example, Rosengren et al. (1994) found that the amount of TV use in preschool was related to aggressive behavior in Grade 5, and this in turn was related to the amount of viewing of TV violence and horror content in Grade 8, which in turn was related to restlessness and lack of concentration in Grade 9.

Explaining Reinforcing Media Behaviors

Explaining how the media reinforce media exposure behaviors over time can be organized by audience factors and message factors (see Exhibit 11.6). Among audience factors, people will become more dependent on media that meet more of their needs (Ball-Rokeach & DeFleur, 1976). People who already have a habit of media exposure will continue with that habit, and the habit will get stronger over time (LaRose & Eastin, 2004; Rosenstein & Grant, 1997), especially among people who are deficient in self-regulation (LaRose & Eastin, 2004).

The demographic of age is also important. Older adults watch more television on average than other age groups (Mares & Woodard, 2006), which is a clear indication of a reinforced habit of television viewing over time. Parents often try different strategies on their younger children to direct them away from increased television viewing. Younger children are more compliant with TV viewing rules when parents use directive language coupled with positive affect but this strategy does not work well with older children (Krcmar, 1996).

Several message factors have also been found to be influential in reinforcing media behaviors. When a television series presents a continuing dramatic story line, viewers are more likely to watch every episode and thereby have their viewing reinforced (Sherman, 1995; Zubayr, 1999). Also, television programmers know that by scheduling a show at the same time every week, they will create and reinforce a viewing habit (Sherman, 1995).

Exhibit 11.6 Further Reading on Reinforcing Behaviors

Audience Factors

Personal needs (Ball-Rokeach & DeFleur, 1976)

Media habits (LaRose & Eastin, 2004; Rosenstein & Grant, 1997)

Personality characteristics

- Deficient self-regulation (LaRose & Eastin, 2004)

Age

- Older adults (Mares & Woodard, 2006)
- Younger children (Krcmar, 1996)

Message Factors

Presence of a continuing dramatic story line (Sherman, 1995; Zubayr, 1999)

Habitual scheduling (Sherman, 1995)

SUMMARY

Behaviors are the overt actions of an individual. Sometimes a person's self-report of his or her own behavior is accurate, but often it is not, so it is important to be skeptical of self-reported behavior.

The media have been found to influence behaviors in four ways. First, people can learn behavioral sequences (both factual and social) from exposure to media messages, although they do not necessarily need to perform those behaviors in order to learn them. Second, the media can trigger behavior, such as media use behavior, imitative behavior, and novel behaviors. A third behavioral effect is the altering of behavioral patterns over time. And the fourth effect is the reinforcement of existing behavioral patterns over the long term.

Review Questions

1. What is a behavioral effect?

2. Why should we be skeptical of research findings that measure a person's behaviors through his or her self-reports?

3. Compare and contrast the learning of a factual behavioral process with a social behavioral process.

4. Compare and contrast the triggering of imitative behavior with the triggering of message-suggested behavior.

5. List the kinds of behaviors that have been found to be altered by the media over time.

6. List the kinds of behaviors that have been found to be reinforced by the media over time.

Further Thinking Questions

1. Look at Exhibits 11. 2 and 11.3, which display many factors that researchers have found to be involved in the triggering of behaviors. Which of those factors do you think are the most influential? You may want to read some of the cited research studies to see how those authors talk about the power of those factors in their discussion sections.

2. Think about the media behaviors you engaged in yesterday. What were the major factors that triggered those specific exposure behaviors?

3. Compare and contrast your two lists from questions 5 and 6 above.
   • In what ways are they the same, that is, do they both share the same kinds of effects?
   • In what ways are they different?

4. Think about your typical media usage habits. What are the major factors that have shaped and reinforced those habits over time?

PART III

Types of Macro-Level Media Effects

This third part of this book is composed of three chapters that examine media effects on macro-level units. Chapter 12 deals with media effects on the public. Chapter 13 shifts attention to media effects on various institutions, and Chapter 14 deals with the effects on society as well as on the media themselves.

Macro-level effects are concerned with aggregates rather than individuals. An aggregate is a combined whole that is formed by the gathering together of all the particular elements. The public is an aggregate because it is the collection of all individuals. Thus public opinion is an aggregate because it is the collection of each individual's opinion on an issue, and it is more concerned with the opinions of the public than the opinions of any one individual. It is usually expressed as a simple percentage about the proportion of individuals who are positive (or negative) about something. For example, you might read that 55% of the public thinks the president is doing a good job. This would mean that 55% of individuals in this country have a positive opinion about the president's job performance.

Given what I have just said, you might be asking yourself why we need a separate treatment of effects on aggregates if aggregates are just collections of individuals—that is, why not deal with public opinion in Chapter 9, on individual attitudes? That is a good question. The answer is that although aggregate effects require the collection of data from individuals and the averaging of those data, the focus changes. When we are concerned with attitudes at the individual level, we want to know who has changed his or her attitude, how big that change is, and why. In contrast, when we are concerned with public opinion we want to know what the average person's opinion is. We do not care about the distribution of opinions, we only care about the average. Recall from Chapter 9 that attitudes are dynamic and continually change. Converse (1962) argued that individuals are not consistent with their opinions; that is, an individual's opinions are likely to change over time almost randomly; also, an individual's opinion is not necessarily related to that individual's beliefs or ideology. However, public opinion is more rational at the aggregate level; it moves in response to events and information (Page & Shapiro, 1992). Thus public opinion is more stable and predictable than any one individual's opinion. Also, public opinion is a better indicator of the overall feeling about social issues in the population, because it takes into consideration the opinions of many people, then reduces all that information down into one indicator, which is the average.

Aggregates are more than the simple collection of all the particular elements. When the elements are combined, something more results. This can be seen most clearly with the macro unit of institutions. While institutions are collections of individual people, they have a structure and a history apart from the individuals who come and go as members (or users) of those institutions. There are sets of procedures, rituals, and values that exist long before any one person joins an institution and exist long after that person leaves. The media can exert an influence on these procedures, rituals, and values.

For all of these reasons, we need to examine media effects on macro units in addition to media effects on individuals. We cannot understand larger social structures simply by adding up data about individuals (Mills, 1956). There is a different dynamic with macro-level units than with individual-level units.

The research literature on macro-level media effects is much smaller than the research literature on individual-level effects. This disparity in size has led some scholars to observe that this relative lack of attention to macro-level effects is a serious shortcoming.

Why is the effects literature on macro units much smaller than the effects literature on individuals? There seem to be two reasons for this. One reason is that the topic of media effects over the years has attracted many more scholars who are interested in micro units—such as the human mind—rather than macro units—such as institutions and society. For example, Shoemaker and Reese (1996) point out that the dominance of psychological studies and paucity of sociological studies biases the accumulation of findings about the media. A second reason for the disparity can be attributed to the research methods used. Scholars who conduct research on individual-level effects typically use the methods of experiment and survey to generate data. Macro-level units require other methods, such as historical analysis, secondary analysis of existing documents, and ethnography. The macro-level methods are typically more time consuming to use well and therefore require many years of data gathering and analysis before a publishable piece with interesting findings can be produced.

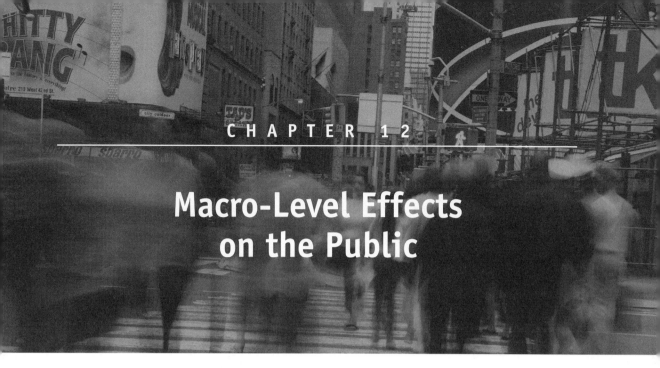

Source: Medioimages/Photodisc/Thinkstock

Effects on Public Knowledge
Information Flow
Effects of News
Effects of Public Information Campaigns
Public Beliefs
Explaining Formation of Public Beliefs
Beliefs of the Public
Public Attitudes and Opinion
Public Affect
Public Behavior
Civic Participation
Social Engagement
Prosocial and Antisocial Behaviors
Summary

Macro-Level Effects on the Public

This chapter looks at how research has documented media influence on the public. It follows a pattern established in the six chapters in Part II on individual-level effects by looking at various types of effects. Paralleling the structure of those previous chapters, this chapter looks at media influence on public knowledge, public beliefs, public attitudes, public affect, and public behavior. While there is no macro analogy with physiology, the other five types of individual-level effects match up with the macro unit of the public.

EFFECTS ON PUBLIC KNOWLEDGE

The media exert an influence on the general level of knowledge in the public by the way they select and present messages. Recall from Chapter 7 that when individual people acquire knowledge, the focus was on differences across individuals and the factors that accounted for those differences. Here we are more concerned with what the public knows. Of course, the public is an aggregation of individuals, and we cannot assess public knowledge without collecting data from individual people. But public knowledge has less to do with what any individual knows and shifts the focus to the general level of knowledge in the public as well as the role the media play in shaping public knowledge.

In this section of the chapter, I first deal with the issue of information flow, then I break down media influence from two kinds of messages: from news and from public information campaigns. News is produced by journalists working for media organizations; their intention is to inform the public about the most important events of the day. Public information campaigns are typically designed and executed by people and organizations who are not employed by the media. These people and organizations have an agenda to inform the public about specific information that they believe would make society better in some way. Exhibit 12.1 presents research on media effects on the public.

Exhibit 12.1   Further Reading on Media Effects on the Public

Effects on Public Knowledge

Explanations

- Two-step flow (Katz & Lazarsfeld, 1955)
- Diffusion of information in the culture (Rogers, 1962, 2000)
- Knowledge gap (Tichenor, Donohue, & Olien, 1970; Rucinski, 2004; Slater, Hayes, Reineke, Long, & Bettinghaus, 2009)

Effects of news

- Collective memory (Barnhurst & Wartella, 1998; Edy, 1999; Peri, 1999)
- Reduction in shared cultural knowledge (Tewksbury, 2003)
- Faulty information (Hardy & Scheufele, 2009; Shah. Cho, Eveland, & Kwak, 2005)

Effects of public information campaigns

- Speed of information flow (DeFleur & Larsen, 1958)
- Drunk driving (Yanovitzky, 2002)

Effects on Public Beliefs

Explanations

- Pictures in our heads (Lippmann, 1922)
- Agenda setting (Cohen, 1963; Dearing & Rogers, 1996; McCombs & Shaw (1972; Meijer & Kleinnijenhuis, 2006; also see Chapter 8)
- Spiral of silence (Noelle-Neumann, 1984)
- Cultivation (Gerbner, Gross, Morgan, & Signorelli, 1980, also see Chapter 8)

Beliefs about institutions (Fan, Wyatt, & Keltner 2001; Moy, Pfau, & Kahlor, 1999)

Beliefs about the government's use of force (Aday, 2010)

Beliefs about family problems (Glynn, Huge, Reineke, Hardy, & Shanahan, 2007)

Faulty beliefs (Shermer, 2002)

Effects on Public Attitudes/Opinion

Political action groups influenced by media workers who create messages that affect the public at large (Andsager, 2000)

- Race relations (Domke, 2000)
- National Organization for Women (Barker-Plummer, 2002)
- Political candidates (Russomanno & Everett, 1995)

Attitudes about institutions (Johnston & Bartels, 2010; Moy et al., 1999)

Consensus of public opinion (Bennett, 1990; Herman & Chomsky, 1988)

Erosion of social trust (Cappella, 2002; Putnam, 2000)

Effects on Public Affect

Feelings of social trust (Cappella, 2002; Putnam, 2000)

Public confidence (Simonson, 1999)

Public fear of crime (Gerbner et al., 1980; Lowry, Ching, Nio, & Leitner, 2003; Romer, Jamieson, & Jamieson, 2003)

Moral panic (Chiricos, 1996)

Effects on Public Behavior

Public discourse (Hardy & Scheufele, 2009; Moy, Domke, & Stamm, 2001; Noelle-Neumann, 1984; Scheufele, Shanahan, & Lee, 2001; Shah, Cho, Eveland, & Kwak, 2005)

Civic engagement (Armstrong, 2007; Cappella, 2002; Hampton, Livio, & Sessions-Goulet, 2010; Hofstetter & Gianos, 1997; Kang & Gearhart, 2010; Matei & Ball-Rokeach, 2003; Pasek, Kenski, Romer, & Jamieson, 2006; Putnam, 2000; Williams, 2006a, 2006b)

Formation of online communities (Becker, Clement, & Schaedel, 2010)

Social movements

- Student protests against the Vietnam War influenced by media coverage of it (Gitlin, 1980; Halloran, Elliot, & Murdock, 1970)
- Feminist movement (Lind & Salo, 2002)

Adoption of innovations (Rogers & Shoemaker, 1971)

Donations to organizations (Simon, 1997)

Civil disorder (Singer, 1970; Spilerman, 1976)

Suicide (Fu, Chan, & Yip, 2009; Phillips & Hensley, 1984; Romer, Jamieson, & Jamieson, 2006)

Rates of violence (Centerwall, 1989; Hennigan, Del Rosario, Heath, Cook, Wharton, & Calder, 1982; Messner, 1986)

Information Flow

Information continually flows from the media to the public. However, not every bit of information is equally successful in making its way into the public's knowledge base. This raises a question about why some information is more influential in shaping public knowledge than is other information. I focus here on three theories that have been influential in explaining this difference: two-step flow, diffusion of information, and knowledge gap.

The *two-step flow theory* explains that information does not typically flow from the media directly to the public at large but instead flows primarily to opinion leaders who then digest the information and pass it along to others in their social networks. This two-step process was first observed by Paul Lazarsfeld (1948) when he analyzed the data from six months of field interviews with voters in the 1940 presidential election. He had conducted the study to determine how people got their information about the political candidates and issues. He found that the media were used extensively by people who were most interested in the campaign. These people made up their minds early about which candidates to support, and they used the media to gather information to reinforce their choices and elaborate their opinions. These people also talked a lot about political issues. Other voters who did not make up their minds early in an election listened to these early deciders, who Lazarsfeld labeled as "opinion leaders." These opinion leaders also served as "gate keepers" of information, because they selected which information to pass along to others. Thus Lazarsfeld found that information was disseminated in a "two-step flow." In the first step, the media transmit information to the opinion leaders. In the second step, these opinion leaders disseminate information to the people in their interpersonal networks.

A second theory, called *diffusion of information,* builds on the two-step model by dividing the public into segments according to how information moves out from the media to a wider and wider range of people in the public. This theory was developed by Everett Rogers (1962) in a major review and synthesis of the literature on how information gets disseminated in societies. Rogers extended the ideas of Lazarsfeld beyond the realm of political information and paid special attention to how information about innovations—especially about agriculture and health—was disseminated. Rogers argued that information about innovations was disseminated in a step-by-step fashion to different groups of people in a society. The first group to receive and use the information were people he labeled as "early adopters." These are people who liked to try new things and were continually monitoring the media to find new things. Rogers said that these early adopters passed their information along to the opinion leaders (à la Lazarsfeld), who then tested out the idea or innovation. If the opinion leaders found they liked the innovation, they passed it along to other people in their interpersonal networks (the "opinion followers"). Finally the information spread out to the "laggards" or "later adopters."

Knowledge gap theory was developed by a team of researchers at the University of Minnesota who spent more than two decades examining the differences across groups in society in terms of how much they learned about current events from the news media (Tichenor et al., 1970). The researchers noticed that certain groups of people learned much more from the media than other groups of people. Thus a "knowledge gap" grew between the people who knew something and the other people who knew nothing about a topic. In a series of studies, these researchers noticed that the knowledge gap was growing larger throughout the 1970s and 1980s. This troubled the researchers, because they had expected that the rise of the mass media would make it possible for everyone to become highly informed, at least about current events. The mass media made so much information available at such a low cost that, the researchers theorized, even the poorest people could gain access to a good deal of information each day. These scholars found that while information was universally available through the mass media, people differed widely in their degree of motivation for seeking out information. They found that the most important predictors of knowledge from the mass media were education and socioeconomic status (SES). Thus people who had higher interest in gaining knowledge about their world were typically driven to higher levels of education and success in life (as indicated by higher incomes and social status). People who had little interest in knowledge usually avoided educational opportunities and therefore had lower information skills, lower incomes, and lower social status. This motivational factor explained why the knowledge gap was growing, not shrinking. The mass media can make a wide range of information universally available, but people have to be motivated to consume it. This knowledge gap is still being found (Grabe, Yegiyan, & Kamhawi, 2008). However, there are some exceptions. For example, Rucinski (2004) found that there are times when there is an inverse knowledge gap, when persons of lower socioeconomic status had greater awareness than did persons of higher socioeconomic status.

Effects of News

The media have always provided information to the public in the form of news, and this news information greatly expands people's knowledge base. Early on in media effects research and thinking, Walter Lippmann (1922) wrote that the media present people with all kinds of information that they cannot get from direct experience in their real lives. For example, people see pictures of the president and can read about legislation passed without ever traveling to Washington, D.C., to experience the workings of government directly. As this information is continually presented to the public, people build their knowledge structures about government and its leaders.

The media have been shown to keep people informed on a daily basis. News messages create and keep alive a collective memory (Edy, 1999) through a communal experience that helps form national identity (Barnhurst & Wartella, 1998).

The Internet has also had an influence on public knowledge. On the one hand, it makes a wide range of information easily available to anyone, which is a positive effect. On the other hand, it presents several negative effects. One such negative effect is the fragmentation of the public as knowledge becomes more specialized and thus moves us away from a common set of shared knowledge. For example, Tewksbury (2005) found that Internet news sites were highly differentiated by audience composition and editorial material; this contributes to fragmentation of public knowledge.

Another negative effect is the Internet's ability to inject inaccurate information into political discussions, then to amplify that inaccurate information (Shah et al., 2005). For example, Hardy and Scheufele (2009) found that when major events are covered by the media in political campaigns, more people start talking about those events; this involves people who are not usually politically active and therefore are less knowledgeable. As a result misinformation and inaccuracies get injected into the public discussion, and this faulty information gets amplified as more people are drawn into political discussions.

Effects of Public Information Campaigns

Researchers have been studying how the media affect public knowledge for more than a century (for a review, see Rogers, 2000). Many of these messages have been designed by government agencies or public action groups who are interested in disseminating information to help make citizens' lives better in some way. For the past half-century they have tried to use television to present PSAs (public service announcements) on matters of health such as drunk driving (Yanovitzky, 2002).

PUBLIC BELIEFS

In this section, we first examine various explanations about how public beliefs are influenced by the media. Then we look at what some of those public beliefs are.

Explaining Formation of Public Beliefs

There are two major theories that explain how the media influence public beliefs. These are the theories of agenda setting and cultivation.

Agenda-setting theory focuses its explanation on how news content in the media shapes the public's beliefs about what is important in society. While he did not use the term "agenda setting," this idea can be traced back to Walter Lippmann (1922), who laid out these ideas in his book *Public Opinion*. Lippmann argued that the news media open a window to a world to which most people do not have access. The news media present pictures of this world that form cognitive maps for us. Thus what the public believes is not influenced by the real world and what we experience directly but instead by the pictures the media provide of that world. Building on Lippmann's idea, Cohen (1963) argued that the news media may not be successful in telling people what to think, but they are stunningly successful in telling people what to think *about*.

The first clear empirical support of this was provided by McCombs and Shaw (1972) in their analysis of the 1968 election campaign for president. They found that when the media present certain issues more saliently than others, those salient issues became the focus of the campaign. The researchers surveyed undecided voters in Chapel Hill, North Carolina, and asked them what they thought were the most important issues in the presidential campaign. They then content analyzed five local and national newspapers, two TV network news programs, and two national news magazines to rank order the coverage of different issues. They found a high degree of correspondence between amount of coverage of certain issues and the public's ranking of those issues as most important. Thus they concluded that media coverage of current events influences the public agenda, which is the rank ordering of the issues that the public believes are the most important at the time. This finding stimulated more than 350 empirical studies of the agenda-setting effect over the course of the next two decades (Dearing & Rogers, 1996).

Over time, this agenda-setting research has also included findings that the media tell us what our beliefs should be on the issues; this is called *second-level agenda setting*. Media messages do not just emphasize issues; they also present informational elements about those issues, and those informational elements tell us what to think about the issue.

When Lippmann (1922) wrote about how the media put pictures in the public's mind, he was referring to print media, primarily newspapers and magazines. With the rise of radio and especially television, media scholars shifted their focus to the "newer" media. By the 1960s, television was regarded as the dominant medium, and it was at the end of this decade that George Gerbner (1969) created his *cultivation theory* explanation for why television was a strong influencer of public beliefs. Gerbner regarded television as the dominant storyteller of the time, arguing that TV presented messages with consistent themes and that people who were exposed to these stories over time came to believe that the themes and patterns in these television stories applied to the real world. Because of the pervasiveness and consistency of the massages, he claimed that the media cultivate a "collective consciousness about elements of existence" (p. 138). Gerbner explains:

> I use the term [cultivation] to indicate that my primary concern in this discussion is not with information, education, persuasion, etc., or with any kind of direct communication "effects." I am concerned with the collective context within which, and in response to which, different individual and group selections and interpretations of messages take place. (p. 139)

Key to cultivation is the focus on public information with an

> awareness that a certain item of knowledge is publicly held (i.e., not only known to many, but *commonly known that it is known to many*) makes collective thought and action possible. Such knowledge gives individuals their awareness of collective strength (or weakness), and a feeling of social identification or alienation. (pp. 139–140)

The media have the ability to make publics by making certain information available that shapes "collective thought and action quickly, continuously, and pervasively across previous boundaries of time, space, and culture" (p. 140). Thus Gerbner is not interested in particular messages but broad patterns across media messages. Also he is not interested in individual interpretations of receivers but instead the beliefs that are shared in the public.

Gerbner explains that the media exert their influence through attention (by focusing attention of the public on certain things through the presence and frequency of certain message elements), emphasis (by the way media messages establish context for priorities and relevance), tendency (by the way media messages present the context of certain things that leads to meaning), and structure (by the way the media show relationships among things).

In the late 1970s, cultivation theory added the constructs of mainstreaming and resonance to extend its explanation of media influence. *Mainstreaming* was defined as the lack of a cultivation effect among heavy viewers of television. It was reasoned that heavy viewers are also strongly influenced by the mainstream of messages in a culture. This is a kind of regression to the mean effect, in which heavy viewers lose their divergent views and are pulled back into the mainstream of a culture. *Resonance* refers to the combined influence of TV acting along with real-world factors particular to an individual to provide a double dose of a message. For example, people who live in high-crime neighborhoods and watch a lot of TV get a double dose of the message that the world is a mean and violent place.

Beliefs of the Public

Many of the beliefs documented by the research studies have already been reported in Chapter 8 on individual beliefs. Those are concerned mainly with cultivated beliefs as well as agenda-setting beliefs. But there are a few other beliefs worth noting here. One set of beliefs concerns beliefs about institutions (Fan et al., 2001; Moy et al., 1999). Another concern has been about public beliefs about the acceptability of the government to use force. For example, Aday (2010) conducted a study to examine how media coverage of the Second Gulf War shaped public beliefs about use of force. The study found that contrary to conventional wisdom, media exerted less influence on public opinion when they report negative or controversial news than when they reflect elite consensus and/or patriotic fervor.

Producers of entertainment programs often present a certain belief continually over time, and audiences acquire this belief. For example, daytime talk shows continually focus on family problems in a way to evoke sympathy among viewers for the people with problems and a desire to want to help them. Researchers have found that people who are heavy viewers of these shows believe there is greater public support for governmental involvement in family problems (Glynn et al., 2007).

It is important to note that many public beliefs are likely to be faulty. In his book, *Why People Believe Weird things: Pseudoscience, Superstition, and Other Confusions of Our Time* (2nd edition), Shermer (2002) provides a long list of public beliefs that have no basis in scientific fact. For example, he points out that in a recent Gallup poll, 22% of Americans believed that aliens have landed on Earth, 35% believed in ghosts, 46% believed in extrasensory perception, 52% of Americans believed in astrology, and 41% believed that dinosaurs and humans existed simultaneously. He argues that even though we live in a scientific age, and there is a lot of accurate information being presented by the media, there is also a lot of inaccurate information. This inaccurate information leads people to believe in things that have no scientific evidence of existence.

PUBLIC ATTITUDES AND OPINION

Public opinion is the aggregate's attitude about something. The media can influence public opinion in three ways. One way the media can influence public opinion is to present a particular attitude repeatedly across many different sources of messages so that many people acquire the same attitude. This is the case with widely advertised products and political candidates (Russomanno & Everett, 1995). Also, there are public relations groups that conduct media campaigns to get the public to acquire positive attitudes about their causes, such as race relations (Domke, 2000) and the National Organization for Women (Barker-Plummer, 2002).

When people think a certain attitude is held by everyone else in society, they will be likely to accept that attitude as their own (Bennett, 1990; Herman & Chomsky, 1988). Because public opinion polling is now so common and the results of such polls so widely available, it is easy for people to find out the issues for which the public opinion is split and for which there is a consensus.

Public opinion about institutions is influenced by messages in the media. For example, television news viewing is positively related to perceptions of the news media and public schools, and newspaper reading was associated with favorable evaluations of the criminal court system and schools (Moy et al., 1999). Also, Johnston and Bartels (2010) found that sensationalist media exposure from newspapers, radio talk shows, and television news reduces support for American courts, both federal and state.

The media also influence public opinion by shaping public standards that the public then uses to make its evaluations on issues. Through repeated coverage, the media give status to the ideas, institutions, and people they portray (Simonson, 1999). This status shapes public standards for which ideas, institutions, and people are interesting and important. For example, there is evidence that over time media messages have eroded social trust (Cappella, 2002; Putnam, 2000), so people are more skeptical; this alters their standards about the value of society and the importance of them participating in it.

PUBLIC AFFECT

This area has attracted less research than other areas, but it has still generated some interesting findings. The media have been found to influence the public feelings about social trust (Cappella, 2002; Putnam, 2000) and public confidence (Simonson, 1999). When the media are critical of government policies, the public comes to feel distrust and even anger about the government and its policies.

Arguably the most widespread emotion engendered by the media is fear. News stories focus on crime and violence around the world and in our own neighborhoods. Fictional programs on television reinforce this feeling that the world is a mean and dangerous place. Cultivation research consistently shows that the public expresses a fear of crime that is higher than warranted (Gerbner et al., 1980; Lowry et al., 2003; Romer et al., 2003).

The news also frequently scares us about the economy, with stories about companies going bankrupt, unemployment increasing, the value of the dollar decreasing, and unsafe products in our stores. News focuses on threats to our health; many foods are depicted as dangerous, as are many substances in our everyday environments. It is no wonder that the public is fearful of its financial and physical health.

Another emotion frequently triggered in the public by the media is anger. The media frequently show people behaving badly in both nonfictional and fictional programming. Often these behaviors offend people and their moral codes. There are times when the public even experiences a moral panic (Chiricos, 1996).

PUBLIC BEHAVIOR

When the media present political information, political discussions about campaign events are triggered (Hardy & Scheufele, 2009). Also, the Internet has been found to trigger political discussion and civic messaging (Shah et al., 2005). However, when the media ignore an issue or event, this has the opposite effect of triggering silence. To explain this phenomenon, Noelle-Neumann (1984) created the spiral of silence theory after observing patterns of news coverage in Western Europe. In her theory, she explains that when the media avoid covering an issue, people typically will not express their beliefs on that issue even if those beliefs are very important to them. They will remain

Source: ©iStockphoto.com/LilliDay

silent, thinking that they are in the minority, and they refrain from expressing their beliefs for fear of being ostracized. Then silence begets more silence, and the belief that the issue is not important gets reinforced over time.

Over the past several decades there has been a growing concern about how the media might be altering public behavior in the areas of civic participation and social engagement. Social critics have argued that with so many media messages so easily available, people spend more and more time with the media and less time participating in society. Also, people watch reports of social problems more, but less actively participate in trying to evoke solutions. These critics argue that people are more isolated and this harms society. This idea of civic participation involves the public volunteering time and money for worthy causes and especially the idea of participating in the political process, which is considered central to a democratic citizenry.

In contrast, other scholars have observed a dramatic increase in social engagement due to the newer media that allow e-mailing, instant messages, calling from anywhere with mobile phones, and continual texting. They say that people are linked together in more and larger social networks than ever before. Let's examine what the research says.

Source: ©iStockphoto.com/apomares

Civic Participation

About a decade ago, Robert Putnam (2000) wrote a widely read book entitled *Bowling Alone* in which he argued that for since the 1970s in America there has been a decline in political and civic participation. He cites falling voter turnout, especially among the younger generation. However, other scholars have challenged Putnam's observations as too general. They argue that public participation in certain forms of civic activities has been decreasing while other forms are increasing. They also argue that certain subgroups of the public have increased their participation while other groups have decreased their participation. For example, a race-based explanation was offered by Beaudoin (2009), who argued that people of different races view civic participation in different ways. In a research study, he found a racial difference in which the association between newspaper exposure and social capital was more positive for Whites than Latinos. Also, the association between TV national news exposure and social capital was found to be less positive for Whites than Blacks. Thus Whites who had high exposure to newspaper messages were more likely to be high in civic participation, whereas among Blacks civic participation was more related to exposure to TV national news.

Another example of differences was found by Pasek, Kenski, Romer, and Jamieson (2006), who examined the role of the media in young people's disengagement from politics. In a nationally representative telephone survey (N = 1,501), young people (ages 14 to 22) reported their habits for 12 different uses of media as well as awareness of current national politics and time spent in civic activities. Contrary to Putnam, Pasek et al. (2006) found that media use, whether information or entertainment oriented, facilitated civic engagement, whereas news media were especially effective in promoting political awareness. Although heavy use of media interferes with both political and civic engagement, the overall effect of media use is favorable.

Arguing that the public is composed of citizens who differ in terms of the rights they expect, Schudson (1998) sees the public as being composed of groups who participate in civic activities in order to monitor and ensure those rights. Schudson says that the key feature of public life is the assertion of rights by a diverse array of groups, each of which is very active but splintered. People are focused much more on personal issues than on the platforms of political parties, so they are less likely to join and participate in traditional political parties. But this does not mean they are any less politically concerned and active.

Motives for civic participation also must be considered. Kang and Gearhart (2010) conducted a Web-based study of citizens' use of city websites with civic engagement and found that surveillance, practical services, and direct democracy features functioned as important conditions for citizens' real-world civic engagement. Results indicated that citizens' use of practical services and direct democracy features of city websites were associated with citizens' civic involvement and political behaviors. The findings suggest that the relationships between citizens' use of city websites and civic engagement differ according to the purpose for which citizens use the sites.

Social Engagement

The research has generally shown that the newer media, especially the Internet, have increased social engagement in the public. For example, Hampton and colleagues (2010) conducted a study to explore the role of urban public spaces and wireless Internet use on social engagement. They observed public behavior in seven parks, plazas, and markets in four North American cities. They found that Internet use within public spaces afforded interactions with existing acquaintances that were more diverse than those associated with mobile phone use. They concluded that online activities in public spaces contribute to broader participation in the public sphere.

The success of online communities depends heavily on economic resources. For example, Becker et al. (2010) analyzed what drives community adoption of the Internet and how direct and indirect financial incentives influence user participation and found that network size significantly affects adoption in newly established communities. They found that offering users the chance to save money had a strong influence on the intention to adopt. Also, the chance to earn money helped increase the network's size without altering user motivation through crowding-out effects. It is interesting to note that the presence of direct financial incentives attracts new users, but it does not increase usage.

Prosocial and Antisocial Behaviors

An important concern is whether the media shape public behavior in a prosocial or antisocial direction. The research shows examples of both. As for prosocial behavior, Simon (1997) examined the relationship between the media's coverage of natural disasters and the public's response. In an aggregate analysis, he found that the amount of U.S. network news coverage of earthquakes was associated with donations by private U.S. citizens.

In the research literature on public behavior, however, there are more examples of antisocial than of prosocial behaviors. One popular area of research has been concerned with violence, aggression, and suicide. For example, Centerwall (1989) looked at changes in rates of violence in the United States, Canada, and South Africa, where television broadcasting was prohibited before 1975. In all three countries, the homicide rates were flat until 10–15 years *after* the introduction of television; then they doubled. Centerwall says that television viewing is linked to about half of all the homicides, rapes, assaults, and other violent crimes committed each year. He also broke the United States down into nine regions and found that homicide rates increased later in those areas where television was introduced later. Also, crime rates on larceny were found to increase with the introduction of television (Hennigan et al., 1982). These authors reasoned that television teaches people about an affluent world of easy-to-obtain material goods, and this leads many people to feel deprived and frustrated enough to steal.

Phillips and Hensley (1984) point out that after highly publicized suicide stories (such as that of Marilyn Monroe), suicides in this country increased significantly. Also, car accidents (drivers of single-car crashes) increased—indicating an increase in suicides. Highly publicized murder-suicides are associated with an increase in multiple-car passenger deaths but not single-car driver deaths. Murder-suicide stories were also found to be related to increases in the number of crashes of private planes. In all cases, the more publicity given to the story, the greater the rise in the number of violent deaths. After heavyweight championship prizefights, the number of U.S. homicides increased, with the person beaten in the fight matching the pattern (in age and race) with the victims of homicides. The researchers concluded that "taken together, the evidence of these studies strongly suggests that some media stories trigger imitative increases in fatal violence" (p. 104). More recently Fu, Chan, and Yip (2009) found influence of media representations of suicides on the subsequent increase of suicide rate.

SUMMARY

Macro-level effects focus our attention on broad patterns in a large aggregate, such as the public, over time. Theories and empirical research have both demonstrated that the media exert an influence on the public. This macro-level effect shows up with the public's knowledge, beliefs, attitudes and opinions, affect, and behaviors.

The media have been shown to raise the level of public knowledge on particular topics through public service campaigns as well as raise the general level of knowledge through the continual presentation of news messages across all media. The media repeatedly present certain kinds of information so that the majority of the public acquires a certain set of knowledge (such as about major ideas, political candidates, or advertised products). The media also alter and reinforce the public's beliefs through a long-term process of socialization. However, there is evidence that there are a significant number of faulty beliefs that the public has acquired over time. The media exert a continuing influence on the public opinion and attitudes as well as the public's mood. And the media exert a continuing influence on public behavior, particularly in the areas of civic participation and social engagement.

Review Questions

1. What is an aggregate, and how is research on aggregate units different from research on individuals?

2. Why is the effects literature on macro units smaller than the effects literature on individuals?

3. What is "information flow" and how is it relevant to public knowledge?

4. How is it possible that a knowledge gap can grow when there is so much information available to everyone so easily?

Further Thinking Questions

1. Think about what you know about public knowledge, that is, do you know in which areas public knowledge is strong and where it is weak?
   - On what topics would you expect the public to have a great deal of knowledge?
   - Are the important topics where you think the public is likely to have little knowledge?

2. Can you think of a public information campaign that had an effect on you?

3. What public beliefs do you think have been cultivated by the media?

4. Think about public opinions.
   - Can you think of any public attitudes that have consensus, that is, on which almost everyone agrees?
   - On which controversial topics do you think the public opinion is most split?

5. Think about the current public mood. Do you think it is more positive or negative now?

6. Think about your own civic participation and social interaction behaviors.
   - Do you think you are more civically active than the public in general (voting, going to rallies, volunteering your time and money, and so on)?
   - Do you think your social networks are as large as the typical person's?

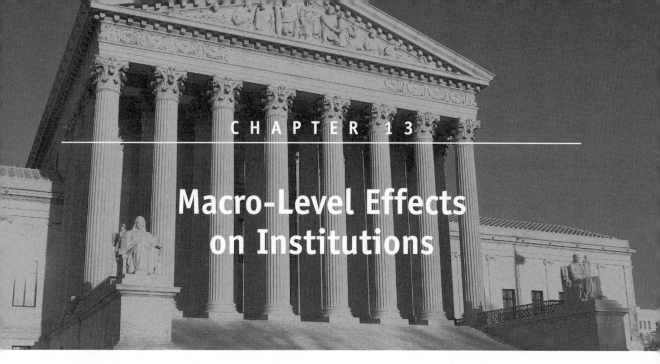

Source: Comstock/Comstock/Thinkstock

CHAPTER 13

Macro-Level Effects on Institutions

Macro-Level Effects on Institutions

$\mathbf{T}$his chapter continues our examination into how the mass media bring about effects in large social structures. Chapter 12 focused on the public. This chapter examines how the mass media affect institutions, specifically the political system, the economic system, family, and religion.

Again, it is important to remember that the individual-level effects and the macro-level effects share the same patterning over time. Regardless of the level of effect, it is useful to think in terms of baseline effects, fluctuation effects, and reinforcement effects. The only difference is the unit that is being influenced by the mass media. With macro-level effects, the unit is an aggregate or a nonhuman entity. Exhibit 13.1 presents research on mass media effects on institutions.

EFFECTS ON POLITICAL SYSTEM

The mass media have always had an influence in shaping the way politics have been conducted. Most of the scholarship on mass media influence on politics focuses on campaigning for the presidency, so the first two topics in this chapter of the book—selection of candidates and campaigns for office—deal mostly with the presidency, but the principles also apply to an increasing degree to other national and even state offices. After these two topics, we shift our attention to media influence on political action groups, the nature of the presidency itself, and Congress.

Selecting Candidates

The way political parties select candidates to run for office—especially the presidency—has profoundly changed because of the mass media. This change is seen with the rise of primary elections and the fall in importance of nominating conventions.

Exhibit 13.1 Further Reading on Mass Media Effects on Institutions

Effects on Political System

Selecting candidates to run for office (Dallek, 2004; Patterson, 1980, 1993; Stuckey & Curry, 2008)

Campaigning for office (Lang & Lang, 1983; Makovsky, 1999; Stuckey & Curry, 2008)

- Internet (Chadwick, 2006; Hofstetter & Gianos, 1997; Mayer & Cornfield, 2008; Shah, Cho, Eveland, & Kwak, 2005)
- Talk radio and comedy programs (Davis & Owen, 1998)

Campaign spending (Comstock, 1980, 1989; Getter, 2004; Lewis, 2000; Will, 1996)

News coverage of campaigns (Iyengar & Kinder, 1987; Jamieson & Waldman, 2003; Lowry & Shidler, 1995; Renner & Lynch, 2008)

Political action groups influencing media workers who create messages that affect the public at large (Andsager, 2000; Vinson, 2008)

- Race relations (Domke, 2000)
- National Organization for Women (Barker-Plummer, 2002)

The presidency (Crouch & Maltese, 2008)

Congress (Rozell & Semiatin, 2008)

Effects on Economic System

Affluent society and consumer culture (Ewen, 1976; Galbraith, 1976; Lasch, 1978)

Stock market (Cuellar-Fernández, Fuertes-Callen, & Lainez-Gadea, 2010; Scheufele, Haas, & Brosius, 2011)

One-dimensional man (Marcuse, 1964)

Globalization (Albarran, 2002; Golding, 1994; Hamelink, 1983; Schiller, 1979; Sinclair, 2004)

Effects on Family

Change in family structure (Douglas, 2003; Irvine, 1999; Perkins, 1996; "U.S. Divorce Statistics," 2002; Whitman, 1996)

Family interaction (Medrich, Roizen, Rubin, & Buckley, 1982; Pipher, 1996)

Effects on Religion

Media regarded as a threat to religion and change this institution in negative ways (Christians, 1997; Ellul, 1964; Emons, Scheepers, & Wester, 2009; Mumford, 1970; Ward, 2009)

- Shift focus (Horsfield, 1997)
- Focus on secular values (Fore, 1987; Horsfield, 1997; Schultze, 1991; Ward, 2009)

- Commodify religion (Fore, 1987; Horsfield, 1997; Schultze, 1991; Ward, 2009)
- Replace ritual (Goethals, 1997; Grimes, 2002; Hoover & Lundby, 1997)
- Replace religion (Fore, 1987; Gerbner & Gross, 1976; Hoover, 1988)

Media helping religion achieve its goals and adapt in society (Alexander, 1997; Association of American Publishers, 2003; Comstock, 1989; Fore, 1987; Hoover, 1988; Horsfield, 1984; Katz & Gurevitch, 1976; Kraus, 2009; Rothenbuhler, 1993; Ward, 2009; Watanabe, 1999)

Primary Elections. The mass media have largely replaced the party elites in the candidate selection process because of the advent of the primary system (Patterson, 1993). The nomination of presidential candidates used to be decided in party caucuses and conventions rather than in primary elections. Up until 1940, primary elections were held in only 13 states. By 1976, 30 states had primaries. Now almost every state has either a primary election or a caucus. This change was stimulated by national television coverage of primaries in states that had them; eventually voters in all states wanted more say in how political parties selected their candidates to run for president.

There are some key benefits to this increase in primary elections and caucuses. As voters, we are given a lot more information about candidates. With this additional information and the opportunity to vote in primaries, we are given more power to select the candidates who will run in the general elections. But there is also a downside: The information we are given about the candidates is usually very superficial and often negative. And the mainstream media set the agenda, thus channeling our interest to a few selected topics and away from all others.

Now, someone who wants to run for president must do well in the early primaries to get press coverage. Those candidates who do not do well are not put on the press's agenda, and the public rarely hears about them, while those candidates who do well get a great deal of media coverage. Thus the media exert a good deal of influence throughout the primaries by labeling certain candidates as front-runners and others as underdogs. Stuckey and Curry (2008) point out that the media give disproportionate coverage to early primaries, which is called *front-loading*. The media have unusual power in defining issues and front-runners in such saturated coverage. Thus media become kingmakers by choosing to feature certain candidates and hasten the departure from the race of other candidates whom the media do not feature or anoint as leaders in the "horse race."

The front-runner is the candidate who wins the very first primary. The press then creates expectations for candidates and the campaign outcome. Throughout the campaign, the press reports polls to set up these expectations about who is winning and by how much. When something different than the expected occurs, it is deemed newsworthy.

Media coverage fluctuates with the performance of the candidates in the preceding contest. The most attention generally goes to the candidate who was the winner or who has emerged surprisingly as the challenger. Candidates who falter become progressively less able to compete because they begin slipping off the media's agenda (Patterson, 1980). For example, before the 2004 primary races, Howard Dean had worked for more than a year to put together a grassroots political organization through the Internet. When the first voter test

Source: "Harrison & Tyler" campaign emblem/ Library of Congress

rolled around—the Iowa caucuses—Massachusetts Senator John F. Kerry unexpectedly came in first in a crowded seven-person field of Democratic candidates. Kerry won with about 125,000 votes or about 22 % of Iowa's Democratic voters (Dallek, 2004). This first caucus was seen as so important that candidates who did not finish well began dropping out, and Howard Dean's "loss" (he still came in second in a field of seven candidates) was something he could not shake. He went on the next week to finish second to Kerry in the New Hampshire primary and again was perceived as a loser. Although he continued to get votes and amass delegates over the course of the next month of primaries, he could not shake his loser image, and he eventually withdrew from the race, leaving Kerry virtually unopposed.

Nominating Conventions. The media have changed the presidential nominating conventions of political parties by focusing so much of the public's attention on them. The historical purpose of these conventions was for loyal party members to gather at a national meeting to exercise their power and to cut deals about party platforms and candidates. The result of all this negotiation was to select a candidate to represent the party in the presidential election. Now, the leading candidate is known well in advance of the "nominating" convention, so those meetings have lost their value as working conventions at which delegates choose their candidates; instead, nominating conventions have been transformed into advertising platforms for the parties. Thus, the delegates are instructed to portray a favorable impression of the party to the public. This means showing harmony and togetherness rather than debating important issues. From the rise of television in the 1950s, the major television networks used to cover both the Democratic and Republican nominating conventions from "gavel to gavel" until the 1990s, when they began cutting back coverage; by 2004, most mass media covered only the major speeches.

Campaigning for Office

Since the founding of the United States, candidates for political office have always relied for publicity on coverage of their campaigns in newspapers and magazines, and they have bought ads in these media to get their messages out to the electorate and to create images for themselves. For example, when William Henry Harrison ran for president in 1840, he wanted to change his image so he would appeal more to the voters who were common people who distrusted the rich. He was afraid of being perceived as an aristocrat because he was the wealthy son of a governor and the owner of a palatial Georgian mansion on a 2,000-acre estate worked by tenant farmers. Instead, he wanted to be perceived as a farmer and backwoodsman to increase his appeal to the electorate. In his newspaper ads, he was shown wearing a coonskin cap and drinking cider by a log cabin. This image was everywhere during the campaign.

About the same time, Daniel Webster created the first political pseudo-event for the press. He camped out with Green Mountain boys in the woods and challenged to a fistfight anyone who called him an aristocrat.

Harrison won his election, but Webster lost his. Using the media does not guarantee victory. But not using the media can guarantee defeat. Candidates for public office, from city council member to president of the United States, must establish name recognition among the electorate, and along with recognized names, they must instill positive images. The media are the channels that make it possible for candidates to achieve these goals quickly and to many people.

When radio came along, politicians used it to reach more of the electorate. In the 1930s, Thomas Dewey, a crusading New York City district attorney, ran for governor. On the final day of the campaign, he was on radio from 6 a.m. until midnight, inviting people to phone in and ask him questions. Most of the calls were from one of his assistants who spent the day in a pay phone booth with a pile of coins.

When television came along in the 1950s, politics began to change dramatically. Since that time, people who want to run for office have been developing much more direct access to the public; thus, there has been a gradual and continual erosion of the amount of influence the political parties are able to exert. This shift in power away from political parties to the public is seen in the areas of primary elections, nominating conventions, campaign staffs, campaign spending, rise of political action committees, content of advertising, news coverage, and the use of new media and vehicles. Clearly the use of the mass media has shaped the behaviors of political candidates (Lang & Lang, 1983).

Over time, the media have become more powerful in political campaigns, and political parties have become less powerful. Stuckey and Curry (2008) said

> The weakening of the political parties as organizing entities has contributed to the rise of candidate-centered campaigns. Candidate-centered campaigns have contributed to the fragmentation and lack of coherence that characterizes our national politics, and that makes polities more difficult for citizens to assimilate and understand. The more confusing politics becomes, the more necessary are the media as interpreters. The cycle, once established, becomes self-reinforcing. (p. 179)

Campaign Staffs. The increase in television involvement in political campaigns has altered the makeup of campaign staffs. The most important person in a campaign used to be the campaign manager, who had extensive contacts among party workers so he or she could cash in favors and get lots of members active in setting up rallies, passing out bumper stickers, and going door to door to hand out party literature. Now the most valued people in the campaign are the public opinion polling expert and the media consultant.

The polling expert finds out what the public wants in a "leader"—that is, how the person should look, how the person should act, and what stands the person should take on important issues. The media consultant then crafts ads and pseudo-events for the media to make the candidate appear similar to that ideal image.

Some U.S. media experts are so successful that they are being hired to influence elections in other countries. For example, both major political parties in Israel hired expensive American consultants to win their 1999 election of prime minister (Makovsky, 1999).

Campaign Spending. Television's increasing importance in political campaigns has resulted in great increases in campaign spending. In the early days of television, expenditures on the media for political advertising increased 600% (adjusted for inflation) between 1952 and 1974 (Comstock, 1980). By 1972, spending was greatly increased in the presidential election, with George McGovern spending $30 million and Richard Nixon $60 million. The reason for the increase was a major shift in the way the campaigns allocated their money. For example, in 1956, 85% of presidential campaign expenditures was spent on setting up rallies for in-person speeches by the candidates. Three presidential elections later, with total expenditures four times greater, more than half the money was spent on television ads (Comstock, 1989). And the television budget continued to increase dramatically, resulting in smaller budgets for field operations such as setting up rallies, local campaign offices, buttons, and bumper stickers.

Shortly after the 1972 presidential election, in which the candidates spent $90 million, Congress passed some campaign reform legislation that placed strict limits and regulations on spending. In the 1976 presidential election, both candidates spent about $9 million.

However, despite the limits imposed by Congress, the money required to run for president has increased dramatically, and a good deal of it is being spent very early in the campaigns. Candidates must spend huge amounts of money early to get name recognition. For example, in 1984, Democratic front-runner Walter Mondale spent more than $30 million to win a single primary. His two challengers (Henry "Scoop" Jackson and Gary Hart) spent a total of more than $21 million in a losing effort—that is, more than $55 million spent by Democratic candidates in a single state! Ronald Reagan, who was an incumbent president at the time, ran unopposed in the Republican primaries and spent $18 million. When the primary campaigns were over, Mondale was nominated as the Democratic candidate and Reagan as the Republican candidate. During the general election that fall, the two presidential candidates were each allowed to spent $40 million, which was the limit then imposed by Congress. But political action committees (PACs), which were not regulated, could raise as much as possible and spend it any way they wanted. The wealthy right-wing National Conservative Political Action Committee spent $14 million to campaign for Reagan.

Politics has become a very big money game. In the 1996 presidential election, more than $152 million of federally approved funds were spent—this is the money raised and spent by the presidential candidates according to limits and procedures imposed by the Federal Election Commission. Also, more than $477 million of federally approved funds were spent on congressional races. In addition to federally approved spending, political action groups can raise their own money and spend it on their own public relations campaigns to support a candidate or to run negative ads against his or her opponents. In 1996, PACs spent $430 million for these campaigns. Thus, more than $1 billion was spent in one year's election campaigns for president and Congress (U.S. Bureau of the Census, 2000). In the 2000 elections for federal offices, media companies donated more than $75 million to candidates (Lewis, 2000).

When people say that "too much" is spent on political advertising, it is not clear what they mean by the "correct" amount. This is the point made by the columnist George Will (1996), who pointed out that the annual sum spent on political campaigning is less than that spent on yogurt. Also, when you take a two-year period and include all the money spent by all candidates campaigning for state and federal offices, it equals the same amount as that spent by the nation's two largest commercial advertisers: Proctor & Gamble and Philip Morris. This $700 million works out to be a combined total across all elections of $1.75 per eligible voter per year.

The 2004 presidential election set records for both spending and for getting around campaign financing laws. During this campaign, about $1 billion was contributed from a total of about 1.23 million contributors, which was more than double the 500,000 people who contributed money to political parties during the 2000 presidential campaigns. Also, campaign regulations increased the allowable donation from $1,000 to $2,000 per person. The $1 billion does not include money spent on the 2004 presidential campaign by PACs and state political parties (Getter, 2004).

News Coverage of Campaigns. Many scholars have criticized the way the press has covered political campaigns, arguing that the characteristics of this coverage have done great harm to the political process. These critics argue that the press focus on superficial aspects rather than fundamental issues, use a horse-race structure for their coverage, and focus on the negative over the positive.

Jamieson and Waldman (2003) published a book called *The Press Effect* in which they argued that the press fail to provide in-depth coverage during political campaigns. That is, journalists rarely do their own research to check the facts and claims of candidates; instead the press simply reports what the candidates say. Part of this problem is that campaigns that are played out in the media are typically dominated by sound bites—short quotes with catchy phrases. Sound bites are so short that they do not give the candidate an opportunity to convey his or her positions with any sophistication or depth. The sound bite has gotten so short that it appears that it cannot shrink any more. Lowry and Shidler (1995) report that in the 1992 presidential campaign, the size of the sound bites stopped shrinking. In 1968, the average sound bite was 43.1 seconds, and it decreased to about 9 to 10 seconds in 1988. In this study, the average sound bite for candidates was 9.4 seconds, and the average for noncandidates was 7.3 seconds. Thus, a 20-year trend seemed to have bottomed out.

Media can directly affect how people process information about political events, and this *priming effect* influences behavior (Iyengar & Kinder, 1987). By focusing on certain issues and ignoring others, the media set the agenda for the campaign. The agenda alters the public's priorities. The high-priority issues then are what the public focuses on when examining the stance of candidates. Thus, if a candidate is strong on many issues and weak on one, and the press makes that one issue a priority, then the public will think that issue to be very important and therefore rate that candidate low.

"The news media also do a fairly poor job when it comes to reporting on polls" (Renner & Lynch, 2008, p. 147). They say that the media do not give the public enough information to be able to evaluate the quality of the polls or their results. Instead, the media report the results of polls using a horse-race perspective to simply tell voters who is ahead and by how much.

New Media and Vehicles. The way political campaigns are conducted has certainly changed over the past 50 years, with the rise of the importance of television as a mass medium. These changes have affected how people participate in the political system (Hofstetter & Gianos, 1997; Shah, Cho, Eveland, & Kwak, 2005).

Internet websites are being used extensively by candidates for all kinds of political offices. Candidates can post information and interact with voters in chat rooms. Also, some of the "older" media are being used in new ways. For example, talk radio is an important outlet for candidates, as are television newsmagazines, electronic town meetings, and MTV (Davis & Owen, 1998). Even entertainment programs such as late-night talk shows (*David Letterman* and *The Tonight Show*) and Comedy Central are being used by candidates to get more exposure. And the Internet has become a source of political campaigning, from raising money to getting particular messages out to particular niches of the electorate. Chadwick (2006) calls this "e-democracy." People who are more strongly involved in political talk radio are also more involved in political and social activities. This relationship holds with controls for demographics (Hofstetter & Gianos, 1997).

Mayer and Cornfield (2008) argue that the Internet has influenced politics positively in four ways: (a) creativity, by allowing a wide variety of people to create content on blogs and the like; (b) interactivity, by letting people participate in conversations continually with many other people; (c) independence, such that people depend less on government and the press for information; and (d) depth, by which people can get more detail on issues and get past superficial media coverage. They say the Internet has also influenced politics negatively in five ways: (a) inequality: the knowledge gap grows; (b) filterlessness: no editors or others to screen good from bad information; (c) blurring: it's harder to determine who is a journalist and who is not; (d) constant surveillance: there is no privacy now that everyone has a cell phone and camera; and (e) cocooning: social isolation and protecting oneself from the flood of information.

Political Action Committees

Political action committees are groups of people who focus on one political issue, then use the media to raise money for their cause and awareness of the importance of their issue to the public. These groups have been very successful and are now a fixture of any political campaign. They force candidates to declare their positions on important issues, then support only those candidates who agree with them. This support is crucial for many candidates, who must spend great sums of money to get name recognition and votes. PACs can produce and pay for media placement of their own ads that support particular candidates, and the money the PACs spend on these activities does not count against federally established limits on campaign financing.

Political action groups influence media workers who create messages that affect the public at large (Andsager, 2000). This has been found by researchers to be the case with the National Organization for Women, which has influenced the way the public thinks and votes about women's issues (Barker-Plummer, 2002). Political action groups have also been influential in shaping issues on race relations and influencing positions of political parties and candidates (Domke, 2000).

By the 1990s, the major political parties began creating and funding their own advocacy groups because, unlike political parties, those groups could spend as much money as they wanted (Vinson, 2008). Thus political parties have redefined their place in the political system by taking advantage of opportunities made possible through the media.

The Presidency

The presidency has changed because of media influence. As Crouch and Maltese (2008) point out, "The president of the United States is the focal point of most political media coverage coming out of Washington, D.C." (p. 19). This puts all of the president's actions under a microscope and therefore puts the candidate under an enormous amount of pressure to act quickly and to explain his or her actions to the American people. Crouch and Maltese say that the White House press corps "demand more information from the president than in the past because there is an increased interest in updated information" (p. 20); many of the news outlets now have a 24-hour news cycle that never stops and continually needs new information to keep the public interested. So the press concentrates on providing new facts but is less able to provide in-depth reporting or to interpret what events mean. This opens the door for commentators who are neither balanced nor objective.

The media have also given the president the opportunity to reach the public directly rather than having his or her message filtered through journalists or commentators. This has served to personalize the presidency and give the public more of a sense of the person who is president.

Congress

Congress as a political institution has been affected by the mass media. Rozell and Semiatin (2008) say

> Fragmentation of the media has decreased incentives for collegiality and disintegrated the structure of norms that characterized an era of good feelings in Congress from the 1940s through the 1960s. Fragmentation has increased the value of personality and decreased the value of institutional responsibility, particularly in the House, where collegiality, which began to wane in the 1970s, has crumbled today. (p. 55)

This fragmentation has made members of Congress less willing to take risks, because any critic can damage their reputations on the Internet. The media have also increased the agenda-setting effect, which puts Congress in more of a responsive than a leadership role.

EFFECTS ON ECONOMIC SYSTEM

Private and Public Goods

The media have an influence on the economic system, not just by influencing public knowledge, public opinion, and public discourse, but also by influencing public values for resources and behaviors of exchange. Almost all of the scholarship that examines the mass media's influence on the economic institution is critical of the practices of the mass media. For example, Galbraith (1976) argued that the mass media through its emphasis on advertising as an essential source of revenue has created a situation in which ad messages pressure people to spend their resources on private goods rather than public goods. He feels that this balance has created an affluent society that benefits those people who have enough money to buy many of these private goods but harms society at large. As an example, if we took all the money that households spend on their personal automobiles, insurance, upkeep, gas, and the like and invested that money in public transportation, we would need far fewer roads, have fewer traffic accidents, and have a much less negative impact on the environment. But instead we use the mass media to advertise hundreds of kinds of automobiles for private consumption, and the resources are consumed much more by individuals than by the public.

This leads to a consumer culture (Ewen, 1976) or even to a culture of narcissism (Lasch, 1978). The consumer culture is one in which the strongest values are shaped and reinforced by advertisers and businesses that market products. Problems are delineated in terms of products that can solve them. And because most of the problems presented by the media are focused on personal appearance and fulfillment, we are trained over time to be focused primarily on ourselves—and superficial aspects of ourselves. Thus we are conditioned to be narcissistic.

Stock Market

The media present a great deal of information about businesses and speculations about the value of their stocks. This raises the question about whether all these media messages are having an effect on the stock market. The research provides mixed results as an answer to this question. For example, one study found that media messages can influence the price of a company's stock both upward and downward (Cuellar-Fernández et al., 2010). This study explored the influence of Web-based corporate reporting on investors' valuation of companies in the information and communications technology industry. This study compiled 8,111 news items issued in the "Press Releases" tab of the firms' websites between January 2003 and April 2005 and analyzed what type of news items affected stock returns. The results show a positive price reaction to news regarding new customers, completion of acquisitions, strategic long-term decisions, and nontechnological alliances. In contrast, the results show a negative price reaction to news regarding the launch of new or upgraded products (Cuellar-Fernández et al, 2010).

Another study looked at the influence of news reports on stock prices and trading volumes. Scheufele, Haas, and Brosius (2011) conducted a content analysis of news reports

Source: ©iStockphoto.com/Nikada

about the selected companies, and a secondary analysis of the daily changes in closing prices and the trading volumes of these companies were combined in a time-series design. The results suggest that media coverage reflects rather than shapes the development at stock exchanges from a short-term perspective (two months). There were almost no hints for a widespread media effect, that is, an impact on so many investors that it will result in a measurable change in stock prices or trading volumes.

Globalization

Media economist Alan Albarran (2002) regards globalization as one of the most important economic trends in recent years. He explains that markets for media messages have been saturated in the United States, so for American media companies to open up even more revenue streams and to increase the flow of income even more, they need to market their messages in other countries.

Globalization is an economic and political trend that is in full swing and is supported by the mass media in several ways. First, the mass media through advertising create awareness and a demand for products produced by global corporations. For many companies, markets are global, not limited to national boundaries. Second, media companies themselves are global. It is not just U.S. companies exerting influence in other countries. Sony, Bertelsmann, and News Corporation, which are based in countries other than the United States, have significant markets throughout the world (Sinclair, 2004). They are so large and powerful that they are able to bring about the removal of regulations that slow down their businesses in various countries.

It has been argued that this globalization leads to cultural homogenization (Sinclair, 2004), which is an extension of the cultural imperialism argument of the twentieth century (Hamelink, 1983; Schiller, 1979). Critics claim that powerful countries such as the United States were exporting their way of life through economic institutions and the mass media. This tended to cause some countries to forsake their indigenous culture and customs and to become Americanized (Schiller, 1969). Now the globalization argument is that the culture being promulgated is not from any one country or culture; rather it is an economically based culture of materialism and consumption that is created and fostered by media stories and advertising (Golding, 1994). Other scholars argue that the mass media present so many alternative cultures that people are able to assert unique identities at the local level and need not conform to a global culture (Hall, 1992).

Sinclair (2004) argued that "the 19th century produced a world dominated by nation-states, the 20th century saw the advent of international institutions set up to coordinate the common interest of national governments on a world scale" (p. 68). Today, media conglomerates are transnational and becoming global. They are more powerful economically than many countries, and culturally they are extremely powerful because they create a global culture of products and ideas that significantly reduce the importance of individual nations.

EFFECTS ON FAMILY

Family Structure

In the span of just one generation, the makeup of the American family has changed radically. The number of traditional two-parent families has shrunk, eclipsed by childless couples, single parents, and people living alone (Perkins, 1996). From the early 1970s to 1998, the percentage of American households made up of married couples with children dropped from 45% to 26%. The percentage of married adults has dropped from 75% of all adults in 1972 to 59% in 2002 (U.S. divorce statistics, 2002). Also, the percentage of children living with single parents went from 4.7% in 1972 to 18.2% in 1998 (Irvine, 1999).

Are the mass media responsible for these changes in the American family? Some scholars say yes, and they argue that changes in the institution of family in the American culture parallel themes in the way the family has been portrayed in the media. For example, Douglas (2003) in his book *Television Families: Is Something Wrong in Suburbia?* traces changes in American families along with changes in families depicted in television programs from the 1940s to the early 2000s. While he acknowledges that real families are different in many ways from television families, he demonstrates that the arc of change in the two are similar. Both showed upward mobility in the 1940s and 1950s. Then, later, both showed a breakdown of the nuclear family, with divorce and blended families more common.

One argument for the cause in the decline of the traditional family is that the rates of divorce are very high in the United States, and they have been climbing since television first penetrated our culture. In 1960, 16% of first marriages ended in divorce, and by 1996, the figure had climbed to 40% (Whitman, 1996). Critics claim that the rise of the divorce rate and the portrayals of broken families on television is not a coincidence; they claim that the television portrayals have socialized people to believe that divorce and having children out of wedlock are acceptable. Critics point out that television too frequently portrays divorce, single-parent households, and alternative lifestyles. These portrayals, presented over many different kinds of shows and over many years, tend to be internalized by viewers. Over time, people become dissatisfied with their own marriages and seek adventure with other partners. Also, popular television series, such as *Married with Children,* portray married life in a negative manner, thus giving young people the idea that marriage is an unattractive lifestyle.

Family Interaction

Television, as well as other media, has the potential to bring the family together to share a common experience. Families can build a bonding ritual around television by agreeing to watch a particular movie or series and then spending time together talking about it after the exposure. Up until the 1970s, many households had only one television, and viewing was a common family activity (Medrich, Roizen, Rubin, & Buckley, 1982).

Now, however, patterns of media use within a family usually indicate that media exposure is an individual rather than a group activity. For example, more than two thirds of all American households have more than one television set, so individual viewing is possible in most homes. Also, with 65% of households having cable and the average cable service providing more than 100 channels, individual viewing is desirable so that family members do not have to compete for the television. Each family member can watch what he or she wants by viewing a separate TV in a separate room.

Even when family members view television together, there is less interaction than if the televisions were off and the family members had to entertain one another. For example, more than one third of families have TV on during meals, and this reduces the conversation among family members.

When it comes to the media, parents have changed their roles over the years. For example, Pipher (1996) points out, "Good parents used to introduce their children into the broader culture; now they try to protect their children from the broader culture. Good parents used to instill the values of the broader culture; now they try to teach their children values very different from the ones the world at large teaches" (p. 11).

Also, parents have reduced the time they spend with their children: 40% less time from the 1950s to the 1990s (Pipher, 1996). Pipher argues, "Rapidly our technology is creating a new kind of human being, one who is plugged into machines instead of relationships, one who lives in a virtual reality rather than a family" (p. 92). "When people communicate by e-mail and fax, the nature of human interaction changes" (p. 88). The conveniences of technology serve to cut us off from face-to-face interaction with others.

Even if we accept the argument that television has influenced the trend toward the breakdown of the traditional family, we must realize that there are also other influences, such as economic ones. For example, in the twenty-first century it takes more money to support a family than in the 1950s. The median household income is now just over $30,000. Both adults are likely to work, and this makes it harder for them to have children and raise them at home. The percentage of women in the labor force has been steadily climbing—in 2011, about 57% of all women 18 years old and older work (U.S. Census Bureau, 2011a).

Another reason that family structure and family interaction have changed is that careers have become more important to many people than their families. Wage earners work longer hours, and this takes them away from the home for a higher proportion of their waking hours. There are strong stressors of time, money, and lifestyle, which make people regard the home as a place to recover from the workplace, not a place where they have high energy. No longer is family of paramount importance in most people's lives (Pipher, 1996).

Clearly, family structures and interaction patterns have been changing over the past five decades. There are many reasons for this. The rise of television use was a key element for decades, but not the only one, in this change. The additional elements of economic demands, the rise in the importance of careers, and changes in lifestyle preferences have all contributed to change in the institution of family. Now with the newer mobile communication technologies, the shared media experience among family members is even more rare.

EFFECTS ON RELIGION

Religion is an important institution in America. Surveys of the U.S. population typically find that about 80% of Americans consider themselves religious and believe in life after death, although only 57% attend a church or synagogue on a regular basis. About two thirds of generation known as the baby boomers—the 76.5 million people who were born between 1946 and 1964—dropped out of organized religion during the 1980s, although some of them were starting to return by the end of that decade (Woodward, 1990). By 2008, 65% of the U.S. adult population identified with a particular religious group (U.S. Census Bureau, 2011b).

Are the mass media a negative force on religion or a positive opportunity? This is a major question that has triggered considerable debate.

Media as a Threat to Religion

For centuries, Western religions have been skeptical and even fearful of technology.

Christianity was an obstacle to technological growth during the Protestant Reformation in the 1600s because technology was regarded as a threat to the natural order that had existed for millennia and as a threat to the traditional value system (Ellul, 1964). Mumford (1970) extended this idea to argue that technology had replaced religion as the arbiter of truth, introduced secular forms of knowledge, and demystified religious symbols.

With the rise of the mass media as technologies of information dissemination, Western religions have had a skeptical and even fearful reaction to the mass media. What is it about the mass media that bothers critics so much when it comes to religion? There seem to be four major reasons.

The Media Shift Focus. One reason that critics are bothered by the rise of technology and the mass media as a threat to religion is that the media shift the population's focus away from spiritual issues and onto secular ones. Christians explain that mass media as technology has manufactured an "instrumentalist order of amoral means and technocratic efficiency, in opposition to the religious imagination" (Horsfield, 1997, p. 65). Thus the mass media continually remind the population of the secular world and how technology and science—rather than religion—provide powerful tools for making one's life better.

Horsfield (1997) goes so far as to say, "The formal institutions of religion in Western culture are all facing major reorganizational, economic, and authority changes, which are described at best as restructuring and at worst as decline" (pp. 167–168). He argues that the media are a reason for this change. He explains, "The movement of the early Christian church out of its parent Jewish culture into Greek culture, for example, was not just a simple process of organizational expansion, but was a movement from a largely oral context into a manuscript context" (p. 173). He continues:

> Developments in electronic media, linked with increasing worldwide affluence and the breaking down of national boundaries in trading arrangements and cultural product dissemination has tended to move social communications away

from an overarching concept of community good mediated through the broader desirability of commercial instrumentality. (p. 175)

This pattern of a reduction in commitment to religion has been found in other countries, such as Holland, where Emons, Scheepers, and Wester (2009) found a shift in the importance of religion both in Dutch culture and Dutch television over time. They analyzed a sample of 503 prime-time programs aired between 1980 and 2005, with a total number of 2,114 identified main characters and found a marked decrease in the proportion of main characters with identifiable religious orientations and the number of programs with religious minor characters over this period of time. The occurrence of religious themes in storylines in programs also had decreased. The researchers also reported that institutional religion had been playing a rapidly decreasing role in Dutch society. They concluded that longitudinal changes in the representation of religion in Dutch television drama seemed to precede changes in the role and perception of religion in Dutch society.

Related to the shift in focus is a shift in values. Fore (1987) details this concern by arguing that the television world emphasizes five themes that are at odds with the central values of religion:

1. Only the strong survive (Social Darwinism).

2. Power and decision making start at the center and move out (Washington, D.C., is the center of political power; New York the center of financial power; Hollywood the center of entertainment power).

3. Happiness consists of limitless material acquisition (consumption is inherently good and people are less important than are property, wealth, and power).

4. Progress is an inherent good (it is good to keep moving, but it is less important to have a goal).

5. There exists a free flow of information. He argues that the mass media divert a major portion of the world's interests, motivations, satisfactions, and energies away from a religious center.

The Media Commodify Religion. Critics argue that the business nature of the mass media has turned religion into a commercial commodity. Horsfield explains:

The competitive nature of the marketplace applies particularly in the dynamic of consumer commoditization, that commercial process whereby noncommercial human activities and services are appropriated, re-formed, packaged, and then sold as commercial products or services. With televangelism, the message of the church is secularized "turning Christ into another consumer product." (Horsfield, 1984, p. 123)

How has this commodification exerted a negative effect on the institution of religion? Fore (1987) argues that the new technological environment encourages the growth of religious concern that rejects or ignores organized religion. People spend more time with electronic devices than they do with people. With increasing channels and content options, people can pick only those things that reinforce already held beliefs. This puts the development of beliefs into the hands of individuals rather than the institution of religion. Thus, communication is treated more as a commodity to serve an individual's immediate needs rather than as a broad cultural phenomenon that brings us together into a large community where the needs of the community are more important than the needs of any individual.

Another example of the mass media pursuing business goals is that they have scrubbed religion of its denominational differences making it nondenominational and thus appealing to a larger group of people (Horsfield, 1984). And the drive to maximize the size of the audience has been getting stronger over time, especially since the 1996 Telecommunications Act, which eliminated national ownership limits and fundamentally liberalized local limits, has had a detrimental effect on religious programs on radio. Ward (2009) argues that before the Telecom Act, religious radio had a long history of economic viability, low turnover, and programming opportunities for independent syndicators of religious programs; this changed after the act. Ward explains that during the 1960s when radio lost its status as the dominant national mass medium, it shifted to a niche orientation and was willing to broadcast religious programming. But since the mid-1990s, ownership of radio stations has been consolidating, and there are now fewer religious radio stations and fewer stations providing religious programming. Ward extends this argument by pointing out that well-known national programs with popular speakers—and the money to afford the rates charged by large group-owned stations—have first claim on airtime because they are proven draws for listeners. Second-tier syndicators are cut off from the top markets, diminishing their ability to reach potential donors who can keep the programs on the air. Smaller media-buying and radio production agencies, which were willing to help lesser-known syndicators develop their programs, may lose their clients and exit the business. As preachers go dark, independent religious stations that often serve lower-tier markets may lose their chief source of revenue. Nor can struggling stations expect help. Thirty years ago, when the religious radio format was still emerging, top syndicators might purchase airtime to help keep stations afloat and preserve the viability of the format on a national scale. Today these syndicators withdraw from underperforming outlets.

The Media Replace Rituals. Another criticism is that the mass media are replacing one of religion's main functions, which is the providing of rituals. The mass media, especially television, are providing rituals that enhance and even replace religious rituals (Grimes, 2002). Television broadcasts religious events such as worship services, weddings, funerals, and the like. They elicit ritualized behaviors such as placing hands on TV or radio receiver to be healed. Goethals (1997) argues that the mass media provide rituals, much like religious rituals, that structure and give meaning to society. These rituals pattern time and space; they offer transcendence. So the media are giving society some things that religion has done in the past, thus explaining why there has been a breaking down of the importance of traditional religions in our society (Hoover & Lundby, 1997).

The Media Replace Religion. Some social critics, such as Hoover (1988), argue that the main effect of the electronic church has not been the changing of people's beliefs. Instead, the main effect of the electronic church has been the changing of the institution of religion in America. How has religious television done this? It has broken down denominational boundaries, thus bringing evangelicals and fundamentalists into the mainstream. And it has changed the way we see politics and religion—the electronic church has taken on a political prominence. In this section of the chapter, we examine how the mass media have influenced the institution of religion in two ways: by providing a substitute for attending religious services and by money.

Television is seen by some as the new American religion. For example, Hoover (1988) says

> Television is the new "cultural storyteller," an agent of norms and values as much as of news and information. Television fulfills this function very much in the way traditional storytellers did—by a process of dialectic, not didactic—where the stories evolve with the culture, retaining most, but not all, of their formal integrity by changing to suit its audiences and new contexts of expression. (p. 241)

Fore (1987) says that television is

> beginning to replace the institution that historically has performed the functions we have understood as religion. Television, rather than churches, is becoming the place where people find a worldview which reflects what to them is the ultimate value, and which justified their behavior and way of life. Television today, whether the viewer knows it or not, and whether the television industry itself knows it or not, is competing not merely for attention and dollars, but for our very souls. . . . Television is itself becoming a kind of religion, expressing the assumptions, values, and belief patterns of many people in our nation, and providing an alternative worldview to the old reality, and to the old religious view based on that reality. (pp. 24–25)

Some scholars think of television as becoming a dominant institution that has taken over some of the functions of religion (Gerbner & Gross, 1976). They say that television implicitly communicates values and interpretations of the world by presenting lessons about success, power, and dominance. By conveying status to certain people, television identifies those people much like priests who guide our thinking.

Media as a Tool for Religion

Many religious leaders have taken a positive view of the mass media, regarding them as tools to spread their messages to the population at large as well as to policy makers. They recognize that the mass media creatively use symbols and images, and by so doing they establish, maintain, and change collective representations, such as beliefs, myths, concepts, and categories (Rothenbuhler, 1993). The primary media to do this have been radio, books, television, and now the Internet.

Radio. Ward (2009) explains that religious leaders have used the mass media, especially radio, successfully for years. He explains that by the 1960s and 1970s, the religious radio format was on the rise. As religious programs came to be heard chiefly on religious stations, the emphasis for radio preachers shifted to "discipling" the already converted. Thus the now-familiar format of program-length radio sermons predominated. Many syndicators continue to believe that "preaching to the choir" is not incongruous with the mission of religious broadcasting in the United States. Radio ministries have never viewed themselves as a replacement for the local church but rather as a supplement. This view holds that programming can aid the church by helping to feed the flock during the week, linking arms with local pastors to train individual church members for the quiet work of making converts, one by one.

Seen in this way, the thrust of religious radio is strategic rather than numerical, with a goal of producing "quality" among evangelical believers rather than quantity. As such, media concentration may be skeptically regarded by those broadcasters who believe that consolidation tends to push programming toward a lower common denominator. Other religious broadcasters, however, have embraced consolidation as a positive development. The measure of success in religious radio, they say, is not in the number of stations or programmers but the number of listeners. Today's large religious radio networks have the resources to make their stations sound more professional, to research and target audience preferences, and to attract more listeners than Mom and Pop could. And with more listeners, they argue, more can be done to advance the mission of religious broadcasting. Perhaps, suggest advocates of consolidation, radio can even recapture its evangelistic function rather than preaching only to the choir.

Books. The Bible is still the all-time best-selling book. Sales continue to grow—up 50% over the past few years. And 91% of all Americans own an average of three versions. However, fewer people are spending time reading it, and there appears to be a problem with Bible illiteracy. More than half of Americans can't name even five of the Ten Commandments, and two thirds don't know the names of the four Gospels. Religious organizations are trying to jazz up the old book, and now there are more than 3,000 different editions designed to appeal to different readers. It is being promoted by celebrities such as M. C. Hammer, the rap artist, and Sinbad, the comedian. Newer versions of the bible include the *TouchPoint Bible,* which is organized by topics such as anger and self-control; the *Positive Thinking Bible,* by Norman Vincent Peale; the *Devotional Bible for Dads,* which is folksy and chatty; and the *Complete Idiot's Guide to the Bible.*

Some newer versions of the Bible display a high degree of political correctness. For example, some versions have changed "Son of Man" to "Human One," and the Lord's Prayer reads, "Our Father-Mother who art in heaven" (Watanabe, 1999).

Television. Religious programs have been on television ever since its earliest days in the 1950s, but it was not until the 1970s that this type of programming became very visible.

There is a controversy about how large the viewing audience is for religious television. The televangelists claim that the audience has been very large. But others, like Fore (1987), have pointed out that the audience for the electronic church is far smaller than claimed. In surveys, about 71 million people say they have watched one of these programs each week. But Nielsen diaries put the figure at about 24.7 million a week, and this is a duplicated audience; the unduplicated figure is about 13.3 million who watch at least 15 minutes a week. The number of people who watch for an hour or more is less than 4 million. Only the top religious programs draw an audience of more than 2 million viewers (Horsfield, 1984). More recently, Alexander (1997) explains that televangelism does not have a big effect on society or religion because only about 5% of the U.S. population regularly watches some form of religious television and these are people who are already committed to a religion. So this message is not reaching the unconverted, nor is it changing the viewers' beliefs, just reinforcing them. The viewers use television religious messages as a ritual; that is, it makes them feel they are part of a community.

What do viewers get from watching religious television programs? Hoover (1988) argues that the electronic church has had a revitalizing effect by recognizing individuals' experiences of dissonance, frustration, and cultural crises. By depicting the culture as out of control, these programs present themselves as offering stability and a clear purpose. They have done this by developing a total, universal explanation of life that proposes to resolve the dissonances felt in contemporary life. Fore (1987) adds that the electronic church appears authoritative at a time when authority appears to be in disarray. It highlights competition between God and the devil. It places emphasis on individuals as the foundational societal unit and charges them to act. And it is generally affirming of the social values most people hold and reinforces this belief system with attractive personalities.

Television is forcing churches to adapt. Comstock (1989) says that "in the case of cultures in which traditional religious observances have a visible and important place, television is one of the central components of modernization that channels public energies toward secular pursuits" (p. 246). As people become more secular, religion has to adapt by fighting against the trend of secularization, thus becoming less relevant to people's everyday lives, or it must change its values. For example, in Israel, television took time away from participation in celebrations and activities associated with Jewish religious practice, so television broadcasting was outlawed on the Sabbath. But the public demanded that the prohibition be lifted, and it was (Katz & Gurevitch, 1976).

Internet. Advocacy groups' use of religious language can shape the public's political attitudes and can influence politicians' legislative behaviors, thereby potentially influencing both public and political agendas. Kraus (2009) conducted a study of websites of a variety of religious groups and found them all to use theological religious themes to influence the public agenda.

In summary, the key benefit of religious messages in the media is that they provide more experiences to worship for those people who are already religious. But critics are concerned that television itself has become a religion, as evidenced by the ritualized viewing by many people. This has critics worried because the values presented on television are very different from the values presented by organized religion.

SUMMARY

The mass media do more than affect individuals; they also shape institutions. This chapter presented evidence that four of our most important institutions have been strongly affected by the influence of the mass media, especially television over the latter half of the twentieth century. The political system has fundamentally changed the way we select candidates who run for national office. The economic system has risen in importance because of the pressure from advertising. The family has changed structure and sense of unity. And religion has used the mass media to offer people all kinds of religious experiences as well as support their rituals; however, the media have triggered critics to complain that the media serve to shift people's attention to more secular matters, supplant religious rituals, and even take the place of religion altogether.

There is no question that these institutions have changed and continue to change from the influence of the mass media. Whether any of these changes is good or bad depends on your perspective.

Review Questions

1. How many ways have the media altered the way campaigns are now conducted for major offices in this country?
   - In what ways have the media made it easier for the average person to get into politics and run for office?
   - In what ways have the media made it more difficult for the average person to get into politics and run for office?

2. What is the difference between private and public goods? How have the media influenced the shift in importance from public goods to private goods?

3. In what ways have the media influenced the economic system?

4. In what ways have the media influenced the institution of family?

5. In what ways have the media influenced religion?

Further Thinking Questions

1. Think about the ways in which you follow political campaigns.
   - In what ways do the media make it easier for you to get involved in these campaigns?
   - In what ways do the media make it more difficult for you to get involved in these campaigns?

2. Think about the way the media cover political events of the three branches of the federal government: executive, legislative, and judicial.

   • Which branch do you think gets the most coverage? Which the least?
   • Are you satisfied with this balance of coverage?

3. Do you think too much money is spent on political campaigns or not enough? If you are not satisfied with the amount, can you think of ways to change it?

4. Do you see anything negative in the way the media have altered facets of the economic system?

5. Are you happy with the changes in family structure and unity that have taken place over the past few generations? If not, can you think of how media should be regulated in order to reduce the changes you do not like?

6. Think about the debate over whether the media have helped or hurt the institution of religion.

   • With which side do you agree more; that is, do you think media influence has helped or hurt religion?
   • If you concluded that media have hurt the institution of religion, can you think of how those negative influences could be reduced?
   • If you concluded that media have helped the institution of religion, can you think of how those positive influences could be enhanced?

Source: Stockbyte/Stockbyte/Thinkstock

CHAPTER 14

Macro-Level Effects on Society, Culture, and Mass Media

Macro-Level Effects on Society, Culture, and Mass Media

T his chapter deals with three broad topics. First we examine how the mass media have influenced society. Then we examine how the mass media have influenced culture. And third, we examine how the media have exerted influences on themselves.

EFFECTS ON SOCIETY

In this section we begin with an examination of the role of information technologies in the shaping of societies, then explore the functions the mass media provide to society. Using these ideas as a foundation, we then examine the debate over whether the mass media serve to integrate individuals into a coherent society or whether the mass media serve to fragment society into many different groups. Exhibit 14.1 presents a list of readings on the effects of mass media on society.

Role of Information Technologies in Shaping Society

Each civilization has been shaped by its technological opportunities and limits (Innis, 1950). For example, the Roman Empire existed because of the emergence of writing on portable documents. Records could be kept and shared across the very large span of geography controlled by the Romans. With the invention of the printing press in Europe during the Middle Ages, it was possible for more people to have voices and to widely distribute their messages. The printing press allowed leaders to communicate with a larger number of people and thus expand societies from small local ones to larger nationalistic ones.

McLuhan (1964) built on these ideas by saying that the medium was the message. He argued that the medium shaped the experience of exposure in a powerful way. Thus new communication technologies changed the personalities of societies. He argued that radio was a "hot" technology that was authoritative and therefore impressed its messages on the

Exhibit 14.1 Mass Media Effects on Society and Culture

Media Influence on Society

Media technology shapes society (Innis, 1950; McLuhan, 1964)

Media functions shape society
- Functional theory (Lasswell, 1948; Merton, 1949; Wright, 1949, 1960)
- Entertainment theory (Mendelsohn, 1966)

Media unify as well as fragment society
- Unifies society into a community (Janowitz, 1952; Meyrowitz & Maguire, 1993; Mollison, 1998; Rogers, 1993; Varan, 1998)
- Fragments society (Donnelly, 1986; Mills, 1956; Putnam, 2000)
- Reduction in public sphere (Dahlgren, 1995; Elliott, 1982)
- Decline in shared experiences (Brown & Pardun, 2004; Eastman, Newton, Riggs, & Neal-Lunsford, 1997; Hindman & Wiegand, 2008)

Media Influence on Culture

Marxism

- Frankfurt School (Adorno & Horkheimer, 1972; Althusser, 1971; Gramsci, 1971)
- Ritual theory (Carey, 1975)

Feminism (van Zoonen, 1994)

British cultural studies (Hall, 1980; Williams, 1961)

Cultural imperialism (Lerner, 1958; Schiller, 1969)

society; in contrast, television was a "cool" medium that allowed people to be more detached from the messages and consider a range of meanings.

Although Innis and McLuhan developed their ideas well before the advent of the newer interactive technologies of computers, digitization of messages, and wireless connections to the Internet, their ideas can be used to explain changes in our society as a result of the widespread use of these newer technologies. These newer technologies are interactive, so users can engage in conversations with one person or many people at the same time through e-mail, instant messaging, and blogs. Users can attract friends and build those friendships through social networking websites. They can actively participate in political and consumer groups by accessing websites of such organizations and contribute their own ideas. This leads to the creation of virtual communities that form around common interests and thus unite people through their interests, even if they are widely scattered geographically. Thus the form of the information technology shapes the character of those communities.

Functionalism

Mass media serve key functions in society, and as new media become available, the functions are altered. This is called the *functional perspective* through which society is regarded as a system of interlocking parts with each part serving its own function. Lasswell (1948) was first to offer a functional explanation for the role of the mass media in our society. He said the media fulfilled the three roles of surveillance, correlation, and transmission. The media, through their news organizations, provide a constant surveillance of the environment and inform people about the most important events, issues, and people. As for correlation, the media socialize people into a common way of thinking that leads to consensus building. By forging and maintaining a common set of values, the media provide continuity. And the mass media transmit a cultural heritage from generation to generation.

Wright (1960) elaborated on these three functions by adding a fourth: entertainment. Wright argued that entertainment provided people with a sense of relaxation and escape from their everyday lives. This helps society by reducing the level of tension (Mendelsohn, 1966). Later a fifth function was added: mobilization. The media can be used by people campaigning for social action to address social, economic, or military problems. Mobilization refers to the function of allowing people to focus the population's attention on certain common objectives (political, governmental, religious, and the like) and motivate people to action.

Integration vs. Fragmentation

Perhaps the biggest debate has been over whether the mass media serve to unite people in a society or to fragment them. Let's examine both sides of this debate.

Integration. Some scholars argue that the mass media serve to pull people together who would otherwise be scattered in some way, such as geographically. By presenting a set of messages simultaneously to a wide range of people, the mass media give people a sense of community; that is, people know that there are many other people who are experiencing the same messages and who are thinking about the same ideas. Over time, the repetition of these ideas shapes society into a coherent whole. Thus the mass media are regarded as formulating societies by attracting people with a common set of values, then reinforcing them with a continual flow of ideas and information (Janowitz, 1952; Rogers, 1993).

The mass media are able to integrate society better than other institutions because of their common messages and pervasive exposure. The media create a public sphere, which is a forum in which ideas get debated and a range of positions gets aired. Over time certain ideas become more accepted, and this builds unity among members of society. Because everyone has such easy access to this continual stream of media messages, everyone can learn the values and norms of society.

The media are breaking down cultural and political boundaries and in so doing they are creating a more unified global culture. For example, scholars point to the influence of television on breaking down the former Soviet Union, because television viewers in that political system found Western-style programming and production techniques, with their

Source: ©iStockphoto.com/hadynyah

references to democracy and capitalism, highly attractive (Mollison, 1998). Thus societies outside the global mainstream get int egrated through processes of *cultural erosion*. Television exerts an erosion effect on cultures, especially when the messages of one culture are introduced into another culture. This erosion effect includes four processes: cultural abrasion, cultural deflation, cultural deposition, and cultural saltation (Varan, 1998).

With the rise of the Internet and digital media, some scholars are more optimistic about a trend toward integration. These scholars contend that the digital media will unify society or homogenize the world through globalization. The unifying argument stems from the ideas of greater networking and faster sharing of information and images. Meyrowitz and Maguire (1993) argue that the digital media have served to integrate all groups of people into a "relatively common experiential sphere."

Fragmentation. Other effects scholars see society fragmenting as a result of mass media. That is, there is a reduction over time of the "public sphere," that is, a shared forum in which people can debate political and cultural issues and form some identity about who they are (Mills, 1956). The media foster social isolation as individuals each pursue their own media exposure agendas. This leads to less public activity and less sharing of values that bind people together into a unified society. There is less civic and social participation (Putnam, 2000). And over time the public sphere grows smaller (Dahlgren, 1995; Elliott, 1982).

Fragmentation has been found among adolescents. In a survey of 2,942 middle schoolers, Brown and Pardun (2004) found that of the 140 television shows listed, only four were watched regularly by at least one third of respondents. For example, few Whites watched any of the Black teens' top 10 shows, and only two of the girls' top 10 shows were on the boys' list. These findings provide little support for the notion of a common youth culture, at least as reflected in recent television programming. Fragmentation of the television audience extends beyond adolescents. Hindman and Wiegand (2008) found that the 25-year decline in the prime-time shares of the top three television networks were not just attributable to technological factors of the penetration of cable and other multiple video programming distribution sources (MVPD) into the nation's households. The decline was correlated even more strongly with indicators of social differentiation, that is, a fragmentation of interests among viewers due to changes in lifestyles.

Donnelly (1986) described this fragmentation of society by calling it an "autonomy generation." He described the autonomy generation as people believing that each individual is the center of all relevant values:

> We are responsible only to ourselves, and we alone can decide which activities and ways of behaving have meaning for us and which do not. We live subjectively according to our own feelings with little need for outside reference. . . . We interpret life in terms of what's in it for us, seek authenticity by transcending society and external value systems, and insist on being ruled only by the laws of our character. . . . We live in the present, responding to momentary perceptions, relationships, and encounters. To us, what is most important is how outside events are perceived and understood by the individual. (p. 178)

He says we experience what Émile Durkheim called *anomie,* the peculiar pain derived from individuals' inability to identify and experience their communities.

Donnelly (1986) says that the new electronic media have five characteristics that affect the nature of society: quantity (availability and use), speed (delivery and satisfaction), weightlessness of images (no context), remoteness (bring faraway information close), and choice (explosion of alternatives). Because the present generation does not possess the cultural tools to absorb such an explosion of information, we will become what Donnelly calls the "confetti generation." The confetti person is inundated by experience but ungrounded in any cultural discipline for arriving at any reality but the self. "We will witness an aggregated version of today when all ideas are equal, when all religions, life-styles, and perceptions are equally valid, and equally indifferent, and equally undifferentiated in every way until given a value by the choice of a specific individual" (pp. 181–182).

Both. As you can see from the previous sections, there are reasons to believe that the mass media fragment as well as integrate society. Characteristics of each medium offer the potential for both fragmentation *and* integration. Some scholars argue that the growing use of digital media will serve to fragment society even further, while other scholars argue that the digital media will unify societies. The fragmenting argument stems from the way the digital media allow individuals to seek out special content and tailor their experiences (see van Dijk, 2004). Keane (1995) goes so far as to say that the idea of a public sphere with public opinion and a common public good is obsolete. The positive effect of this fragmentation trend is that diversity of programming will increase because digitization allows for more voices to be heard (Berger & Huntington, 2002; Cowan, 2002). (For more on this debate see Waisbord, 2004.)

A few research studies have demonstrated both trends. For example, Internet connectedness has both a positive and negative effect on communities. In a positive sense, the Internet connects people and builds civic participation and ethnic assimilation; however there is also evidence that technologically savvy residents become disengaged from their neighborhoods (Matei & Ball-Rokeach, 2003). Also, a one-month panel study of an immersive online video game investigated its social and civic impact. The data revealed mixed effects. Although the game led to an improved global outlook and some online community improvements, some kinds of existing friendships eroded and the most social players became more insular, but family interactions were unaffected (Williams, 2006).

CULTURE

Culture is socially constructed; that is, it does not exist in some objective lasting form, but instead it is created by humans in their everyday lives (Berger & Luckmann, 1966). Culture represents a process of producing and using symbols that convey meaning and allow people to share experiences—aesthetic, religious, and personal experiences (Carey, 1975). There is a ritual aspect to this sharing that goes beyond the transmitting of information. That is, the ritualized experience of sharing experiences shapes our culture, and by studying these rituals we can develop a greater understanding about the values underlying that culture and the meaning people attribute to those experiences.

In this section, I present four explanations for how the media shape culture. Each of these four—Marxism, feminism, British cultural studies, and cultural imperialism—generally share two ideas. They all believe the media play a very important role in creating and shaping cultures. They also believe that media messages present discourses—consistent themes about meaning—that underlie most messages.

Marxism

Karl Marx developed a grand theory of the economic and political systems dominant in Europe in the late 1800s. Marx argued that the problems with industrialization and urbanization were not bad per se; rather society's problems could be traced to the greedy robber barons who used the capitalist system to exploit workers by paying them reduced wages so the capitalists could grow fabulously wealthy. He called for the workers to unite, rise up, and abolish the oppressive class system and to replace it with an egalitarian system with a democratic social order.

Source: Library of Congress Digital Collections

Marx blamed the hierarchical class system as being at the root of society's problems. The power elites maintained their hold on power by controlling the superstructure of society—culture. The elites created an ideology that was a drug for the masses. This ideology was simply accepted by the masses as the natural way, even though it undermined their personal interests.

The Marxist approach exerted enormous influence on scholarly thinking from the 1930s through the 1980s as it evolved into other explanations that applied to the changes in our culture. The scholars who adapted Marxism to media applications were called neo-Marxists and included the scholars of the Frankfurt School as well as some British cultural scholars. These scholars elaborated the idea of ideology and argued that the mass media were a powerful tool that disseminated the ideology and supported the superstructure that kept the working class enslaved in a false consciousness. These scholars argue that the power elites use the mass media to promulgate their ideology and socialize people to accept the current systems (Althusser, 1971). The population then accepts these ideas and values as being natural and unchangeable, so they do not challenge them (Gramsci, 1971). These neo-Marxists were largely scholars critical of dominant ideologies in cultures and the way the media foster those ideologies.

The Frankfurt School arose in the 1930s at the University of Frankfurt in Germany under the leadership of Theodor Adorno and Max Horkheimer (1972). These scholars made a distinction between high culture and low culture. They argued that high culture included things like great literature, symphonic music, and art. High culture had its own integrity and could not be subverted by the elites. In contrast, low culture, presented by the mass media of popular magazines, newspapers, cheap novels, movies, and radio, could have its content manipulated to serve the aims of the elites. These scholars complained that the mass media were conduits of low rather than high culture.

Feminism

Feminist theory is similar to Marxist theory in the sense that the media are believed to espouse an ideology that creates a false consciousness in their audiences. With feminism, the ideology is a patriarchal one where there is a male-dominated social order that people assume to be natural and just. Women are weaker and less capable than are men, so women gain their identity through their association with male characters.

Feminist theory claims that audiences come to accept this power structure without questioning it. Therefore the male-dominated social order uses the mass media to preserve itself through the continual repetition of their paternalistic themes (van Zoonen, 1994).

British Cultural Studies

The British cultural studies movement was called the "Birmingham School." These scholars were influenced by the work of Raymond Williams, who rejected the notion that high culture was somehow better for individuals and society. He argued that each group develops its own folk culture. However, he was skeptical of the value of the mass media in repackaging folk cultures (Williams, 1961).

British cultural studies were further enhanced by the influential ideas of Stuart Hall, who argued that the mass media served as pluralistic public forums in which various groups struggle to define and shape culture. Hall (1980) believed that elites did not control this negotiation of culture but that they did enjoy an advantage because the existing superstructure already supported them in their dominant position.

Cultural Imperialism

Some critics see a danger in the way a dominant culture can use the mass media to impose its culture on other cultures. Thus one culture, such as the United States, can spread its ideas and values by disseminating technological channels of information and then controlling those channels with particular messages. This is cultural imperialism. For example, after World War II the U.S. government funded projects to modernize traditional societies by introducing media technology along with Western ideas into those ancient cultures, especially in Asia, Africa, and Latin America (Lerner, 1958; Schiller, 1969). The motives of the U.S. government were to instill democratic ideals along with capitalistic economic systems in those countries so that the countries would be more resistant to the spread of communism from the Soviet Union. But critics complained that the values and cultural practices of those countries were being eroded. The tribal nature of many of these societies was important to the functioning of their institutions and family life, so the changes in values were eliminating the fundamental elements of their societies that had formed the character of their cultures over centuries.

EFFECTS ON THE MASS MEDIA THEMSELVES

The media also exert an influence on themselves. When the media create alterations in the public, institutions, society, and culture, those alterations influence changes in media structures and practices. Thus the mass media adapt to markets, the economy, and the culture they help shape. They are not a meta-influence that sits above everything and directs a one-way authoritative influence on others; the media are part of a complex system that they influence and are influenced by. Exhibit 14.2 presents a list of readings on the effects of mass media on themselves.

The media influence can be seen most clearly in three areas: adaptations to new technologies, changes in concentration of ownership, and socialization of their workers.

Exhibit 14.2   Further Reading on Effects on the Mass Media Themselves

New Technologies

Day-to-day activities of media workers

- New multimedia technologies work practices and organizational structures in newsrooms for online newspapers (Boczkowski, 2004)
- New technology that allows live reporting changing TV local news (Tuggle & Huffman, 1999)

Conceptualization of audiences (Lin, 1995)

Redefining purpose (Ahn & Litman, 1997; Chan-Olmsted & Ha, 2003; Schaefer & Martinez, 2009; Yan & Park, 2009)

Ownership and Control

Media industries increased in concentration of ownership (Ahn & Litman, 1997; Bagdikian, 1992, 2000; Noam, 2009)

Trend toward concentration harmful to consumers (Altschull, 1984; Blevins & Brown, 2010; Murdock, 1990; Napoli, 1999; Yanich, 2010)

Trend toward concentration not harmful to consumers (Einstein, 2004; Hofmeister, 2005; Lacy & Riffe, 1994; Naom, 2009; Picard, Winter, McCombs, & Lacy, 1988)

Socialization Effects

Media logic (Altheide & Snow, 1979)

Shaping values of workers (Berkowitz & TerKeurst, 1999; Bogart, 1995; Janowitz, 1975; Lippmann, 1922; McManus, 1994; Rodgers & Thorson, 2003; Schudson, 1978; Shoemaker & Reese, 1991; Tuchman, 1978; Weaver & Wilhoit, 1986)

New Technologies

As a result of new communication technologies, the everyday activities of media workers as well as the business practices of media companies have been forced to change in many ways. For example, the practice of journalism has changed with new technological developments. New technology that allows live reporting is changing local TV news (Tuggle & Huffman, 2001). New multimedia technologies have changed work practices and organizational structures in newsrooms for online newspapers (Boczkowski, 2004).

The newer technologies are giving people greater choice, and traditional patterns of media use are breaking down. For example, television programmers had developed strategies to attract and condition audiences for repeated exposures, but these strategies have lost a good deal of their usefulness. One of these strategies was to stack similar programs in a sequence so viewers would be likely to continue watching a channel throughout an entire evening. The prediction of the rating of a TV show from a combination of inheritance effect (the rating of its lead-in show) and degree of competition (strength of competing TV shows on at the same time) has declined from 80% to about 55%. This means that more viewers are making the choice to switch channels after a program rather than follow the habit of flowing into the next program. To combat this choice to switch channels, programmers are using new forms of transitions between programs to hold their audiences, and these transition effects account for as much as 9% of the ratings (Eastman et al., 1997).

The newer technologies have forced media companies to rethink their concepts of audiences and their purposes. For example, broadcast and cable TV have had to adapt with the rise of the Internet and digital technology. Television networks changed their programming strategies throughout the 1980s in response to competition from cable channels and other media. They were motivated to optimize viewing shares and consolidate potential risk (Lin, 1995). Chan-Olmsted and Ha (2003) found that the television stations have focused their online activities on building audience relationships rather than generating online ad sales. The Internet is used mostly as a "support" to complement the stations' offline core products.

New technological developments have also changed the structure of mass media industries. Vertical integration in the cable TV industry has resulted in greater program diversity and lower prices (Ahn & Litman, 1997). Media companies are now much less focused on channel and more on message. Over time, newspapers think of themselves less as paper media and more as news organizations that deliver current events through paper and Internet channels. Yan and Park (2009) found that local television stations significantly increased their local news programming from 1997 to 2003. The increases were attributable to the top four stations in each market.

With greater competition, television stations have changed the composition of their news messages by using editing techniques. For example, in a content analysis of U.S. commercial network editing that spanned a 36-year period, Schaefer and Martinez (2009) found that network news editors embraced faster pacing, shorter sound bites, and more special effects between 1969 and 2005. When taken together, the results suggest that U.S. network television journalism has evolved from more "camera of record" and realistic news techniques in favor of a variety of synthetic editing strategies that convey complex audiovisual arguments.

Concentration of Ownership

Ownership patterns of media companies have become more concentrated over the past three decades. To illustrate, Bagdikian conducted an analysis of media ownership patterns in 1983 and found that the control of the media was essentially in the hands of 50 people. These were the CEOs of the largest media companies that, in combination, controlled more than half of the revenues and audiences in their media markets. Less than a decade later, Bagdikian (2000) found that the number had shrunk to 23 CEOs of corporations that control most of the business in the country's 25,000 media businesses.

Eleven companies controlled most of the daily newspaper circulation. In magazine publishing, a majority of the total annual industry revenues went to two firms. Five firms controlled more than half of all book sales. Five media conglomerates shared 95% of the recordings market, with Warner and CBS alone controlling 65% of that market. Eight Hollywood studios accounted for 89% of U.S. feature film rentals. Three television networks earned more than two thirds of the total U.S. television revenues (Bagdikian, 1992). In 2000, Bagdikian published an updated version of his analysis and concluded that "six firms dominate all American mass media" (Bagdikian, 2000, p. x). Each of these six companies (Bertelsmann, Disney, General Electric, News Corp., Time Warner, and Viacom) owned media vehicles in almost all of the mass media. All six own subsidiaries in many countries and market their messages all over the world.

In a more recent analysis, Noam (2009) points out that concentration indexes show that concentration in the traditional mass media industries doubled from 1984 and 2005, but that it is still low compared to other industries. And when we take a broader perspective and look at the overall information sector—encompassing 100 separate industries—the indexes of concentration are 25% lower in 2005 compared to 1984.

This trend toward media concentration has stimulated a debate about whether this is a good or bad thing for consumers. Let's examine this debate in some detail.

Concentration Is Harmful. The critics of the trend toward greater concentration are especially concerned about the media industries. They argue that the mass media have a special responsibility to the public that businesses in other industries do not have. That is, the media provide a forum for ideas and that it is important to protect this forum so that it stays open to all ideas, not just ideas that are the most marketable to businesses. The broadcast and telecommunication parts of the mass media are regulated by the Federal Communication Commission (FCC). The FCC uses a "marketplace of ideas" metaphor in guiding their regulations, especially deregulation of broadcasting. That is, they are trying to achieve open markets in which as many ideas as possible can be expressed (Napoli, 1999), but with fewer owners, the variety of messages is reduced. For example, Murdock (1990) argues that just because the powerful media companies produce a great number of media vehicles and messages, this does not mean that the messages are different from one another and that instead it means the same basic commodity appears "in different markets and in a variety of packages" (p. 8).

Critics also argue that as competition among media companies decreases, the content of messages changes. Furthermore, these content changes are in a negative way, such as a loss of quality or a shift toward content that is harmful to audiences in some way. For example, Altschull (1984) pointed out that an axiom of journalism is that the contents of the media always reflect the interests of those who finance them. So if there are fewer owners of huge media conglomerates and fewer CEOs of huge manufacturing conglomerates that use the mass media to advertise their products and services, this is a dangerous trend. Critics argue that the few powerful elites will limit range of expression so that many voices will be silenced.

Blevins and Brown (2010) conducted an analysis of the studies used by the FCC in its media ownership proceedings from 2002 to 2007 and found a disproportionate use of economic research to support the agency's rule changes. The use of this research in policy making is important because the FCC's reliance on economic literature may have helped justify a "procedural" definition of what constitutes the public interest, and a "neoliberal" faith in the wisdom of market forces to ensure that the public interest is being served. The findings suggest that the inclusion of a broader range of scholarship, especially media research, would not have supported the FCC's decision to further relax media ownership rules.

Concentration Is Not Harmful. On the other side of the debate are people who argue that concentration in the media industries is not harmful to consumers and actually has some positive benefits for them. When companies are large, they enjoy greater economies of scale, thus reducing costs, and can operate more efficiently and pass those savings along to consumers or keep the profits and pass those benefits along to shareholders. Because the large media companies are publically held, their shares of stock are widely held by institutions (such as insurance companies and retirement funds) so the average person is also likely to benefit. Noam (2009) points out that much of the media is owned by institutions, such as pension funds like TIAA-CREF, mutual funds, and institutional investors. These institutions let media managers run their businesses in a micro-sense, their only interest being a profit orientation. They are not interested in promoting an ideology, as the so-called media moguls are sometimes accused of.

Also, greater economic power is needed to fund the high risk of producing media messages. It takes a great deal of resources to invest in a new type of message (new movies when costs exceed $100 million per film), a TV series, a new magazine, and such).

Scholars on this side of the debate also point out that many of the fears of critics of concentration are unfounded. There is no evidence that the quality of media messages has declined due to concentration. For example, research has not found that when a radio station is bought by a conglomerate the content degrades. Lacy and Riffe (1994) looked at the news content of radio stations and compared group ownership effects. They found that group ownership had no impact on the financial commitment or the local and staff emphasis of news coverage. Also, a study done on newspaper content could find no change in content after a newspaper was bought by a chain (for example, see Picard et al., 1988). No evidence of change was found with the stories, the range of opinions on the editorial page, or the proportion of the newspaper displaying news. However, in a study examining the relationship between local news content and ownership structure in 17 television markets in the United States, Yanich (2010) found that ownership does matter in the production of news on local broadcasts. The more concentrated in ownership were the TV stations in a local market, the lower the proportion of local news presented in the entire designated market area.

Neither has the concentration of ownership led to an increase in harmful content. This has not yet been tested directly, but there is indirect evidence that concentration of ownership in the radio industry is associated with an increase in negative speech and obscenity. One research study found that as big broadcasters buy more radio stations, shock-jock programming often replaces local content. From 2000 to 2003, the nation's four largest radio companies racked up 96% of the fines handed out by the FCC, although their stations accounted for only about half the country's listening audience (Hofmeister, 2005).

This criticism that concentration of ownership reduces competition in a market seems valid on the surface, but it breaks down when analyzed. To illustrate, let's say a city has two newspapers. A chain buys one of those newspapers. The chain-owned newspaper cuts subscription costs and ad rates. Readers and advertisers switch to the chain newspaper because it is less expensive. Eventually, the other newspaper goes out of business. The degree of concentration in that market goes up. But this does not mean that the newspaper has no competition simply because it is the only newspaper in the market. The newspaper must compete for audiences and advertisers along with the radio, television, and cable stations in the market. Thus, if the newspaper degrades its news product, people will drop their subscriptions and turn to other sources of news. With lower circulation rates, the newspaper will need to drop the rate it charges advertisers, and this will produce less revenue. With less revenue, the newspaper will need to lay off reporters, and the news product further degrades. This downward cycle continues until the newspaper is out of business. But this almost never happens because chain-owned newspapers are driven by making large profits, and to do that, they must do everything they can to expand their circulations and hence their appeal to advertisers.

Newspapers, as well as all the other media, expand their revenues only by providing more and better services to consumers. How do they know what consumers want? They are continually doing market research to test out new ideas. Also, they carefully monitor the public reactions, verbal as well as monetary, to their messages. When the public's tastes or wants change, the media know this, and they offer new types of products and messages.

Although the businesspeople in media organizations generally leave the creative people alone to do what they do best and attract large audiences, the business side can spill over onto the editorial side at newspapers in some cases. This was clearly illustrated in the fall of 1999, when the *Los Angeles Times Magazine* devoted coverage of the Staples Center, a new sports arena. The publisher, Kathryn M. Downing, had entered into a partnership agreement on the issue with the Staples Center, agreeing to have the Staples Center promote the magazine in return for sharing profits. Downing did not tell her reporters or editors about the business partnership. When the journalists found out, they complained about not knowing the magazine had been turned into a public relations device for the Staples Center. Downing, whose background was as a business manager and not as a journalist, apologized, saying that she did not realize that her actions would damage the journalistic integrity of the newspaper ("*L.A. Times* Publisher Errs, Apologizes," 1999).

At the same time as we see concentration of usage of websites, there is little evidence of vertical integration among companies providing computer services and hardware. "The computer industry is hugely splintered. Some firms sell components (Intel, AMD); some, software (Microsoft, SAP); some, services (IBM, EDS); some, hardware (Dell, Apple). There's overlap, but not much" (Samuelson, 2006, p. 45). Also, the Internet is dominated by newer companies, such as Google, eBay, and Yahoo, not the older established companies.

Critics argue that as concentration increases, the individual's access to the media is reduced. *Access* here can mean two different things. One meaning is ownership; that is, how much access does an individual have to own a media property? Because most media companies are public corporations, any individual can buy a share of any company. But can a person own a media property fully? The answer still is yes. There are comparatively low barriers to entry in the magazine, book publishing, weekly newspaper, and computer industries. With several thousand dollars, a desktop computer, and a strong initiative, most people could begin a company in one of these media industries. Of course, he or she should be prepared to face very stiff competition to gain the attention of an audience and the confidence of advertisers. But it is possible to create one's own media voice in those industries. In contrast, barriers to entry are much higher in the radio, television, cable, and film industries, and the conglomerate mergers over the past several decades have raised those barriers much higher, almost to the point of being prohibitive for anyone except the wealthiest individuals and the biggest companies.

Access can also mean the ability to get your point of view heard through someone else's media property. This is still relatively easy to do at the local level, such as with newspapers and small-circulation magazines. Most still print letters to the editors, and most buy articles from people with little journalistic experience. Also, most markets have call-in radio programs through which you can get your voice heard. In contrast, to get your voice heard in national media properties such as *Newsweek* magazine or a TV or cable network requires a great deal of skill and good connections because the competition to use those channels is so strong.

Many critics argue that the media industries lose diversity when the industries become more concentrated. Fewer voices should mean fewer opinions getting aired. However, Einstein (2004) points out that "in study after study, scholars have determined that there is no proven causality between media ownership and programming content" (p. vii). Einstein argues that the reduction in the number of program choices is not due to consolidation but to television's reliance on advertising as its primary source of revenue. Because of this reliance, there are severe limits on content, which include timelines for length of program, the "lowest common denominator" mentality, and an avoidance of controversy. In an analysis of the TV industry over the past four decades, Einstein reveals that as the industry became more concentrated, programming became more diverse. She said that diversity was at its peak in the late 1960s and then declined when the FCC imposed regulations about sharing programs through syndication. Then, when those syndication rules were relaxed and broadcasters could keep the programs they produced to themselves, diversity increased sharply in prime time.

Socialization Effects

The mass media socialize their workers into certain types of roles that serve to preserve the functioning of those organizations. Altheide and Snow (1979) have called this perspective "media logic" to refer to the values that are instilled in this socialization process. The more that media workers accept this socialization, integrate certain values, and exhibit certain procedures, the more successful they become in media organizations.

This socialization process has been studied most in the area of journalism. For example, Berkowitz and TerKeurst (1999) studied how journalists were socialized into an interpretive community in which members construct meanings in interactions among themselves as well as in interactions with news sources. Rodgers and Thorson (2003) studied the socialization procedures of both men and women into the professional of journalism and found important gender differences. Men were more likely to be given opportunities for advancement and responsibility, while women were discouraged.

The most important value socialized into journalists is the importance of objectivity (Janowitz, 1975; Lippmann, 1922; Schudson, 1998; Tuchman, 1978). In addition, there are other values that journalists acquire through socialization in the profession over time, such as the values of dissemination, interpretation, and adversary (Weaver & Wilhoit, 1986). *Dissemination* refers to getting information to the public quickly. *Interpretation* refers to analyzing and interpreting complex issues. And the *adversary* role was serving as a social critic and pointing out faulty practices of government and business. Weaver and Wilhoit (1986), observed that the role of adversary has been weakening over time, while other values have been strengthening over time. The values that have been growing stronger relate to the business nature of journalism and thus bringing the values of journalism more in line with the values of advertisers (Bogart, 1995; Shoemaker & Reese, 1996). McManus (1994) shows that journalism has been shaped by the pressures of what he calls the "market model." He says that news selection is influenced by cost, perceptions of audience interest, and threats to business interest. That is, the probability that something will be covered by a journalist is inversely proportional to its cost of covering it, directly proportional to perceptions of audience interest, and inversely proportional to the harm it will impact on the business values to the owners or advertisers.

SUMMARY

The mass media significantly influence society, cultures, and themselves. The form of this influence changes over time with newer technologies of information dissemination and with changes in their functions. It appears that some of this influence serves to fragment society, while other influence serves to unify disparate people into communities.

The mass media influence culture. Through the way they tell their stories they create and alter the common interpretation of the major themes in cultures. And the mass media exert an influence on themselves as they grow and adapt to new challenges and opportunities, such as those arising from the availability of newer technologies. The media must socialize new workers. This has been studied especially in the area of journalism. This socialization reflects a blending of the older, more traditional journalistic values of objectivity with the newer business-oriented values concerning the maintenance of audiences and the satisfaction of advertisers. New generations of media workers must learn these values and practices if they are to be useful to the media organizations.

Review Questions

1. How have different information technologies changed society?

2. What does *functionalism* mean?

3. How is functionalism related to media effects?

4. In what ways have the media served to unify society?

5. In what ways have the media served to fragment society?

6. What is culture?

7. How do the media shape culture?

8. How do the media socialize their workers?

Further Thinking Questions

1. Which technological innovation do you think has had the greatest impact on changing society?

2. Do you think the media have done more to unify or fragment society?

3. Which of the four cultural approaches do you think explains the media's role the best?

4. Do you think the ownership of the media companies is in the hands of too few people?
   - If you think that ownership is too concentrated, what do you think should be done? What should the limit on ownership be and how should this be enforced?
   - If you do not think that ownership is too concentrated, how would you answer the critics?

5. Do you think the values being socialized in workers in the new media (computers and Internet companies) is different from the values being socialized in the workers in the older media (such as print, film, radio, and television)?

PART IV

The Big Picture

This fourth and final part of the book is composed of two chapters that focus on the "big picture" of media effects. Now that you have worked your way through all the details presented in the previous 14 chapters, it is time to step back and think more broadly about media effects.

We begin this examination of the big picture in Chapter 15 with an overview of some of the cautions you should experience when thinking about the many research findings presented in the book. All research literatures have their flaws and limitations; however, this does not mean that research literatures are not valuable. The research literature on media effects is extremely valuable, but you need to be able to recognize some of its flaws if you want to be an educated consumer of this knowledge.

Chapter 16 concludes the book with a brief summary of the major ideas about the nature of audiences, effects, media influence, and the media effects research literature. Then I present a general strategy for helping you manage those effects in your everyday life.

The purpose of this book has been to help you develop a broader perspective on media influence and the effects in your lives that result from that influence. These final two chapters help you make the transition from a learner of media effects to a user of this knowledge.

CHAPTER 15

Cautions

Source: Jupiterimages/Comstock/Thinkstock

Cautions

You don't need to be an expert in research methods in order to be an informed consumer of the media effects research literature. But you do need a little guidance on what to be cautious about when determining the degree of confidence you can have in the findings from this literature. In this chapter, I help you be a more critical reader of the media effects literature by first pointing out four methodological cautions you should keep in mind when you think about this literature. Second, I address the issue concerning the extent to which the findings in this literature can be applied in a person's everyday life.

METHODOLOGICAL CAUTIONS

All research literatures have flaws, and the research literature on media effects is no exception. In order for you to be a sophisticated consumer of the findings in this literature, you need to recognize the important shortcomings in this literature. In this section, I highlight what I believe to be the four most important of these shortcomings. These concern the use of self-reports, the use of repeated measures, the use of attribute variables, and the calibration of influences.

Use of Self-Reports

The media effects literature is dominated by research participants' self-reports on media effects. This is what I found after analyzing the media effects literature of studies recently published (odd years from 1995 to 2009) in eight of the top communication journals. In those 64 journal/years, I found 575 articles dealing with media effects on individuals, which included 696 individual effects being tested. Among those 696 effects, 82% were measured using self-reports. Of course, with some types of effects, self-reported measures are the most appropriate. After all, how else can we measure people's current knowledge, attitudes, and beliefs unless we ask them to tell us? When we study behavioral effects, we have alternatives to self-report, yet 88.3% (151 out of 171) of all studies of behavioral effects relied on self-report and only 11.7% used observation, interview, or electronic recording of the behavior.

The use of self-reported data on behaviors should be regarded as highly suspect, because it has been well documented that self-reported behavior is often very different from actual behavior (Morgan, Movius, & Cody, 2009; Prior, 2009). There are two reasons for this difference. One reason is that our intentions for behavior are usually better (more ambitious or more socially acceptable) than what we end up actually doing. For example, most of us have the best intentions to perform all sorts of healthy behaviors (such as eating well, exercising regularly, and avoiding risky behaviors), but the actual behaviors we perform are often less than our intentions. Also, when people are asked what they watch on television, they tend to underreport shows considered trashy and overreport things like news viewing. For example, Prior compared people's self-reports of TV usage with Nielsen data on actual television exposure and found a "severe over-reporting" of news exposure. He found that people overreport their exposure to news by a factor of 3 on average and as much as eightfold within some demographic groups.

A second reason for the difference between self-reported behaviors and actual behaviors is that we are often unaware of what our actual behavior is, especially when we are asked about our mundane everyday behaviors that we perform as habits. Because many of our media exposure behaviors are so automatic and habitual that we have no memory to draw from, our self-reports of media behaviors are often nothing more than wild guesses. For example, recall from Chapter 11 when I described the Ferguson (1992) study that asked people how often they had changed channels during a television viewing session that ended just minutes before and found that there was no relationship between their actual behavior and their reported behavior. That is, everyone was making wild guesses and participants were as likely to underestimate their channel changes as they were to overestimate them.

Self-reporting is the least expensive—and most efficient—way for researchers to generate behavioral data. However, this data-gathering technique is open to all sorts of biases; that is, people might not want to tell you private things about themselves or things that would make them look bad, so they are likely to "enhance" the data.

Self-report measures of physiological responses are also highly suspect, because people do not typically have an accurate perception of how physiologically aroused they are in many situations. For example, Ravaja (2004a) conducted an experiment on the influence of broadcast news story elements on participants and found that self-reported arousal was not related to a person's physiological arousal (electrodermal activity). Also he took physiological measures of facial electromyographic and respiratory sinus arrhythmia, which are an index of attention and improved memory performance for positive messages. These measures should have been related to a person's self-report of pleasure with the news stories, but Ravaja did not find such a relationship in his study. This study clearly found—as do many other studies—that many times people do not have an accurate perception of their physiological reactions.

While self-reports of behavioral and physiological effects should be regarded as relatively having low validity for the reasons just expressed, self-reports are highly suspect with other kinds of effects. Problems with the validity of self-reported data have been documented when participants are asked about their attitudes (Sturgis, Roberts, & Allum, 2005), affect (Sparks, Pellechia, & Irvine, 1999), and cognitions (Slater, Goodall, & Hayes, 2009). Often research participants will not have an attitude on a particular issue but will express one anyway when asked. Often research participants will not be aware of all their emotions and moods or will not be able to recall them accurately when they are later asked on a survey instrument. And often people will not be willing to express what they are really thinking or feeling, because they believe it might not be socially acceptable.

When researchers measure individuals' behaviors, they have alternatives to self-reporting. Exhibit 15.1 displays different types of behavioral measures in a rank-ordered manner that indicates the degree of confidence we can have in the data based on the method that

---

Exhibit 15.1 Examples of Types of Behavioral Measures

Example 1: Television Viewing

Self-Report. People are often asked on surveys about their TV viewing habits. Also, the Nielsen Company mails to American households TV viewing diaries on which people mark on paper which shows they have watched over a two-week period then mail it back to the Nielsen Company. Often people will wait until it is time to mail the dairy back before recording their viewing behavior; in this case people can forget about many of the shows they watched and how many times they changed the channels.

Observations From Untrained Coders. Researchers interested in children's viewing patterns will ask parents to list their children's favorite TV shows and how often their children watch each of those shows. Because parents are not always in the room to monitor what their children are watching, their observations can be partial or self-serving.

Observation From Trained Coders. There are some researchers who train coders to observe their research subjects, then to record their observations.

Electronic Recording. The Nielsen Company gathers audience data with a device known as a "peoplemeter," which is attached to television receivers in a person's home. The peoplemeter begins recording information whenever the TV receiver is turned on and continues until the TV receiver is turned off. The peoplemeter records the station the TV receiver is tuned to as well as the people who were in the room with the TV receiver.

Example 2: Aggressive Behavior

Self-Report. On a survey instrument, people are asked to list the number of times they behaved aggressively over the previous two weeks. On a 7-point Likert scale (1 = very strong, 2 = strong, 3 = somewhat strong, 4 = neutral, 6 = somewhat weak, 6 = weak, 7 = very weak) they are asked to rate how aggressive their behavior usually is.

Observation From Untrained Coders. On a survey form, people are asked to list their friends. Then for each friend, respondents are asked to list any acts of aggression that friend exhibited over the previous two weeks.

Observation From Trained Coders. Children are put in a room with a variety of toys, such as building blocks, clay, hammers, and plastic swords. Trained coders observe children's play behavior and record how many times those children act aggressively.

Electronic Recording. College students participate in a research study in which they play a computer game. They are told that each of the avatars on the screen is controlled by other college students playing the game. The avatars must compete with each other for valuable rewards. In this competition, game players use weapons to destroy their opponents. The computer records how many times each player uses a weapon to harm another avatar.

researchers used to generate those data. In general, electronically recorded measures of behavior are the most valid because they avoid threats to validity introduced by human error. Electronic measures are typically recordings of time spent with the media or counts of audience actions gathered automatically, such as computer keystrokes or Web pages visited and for how many seconds each.

Next best as measures of behaviors are observations from trained coders, followed by observations from untrained coders; these measures are usually more objective than self-reported behaviors. The quality of the data from observation depends on how well the observers were trained to recognize certain behaviors and the consistent precision used by those observers. Many studies that use observation of behavior do not train their observers and instead rely on the impressions of people who have spent time with the audience members of whom they are measuring.

Use of Repeated Measures

Much of the media effects literature is concerned with long-term effects on individuals, such as with the altering and reinforcing functions (see chapters in Part II). Yet despite this focus in the research, studies rarely employ repeated measures over time to make adequate assessments of change or non-change in the case of reinforcement. Referring to my content analysis of scholarly journal articles once again, of the 696 individual effects that were tested in this literature, 262 of these made claims for testing long-term effects. However, only 24 (9.2%) of these studies that purportedly tested for long-term effects took a measure of the effect at more than one point in time. One example to illustrate this pattern is with tests of the cultivation effect, with its prediction that each exposure to the television world gradually alters a person's belief—like a drip, drip, drip of meaning—away from a real-world-fashioned belief and into a belief that conforms more to the television world. However, the typical test of a cultivation effect is a cross-sectional survey in which participants are asked about their current beliefs and current television viewing. Thus the researchers involved in these 24 studies are assuming the stability of television viewing and the instability of beliefs over time. In a larger sense, all studies that claim to test a socialization influence by the media are in essence claiming that the media gradually alter a person over the long term or else serve to reinforce existing effects. Therefore it would seem that any media effects study claiming to document a longer-term effect would necessarily need to collect a measure of the effect at more than one point in time in order to "connect the dots" across the multiple measures of that effect and thereby plot the arc of change or non-change; however, a very small percentage of media effects studies do this.

Use of Attribute Variables

Attribute variables are the measure of a superficial characteristic of a person, such as sex or age. Attribute variables are easy to measure, so they are useful in the early formative stages of a research field. However, in order for a research field to move out of an initial exploratory phase and into a more sophisticated phase of prediction and explanation of the phenomenon the research must identify the active forces that exert an influence on the phenomenon. Therefore, shift of attention from attribute to active variables is a sign of increasing precision in the growth of a research field.

There are two attribute variables—gender and age—that are frequently used in media effects research and have provided some value in the past when research was primarily exploratory. For example, biological sex (male or female) has been an easy attribute variable to measure and use. If a researcher is willing to assume uniformity within a sex value (that is, all females are exactly the same) and important differences across the values (males are different than females), then it makes sense to be satisfied with attribute variables. If we are interested in the phenomenon of hormonal development in humans, then the use of biological sex is an important variable. But with media effects research, sex is typically used to represent something more than a biological determination; that is, sex is used in many research studies as an indicator of something more active like a pattern of role socialization or a complex of personality characteristics (for example., degree of aggressiveness, empathy, nurturing, and the like). Using biological sex as a surrogate for gender role socialization guarantees that its use in predicting effects will be fuzzy at best, because not all people of the same biological sex have the same degree or type of gender role socialization.

A child's age has been used as a variable to indicate the child's cognitive development level, as claimed by Piaget's stage theory (Pulaski, 1980). However, researchers have found that people who share an age do not also share the same level of cognitive development; nor do they share the same level of emotional development, moral development, or even experience with the media (Potter, 2011). For example, Piaget's theory says that children are fully developed cognitively and therefore are capable of adult thinking (formal operations) at age 13. However, King (1986) conducted a review of the published literature that

Source: Hemera Technologies/PhotoObjects.net/Thinkstock

tested the formal reasoning abilities of adults and concluded that "a rather large proportion of adults do not evidence formal thinking, even among those who have been enrolled in college" (p. 6). This conclusion holds up over the 25 studies she analyzed, including a variety of tests of formal reasoning ability and a variety of samples of adults 18 to 79 years old. In one third of the samples, fewer than 30% of the respondents exhibited reasoning at the fully formal level, and in almost all samples no more than 70% of the adults were found to be fully functioning at the formal level.

Also, despite the assumption that children develop morally as they age, the ability to reason morally has also been shown to have a weak relationship with age. For example, Van der Voort (1986) found no evidence that children judge violent behavior more critically in a moral sense as they age. There is a range of moral development among people of any given age.

Calibration of Influences

A fourth caution is to look for a calibration of media effects and the factors that bring them about. Not all effects are equally powerful or prevalent—some are much stronger than others and some affect many more people than do others.

One of the shortcomings in the media effects literature is that researchers typically are more concerned with statistical significance than with substantive significance. This means that when researchers run their data through statistical programs, they focus on statistical significance, which is the probability that their observed effect could not have occurred by chance alone. When they find statistical significance, they know they have a greater chance of having their research study published. Therefore the media effects literature is full of studies with statistical significance, but the authors of those studies frequently background (or ignore altogether) the more important issues about prevalence (whether the media effect they found is likely to occur in 100 people or in 30 million people), frequency (whether the effect is likely to occur only once or repeatedly), or strength (whether the effect is strong or so weak that people are not likely to notice it or care about it).

Over time, mature research literatures compare and contrast various effects on prevalence, frequency, and strength so that there is a kind of rank ordering of effects. With the media effects literature, there is very little calibration of the relative importance across different effects.

MEDIA EFFECTS VS. MASS MEDIA EFFECTS

The terms *mass* media and *mass* communication are in common use. Yet perhaps you have noticed that I have rarely used either of these terms in this book. Why is that? There are two reasons. First, scholars have had a very difficult challenge in defining these terms. Scholars continue to use these terms to label books, bodies of research, and even academic departments. However, very few scholars have even attempted to define these terms, and we are left with a fuzzy meaning at best. A second—and more important—reason that I have largely avoided using these terms in the book to this point is that the research literature is much more oriented toward media effects, instead of "mass" media effects. But now it is time to try clearing up these two issues about (1) What does *mass* mean, and (2) How can I make the claim that the effects research literature is much more oriented toward media effects than it is toward "mass" media effects? As you will see by the end of this section of the chapter, it makes a difference how we define "mass" media, and this difference has important implications for the confidence we can have in translating the findings from this research literature into our everyday lives.

What Are the "Mass" Media?

It is ironic that the term *mass media* is both so widely used and so little understood. Media researchers typically treat the term as if everyone understands what it means; that is, they rarely bother to present a definition of it. And those scholars who do try to define it run into a great deal of difficulty and usually end up talking about how the mass media should *not* be defined rather than trying to explicate the key essence of this phenomenon.

In this section, I show you the more popular definitional elements that have been used to clarify what mass media are. Notice how each one has been found to be faulty. This section concludes with a definition that avoids the problems with faulty elements and keeps the focus on the central essence of what scholars seem to mean when they refer to the "mass" media.

Source: ©iStockphoto.com/Moodboard_Images

Size of Audience. The most popular way to define the mass media is to say that the audience must be large. This is typically the central criterion used by the public. This definitional element of audience size does have some usefulness, because it serves to rule out some things that we would all agree are not mass media—things like mailing a personal letter, a phone call with a friend, and photographs on your refrigerator. However, when we use audience size as a criterion for defining mass media, we quickly run into a problem as we confront the question: How large must the audience be? Does it need to be 500 people? Is that large enough? Probably not. Then what about 1,000? What is the magic threshold number? Unfortunately, no one has ever been able to define *large* in a satisfactory way. It is always arbitrary. There is no magic number that can be used for a threshold for how large an audience must be.

Perhaps size can be determined in a relative manner. Webster and Phalen (1997) try to get around the threshold problem by arguing that the audience "must be of sufficient size that individual cases (e.g., the viewer, the family, the social network) recede in importance and the dynamic of a larger entity emerges. This is the essence of statistical thinking" (p. 9). They show that this conception of the mass audience was tied to the rise of statistical methods of determining exposure to various media vehicles, especially radio, for the purpose of renting them to advertisers. This argument helps a bit by saying that the audience, in essence, has to be large relative to the number of people one can talk with in personal groups. But again it does not leave us with a clear guideline to define the mass media. To illustrate, think about a local radio station with 1,000 daily listeners in a small town; most people would regard this as a mass medium. Now think about a high school football game with 10,000 fans in the stands watching the game and listening to the announcer on the public address system; most people would not regard this as a mass medium.

Size alone (whether it be thought of as an absolute number that could be regarded as a threshold or a relative ratio) does not help us separate the mass media from the non-mass media. Therefore there must be something else to the definition.

Type of Audience. A second type of definition is based on the character of the audience. Early sociologists reasoned that in order to have *mass* media, we needed to have *mass* audiences. These thinkers argued that people in mass audiences were mass-produced products, much like cars, bars of soap, and boxes of cereal. That is, the mass media acted like factories in mass producing audiences. Following from this reasoning, they defined a "mass" audience as having four characteristics. First, the audience composition was heterogeneous. This means that the audience was composed of people of all kinds, and no one was excluded. Second, the audience members were anonymous. The message designers didn't know the names of anyone in the audience nor did they care to, because the designers regarded everyone to be the same and interchangeable. Third, there was little interaction among the members in the audience. People didn't talk to each other about the media messages, so the meanings of the messages did not get modified in conversations. Instead, those messages had a direct effect on each person in a uniform manner. And fourth, there was no leadership. The mass was very loosely organized and was not able to act with the unity that marks a crowd (Blumer, 1946).

The idea of the *mass society* arose with the Industrial Revolution in the mid-1800s. The United States and Western European countries were regarded as having "mass" societies because the countries were heavily industrialized. These countries had many factories that mass-produced all kinds of products on assembly lines, so that all products coming off a particular assembly line were the same. It was believed that this same technological process that led to factories and mass-produced goods also led to mass-produced audiences. The mass media produced the same types of messages over and over, and people who continually experienced these messages came to think the same things. Less industrialized countries did not have mass societies, because people there were tightly integrated into social networks in which they interacted continually with others on a daily basis. So the United States was regarded as having a mass society and India was not; the population of India was much larger than that of the United States, but the *type* of audience in the United States was very different than the type of audience in India.

Because it was believed that communication did take place in a mass-like fashion, it was assumed that a message reached everyone in the same way and was processed by everyone in the same manner. It was also believed that the processing itself was very simple; that is, people were vulnerable, they had no psychological defenses against messages, because they did not discuss messages with other people.

As evidence for this position, social critics pointed to the way that Adolph Hitler used the mass medium of radio in the 1930s to mobilize the German population to support him. Another often cited example of the public's seeming lack of defense against media messages is provided by the widespread reaction to Orson Welles's 1939 Mercury Theater presentation of *War of the Worlds,* which was a fictional radio play presented as if it were a newscast. It was alleged that listeners of this show accepted the literal meaning of the fictional radio play and believed that the Earth was actually being invaded by Martians. These examples led some sociologists of the 1930s and 1940s to be very vocal in their warnings about the dangers of the mass media. However, a more careful analysis of these examples mentioned reveals that most people were not affected by those messages (Cantril, 1947). Further, it was later shown that the people who were affected were not all affected in the same manner, nor did they all react in the same way. The mass media were not powerful factory-like entities that mass-produced a mass audience in which everyone was affected the same way. There was no "mass" audience; even in highly industrialized countries, people think for themselves. For any given media message, there are many different types of audiences, because people interpret the meaning of messages differently. Therefore the *type* of audience cannot be the key to defining the mass media; there must be something else.

Channel of Transmission. Another type of definition is a channel-based one; that is, it places the focus on the channels that are used to transmit information. Some people define *mass media* as the technological means of disseminating messages. For example, Janowitz (1968) defined *mass communication* as communications in which "specialized groups employ technological devices (press, radio, films, etc.) to disseminate symbolic content" (p. 41). These channels are usually categorized as print (newspapers, books, magazines) or electronic (radio, CDs, film, television, computers).

Defining the mass media by channels of transmission is also faulty. To illustrate this point, consider the question: Is television a mass medium? Most people would say yes, envisioning the television set hooked up to a cable transmission service. But what if the television set is hooked up to a DVD playing back your niece's birthday party? It is still the same TV set, but now it doesn't seem accurate to regard it as a *mass* medium. People now watch a TV screen for lots of different reasons—to watch a broadcast TV show, a cable TV magazine-type show, a video recording of a Hollywood movie, a newspaper's website on the Internet, an abstract visual while playing back a CD, to read an electronic book, and the list goes on. Sometimes the channel of TV seems to be a mass medium, and other times it seems more private and personal.

Now consider your telephone. Is that a mass medium? Most people would say no. But what if your phone is an iPhone on which you play popular music, surf the Web, and watch your favorite TV shows from the night before? With digitization, messages can move seamlessly through different channels, so the idea of channel is becoming confused. Thus digitization has blurred the line between channels of transmission. A phone is more than a telephone, and a video screen is more than a television. Therefore it is no longer useful to key the definition of *mass media* to certain channels of transmission, because doing so will lead to more confusion than clarity. There must be something else that distinguishes between the mass media and non-mass media.

The Something Else. What is the "something else"? When we read through the work of scholars who use this term, it appears that they are referring to the technological channels that are used by certain types of organizations that are trying to attract the largest number of people within their targeted niches and then condition those audience members for continual, habitual exposures. The key elements of such a definition are the intentions of the senders of those messages in combination with the channels of transmission they use. Also, key to the definition are the ideas of attracting and conditioning in an environment in which people are overwhelmed with media and message choices. Let's examine these ideas in more detail.

With the mass media, the intention of the sender is to assemble an audience and keep the audience for repeated, habitual exposures to their messages. Therefore the mass media are not concerned about presenting a single message and attracting an audience for that one message. Instead, the mass media are in it for the long haul; that is, they want to build audiences that they can maintain over time and depend on for repeated exposures.

This intention is the most important element that distinguishes the mass media from other media and other forms of communication. A concert promoter who sells 100,000 tickets to a Saturday night concert is not a mass medium. But a radio station that has 1,000 listeners tuned in every day is a mass medium. Of course the radio station may try to attract 100,000 listeners every day, but the failure to attract a large number of listeners does not disqualify it as a mass medium as long as the radio station's intention is to provide programming every day to keep its listeners listening. It doesn't matter how large the audience is; what matters is the sender's motive to attract as many people as possible and to condition them for repeat exposures.

The mass media use technological channels to disseminate their messages. They use the technology as tools to achieve their intention of constructing and maintaining audiences. These technological channels are necessary tools to make the messages widely available to all members of the targeted audience at the same time. These channels are available for repeated use, and this serves the intention of conditioning the audience for repeat exposures.

The mass media are organizations, not individuals. Individuals can often use a mass medium platform to send messages, but the individual is not the mass medium. For example, you might have a page on Facebook and use it as a platform to send out messages to your friends. However, it is Facebook instead of you that is the mass medium, because it is Facebook that has created and maintains the technological channel that makes it possible for messages to be sent out widely and immediately. And it is Facebook that has created features that attracted your usage and conditions you for continued usage.

Given these arguments, the essence of the "mass" media is that they are organizations that use technological channels of distributing messages with the purpose of creating and maintaining audiences within the everyday environment of choice. Notice that the definition of mass media is not keyed to the qualities of the audience, as early sociologists did when they conceptualized the mass audience and how it was affected by newly developed channels of communication in the first half of the twentieth century. Nor is the definition keyed to the size of the audience or to particular channels. Television might or might not be a mass medium; whether it is or not depends not on the size of the audience but on how it is used. Nor is the definition keyed to particular technological channels; instead, the definition is keyed to *how* the channel is used. The focus is on the intention of the sender.

CAUTION IN TRANSLATING

Given the definition of "mass" media developed here, we can see that while all of the research studies cited in the previous chapters examine media, almost none of them examined the media under "mass" conditions. Given the definition, the essence of "mass" media effects lies in what happens in people's everyday lives when they are inundated with choice among thousands of media messages as well as other demands on their time. The really important questions then are, How do certain media messages break through all that clutter to trigger attention—or more precisely, what is it about particular media messages that triggers the attention of certain kinds of people while being ignored by other types of people? Which effects are likely to occur in a person's everyday life when they are largely in a state of automaticity? And, what are the natural dynamics in everyday life that are shaped and maintained by the media that lead to certain effects? In order to generate valid answers to these questions, studies need to observe people in their naturalistic environments to determine what happens as they filter messages and process that information on the way to experiencing effects.

The large literature on media effects is composed of studies that do not observe how people use the media in their everyday lives and how the effects occur in that mundane flow. Instead, the media effects literature relies more on artificially generated data than on naturally occurring exposures and effects. The data are generated through experiments and surveys. With experiments, participants are removed from their everyday lives and brought into a laboratory where they are exposed to carefully crafted stimulus material and then subjected to measurement that is very unlike their real-world experiences. Laboratory experiments remove research participants from their everyday lives so that researchers can control the situation and thereby isolate a particular factor they expect to be influential in bringing about a media effect. This control is necessary in the design of an experiment, so that it places the focus on that one factor and avoids the messiness of all kinds of other factors contaminating the interpretation of their results. But real life is messy, with many factors simultaneously interacting at any one time. The key to understanding real-life phenomena is not to sterilize it by creating artificial treatment conditions but to confront the phenomenon and try to understand it as it exists.

With surveys, participants are asked to recall their mundane behaviors (such as media exposures, interactions with other people) well after they have been performed. Also, when research participants are asked about their feelings, attitudes, and beliefs on Likert scales (for example, 1 = very strong, 2 = strong, 3 = neutral, 4 = weak, 5 = very weak), it is difficult to respond well because participants typically do not think in those terms. So research participants must translate those things into a number as required by the research questions, and this translation moves the response far away from an expression of the actual experience.

Thus the data generated by these artificial means are an indirect measure of what goes on in a person's everyday life. As such, the data are valuable as indicators about potentials, that is, the potential of what effects may be occurring in everyday life. But the findings of this large literature rarely address the effects that occur in a way that documents their actual prevalence or strength.

These conditions of the literature prevent it from being a "mass" media effects literature. This is not to say that it is not useful. This large literature of media effects is extremely valuable as a basis for the eventual study of "mass" media effects. Until we are able to build a strong literature on "mass" media effects, we can use the findings from the media effects literature as a useful guide to predict what the actual everyday effects are—that is, the "mass" media effects.

SUMMARY

My final caution is that you keep your focus on the big picture and not let individual flaws in a research literature lead you to a negative attitude about the media effects literature. All research literatures have shortcomings, because all research studies have flaws; no study generates completely valid findings. Do not fall into the black-and-white trap of thinking that if something is not perfect, it is useless.

By presenting the four methodological cautions and the concern about translating the research findings into everyday practice, my intention was to help you recognize the stronger studies when you read the research literature for yourself. When you read the media effects literature more critically, you can better extract the value from this large literature and not be pulled toward inaccurate conclusions.

It would also be a mistake to discount the media effects literature as not having any usefulness. To the contrary, it has been highly useful in forming a foundation for "mass" media effects understanding by providing indications about which effects may be occurring and the factors that may be responsible for those effects. This literature has been very valuable in moving us far away from the days of wild speculation about certain effects being very powerful or nonexistent. Those speculations had no empirical basis. Now, after so much testing, we have a good idea about what many of the media effects are; now we need to test them in more naturalistic settings and then carefully calibrate them so we can understand their relative pervasiveness, strength, and importance.

Review Questions

1. What are the four methodological cautions outlined in this chapter?

2. With each of those four cautions, what is the methodological shortcoming and how can it be overcome?

3. What are the struggles that scholars have had in defining the "mass" media?

4. What is the definition of "mass" media developed in this chapter?

5. Why is it a problem to translate the findings from the media effects literature directly into your everyday life?

Further Thinking Questions

1. Which of the four methodological cautions do you think is the most serious, that is, which does the most to limit your trust in the findings?

2. Can you think of any findings presented in the previous nine chapters that seemed to be developed from observations of people in their everyday lives?

3. Pick a finding that you think was developed in an artificial manner and think about how you would conduct a research study to examine this as a "mass" media effect.

CHAPTER 16

Springboard

Source: ©iStockphoto.com/Xaviarnau

Springboard

The purpose of this book has been to help you develop a broader perspective on media influence and the effects in your lives that result from that influence. In this chapter, I first remind you of the most important ideas about the nature of audiences, effects, media influence, and the media effects research literature. Then I help you extend your understanding of media effects a bit by considering how some effects are more primary and foundational than other effects. Finally, I present a brief, general strategy for helping you manage those effects in your everyday lives.

REVIEWING KEY IDEAS

This section presents a big picture overview in four areas. These four areas are the nature of the audience, nature of media effects, nature of media influence, and nature of the media effects research.

Nature of Audience

We are the audience for media messages every day of the year, every year of our lives. However, this does not mean that we are all members of the same audience; instead, we each have our own special needs for information and entertainment, so we each have our own particular patterns of media exposure. Because our culture is composed of thousands of specialized audiences, each of us can follow a unique pattern of exposure. Therefore each of us experiences a unique pattern of media effects.

While our exposure patterns differ, we all share two things in common. First, we all spend a great deal of time being exposed to media messages every day. Second, we all navigate through this huge cafeteria of media messages primarily in a state of automaticity, which allows us to filter messages very efficiently. That is, our minds use our preprogrammed algorithms to screen out almost all media messages and let in only those few messages that meet our particular needs. When we screen in a message, we typically experience it in one of three exposure states: attentional, transported, or self-reflexive. When we screen in a message, we engage in meaning-matching tasks, when our minds at times act like efficient machines that quickly identify symbols and access the denoted meaning that we have stored in our algorithms. This process allows us to share meaning and enjoy an experience common to other audience members who attend to the same message. However, we can also go beyond meaning matching to meaning construction, when we engage in personal interpretive processes and create nuances of meaning that make us different from everyone else.

Therefore we cannot avoid being a part of many different audiences for media messages as we go through our everyday lives. And in that ever-changing flow of media messages, we continually experience the interplay of sharing common meanings with others while at the same time creatively altering those meanings to better suit our needs.

Nature of Media Effects

It is important to develop a broad perspective on what a media effect is. Recall from Chapter 3 that effects can differ by level (micro vs. macro), by timing (immediate vs. long term), by duration (temporary vs. permanent), by directness (direct media influence vs. indirect), by intention (or non-intention), by change (difference vs. no difference), by valence (negative or positive), and by manifestation (observable vs. latent). When we consider all these elements, *media effects* is defined as those things that occur as a result—either in part or in whole—from media influence. They can affect individual people as well as all people in the form of the public. They can affect institutions, society, and the workings of the media themselves. They can occur immediately during exposure to a media message, or they can take a long time to occur after any particular exposure. They can last for a few seconds or an entire lifetime. They can act directly on a target (a person, the public, an institution, society, or the media industries) or they can act indirectly. They can occur whether the media have an intention for them to occur or not. They can show up as changes, but they can also reinforce existing patterns, in which case the effects appear as no changes. They can be positive as well as negative. And finally, they can be easily observable (as in manifest effects) or they can be latent (as in process effects).

Nature of Media Influence

Media influence is continual and ongoing in three ways. First, the media exert their influence directly on us during exposures to messages. This is a considerable amount of time, because the average person spends more time with the media than with any other activity, including sleeping. Second, the media exert their influence on us indirectly when we interact with other people or institutions that themselves have been influenced by media messages. Third, and perhaps most profoundly, the media exert their influence on us whenever we use our mental algorithms to make our selection of messages, to trigger meaning matching, and to guide meaning construction. Because the media have had an influence in programming our algorithms, that influence continues whenever we access those algorithms. Because the media have shaped our beliefs, the media influence us later when we recall those beliefs. Because the media have influenced our standards, the media then influence our processes of evaluation later when we use those standards. Because the media have reinforced our behavior, the media show their influence as we enact those behaviors in the many automatic routines we habitually use each day. And because the media shape how we think about things, they influence us each time we think.

Often this media influence cannot be easily observed, but this does not mean that the media influence is not continuing. This is why it is important to consider both manifestation and process effects. Not all media-influenced effects provide easy-to-spot manifestations. Some media-influenced effects take a long time to emerge, so by the time we observe an effect, it is difficult to make a case that the effect was influenced by media exposures. For example, after several years of watching news commentators criticize the president, your otherwise positive attitude of the president might have eroded so that you are now neutral or even negative about the president. No one media exposure caused you to change your attitude. Also, your attitude change took place during a time period when you were likely to be discussing presidential performance with your friends, so those conversations must be considered part of the process of media influence; that is, perhaps you are an opinion leader in political matters, so you acquire information from the media and pass it along to your friends as you monitor your friends' reactions, which stimulates you to seek out more information from the media to strength your arguments. Thus your media exposures interact with your conversations with friends in a cyclical process of media influence.

Some media-influenced effects never produce characteristics that can be observed. For example, perhaps you have a friend who developed a behavioral intention to learn to play a musical instrument after years of listening to music, but for one reason or another never bought a musical instrument, took a lesson, or tried to play. He or she never talks about this behavioral intention because it would be too embarrassing, but the intention to learn to play a musical instrument gets stronger and stronger with more and more exposures to musical recordings on radio, TV, and the Internet.

Some media-influenced effects exhibit themselves as non-changes, so it is difficult to make a case that the continuing of the status quo represents a media effect. For example, let's say you are a loyal Coke drinker. Over time you continue to drink only Coke, despite repeated exposures to other kinds of soft drinks in the media. It appears that the media have no influence when you think about all the ads for soft drinks to which you have been exposed and their total lack of influence on getting you to try other soft drinks. However, you should not overlook the influence that Coke ads have had on reinforcing your brand loyalty.

While the media influence can be observed in many effects, that influence is often difficult or impossible to observe with other effects. Remember that our inability to observe a particular manifestation does not automatically mean that the media are not exerting an influence. Many effects are "process" effects, which means that changes are in process and building below the surface, and they have not yet erupted into manifestations yet. If we limited our thinking about effects to only those effects that were clearly manifested, we would miss a good deal about how the mass media continually influence effects.

When considering media influence, it is important to think of patterns over time, such as baselines and fluctuations. The baseline, which is shaped by media influence over long periods of time, is the best estimate of a person's degree of effect at any given time. Fluctuations are short-term deviations from the baseline.

Baselines differ in slope, degree, and elasticity. *Slope* refers to the direction of the angle of the baseline; an upward slope indicates a generally increasing level of an effect over time, while a downward slope indicates a generally decreasing level of an effect. *Degree* refers to the steepness of the angle; a sharp angle reflects a relatively large degree of change in effects level, while a relatively flat slope reflects a continuing level in the baseline. *Elasticity* reflects how entrenched the baseline is. Over time a baseline that has been reinforced continually by the same kind of media messages will become highly entrenched, making it less and less likely that there will be fluctuations off the baseline, and when there are fluctuation spikes, those fluctuation spikes are smaller and smaller over time.

Fluctuations have three characteristics: duration, magnitude, and direction. The *duration* refers to how long the fluctuation lasts before returning to the baseline. *Magnitude* refers to how far the fluctuation spike deviates from the baseline. And *direction* refers to whether the fluctuation spike moves upward (thus representing an increase in the level) or downward (thus representing a decrease in the level).

Nature of Media Effects Research

Scholars have developed a very large literature examining wide variety of media effects. This literature, which has been estimated to be as large as 10,000 studies, documents hundreds of different effects on individuals as well as aggregates such as the public, institutions, society, culture, and the media themselves. Also, scholars have developed well over a hundred theories to identify various effects and to test the factors that lead to those effects.

Theories, however, were not used in this book to organize the wide range of media effects, because less than one third of the research literature has dealt with theory. Instead, the perspective in this book was to display the full range of the research, so a pair of METs (Media Effects Templates) were developed—one for effects on individuals and one for macro-level effects. The individual-level MET (shown in Figure 3.1) is structured by type of media effects (physiology, cognitions, beliefs, attitudes, affects, and behaviors) and by media influence functions (acquiring, triggering, altering, and reinforcing). The macro-level MET (shown in Figure 3.2) is structured by five types of effects (cognition, belief, attitude, affect, and behavior) and five macro units (the public, institutions, society, culture, and the mass media themselves). This macro-level MET is an alteration of the individual-level MET so that it can better organize the literature of media effects on larger aggregates, which is much smaller than the research literature of effects on individuals.

While the media effects literature has been very useful in identifying a wide range of effects and their influences, it has been less successful in determining the relative importance among those effects in their everyday prevalence and strength. The reason for this is that the literature is built largely from designs that have used laboratory experiments rather than field experiments and that used survey methods in which participants self-report rather than observations of real-world occurrences. Furthermore, the literature makes many claims about effects over time (both changes to as well as reinforcements of the status quo) without observing participants or asking participants about their knowledge, attitudes, beliefs, affects, and behaviors at more than one point in time. For these reasons, the findings that emerge from this literature are more suggestive than definitive. However, this literature has established a very useful foundation that will support the research field as it moves out of its largely exploratory beginning and into a more rigorous phase of documenting media influence in the everyday lives of us all, where we are overwhelmed with choices.

EXTENDING YOUR UNDERSTANDING

Now that you have reviewed the major ideas, it is possible to take one more step toward focusing even more on the big picture, and that is to address the question: Are all media effects equally important? We will have to wait for a full answer to this question until after the research field is able to more fully calibrate the relative prevalence and strength among the many effects it has uncovered. However, in the meantime we can use the wisdom in the existing literature to direct our attention to some types of effects as more primary than others. By *primary*, I mean that if certain of these effects do not occur in an individual, then other types will not follow in succession. Specifically, physiological and cognitive effects are more primary than the other four types. That is, something physiological or cognitive must occur in an individual in order for a belief, attitudinal, affective, or behavioral effect to occur.

Why is this so? In the set of six types of media effects, cognitive and physiological effects are relatively independent from the others in the sense that they can occur with no antecedent from the other four; however, the other four are dependent on an antecedent from cognition or physiology or both. For example, a person can be exposed to a media message and learn a fact. That is a purely cognitive effect. The person can then do something with that fact and derive another type of effect, such as an attitude or a belief. Media influenced attitudes begin with the media a providing of information to a person in the form of an attitude which is then either (a) retained by the person (much like the retention of factual information) as his or her own attitude, or (b) triggers a thought process of evaluation. Likewise, media-influenced beliefs begin with the media providing information to a person in the form of a belief that is then either (a) retained by the person (much like the retention of factual information) as his or her own belief, or (b) triggers a thought process of pattern construction and generalization from the pattern elements to the world. In a chapter entitled "Cognitive Processes in Attitude Formation and Change" in the *Handbook of Attitudes,* Wegener and Carlston (2005) argue that the "cognitive process has been at the heart of research on attitudes virtually since that research began" (p. 493). And more generally they say, "If the human brain is involved, a process is cognitive, and because the human brain is almost always involved, few human activities fall outside the cognitive umbrella" (p. 494).

Media-influenced affective effects begin with the media stimulating a physiological reaction that is then labeled in a cognitive process, either consciously or unconsciously. Media-influenced behavioral effects begin with an idea planted in a person's mind about a behavioral sequence and a physiological reaction that is needed to energize the action.

Some of the behavioral effects are automatic, so that they require only the energy to enact (for example, imitation) and thus circumvent the thinking processes. Other behavioral effects require a significant degree of cognition as people think about how to behave, construct a sequence of novel acts, and rehearse the sequence before performing it. The manifestation consists of behaviors, but in order to understand the manifestation, we need to examine the process leading up to it, which involves cognitions.

Another reason to make a distinction between primary and derived types of effects is that derived effects are typically more complex than primary effects and they require more drive energy to undertake and complete successfully. Furthermore, the derived effects get their drive energy from the primary effects. For example, behaving aggressively requires more energy than imagining oneself behaving aggressively. Crossing the line between thinking about something and doing something requires arousal, and that is a physiological effect. Another example is changing one's attitude about something. It requires more energy to reevaluate and rethink than to keep the same attitude. It requires drive energy to do the reevaluation and rethinking. The cognitive state of dissonance has been found to create such drive energy. Humans experience a drive for consistency and will be motivated to expend the energy needed to achieve this goal of consistency.

So for the time being, we still have a lot to learn about which of the hundreds of media-influenced effects are the strongest and the most prevalent. But we do know that cognitive and physiological effects are primary; without something happening in one or both of these types, we cannot have a belief, attitude, affective, or behavioral effect.

MANAGING EFFECTS ON OURSELVES

There is not much we can do as individuals to change the way the media tell their stories, the way they try to attract our attention, and the way they condition us for repeated exposures. Producers have carefully developed their formulas over decades of trial and error. These formulas work very well for attracting and holding our attention. It is foolhardy for us to complain to producers that their formulas work too well and to expect producers to change their storytelling practices when such changes would serve to make them less successful. Instead, if we are bothered by certain media effects that we are experiencing, then we need to change our own practices and habits. This type of change is likely to be much more successful than spending all our time writing letters to producers or complaining to the people around us.

What are the changes we can make? I suggest following a five-step procedure. The more often you go through these five steps, the more you will understand the media influences on your life and the more you will be able to control this process.

Step 1: Increase Awareness of Your Goals

You can begin by asking yourself a series of questions: What do I want to achieve in life? What do I want to achieve this year, this week, and today? What do I want to achieve right now? What makes me happy? What things do I want to avoid and why?

Source: Comstock Images/Comstock/Thinkstock

Some people are fairly introspective and know themselves well; they can provide detailed answers to all of these questions at any given time. Other people can only give fuzzy answers or no answers at all to some (or all) of these questions. The more you are satisfied with the clarity and detail in your answers, the more you know yourself.

Once you have confronted your answers to these questions, move onto the really big question: How many of my goals are really me and how many have been programmed by the mass media? This is not an easy question to answer because it is not a question that can be answered without a lot of thinking and self-monitoring over time. After all, the media have been subtly shaping your expectations for many years, so it will take some time to get your perspective on these shaping influences and to spot differences between your natural beliefs and those imposed by the mass media. But if you keep thinking about this over time, you will start to notice instances when your media exposure habits are not delivering the kinds of feelings and information you want. When this happens, you have identified a place where the media have programmed you in a way that is not satisfying your own goals.

Step 2: Think About How You Can Use the Media as Your Tools

Given your goals, which media, vehicles, genres of messages, and individual messages serve your needs best? Look at your answer and think about how you can use the media to reach these goals rather than have the media train you into habitual, mindless exposures so that you will help *them* reach *their* goals. If you want entertainment, are you finding the best shows to entertain you? Or has the long-term media programming of your algorithms narrowed your search so much that you feel you have no alternatives? If it is the latter, then get out of your programmed rut and explore.

Step 3: Monitor Your Media Exposures

Many of us do not have a clear idea of our media exposures. We think we have one pattern of media exposure when in reality our pattern is very different. This is because most media exposure is habitual and we do not keep a running tally in our minds about all the time we spend with any given medium. Also, we do not catalogue each message exposure. Instead, we have some fuzzy idea of which media and which messages we spend time with, but this idea is often highly inaccurate. So it is important periodically to monitor your exposures. This is hard to do because it can be exhausting, so this is not something you should do every day. But you should try it periodically to check the accuracy of your beliefs about your exposure patterns.

What should be monitored? We need to think beyond simply recording how much time we spend with each medium, such as the Internet, recorded music, television, and so on. We also need to be aware of how much time we spend in various exposure states. Are you spending enough time in the transported state, where you are fully engrossed in the experience? Are you spending enough time in the self-reflexive state, where you critically analyze what you are doing and why?

We need to monitor our feelings of satisfaction with our exposures. Are we getting the full level of satisfaction we expect, or are we following our habits of exposure because we have nothing else better to do?

Step 4: Alter Your Reactions to Messages

When you identify patterns of exposure that are not meeting your needs well enough, try altering what you think about the messages during those exposures. The first thing to do is to try exposing yourself to messages less in the automatic exposure state and more in the attentional or—better still—in the self-reflexive state. Be active in asking yourself about your degree of arousal and why you are aroused like you are. Ask yourself about the point of view of the message designer and whether there are other points of view you could use when constructing your own meaning from the message. Think about the consequences of your actions and ask yourself whether similar consequences would happen to you in your everyday life. Think about the range of consequences for your actions and whether the media portrayals fall within that range; if they do not, then perhaps they are not realistic enough for you to consider the possibility of adapting them in your own life. But perhaps they are probable, even though you have not experienced them in your own life.

The essence of thinking about our reactions to the messages is keyed to our perceptions of their reality. And by reality, I do not simply mean whether they have occurred in our real lives, but whether it is probable that they could occur if we are motivated to do what it takes to make them occur. One of the very attractive features of media stories is that they show us people and events beyond our current grasp. This is a bad thing if all it does is make us feel frustrated or if we keep telling ourselves that we could experience those things but then do nothing in our real lives to make those experiences a reality for us. But this can be a good thing if it motivates us to extend our real lives.

Step 5: Alter Your Exposure Patterns

After making a habit of altering your reactions to certain types of media content, you will find yourself motivated to alter your exposure patterns. Why is this? Because when your reactions regard certain content as silly and useless for your purposes, you will have little motivation to continue with those types of exposures. Also, as others of your reactions find deeper and more interesting meanings in other types of content, you will find yourself drawn more to that content. Thus what you are doing is allowing your needs to come forth and shift your needs for media content. As your needs shift, you will be exposing yourself to different kinds of content. There is a lot of different kind of content across the mass media, so do not think that you will evolve into a need for which there is no media content.

Do not feel that you need to make a radical shift in your exposure patterns. Let your evolving awareness of your needs determine the flow. As you shift your exposure patterns, you will discover new needs that you will want to satisfy, so return to Step 1 and work through the sequence of steps again. These five steps are a process that is best repeated over and over. Each time you will learn something more about yourself and your ability to see more in the same media messages. Gradually you will shift the balance of influence away from the media and more inside your control. In short, you will be increasing your control over the media effects process.

SUMMARY

Now that you know a lot more about what media effects are, how the mass media exert their influence, and how to gain more control over those effects in your everyday life, the rest is up to you. The book and the course are finished, only you can decide whether this is the end of your learning about media effects or only the beginning.

Review Questions

1. What are the most important ideas about the nature of the audience?

2. What are the most important ideas about the nature of media effects?

3. What are the most important ideas about the nature of media influence?

4. What are the most important ideas about the nature of media effects research?

5. Why are cognitive and physiological effects more primary than the other four types of effects of belief, attitude, affect, and behavior?

6. What are the five steps in managing media effects on yourself?

Further Thinking Question

From this point onward, there really is only one question: What will you do with the information you learned from this book to help control the media effects in your own life?

References

Abelman, R. (1995). Gifted, LD, Gifted/LD children's understanding of temporal sequencing on television. *Journal of Broadcasting & Electronic Media, 39*, 297–312.

Abramson, P. R., Perry, L., Seeley, T., Seeley, D., & Rothblatt, A. (1981). Thermographic measurement of sexual arousal: A discriminant validity analysis. *Archives of Sexual Behavior 10*(2), 175–176.

Aday, S. (2010). Leading the charge: Media, elites, and the use of emotion in stimulating rally effects in wartime. *Journal of Communication, 60,* 440–465.

Adorno, T., & Horkheimer, M. (1972). *The dialectic of enlightenment*. New York: Herder & Herder.

Ahn, H., & Litman, B. R. (1997). Vertical integration and consumer welfare in the cable industry. *Journal of Broadcasting & Electronic Media, 41,* 453–477.

Ajzen, I., & Fishbein, M. (1977). Attitude-behavior relations: A theoretical analysis and review of empirical research. *Psychological Bulletin, 84,* 888–918.

Ajzen, I., & Fishbein, M. (2005). The influence of attitudes on behavior. In D. Albarracin, B. T. Johnson, & M. P. Zanna (Eds.), *The handbook of attitudes* (pp. 173–221). Mahwah, NJ: Erlbaum.

Albarracin, D., Johnson, B. T., & Zanna, M. P. (Eds.). (2005). *The handbook of attitudes*. Mahwah, NJ: Erlbaum.

Albarracin, D., Zanna, M. P., Johnson, B. T., & Kumkale, G. T. (2005). Attitudes: Introduction and scope. In D. Albarracin, B. T. Johnson, & M. P. Zanna (Eds.), *The handbook of attitudes* (pp. 3–19). Mahwah, NJ: Erlbaum.

Albarran, A. B. (2002). *Media economics: Understanding markets, industries and concepts* (2nd ed.). Ames: Iowa State University Press.

Alexander, B. C. (1997). Televangelism: Redressive ritual within a larger social drama. In S. M. Hoover & K. Lundby (Eds.), *Rethinking media, religion, and culture* (pp. 194–208). Thousand Oaks, CA: Sage.

Allen, M., D'Alessio, D., Brezgel, K. (1995). Meta-analysis summarizing the effects of pornography II: Aggression after exposure. *Human Communication Research, 22,* 258–283.

Allport, F. H. (1924). *Social psychology.* Boston: Houghton Mifflin.

Allport, G. W. (1935). Attitudes. In C. Murchison (Ed.), *Handbook of social psychology* (pp. 798–884). Worcester, MA: Clark University Press.

Altschull. J. H. (1984). *Agents of power: The role of the news media in human affairs.* New York: Longman.

Althaus, S. L., & Tewksbury, D. (2002). Agenda setting and the "new" news: Patterns of issue importance among readers of the paper and online versions of the New York Times. *Communication Research, 29,* 180–207.

Altheide, D. L., & Snow, R. P. (1979). *Media logic.* Beverly Hills, CA: Sage.

Altheide, D. L., & Snow, R. P. (1991). *Media worlds in the postjournalism era.* New York: Aldine/de Gruyter.

Althusser, L. (1971). *Lenin and philosophy and other essays.* Translated from the French by Ben Brewster. London: New Left Books.

Anderson, D. R., & Burns, J. (1991). Paying attention to television. In J. Bryant & D. Zillmann (Eds.), *Responding to the screen: Reception and reaction processes* (pp. 3–25). Hillsdale, NJ: Erlbaum.

Anderson, D. R., Collins, P. A., Schmitt, K. L., & Jacobvitz, R. S. (1996). Stressful life events and television viewing. *Communication Research, 23,* 243–260.

Anderson, D. R., Huston, A. C., Wright, J. C., & Collins, P. A. (1998). *Sesame Street* and educational television for children. In R. G. Noll & M E. Price (Eds.), *A communications cornucopia: Markle Foundation essays on information policy* (pp. 279–296). Washington, DC: Brookings Institution Press.

Anderson, J. R. (1983). *The architecture of cognition.* Cambridge, MA: Harvard University Press.

Andison, F. S. (1977). TV violence and viewer aggression: A cumulation of study results. *Public Opinion Quarterly, 41,* 314–331.

Andsager, J. L. (2000). How interest groups attempt to shape public opinion with competing news frames. *Journalism & Mass Communication Quarterly, 77,* 577–592.

Andsager, J. L., Austin, E. W., & Pinkleton, B. E. (2001). Questioning the value of realism: Young adults' processing of messages in alcohol-related public service announcements and advertising. *Journal of Communication, 51*, 121–142.

Andsager, J. L., Austin, E. W., & Pinkleton, B. E. (2002). Gender as a variable in interpretation of alcohol-related messages. *Communication Research, 29*, 246–269.

Appel, M. (2008). Fictional narratives cultivate just-world beliefs. *Journal of Communication, 58*, 62–83.

Appiah, O. (2002). Black and White viewers' perception and recall of occupational characters on television. *Journal of Communication, 52*, 776–793.

Armstrong, G. B. (2002). Experimental studies of the cognitive effects of the use of television as background to intellectual activities. In A. V. Stavros (Ed.), *Advances in communications and media research* (Vol. 1, pp. 21–56). New York: Nova Science Publishers.

Armstrong, J. S. (2007). Constructing television communities: The FCC, signals, and cities, 1948–1957. *Journal of Broadcasting & Electronic Media, 51*, 129–146.

Arpan. L. M., & Peterson, E. M. (2008). Influence of source liking and personality traits on perceptions of bias and future news source selection. *Media Psychology, 11*, 310–329.

Association of American Publishers. (2003, May 7). March numbers show book sales still uneven. Retrieved July 23, 2004, from http://www.publishers.org/press/releases

Aubrey, J. S. (2006). Effects of sexually objectifying media on self-objectification and body surveillance in undergraduates: Results of a 2-year panel study. *Journal of Communication, 56*, 366–386.

Aubrey, J. S., & Taylor, L. D. (2009). The role of lad magazines in priming men's chronic and temporary appearance-related schemata: An investigation of longitudinal and experimental findings. *Human Communication Research, 35*, 28–58.

Austin, E. W., & Pinkleton, B. E. (1995). Positive and negative effects of political disaffection on the less experienced voter. *Journal of Broadcasting & Electronic Media, 39*, 215–235.

Austin, E. W., Pinkleton, B. E., & Funabiki, R. P. (2007). The desirability paradox in the effects of media literacy training. *Communication Research, 34*, 483–507.

Baek, Y. M., & Wojcieszak, M. E. (2009). Don't expect too much! Learning from late-night comedy and knowledge item difficulty. *Communication Research, 36*, 783–809.

Bagdikian, B. (1992). *The media monopoly* (4th ed.). Boston: Beacon Press.

Bagdikian, B. (1997). *The media monopoly* (5th ed.). Boston: Beacon Press.

Bagdikian, B. H. (2000). *The media monopoly* (6th ed.). Boston: Beacon Press.

Baker, R. K., & Ball, S. J. (1969). *Violence and the media.* Washington, DC: U. S. Government Printing Office.

Baker, W. E., Honea, H., & Russell, C. A. (2004). Do not wait to reveal the brand name: The effect of brand-name placement on television advertising effectiveness. *Journal of Advertising, 33*(3), 77–85.

Ball-Rokeach, S. J., & DeFleur, M. (1976). A dependency model of mass-media effects. *Communication Research, 3*, 3–21.

Bandura, A. (1977). Self-efficacy: Toward a unifying theory of behavioral change. *Psychological Review, 84*, 191–215.

Bandura, A. (1986). *Social foundations of thought and action: A social cognitive theory.* Englewood Cliffs, NJ: Prentice Hall.

Bandura, A. (1994). Social cognitive theory of mass communication. In J. Bryant & D. Zillmann (Eds.), *Media effects* (pp. 61–90). Hillsdale, NJ: Erlbaum.

Bandura, A. (2001). Social cognitive theory of mass communication. *Media Psychology, 3*, 265–299.

Bandura, A. (2002). Social cognitive theory of mass communication. In J. Bryant & D. Zillmann (Eds.), *Media effects: Advances in theory and research* (2nd ed., pp. 121–153). Mahwah, NJ: Erlbaum.

Bantz, C. R., McCorkle, S., & Baade, R. C. (1980). The news factory. *Communication Research, 7*, 45–68.

Bargh, J. A. (1984). Automatic and conscious processing of social information. In R. S. Wyer & T. K. Srull (Eds.), *Handbook of social cognition* (Vol. 3, pp. 1–43). Hillsdale, NJ: Erlbaum.

Bargh, J. A. (1997). The automaticity of everyday life. In R. S. Wyer (Ed.), *Advances in social cognition* (pp. 1–61). Mahwah, NJ: Erlbaum.

Barker-Plummer, B. (2002). Producing public voice: Resource mobilization and media access in the National Organization for Women. *Journalism & Mass Communication Quarterly, 79*, 188–205.

Barnhurst, K. G., & Wartella, E. (1998). Young citizens, American TV newscasts and the collective memory. *Critical Studies in Mass Communication, 15*, 279–305.

Basil, M. D. (1996). Identification as a mediator of celebrity effects. *Journal of Broadcasting & Electronic Media, 40*, 478–495.

Basil, M. D., Brown, W. J., & Bocarnea, M. C. (2002). Differences in univariate values versus multivariate relationships: Findings from a study of Diana, Princess of Wales. *Human Communication Research, 28*, 501–514.

Bass, A. Z. (1969). Refining the gatekeeper concept. *Journalism Quarterly, 46*, 69–71.

Baudrillard, J. (1983). *Simulations*. Translated by Paul Foss, Paul Patton, & Philip Beitchman. New York: Semiotext(e).

Baumgartner, J. C., & Morris, J. S. (2008). One "nation," under Stephen? The effects of the Colbert Report on American youth. *Journal of Broadcasting & Electronic Media, 52*, 622–643.

Beaudoin, C. E. (2009). Exploring the association between news use and social capital: Evidence of variance by ethnicity and medium. *Communication Research, 36*, 611–636.

Becker, J. U., Clement, M., & Schaedel, U. (2010). The impact of network size and financial incentives on adoption and participation in new online communities, *Journal of Media Economics, 23*, 165–179.

Becker, L. B., & Whitney, D. C. (1980). Effects of media dependencies: Audience assessments of government. *Communication Research, 7*, 95–120.

Bem, D. J. (1972). Self perception theory. In L. Berkowitz (Ed.), *Advances in experimental social psychology* (Vol. 6, pp. 1 – 62). New York: Academic Press.

Bennett, S. E. (1989). Trends in Americans' political information, 1967–1987. *American Politics Quarterly, 17*(4), 422–435.

Bennett, W. L. (1990). Toward a theory of press-state relationship in the United States. *Journal of Communication, 40*(2), 103–125.

Benoit, W. L., & Hansen, G. J. (2004). Presidential debate watching, issue knowledge, character evaluation, and vote choice. *Human Communication Research, 30*, 121–144.

Berelson, B., Lazarsfeld, P. F., & McPhee, W. N. (1954). *Voting: A study of opinion formation in a presidential campaign*. Chicago: University of Chicago Press.

Bergen, L. Grimes, T., & Potter, D. (2005). How attention partitions itself during simultaneous message presentations. *Human Communication Research, 31*, 311–336.

Berger, C.R. (1998). Processing quantitative data about risk and threat in news reports. *Journal of Comunication, 48*, 87–106.

Berger, C. R. (2000). Quantitative depictions of threatening phenomena in news reports: The scary world of frequency data. *Human Communication Research, 26*, 27–52.

Berger, C. R. (2005). Slippery slopes to apprehension: Rationality and graphical depictions of increasingly threatening trends. *Communication Research, 32*, 3–29.

Berger, P. L., & Huntington, S. P. (2002). *Many globalizations: Cultural diversity in the contemporary world*. New York: Oxford University Press.

Berger, P. L., & Luckmann, T. (1966). *The social construction of reality*. Garden City, NY: Anchor.

Berkowitz, D., & TerKeurst, J. V. (1999). Community as interpretive community: Rethinking the journalist-source relationship. *Journal of Communication, 49*, 125–136.

Berkowitz, L. (1965). Some aspects of observed aggression. *Journal of Personality & Social Psychology, 2*, 359–369.

Berkowitz, L. (1984). Some effects of thoughts on anti- and prosocial influences of media events: A cognitive-neoassociationist analysis. *Psychological Bulletin, 95*, 410–427.

Berkowitz, L. (2000). *Causes and consequences of feelings*. New York: Cambridge University.

Berlyne, D. E. (1960). *Conflict, arousal, and curiosity*. New York: McGraw-Hill.

Berman, R. (1981). *Advertising and social change*. Beverly Hills, CA: Sage.

Berney-Reddish, I. A., & Areni, C. S. (2006). Sex differences in responses to probability markers in advertising claims. *Journal of Advertising, 35*(2), 7–16.

Berscheid, E., & Walster, E. (1974). Physical attractiveness. In L. Berkowitz (Ed.), *Advances in experimental social psychology* (pp. 157–215). New York: Academic Press.

Bilandzic, H. (2006). The perception of distance in the cultivation process: A theoretical consideration of the relationship between television content, processing experience, and perceived distance. *Communication Theory, 16*, 333–355.

Bilandzic, H., & Busselle, R. W. (2008). Transportation and transportability in the cultivation of genre-consistent attitudes and estimates. *Journal of Communication, 58*, 508–529.

Bird, S. E. (1999). Gendered construction of the American Indian in popular media. *Journal of Communication, 49*, 61–83.

Bissell, K. L., & Zhou, P. (2004). Must-see TV or ESPN: Entertainment and sports media exposure and body-image distortion in college women. *Journal of Communication, 54*, 5–21.

Bleakley, A., Hennessy, M., Fishbein, M., & Jordan, A. (2008). It works both ways: The relationship between exposure to sexual content in the media and adolescent sexual behavior. *Media Psychology, 11*, 443–461.

Blevins, J., & Brown, D. H. (2010). Concerns about the disproportionate use of economic research in the FCC's Media Ownership Studies from 2002–2007. *Journal of Broadcasting & Electronic Media, 54*, 603–620.

Blumer, H. (1946). The field of collective behavior. In A. M. Lee (Ed.), *New outline of the principles of sociology* (pp. 167–222). New York: Barnes & Noble.

Boczkowski, P. J. (2004). The processes of adopting multimedia and interactivity in three online newsrooms. *Journal of Communication, 54,* 197–213.

Bogart, L. (1995). *Commercial culture: The media system and the public interest.* New York: Oxford University Press.

Bolls, P. D., & Lang, A. (2003). I saw it on the radio: The allocation of attention to high-imagery radio advertisements. *Media Psychology, 5,* 33–55.

Bolls, P. D., Lang, A., & Potter, R. F. (2001). The effects of message valence and listener arousal on attention, memory, and facial muscular responses to radio advertisements. *Communication Research, 28,* 627–651.

Boorstin, D. (1961). *The image.* New York: Atheneum.

Botta, R. A. (1999). Television images and adolescent girls' body image disturbance. *Journal of Communication, 49,* 22–41.

Botta, R. A. (2000). The mirror of television: A comparison of black and white adolescents' body image. *Journal of Communication, 50,* 144–159.

Boyd-Barrett, O. (1977). Media imperialism: Towards an international framework for the analysis of media systems. In J. Curren, M. Gurevitch, & J. Woollacott (Eds.), *Mass communication and society* (pp. 116–135). Beverly Hills, CA: Sage.

Bracken, C. C. (2005). Presence and image quality: The case of high-definition television. *Media Psychology, 7,* 191–205.

Bracken, C. C. (2006). Perceived source credibility of local television news: The impact of television form and presence. *Journal of Broadcasting & Electronic Media, 50,* 723–741.

Bracken, C. D., & Lombard, M. (2004). Social presence and children: Praise, intrinsic motivation, and learning with computers. *Journal of Communication, 54,* 22–37.

Bradley, S. D., & Shapiro, M. A. (2004). Parsing reality: The interactive effects of complex syntax and time pressure on cognitive processing of television scenarios. *Media Psychology, 6,* 307–333.

Bramlett-Solomon, S., & Wilson, V. (1989). Images of the elderly in *Life* and *Ebony,* 1978–87. *Journalism Quarterly, 66,* 185–188.

Braun-LaTour, K. A., & LaTour, M. S. (2004). Assessing the long-term impact of a consistent advertising campaign on consumer memory. *Journal of Advertising, 33*(2), 49–61.

Braun-LaTour, K. A., & LaTour, M. S. (2005). Transforming consumer experience: When timing matters. *Journal of Advertising, 34*(3), 19–30.

Braun-LaTour, K. A., LaTour, M. S., Pickrell, J. E., & Loftus, E. F. (2004). How and when advertising can influence memory for consumer experience. *Journal of Advertising, 33*(4), 7–25.

Brewer, P. R., & Cao, X. (2006). Candidate appearances on soft news shows and public knowledge about primary campaigns. *Journal of Broadcasting & Electronic Media, 50,* 18–35.

Brosius, H-B., Donsbach, W., & Birk, M. (1996). How do text-picture relations affect the informational effectiveness of television newscasts? *Journal of Broadcasting & Electronic Media, 40,* 180–195.

Brown, J. D., & L'Engle, K. L. (2009). X-rated: Sexual attitudes and behaviors associated with U.S. early adolescents' exposure to sexually explicit media. *Communication Research, 36,* 129–151.

Brown, J. D., & Pardun, C. J. (2004). Little in common: Racial and gender differences in adolescents' television diets. *Journal of Broadcasting & Electronic Media, 48,* 266–278.

Bryant, J., Carveth, R. A., & Brown, D. (1981. Television viewing and anxiety: An experimental examination. *Journal of Communication, 31,* 106–119.

Bryant, J., & Miron, D. (2002). Entertainment as media effect. In J. Bryant & D. Zillmann (Eds.), *Media effects: Advances in theory and research* (2nd ed., pp. 549–582). Mahwah, NJ: Erlbaum.

Bucy, E. P., & Newhagen, J. E. (1999a). The emotional appropriateness heuristic: Processing televised presidential reactions to the news. *Journal of Communication, 49,* 59–79.

Bucy, E. P., & Newhagen, J. E. (1999b). The micro- and macrodrama of politics on television: Effects of media format on candidate evaluations. *Journal of Broadcasting & Electronic Media, 43,* 193–210.

Buijzen, M., & Valkenburg, P. M. (2000). The impact of television advertising on children Christmas wishes. *Journal of Broadcasting & Electronic Media, 44,* 456–470.

Buijzen, M., & Valkenburg, P. M. (2005). Parental mediation of undesired advertising effects. *Journal of Broadcasting & Electronic Media, 49,* 153–166.

Burgoon, M., Pfau, M., & Birk, T. S. (1995). An inoculation theory explanation for the effects of corporate issue/advocacy advertising campaigns. *Communication Research, 22,* 485–505.

Burke, M. C., & Edell, J. A. (1989). The impact of feelings on ad-based affect and cognition. *Journal of Marketing Research, 26*(1), 69–83.

Busselle, R. W. (2001). Television exposure, perceived realism, and exemplar accessibility in the social judgment process. *Media Psychology, 3,* 43–67.

Byrne. S., Linz, D., & Potter, W. J. (2009). A test of competing cognitive explanations for the boomerang effect in response to the deliberate disruption of media-induced aggression. *Media Psychology, 12,* 227–248.

Cacioppo, J. T., Gerdner, W. L., & Bernston, G. G. (1999). The affect system has parallel and integrative processing components: Form follows function. *Journal of Personality & Social Psychology, 76,* 839–855.

Calzo, J. P., & Ward, L. M. (2009). Media exposure and viewers' attitudes toward homosexuality: Evidence for mainstreaming or resonance? *Journal of Broadcasting & Electronic Media, 53,* 280–299.

Campbell, H. J. (1973). *The pleasure areas: A new theory of behavior.* New York: Delacorte.

Cantor, J. (1994). Fright reactions to mass media. In J. Bryant & D. Zillmann (Eds.), *Media effects: Advances in theory and research* (pp. 213–245). Hillsdale, NJ: Erlbaum.

Cantor, J. (2002). Fright reactions to mass media. In J. Bryant & D. Zillmann (Eds.), *Media effects: Advances in theory and research* (2nd ed., pp. 287–306). Mahwah, NJ: Erlbaum.

Cantor, J., & Hoffner, C. (1990). Children's fear reactions to a televised film as a function of perceived immediacy of depicted threat. *Journal of Broadcasting & Electronic Media, 34,* 421–442.

Cantor, J., & Nathanson, A. I. (1996). Children's fright reactions to television news. *Journal of Communication, 46*(4), 139–152.

Cantor, J., & Nathanson, A. I. (1997). Predictors of children's interest in violent television programs. *Journal of Broadcasting & Electronic Media, 41,* 155–167.

Cantor, J., & Sparks, G. C. (1984). Children's fear responses to mass media: Testing some Piagetian predictions. *Journal of Communication, 34*(2), 90–103.

Cantor, J., & Wilson, B. J. (1984). Modifying fear responses to mass media in preschool and elementary school children. *Journal of Broasdcasting, 28,* 431–443.

Cantor, J., & Wilson, B. J. (1988). Helping children cope with frightening media presentations. *Current Psychology: Research & Reviews, 7,* 58–75.

Cantor, J., Wilson, B. J., & Hoffner, C., (1986). Emotional responses to a televised nuclear holocaust film. *Communication Research, 13,* 257–277.

Cantor, J., Ziemke, D., & Sparks, G. G. (1984). Effects of forewarning on emotional responses to a horror film. *Journal of Broadcasting, 28,* 21–31.

Cantor, J., Zillamn, D., & Bryant, J. (1975). Enhancement of experienced sexual arousal in response to erotic stimuli through misattribution of unrelated residual excitation. *Journal of Personality and Social Psychology, 32,* 69–75.

Cantril, H. (1940). *The invasion from Mars: A study of the psychology of panic.* Princeton, NJ: Princeton University Press.

Cappella, J. N. (2002) Cynicism and social trust in the new media environment. *Journal of Communication, 52,* 229–241.

Cappella, J. N., & Jamieson, K. H. (1997). *The spiral of cynicism: The press and the public good.* New York: Oxford University Press.

Carey, J. (1975). A cultural approach to communications. *Communications, 2,* 1–22.

Carlson, M., Marcus-Newhall, A., & Miller, N. (1990). Effects of situational aggression cues: A quantitative review. *Journal of Personality & Social Psychology, 58,* 622–633.

Carpentier, F. R. D. (2009). Effects of priming social goals on personal interest in television news. *Journal of Broadcasting & Electronic Media, 53,* 300–316.

Carpentier, F. R. D., Roskos-Ewoldsen, D. R., & Roskos-Ewoldsen, B. B. (2008). A test of the network models of political priming. *Media Psychology, 11,* 186–206.

Carragee, K. M. (1990). Interpretive media study and interpretive social science. *Critical Studies in Mass Communication, 7,* 81–96.

Cartwright, D. (1949). Some principles of mass persuasion. *Human Relations, 2,* 253–267.

Centerwall, B. S. (1989). Exposure to television as a risk factor for violence. *Journal of Epidemiology, 129,* 643–652.

Chadwick, A. (2006). *Internet politics: States, citizens, and new communication technologies.* New York: Oxford University Press.

Chaffee, S. H. (1972). The interpersonal context of mass communication. In F. G. Kline & P. J. Tichenor (Eds.), *Current perspectives in mass communication research* (pp. 95–120). Beverly Hills: Sage.

Chaiken, S., Liberman, A., & Eagly, A. H. (1989). Heuristic and systematic processing within and beyond the persuasion context. In J. S. Uleman & J. A. Bargh (Eds.), *Unintended thought* (pp. 212–252). New York: Guilford.

Chan-Olmsted, S. M., & Ha, L. S. (2003). Internet business models for broadcasters: How television stations perceive and integrate the Internet. *Journal of Broadcasting & Electronic Media, 47,* 597–617.

Chandler, J., Konrath, S., & Schwarz, N. (2009). Online and on my mind: Temporary and chronic accessibility moderate the influence of media figures. *Media Psychology, 12,* 210–226.

Chang, C. (2002). Self-congruency as a cue in different advertising-processing contexts. *Communication Research, 29,* 503–536.

Chang, C. (2004). Country of origin as a heuristic cue: The effects of message ambiguity and product involvement. *Media Psychology, 6,* 169–192.

Chang, C. (2006). Beating the news blues: Mood repair through exposure to advertising. *Journal of Communication, 56,* 198–217.

Chang, C. (2007). The relative effectiveness of comparative and noncomparative advertising. *Journal of Advertising, 36,* 21–25.

Chang, H-c. (1998). The effect of news teasers in processing TV news. *Journal of Broadcasting & Electronic Media, 42,* 327–339.

Chaudhuri, A., & Buck, R. (1995). Media differences in rational and emotional responses to advertising. *Journal of Broadcasting & Electronic Media, 39,* 109–125.

Check, J. V. P. (1985). *The effects of violent and nonviolent pornography.* Ottawa: Department of Justice for Canada.

Chia, S. C. (2006). How peers mediate media influence on adolescents' sexual attitudes and sexual behavior. *Journal of Communication, 56,* 585–606.

Chiricos, T. (1996). Moral panic as ideology: Drugs, violence, race and punishment in America. In *Justice with prejudice: Race and criminal justice in America* (pp. 19–48). New York: Harrow & Heston.

Cho, H., & Boster, F. J. (2008). First and third person perceptions on anti-drug ads among adolescents. *Communication Research, 35,* 169–189.

Cho, J. (2005). Media, interpersonal discussion, and electoral choice. *Communication Research, 32,* 295–322.

Cho, J., & McLeod, D. M. (2007). Structural antecedents to knowledge and participation: Extending the knowledge gap concept to participation. *Journal of Communication, 57,* 205–228.

Chock, T. M., Fox, J. R., Angelini, J. R., Lee, S., & Lang, A. (2007). Telling me quickly: How arousing fast-paced PSAs decrease self-other differences. *Communication Research, 34,* 618–638.

Chory-Assad, R. M., & Tamborini, R. (2003). Television exposure and the public's perceptions of physicians. *Journal of Broadcasting & Electronic Media, 47,* 197–215.

Chory-Assad, R. M., & Yanen, A. (2005). Hopelessness and loneliness as predictors of older adults' involvement with favorite television performers. *Journal of Broadcasting & Electronic Media, 49,* 182–201.

Christians, C. G. (1997). Technology and triadic theories of mediation. In S. M. Hoover & K. Lundby (Eds.), *Rethinking media, religion, and culture* (pp. 65–82). Thousand Oaks, CA: Sage.

Cicchirillo, V., & Chory-Assad, R. M. (2005). Effects of affective orientation and video game play on aggressive thoughts and behaviors. *Journal of Broadcasting & Electronic Media, 49,* 435–449.

Cline, T. W., & Kellaris, J. J. (2007). The influence of humor strength and humor-message relatedness on ad memorability: A dual process model. *Journal of Advertising, 36,* 55–67.

Cline, V. B., Croft, R. G., & Courier, S. (1973). Desensitization of children to television violence. *Journal of Personality & Social Psychology, 27*(3), 260–265.

Clore, G. L., & Schnall, S. (2005). The influence of affect on attitudes. In D. Albarracin, B. T. Johnson, & M. P. Zanna (Eds.). *The handbook of attitudes* (pp. 437–489). Mahwah, NJ: Erlbaum.

Coe, K., Tewksbury, D., Bond, B. J., Drogos, K. L., Porter, R. W., Yahn, A., & Zhang, Y. (2008). Hostile news: Partisan use and perceptions of cable news programming. *Journal of Communication, 58,* 201–219.

Cohen, B. C. (1963). *The press and foreign policy.* Princeton, NJ: Princeton University Press.

Cohen, J. (1997). Parasocial relations and romantic attraction: Gender and dating status differences. *Journal of Broadcasting & Electronic Media, 41,* 516–529.

Cohen, J. (2002). Television viewing preferences: Programs, schedules, and the structure of viewing choices made by Israeli adults. *Journal of Broadcasting & Electronic Media, 46,* 204–221.

Cohen, J., & Tsfati, Y. (2009). The influence of presumed media influence on strategic voting. *Communication Research, 36,* 359–378.

Cohen, J., & Weimann, G. (2008). Who's afraid of reality shows? Exploring the effects of perceived influence of reality shows and the concern over their social effects on willingness to censor. *Communication Research, 35,* 382–397.

Collins, W. A. (1973). Effect of temporal separation between motivation, aggression, and consequences: A developmental study. *Developmental Psychology, 8*(2), 215–221.

Collins, W. A., Berndt, T. J., & Hess, V. L. (1974). Observational learning of motives and consequences for television aggression: A developmental study. *Child Development, 45,* 799–802.

Comisky, P., & Bryant, J. (1982). Factors involved in generating suspense. *Human Communication Research, 9,* 49–58.

Comstock, G. A. (1980). *Television in America.* Beverly Hills, CA: Sage.

Comstock, G.A. (1989). *The evolution of American television*. Newbury Park, CA: Sage.

Comstock, G., Chaffee, S. Katzman, N., McCombs, M., & Roberts, D. (1978). *Television and human behavior*. New York: Columbia University Press.

Converse, P. E. (1962). Information flow and the stability of partisan attitudes. *Public Opinion Quarterly, 26*(4), 578–599.

Cooper, R., & Tang, T. (2009). Predicting audience exposure to television in today's media environment: An empirical integration of active-audience and structural theories. *Journal of Broadcasting & Electronic Media, 53,* 400–418.

Corner, J. (1999). *Critical ideas in television studies*. Oxford, UK: Clarendon Press.

Coser, L. A. (1956). *The functions of social conflict*. New York: Free Press.

Coser, L. A., Kadushin, C., & Powell, W. W. (1982). *Books: The culture and commerce of publishing*. New York: Basic Books.

Coulter, D. S., & Punj, G. N. (2004). The effects of cognitive resource requirements, availability, and argument quality on brand attitudes: A melding of elaboration likelihood and cognitive resource matching theories. *Journal of Advertising, 33*(4), 53–64.

Cowan, T. (2002). *Creative destruction: How globalization is changing the world's cultures*. Princeton, NJ: Princeton University Press.

Craik, F. I. M., & Lockhart, R. S. (1972). Levels of processing: A framework for memory research. *Journal of Verbal Learning and Verbal Behavior, 11,* 671–684.

Croteau, D., & Hoynes, W. (2001). *The business of media: Corporate media and the public interest*. Boston: Pine Forge Press.

Crouch, J., & Maltese, J. A. (2008). The presidency and the news media. In M. J. Rozell & J. D. Mayer (Eds.) *Media power, media politics* (2nd ed., pp. 19–41). New York: Rowman & Littlefield.

Csikszentmihalyi, M. (1988). The flow experience and its significance for human psychology. In M. Csikszentmihalyi & I. S. Csikszentmihalyi (Eds.), *Optimal experience: Psychological studies of flow in consciousness* (pp. 15–35). New York: Cambridge University Press.

Cuellar-Fernández, B., Fuertes-Callén, Y., & Laínez-Gadea, J. (2010). The impact of corporate media news on market valuation. *Journal of Media Economics, 23,* 90–110.

Cwalina, W., Falkowski, A., & Kaid, L. L. (2000). Role of advertising in forming the image of politicians: Comparative analysis of Poland, France, and Germany. *Media Psychology, 2,* 119–146.

Dahlgren, P. (1995). *Television and the public sphere*. London: Sage.

Dallek, M. (2004, January 25). Primaries make voters secondary. *Los Angeles Times,* p. M2.

David, C. C. (2009). Learning political information from the news: A closer look at the role of motivation. *Journal of Communication, 59,* 243–261.

David, P., & Johnson, M. A. (1998). The role of self in third-person effects about body image. *Journal of Communication, 48*(4), 37–58.

David, P., Liu, K., & Myser, M. (2004). Methodological artifact or persistent bias? Testing the robustness of the third-person and reverse third-person effects for alcohol messages. *Communication Research, 31,* 206–233.

David, P., Morrison, G., Johnson, M. A., & Ross, F. (2002). Body image, race, and fashion models: Social distance and social identification in third-person effects. *Communication Research, 29,* 270–294.

Davis, M. H., & Kraus, L. A. (1989). Social contact, loneliness and mass media use: A test of two hypotheses. *Journal of Applied Social Psychology, 19,* 1100–1124.

Davis, S., & Mares, M-L. (1998). Effects of talk show viewing on adolescents. *Journal of Communication, 48*(2), 69–86.

Davis, R., & Owen, D. (1998). *New media and American politics*. New York: Oxford University Press.

Davison, W. P. (1983). The third-person effect in communication. *Public Opinion Quarterly, 47,* 1–15.

Dearing, J. W., & Rogers, E. M. (1996). *Agenda setting*. Thousand Oaks, CA: Sage.

DeFleur, M. L. (1970). *Theories of mass communication* (2nd ed.). New York: David McKay.

DeFleur, M. L., & Ball-Rokeach, S. (1975). *Theories of mass communication* (3rd ed.). New York: David McKay.

DeFleur, M. L., & Larsen, O. N. (1958). *The flow of information*. New York: Harper & Brothers.

Denenberg, V. H. (1987). Animal models and plasticity. In J. Gallagher & C. Ramey (Eds.), *The malleability of children*. Baltimore: Paul H. Brookes.

Denham, B. E. (2004). Toward an explication of media enjoyment: The synergy of social norms, viewing situations, and program content. *Communication Theory, 14,* 370–387.

Detenber, B. H., & Reeves, B. (1996). A bio-informational theory of emotion: Motion and image size effects on viewers. *Journal of Communication, 46*(3), 66–84.

Detenber, B. H., Simons, R. F., & Bennett, G. G., Jr. (1998). Roll 'em!: The effects of picture motion on emotional responses. *Journal of Broadcasting & Electronic Media, 42,* 113–127.

Detenber, B. H., Simons, R. F., & Reiss, J. E. (2000). The emotional significance of color in television presentations. *Media Psychology, 2,* 331–355.

De Vreese, C. H., & Semetko, H. A. (2002). Cynical and engaged: Strategic campaign coverage, public opinion, and mobilization in a referendum. *Communication Research, 29,* 615–641.

Diamond, M. (1988). *Enriching heredity.* New York: Free Press.

Diar, F., & Sundar, S. S. (2004). Orienting response and memory for Web advertisements: Exploring effects of pop-up window and animation. *Communication Research, 31,* 537–567.

Dixon, T. L. (2008). Crime news and racialized beliefs: Understanding the relationship between local news viewing and perceptions of African Americans and crime. *Journal of Communication, 58,* 106–125.

Dixon, T. L., & Azocar, C. L. (2006). Priming crime and activating Blackness: Understanding the psychological impact of the overrepresentation of Blacks as lawbreakers on television news. *Journal of Communication, 56,* 229–253.

Dolich, I. J. (1969). Congruence relationships between self images and product brands. *Journal of Marketing Research, 6,* 80–83.

Domke, D. (2000). Strategic elites, the press, and race relations. *Journal of Communication, 50,* 115–140.

Donnelly, W. J. (1986). *The confetti generation: How the new communications technology is fragmenting America.* New York: Holt.

Donohew, L., & Tipton, L. (1973). A conceptual model of information seeking, avoiding, and processing. In P. Clark (Ed.), *New models for mass communication research* (pp. 243–268). Beverly Hills, CA: Sage.

Dorr, A. (1980). When I was a child I thought as a child. In S. B. Withey & R. P. Abeles (Eds.), *Television and social behavior: Beyond violence and children* (pp. 191–230). Hillsdale, NJ: Erlbaum.

Douglas, W. (2003). *Television families: Is something wrong in suburbia?* Mahwah, NJ: Erlbaum.

Dulany, D. E. (1968). Awareness, rules, and propositional control: A confrontation with S-R behavior theory. In T. Dixon & D. Horton (Eds.), *Verbal behavior and behavior theory* (pp. 340–387). New York: Prentice Hall.

Duncan, C. P., & Nelson, J. E. (1985). Effects of humor in a radio advertising experiment. *Journal of Advertising, 14,* 33–40.

Dutta-Bergman, M. J. (2004). Complementarity in consumption of news types across traditional and new media. *Journal of Broadcasting & Electronic Media, 48,* 41–60.

Dysinger, W. S., & Ruckmick C. A. (1933). *The emotional responses of children to the motion picture situation.* New York: Macmillan.

Eagly, A. H., & Chaiken, S. (1998). Attitude structure and function. In D. T. Gilbert, S. T. Fiske, & G. Lindzey (Eds.), *Handbook of social psychology* (4th ed., Vol. 1, pp. 269–322). New York: McGraw-Hill.

Eastin, M. S. (2006). Video game violence and the female game player: Self- and opponent gender effects on presence and aggressive thoughts. *Human Communication Research 32,* 351–372.

Eastin, M. S., Appiah, O., & Cicchirillo, V. (2009). Identification and the influence of cultural stereotyping on postvideogame play hostility. *Human Communication Research, 35,* 337–356.

Eastman, S. T. (1993). *Broadcast/cable programming: Strategies and practices* (4th ed.). Belmont, CA: Wadsworth.

Eastman, S. T., & Newton, G. D. (1998). The impact of structural salience within on-air promotion. *Journal of Broadcasting & Electronic Media, 42,* 50–79.

Eastman, S. T., Newton, G. D., & Pack, L. (1996). Promoting prime-time programs in megasporting events. *Journal of Broadcasting & Electronic Media, 40,* 366–388.

Eastman, S. T., Newton, G. D., Riggs, K. E., & Neal-Lunsford, J. (1997). Accelerating the flow: A transition effect in programming theory? *Journal of Broadcasting & Electronic Media, 41,* 265–283.

Eccles, A., Marshall, W. L., & Barbaree, H. E. (1988). The vulnerability of erectile measures to repeated assessments. *Behavior Research & Therapy, 26,* 179–183.

Edell, J. A. (1988). Effects in advertisements: A review and synthesis. In S. Hecker & D. W. Stewart (Eds.), *Nonverbal communication in advertising* (pp. 11–28). Lexington, MA: D. C. Heath.

Edy, J. A. (1999). Journalistic uses of collective memory. *Journal of Communication, 49,* 71–85.

Edy, J. A., & Meirick, P. C. (2007). Wanted, dead or alive: Media frames, frame adoption, and support for the war in Afghanistan. *Journal of Communication, 57,* 19–141.

Eggermont, S. (2004). Television viewing, perceived similarity, and adolescents' expectations of a romantic partner. *Journal of Broadcasting & Electronic Media, 48,* 244–265.

Eggermont, S. (2006). Developmental changes in adolescents' television viewing habits: Longitudinal trajectories in a three-wave panel study. *Journal of Broadcasting & Electronic Media, 50,* 742–761.

Einstein, M. (2004). *Media diversity: Economics, ownership, and the FCC.* Mahwah, NJ: Erlbaum.

Elliott, P. (1982). Intellectuals, the information society and the disappearance of the public sphere. *Media, Culture & Society, 4,* 243–253.

Ellul, J. (1964). *The technological society.* New York: Knopf.

Emons, P., Scheepers, P., & Wester, F. (2009). Longitudinal changes in religiosity in Dutch society and drama programs on television, 1980–2005. *Journal of Media & Religion, 8,* 24–39.

Escalas, J. E. (2004). Imagine yourself in the product: Mental stimulation, narrative transportation, and persuasion. *Journal of Advertising, 33*(2), 37–48.

Eveland, W. P. Jr. (2001). The cognitive mediation model of learning from the news: Evidence from nonelection, off-year election, and presidential election contexts. *Communication Research, 28,* 571–601.

Eveland, W. P. Jr. (2002). News information processing as mediator of the relationship between motivations and political knowledge. *Journalism & Mass Communication Quarterly, 79,* 26–40.

Eveland, W. P. Jr., Cortese, J., Park, H., & Dunwoody, S. (2004). How web site organization influences free recall, factual knowledge, and knowledge structure density. *Human Communication Research, 30,* 208–233.

Eveland, W. P. Jr., & Dunwoody, S. (2001). Applying research on the uses and cognitive effects of hypermedia to the study of the World Wide Web. In W. B. Gudykunst (Ed.), *Communication yearbook 25* (pp. 79–113). Mahwah, NJ: Erlbaum.

Eveland, W. P Jr., & Dunwoody, S. (2002). An investigation of elaboration and selective scanning as mediators of learning from the web versus print. *Journal of Broadcasting & Electronic Media, 46,* 34–53.

Eveland, W. P. Jr., Marton, K., & Seo, M. (2004). Moving beyond "just the facts": The influence of online news on the content and structure of public affairs knowledge. *Communication Research, 31,* 82–108.

Ewen, S. (1976). *Captains of consciousness.* New York: McGraw-Hill.

Ex, C.T.G.M., Janssens, J.M.A.M., & Korzilius, H. P. L. M. (2002). Young females' images of motherhood in relation to television viewing. *Journal of Communication, 52,* 955–971.

Eyal, K., & Cohen, J. (2006). When good friends say goodbye: A parasocial breakup study. *Journal of Broadcasting & Electronic Media, 50,* 502–523.

Eyal, K., & Kunkel, D. (2008). The effects of sex in television drama shows on emerging adults' sexual attitudes and moral judgments. *Journal of Broadcasting & Electronic Media, 52,* 161–181.

Fabrigar, L. R., MacDonald, T. K., & Wegener, D. T. (2005). The structure of attitudes. In D. Albarracin, B. T. Johnson, & M. P. Zanna (Eds.), *The handbook of attitudes* (pp. 79–124). Mahwah, NJ: Erlbaum.

Fan, D. P., Wyatt, R. O., & Keltner, K. (2001). The suicidal messenger: How press reporting affects public confidence in the press, the military, and organized religion. *Communication Research, 28,* 826–852.

Farrar, K. M., Krcmar, M., & Nowak, K. L. (2006). Contextual features of violent video games, mental models, and aggression. *Journal of Communication, 56,* 387–405.

Fazio, R. H. (1986). How do attitudes guide behavior? In R. M. Sorrentino & E. T. Higgins (Eds.), *Handbook of motivation and cognition* (pp. 204–243). New York: Guilford.

Fazio, R. H. (1990). A practical guide to the use of response latency in social psychological research. *Research Methods in Personality and Social Psychology, 11,* 74–97.

Ferguson, D. A. (1992). Channel repertoire in the presence of remote control devices, VCRs, and cable television. *Journal of Broadcasting & Electronic Media, 36,* 83–91.

Ferguson, D. A., & Perse, E. M. (1993). Media and audience influences on channel repertoire. *Journal of Broadcasting & Electronic Media, 37,* 31–47.

Ferris, A. L., Smith, S. W., Greenberg, B. S., & Smith, S. L. (2007). The content of reality dating shows and viewer perceptions of dating. *Journal of Communication, 57,* 490–510.

Feshbach, N. D., & Roe, K. (1968). Empathy in six- and seven-year-olds. *Child Development, 39,* 133–145.

Feshbach, S. (1961). The stimulating effects of a vicarious aggressive activity. *The Journal of Abnormal and Social Psychology, 63,* 381–385.

Festinger, L. (1957). *A theory of cognitive dissonance.* Evanston, IL: Row, Peterson.

Fisch, S. M. (2000). A capacity model of children's comprehension of educational content on television. *Media Psychology, 2,* 63–91.

Fishbein, M., & Ajzen, I. (1975). *Belief, attitude, intention, and behavior: An introduction to theory and research.* Reading, MA: Addison-Wesley.

Fishbein, M., & Cappella, J. N. (2006). The role of theory in developing effective health communications. *Journal of Communication, 56,* S1–S17.

Fischer, C. (1992). *America's calling*. Berkeley: University of California Press.

Fisher, D. A., Hill, D. L., Grube, J. W., Bersamin, M. M., Walker, S., & Gruber, E. L. (2009). Televised sexual content and parental mediation: Influences on adolescent sexuality. *Media Psychology, 12,* 121–147.

Fiske, J. (1986). MTV and the politics of postmodern pop. *Journal of Communication Inquiry, 10,* 80–91.

Fiske, S. T., & Taylor, S. E. (1991). *Social cognition* (2nd ed.). New York: McGraw-Hill.

Flanagin, A. J., & Metzger, M. J. (2000). Perceptions of Internet credibility. *Journalism & Mass Communication Quarterly, 77,* 515–540.

Folkerts, J., & Lacy, S. (2001). *The media in your life: An introduction to mass communication* (2nd ed.). Needham Heights, MA: Allyn & Bacon.

Ford, T. (1997). Effects of stereotypical television portrayals of African-Americans on person perception. *Social Psychology Quarterly, 60,* 266–278.

Fore, W. F. (1987). *Television in religion*. Minneapolis, MN: Augsburg.

Fox, J. R. (2004). A signal detection analysis of audio/video redundancy effects in television news video. *Communication Research, 31,* 524–536.

Fox, J. & Bailenson, J. N. (2009). Virtual self-modeling: The effects of vicarious reinforcement and identification on exercise behaviors. *Media Psychology, 12,* 1–25.

Fox, J. R., Lang, A., Chung, Y. Lee, S., Schwartz, N., & Potter, D. (2004). Picture this: Effects of graphics on the processing of television news. *Journal of Broadcasting & Electronic Media, 48,* 646–674.

Fox, J. R., Park, B., & Lang, A. (2007). When available resources become negative resources: The effects of cognitive overload on memory sensitivity and criterion bias. *Communication Research, 34,* 277–296.

Freedman, J. L., & Sears, D. (1966). Selective exposure. In L. Berkowitz (Ed.), *Advances in experimental social psychology*. New York: Academic Press.

Frijda, N. H., & Zeelenberg, M. (2001). Appraisal processes in emotion: Theory, methods, research. In K. R. Scherer & A. Schorr (Eds.), *Appraisal processes in emotion: Theory, methods, research* (pp. 141–155). London: Oxford University Press.

Fu, K-W, Chan, Y-Y, & Yip, P. S. F. (2009). Testing a theoretical model based on social cognitive theory for media influences on suicidal ideation: Results from a panel study. *Media Psychology, 12,* 26–49.

Fujioka, Y. (2005). Emotional TV viewing and minority audience: How Mexican Americans process and evaluate TV news about in-group members. *Communication Research, 32,* 566–593.

Funk, J. B., & Buchman, D. D. (1996). Playing violent video and computer games and adolescent self-concept. *Journal of Communication, 46*(2), 19–32.

Galbraith, J. K. (1976). *The affluent society*. New York: New American Library.

Gantz, W., Gartenberg, H. M., & Rainbow, C. K. (1980). Approaching invisibility: The portrayal of the elderly in magazine advertisements. *Journal of Communication, 30*(1), 56–60.

Gantz, W., Wang, Z., Paul, B., & Potter, R. F. (2006). Sports versus all comers: Comparing TV sports fans with fans of other programming genres. *Journal of Broadcasting & Electronic Media, 50,* 95–118.

Gardner, M. P., & Hill, R. P. (1988). Consumers' mood states: Antecedents and consequences of experimental versus informational strategies for brand choice. *Psychology & Marketing, 5*(2), 169–182.

Garramone, G. M., & Atkin, C. K. (1986). Mass communication and political socialization: Specifying the effects. *Public Opinion Quarterly, 50*(1), 76–86.

Geen, R. G. (1975). The meaning of observed violence: Real vs. fictional violence and consequent effects on aggression and emotional arousal. *Journal of Research in Personality, 9,* 270–281.

Geen, R. G., & Berkowitz, L. (1967). Some conditions facilitating the occurrence of aggression after the observation of violence. *Journal of Personality, 35,* 666–676.

Geen, R. G., & Rokosky, J. J. (1973). Interpretations of observed aggression and their effect on GSR. *Journal of Experimental Research in Personality, 6,* 289–292.

Gerbner, G. A. (1969). Towards "cultural indicators": The analysis of mass mediated message systems. *AV Communication Review, 17,* 137–148.

Gerbner, G., & Gross, L. (1976). Living with television: The violence profile. *Journal of Communication, 26*(2), 173–199.

Gerbner, G., Gross, L., Jackson-Beeck, M., Jeffries-Fox, S., & Signorielli, N. (1978). Cultural indicators: Violence profile no. 9. *Journal of Communication, 28*(3), 176–207.

Gerbner, G., Gross, L., Morgan, M., & Signorielli, N. (1980). The mainstreaming of America: Violence profile no. 11. *Journal of Communication, 30* (3), 10–29.

Getter, L. (2004, May 4). Bush, Kerry awash in money. *Los Angeles Times*, pp. A1, A20.

Gibbons, J. A., Lukowski, A. F., & Walker, W. R. (2005). Exposure increases the believability of unbelievable news headlines via elaborate cognitive processing. *Media Psychology, 7,* 273–300.

Gibson, R., & Zillmann, D. (2000). Reading between the photographs: The influence of incidental pictorial information on issue perception. *Journalism & Mass Communication Quarterly, 77,* 355–366.

Gitlin, T. (1980). *The whole world is watching: The role of the news media in the making and unmaking of the new left.* Berkeley: University of California Press.

Gitlin, T. (1985). *Inside prime time.* New York: Pantheon.

Givens, S. M. B., & Monahan, J. L. (2005). Priming mammies, Jezebels, and other controlling images: An examination of the influence of mediated stereotypes on perceptions of an African American woman. *Media Psychology, 7,* 87–106.

Glynn, C. J., Huge, M., Reineke, J. B., Hardy, B. W., & Shanahan, J. (2007). When Oprah intervenes: Political correlates of daytime talk show viewing. *Journal of Broadcasting & Electronic Media, 51,* 228–244.

Goethals, G. (1997). Escape from time: Ritual dimensions of popular culture. In S. M. Hoover & K. Lundby (Eds.), *Rethinking media, religion, and culture* (pp. 117–132). Thousand Oaks, CA: Sage.

Goffman, E. (1974). *Frame analysis: An essay on the organization of experience.* Cambridge, MA: Harvard University Press.

Goffman, E. (1979). *Gender advertisements.* New York: Harper Colophon.

Goidel, R. K., Freeman, C. M., & Procopio, S. T. (2006). The impact of television viewing on perceptions of juvenile crime. *Journal of Broadcasting & Electronic Media, 50,* 119–139.

Golan, G., & Wanta, W. (2001). Second-level agenda setting in the New Hampshire primary: A comparison of coverage in three newspapers and public perceptions of candidates. *Journalism & Mass Communication Quarterly, 78,* 247–259.

Goldberg, M. E., & Gorn, G. J. (1987). Happy and sad TV programs: How they affect reactions to commercials. *Journal of Consumer Research, 14,* 387–403.

Golding, P. (1994). The communication paradox: Inequity at the national and international levels. *Media Development, 4,* 7–9.

Goleman, D. (1995). *Emotional intelligence.* New York: Bantam.

Goranson, R. (1969). *Observed violence and aggressive behavior: The effects of negative outcomes to the observed violence.* Unpublished doctoral dissertation. University of Wisconsin, Madison.

Gorham, B. W. (2006). News media's relationship with stereotyping: The linguistic intergroup bias in response to crime news. *Journal of Communication, 56,* 289–308.

Gorn, G. J. (1982). The effects of music in advertising on choice behavior: A classical conditioning approach. *Journal of Marketing, 46*(1), 94–101.

Grabe, M. E., & Drew, D. G. (2007). Crime cultivation: Comparison across media genres and channels. *Journal of Broadcasting & Electronic Media, 51,* 147–171.

Grabe, M. E., & Kamhawi, R. (2006). Hard wired for negative news? Gender differences in processing broadcast news. *Communication Research, 33,* 346–369.

Grabe, M. E., Yegiyan, N., & Kamhawi, R. (2008). Experimental evidence of the knowledge gap: Message arousal, motivation, and time delay. *Human Communication Research, 34,* 550–571.

Grabe, M. E., Zhou, S., Lang, A., & Bolls, P. D. (2000). Packing television news: The effects of tabloid on information processing and evaluative responses. *Journal of Broadcasting & Electronic Media, 44,* 581–598.

Graber, D. A. (1980). *Crime news and the public.* New York: Praeger.

Graber, D. A. (1988). *Processing the news: How people tame the information tide* (2nd ed.). New York: Longman.

Graesser, A. C., & Nakamura, G. V. (1982). The impact of a schema on comprehension and memory. In G. H. Bower (Ed.), *The psychology of learning and motivation: Advances in research and theory* (Vol. 16, pp. 66–109). New York: Academic Press.

Gramsci, A. (1971). *Selections from the prison notebooks.* London: Lawrence & Wishart.

Green, M. C., & Brock, T. C. (2000). The role of transportation in the persuasiveness of public narratives. *Journal of Personality & Social Psychology, 79,* 701–721.

Green, M. C., Brock, T. C., & Kaufman, G. F. (2004). Understanding media enjoyment: The role of transportation into narrative worlds. *Communication Theory, 14,* 311–327.

Green, M. C., Kass, S., Carrey, J., Herzig, B., Feeney, R., & Sabini, J. (2008). Transportation across media: Repeated exposure to print and film. *Media Psychology, 11,* 512–539.

Greenberg, B. S. (1964). The diffusion of news about the Kennedy assassination. *Public Opinion Quarterly, 28,* 225–232.

Greenberg, B. S. (1988). Some uncommon television images and the drench hypothesis. In S. Oskamp (Ed.), *Television as a social issue* (pp. 88–102). Newbury Park, CA: Sage.

Greenberg, B. S., & Brand, J. E. (1993). Cultural diversity on Saturday morning television. In G. Berry & J. K. Asamen (Eds.), *Children and television in a changing socio-cultural world* (pp. 132–142). Newbury Park, CA: Sage.

Greenberg, B. S., & Parker, E. (Eds.). (1965). *The Kennedy assassination and the American public.* Stanford, CA: Stanford University Press.

Greene, K., Krcmar, M., Rubin, D. L., Walters, L. H., & Hale, J. L. (2002). Elaboration in processing adolescent health messages: The impact of egocentrism and sensation seeking on message processing. *Journal of Communication, 52,* 812–831.

Greenwald, A. G. (1968). Cognitive learning, cognitive response to persuasion, and attitude change. In A. Greenwald, T. Brock, & T. Ostrom (Eds.), *Psychological foundations of attitudes* (pp. 147–170). New York: Academic Press.

Greenwood, D. N., & Long, C. R. (2009). Psychological predictors of media involvement: Solitude experiences and the need to belong. *Communication Research, 36,* 637–654.

Griffin, R. J., Neuwirth, K., Dunwoody, S., & Giese, J. (2004). Information sufficiency and risk communication. *Media Psychology, 6,* 23–61.

Grimes, R. L. (2002). Ritual and the media. In S. M. Hoover & L. S. Clark (Eds.), *Practicing religion in the age of the media: Explorations in media, religion, and culture* (pp. 219–234). New York: Columbia University Press.

Grimes, T., Bergen, L., Nicholes, K., Vernberg, E., & Fonagy, P. (2004). Is psychopathology the key to understanding why some children become aggressive when they are exposed to violent television programming? *Human Communication Research, 30,* 153–181.

Groebel, J., & Krebs, D. (1983). A study of the effects of television on anxiety. In C. D. Spielberger & R. Diaz-Guerrero (Eds.), *Cross-cultural anxiety* (Vol. 2, pp. 89–98). New York: Hemisphere.

Groenendyk, E. W., & Valentino, N. A. (2002). Of dark clouds and silver linings: Effects of exposure to issue versus candidate advertising on persuasion, information retention, and issue salience. *Communication Research, 29,* 295–319.

Gross, K., & Aday, S. (2003). The scary world in your living room and neighborhood: Using local broadcast news, neighborhood crime rates, and personal experience to test agenda setting and cultivation. *Journal of Communication, 53,* 411–426.

Gunter, B. (1985). *Dimensions of television violence.* Aldershot, UK: Gower.

Gunter, B., & Furnham, A. (1984). Perceptions of television violence: Effects of programme genre and type of violence on viewers' judgements of violent portrayals. *British Journal of Social Psychology, 23,* 155–164.

Gunther, A. C. (1991). What we think others think: Cause and consequence in the third-person effect. *Communication Research, 18,* 355–372.

Gunther, A. C., Bolt, D., Borzekowski, D. L. G., Liebhart, J. L., & Dillard, J. P. (2006). Presumed influence on peer norms: How mass media indirectly affect adolescent smoking. *Journal of Communication, 56,* 52–68.

Gunther, A. C., & Chia, S. C-Y. 2001). Predicting pluralistic ignorance: The hostile media perception and its consequences. *Journalism & Mass Communication Quarterly, 78,* 688–701.

Gunther, A. C., & Christen, C. T. (2002). Projection of persuasive press? Contrary effects of personal opinion and perceived news coverage on estimates of public opinion. *Journal of Communication, 52,* 177–195.

Gunther, A. C., & Liebhart, J. L. (2006). Broad reach or biased source? Decomposing the hostile media effect. *Journal of Communication, 56,* 449–466.

Gunther, A. C., Miller, N., & Liebhart, J. L. (2009). Assimilation and contrast in a test of the hostile media effect. *Communication Research, 36,* 747–764.

Gunther, A. C., & Schmitt, K. (2004). Mapping boundaries of the hostile media effect. *Journal of Communication, 54,* 55–70.

Gunther, A. C., & Storey, J. D. (2003). The influence of presumed influence. *Journal of Communication, 53,* 199–215.

Hale, J. L., Lemieux, R., & Mongeau, P. A. (1995). Cognitive processing of fear-arousing message content. *Communication Research, 22,* 459–474.

Hall, A. (2003). Reading realism: Audiences' evaluations of the reality of media texts. *Journal of Communication, 53,* 624–641.

Hall, A. (2005). Audience personality and selection of media and media genres. *Media Psychology, 7,* 377–398.

Hall, A. (2009). Perceptions of the authenticity of reality programs and their relationships to audience involvement, enjoyment, and perceived learning. *Journal of Broadcasting & Electronic Media, 53,* 515–531.

Hall, S. (1980). Encoding and decoding in the television discourse. In S. Hall et al. (Eds.), *Culture, media, language* (pp. 197–208). London: Hutchinson.

Hallahan, K. (1994, August). *Product news versus advertising: An exploration within a student population.* Paper presented at the annual conference of the

Association for Education in Journalism and Mass Communication, Atlanta.

Halloran, J. D., Elliott, P., & Murdock, G. (1970). *Communications and demonstrations.* Harmondsworth, UK: Penguin.

Hamelink, C. (1983). *Cultural autonomy in global communications.* New York: Longman.

Hampton, K. N., Livio, O., & Sessions Goulet, L. (2010). The social life of wireless urban spaces: Internet use, social networks, and the public realm. *Journal of Communication, 60,* 701–722.

Hapkiewicz, W. G. (1979). Children's reactions to cartoon violence. *Journal of Clinical Child Psychology, 8,* 30–34.

Hardy, B. W., & Scheufele, D. A. (2005). Examining differential gains from internet use: Comparing the moderating role of talk and online interactions. *Journal of Communication, 55,* 71–84.

Hardy, B. W., & Scheufle, D. A. (2009). Presidential campaign dynamics and the ebb and flow of talk as a moderator: Media exposure, knowledge, and political discussion. *Communication Theory, 19,* 89–101.

Hare, R. D., & Blevings, G. (1975). Defense responses to phobic stimuli. *Biological Psychology, 3,* 1–13.

Harris, R. J., Hoekstra, S. J., Scott, C. L., Sanborn, F. W., Dodds, L. A., & Brandenburg, J. D. (2004). Autobiographical memories for seeing romantic movies on a date: Romance is not just for women. *Media Psychology, 6,* 257–284.

Harris, R. J., & Scott, C. L. (2002). Effects of sex in the media. In J. Bryant & D. Zillmann (Eds.), *Media effects: Advances in theory and research* (2nd ed., pp. 307–331). Mahwah, NJ: Erlbaum.

Harrison, K. (1997). Does interpersonal attraction to thin media personalities promote eating disorders? *Journal of Broadcasting and Electronic Media, 41,* 478–500.

Harrison, K. (2000). The body electric: Thin-ideal media and eating disorders in adolescents. *Journal of Communication, 50,* 119–143.

Harrison, K. (2006). Scope of self: Toward a model of television's effects on self-complexity in adolescence. *Communication Theory, 16,* 251–279.

Harrison, K., & Cantor, J. (1997). The relationship between media consumption and eating disorders. *Journal of Communication, 47*(1), 40–67.

Harrison, K., & Fredrickson, B. L. (2003). Women's sports media, self-objectification, and mental health in Black and White adolescent females. *Journal of Communication, 53,* 216–232.

Harrison, K., Taylor, L. D., & Marske, A. L. (2007). Women's and men's eating behavior following exposure to ideal-body images and text. *Communication Research, 33,* 507–530.

Harrison, L. F., & Williams, T. M. (1977, June). *Television and cognitive development.* Paper presented at the meeting of the Canadian Psychological Association, Vancouver.

Harwood, J. (1997). Viewing age: Lifespan identity and television viewing choices. *Journal of Broadcasting & Electronic Media, 41,* 203–213.

Harwood, J. (1999). Age identification, social identity gratifications, and television viewing. *Journal of Broadcasting & Electronic Media, 43,* 123–136.

Hawkins, R. P., & Pingree, S. (1980). Some processes in the cultivation effect. *Communication Research, 7* (2), 193–226.

Hawkins, R. P., & Pingree, S. (1981). Using television to construct social reality. *Journal of Broadcasting, 25,* 347–364.

Hawkins, R. P., Tapper, J., Bruce, L., & Pingree, S. (1995). Strategic and nonstrategic explanations for attentional inertia. *Communication Research, 22,* 188–206.

Hawkins, R. P., & Pingree, S. (1982). Television's influence on social reality. In D. Pearl, L. Bouthilet, & J. Lazar (Eds.), *Television and behavior: Ten years of scientific progress and implications for the eighties.* DHHS publication No. ADM 82–1196, Vol. 2, pp. 224–247. Washington, DC: U.S. Government Printing Office.

Hazlett, R. L., & Hazlett, S. Y. (1999). Emotional response to television commercials: Facial EMG vs. self-report. *Journal of Advertising Research, 39*(2), 7–23.

Hay, J. (1989). Advertising as a cultural text (Rethinking message analysis in a recombinant culture). In B. Dervin, L. Grossberg, B. J. O'Keefe, & E. Wartella (eds.), *Rethinking communication: Volume 2, Paradigm exemplars.* Newbury Park, CA: Sage.

Healy, J. M. (1990). *Endangered minds: Why children don't think and what we can do about it.* New York: Simon & Schuster.

Hearold, S. (1986). A synthesis of 1043 effects of television on social behavior. In G. Comstock (Ed.), *Public communication and behavior* (Vol. 1, pp. 65–133). San Diego: Academic Press.

Hennigan, K., M., Del Rosario, M. L., Heath, L., Cook, T. D., Wharton, J. D., & Calder, B. J. (1982). Impact of the introduction of television on crime in the United States: Empirical findings and theoretical implications. *Journal of Personality & Social Psychology, 42,* 461–477.

Herman, E., & Chomsky, N. (1988). *Manufacturing consent: The political economy of mass media.* New York: Pantheon.

Hetsroni, A., & Tukachinsky, R. H. (2006). Television-world estimates, real-world estimates, and television viewing: A new scheme for cultivation. *Journal of Communication, 56,* 133–156.

Himmelweit, H. T., Oppenheim, A. N., & Vince, P. (1958). *Television and the child.* London: Oxford University Press.

Himmelweit, H. T., Swift, B., & Jaeger, M. E. (1980). The audience as critic: A conceptual analysis of television entertainment. In P. H. Tannenbaum (Ed.) *The entertainment functions of television* (67–106). Hillsdale, NJ: Erlbaum.

Hindman, D. B., & Wiegand, K. (2008). The big three's prime-time decline: A technological and social context. *Journal of Broadcasting & Electronic Media, 52,* 119–135.

Hitchon, J. C., & Chang, C. (1995). Effects of gender schematic processing on the reception of political commercials for men and women candidates. *Communication Research, 22,* 430–458.

Hitchon, J. C., & Thorson, E. (1995). Effects of emotion and product involvement on experience of repeated commercial viewing. *Journal of Broadcasting & Electronic Media, 39,* 356–389.

Hoffner, C. (1995). Adolescents' coping with frightening mass media. *Communication Research, 22,* 325–346.

Hoffner, C. (1996). Children's wishful identification and parasocial interaction with favorite television characters. *Journal of Broadcasting and Electronic Media, 40,* 389–402.

Hoffner, C. (1997). Children's emotional reactions to a scary film: The role of prior outcome information and coping style. *Human Communication Research, 23,* 323–341.

Hoffner, C., Plotkin, R. S., Buchanan, M., Anderson, J. D., Kamigaki, S. K., Hubbs, L. A., Kowalcyk . . . Pastorek, A. (2001). The third-person effect in perceptions of the influence of television violence. *Journal of Communication, 51,* 283–299.

Hoffner, C., & Buchanan, M. (2002). Parents' responses to television violence: The third-person perception, parental mediation, and support for censorship. *Media Psychology, 4,* 231–252.

Hoffner, C., & Cantor, J. (1990). Forewarning of threat and its successful outcome: Effects on children's emotional responses to a film sequence. *Human Communication Research, 16,* 323–354.

Hoffner, C. A., & Levine, K. J. (2005). Enjoyment of mediated fright and violence: A meta-analysis. *Media Psychology, 7,* 207–237.

Hoffner, C. A., Levine, K. J., & Toohey, R. A. (2008). Socialization to work in late adolescence: The role of television and family. *Journal of Broadcasting & Electronic Media, 52,* 282–302.

Hoffman, L. H., & Thomson, T. L. . (2009). The effect of television viewing on adolescents' civic participation: Political efficacy as a mediating mechanism. *Journal of Broadcasting & Electronic Media, 53,* 3–21.

Hofmeister, S. (2005, September 8). Study ties indecency to consolidation of media. *Los Angeles Times,* C1, C11.

Hofstetter, C. R., & Gianos, C. L. (1997). Political talk radio: Actions speak louder than words. *Journal of Broadcasting & Electronic Media, 41,* 501–515.

Holbert, R. L. (2005). Debate viewing as mediator and partisan reinforcement in the relationship between news use and vote choice. *Journal of Communication, 55,* 85–102.

Holbert, R. L., & Hansen, G. J. (2008). Stepping beyond message specificity in the study of emotion as mediator and inter-emotion associations across attitude objects: Fahrenheit 9/11, anger, and debate superiority. *Media Psychology, 11,* 98–118.

Holbert, R. L., Kwak, N., & Shah, D. V. (2003). Political implications of prime-time drama and sitcom use: Games of representation and opinions concerning women's rights. *Journal of Communication, 53,* 45–60.

Holbert, R. L., Shah, D. V., & Kwak, N. (2003). Political implications of prime-time drama and sitcom use: Genres of representation and opinions concerning women's rights. *Journal of Communication, 53,* 45–60.

Holbrook, M. B., & Westwood, R. A. (1989). The role of emotion in advertising revisited: Testing a typology of emotional responses. In P. Cafferata & A. M. Tybout (Eds.), *Cognitive and affective responses to advertising* (pp. 353–371). Lexington, MA: D. C. Heath.

Hollander, B. A. (2005). Late-night learning: Do entertainment programs increase political campaign knowledge for young viewers? *Journal of Broadcasting & Electronic Media, 49,* 402–415.

Holmstrom, A. J. (2004). The effects of the media on body image: A meta-analysis. *Journal of Broadcasting & Electronic Media, 48,* 196–216.

Homer, P. M. (2006) Relationships among ad-induced affect, beliefs, and attitudes. *Journal of Advertising. 35,* 35–51.

Hoover, S.M. (1988).*Mass media religion: The social sources of the electronic church*. Newbury Park, CA: Sage.

Hoover, S. M., & Lundby, K. (1997). Introduction: Setting the agenda. In S. M. Hoover & K. Lundby (Eds.), *Rethinking media, religion, and culture* (pp. 3–14). Thousand Oaks, CA: Sage.

Hopkins, R., & Fletcher, J. E. (1994). Electrodermal measurement: Particularly effective for forecasting message influence on sales appeal. In A. Lang (Ed.), *Measuring psychological responses to media* (pp. 113–132). Hillsdale, NJ: Erlbaum.

Horsfield, P. (1984). *Religious television: The American experience*. New York: Longman.

Horsfield, P. G. (1997). Changes in religion in periods of media convergence. In S. M. Hoover & K. Lundby (Eds.), *Rethinking media, religion, and culture* (pp. 167–183). Thousand Oaks, CA: Sage.

Horton, D., & Wohl, R. R. (1956). Mass communication and para-social interaction. *Psychiatry, 19*, 215–229.

Horvath, C. W. (2004). Measuring television addiction. *Journal of Broadcasting & Electronic Media, 48*, 378–398.

Hovland, C. I., Lumsdaine, A., & Sheffield, F. (1949). *Experiments on mass communication*. Princeton, NJ: Princeton University Press.

Hsia, H. J. (1977). Redundancy: Is it the lost key to better communication? *AV Communication Review, 25*(1), 63–85.

Huang, L-N. (2000). Examining candidate information search processes: The impact of processing goals and sophistication. *Journal of Communication, 50*, 93–114.

Huh, J., Delorme, D. E., & Reid, L. N. (2004). The third-person effect and its influence on behavioral outcomes in a product advertising context: The case of direct-to-consumer prescription drug advertising. *Communication Research, 31*, 568–599.

Hullett, C. R. (2005). The impact of mood on persuasion: A meta-analysis. *Communication Research, 32*, 423–443.

Huntemann, N., & Morgan, M. (2001). Mass media and identity development. In D. G. Singer & J. L. Singer (Eds.), *Handbook of children and the media* (pp. 309–322). Thousand Oaks, CA: Sage.

Hwang, H., Gotlieb, M. R., Nah, S., & McLeod, D. M. (2007). Applying a cognitive-processing model to presidential debate effects: Postdebate news analysis and primed reflection. *Journal of Communication, 57*, 40–59.

Hwang, H., Pan, Z., & Sun, Y. (2008). Influence of hostile media perception on willingness to engage in discursive activities: An examination of mediating role of media indignation. *Media Psychology, 11*, 76–97.

Hwang, Y., & Southwell, B. G. (2009). Science TV news exposure predicts science beliefs: Real world effects among a national sample. *Communication Research, 36*, 724–742.

Hyman, H., & Sheatsley, P. (1947). Some reasons why information campaigns fail. *Public Opinion Quarterly, 11*, 412–423.

Igartua, J-J, & Cheng, L. (2009). Moderating effect of group cue while processing news on immigration: Is the framing effect a heuristic process? *Journal of Communication, 59*, 726–749.

Infoniac.com. (2008, March 13). The amount of digital information reached 281 exabytes (281 billion gigabytes). Retrieved Sept. 11, 2009, from http://www.infoniac.com/

Innis, H. A. (1950). *Empire and communications*. Oxford, UK: Oxford University Press.

Irvine, M. (1999, November 25). Married couples are the new endangered species. *Tallahassee Democrat*, p. 6B.

Isen, A. M. (2000). Positive affect and decision making. In M. Lewis & J. M. Haviland-Jones (Eds.), *Handbook of emotions* (2nd ed., pp. 417–435). New York: Guilford.

Iyengar, S. (1991). *Is anyone responsible? How television frames political issues*. Chicago: University of Chicago Press.

Iyengar, S., & Kinder, D. R. (1987). *News that matters: Television and American opinion*. Chicago: University of Chicago Press.

James, W. (1894). The physical basis of emotion. *Psychological Review, 1*, 516–529.

Jamieson, K. H., & Waldman, P. (2003). *The press effect: Politicians, journalists, and the stories that shape the political world*. New York: Oxford University Press.

Janowitz, M. (1952). *The community press in an urban setting*. Glencoe, IL: Free Press.

Janowitz, M. (1968). The study of mass communication. In the *International Encyclopedia of the Social Sciences* (Vol. 3, pp. 41–53). New York: Macmillan.

Janowitz, M. (1975). Sociological theory and social control. *American Journal of Sociology, 81*, 82–108

Jansz, J. (2005). The emotional appeal of violent video games for adolescent males. *Communication Theory, 15*, 219–241.

Jeffres, L. W. (1994). *Mass media processes* (2nd ed.). Prospect Heights, IL: Waveland.

Jensen, J. D., & Hurley, R. J. (2005). Third-person effects and the environment: Social distance, social desirability, and presumed behavior. *Journal of Communication, 55*, 242–256.

Jhally, S. (ed.) (1987). *The codes of advertising: Fetishism and the political economy of meaning in the consumer society*. New York: St. Martin's Press.

Jhally, S., & Livant, (1986). Watching as working: The valorization of audience consciousness. *Journal of Communication, 36*(3), 124–143.

Jo, E., & Berkowitz, L. (1994). A priming effect analysis of media influences: An update. In J. Bryant & D. Zillmann (Eds.), *Media effects: Advances in theory and research* (pp. 43–60). Hillsdale, NJ: Erlbaum.

Johnson, T. J., & Kaye, B. K. (1998). Cruising is believing? Comparing Internet and traditional sources on media credibility measures. *Journalism & Mass Communication Quarterly, 75*, 325–340.

Johnson-Laird, P. N., & Oatley, K. (2000). Cognitive and social construction of emotions. In M. Lewis & J. M. Haviland-Jones (Eds.), *Handbook of emotions* (2nd ed., pp. 458–475). New York: Guilford.

Johnston, C. D., & Bartels, B. L. (2010). Sensationalism and sobriety: Differential media exposure and attitudes toward American courts. *Public Opinion Quarterly, 74*, 260–285.

Johnston, D. D. (1995). Adolescents' motivations for viewing graphic horror. *Human Communication Research, 21*, 522–552.

Juanillo, N. K. Jr., & Scherer, C. W. (1991, May). *Patterns of family communication and health lifestyle*. Paper presented at the annual conference of the International Communication Association, Chicago.

Kaiser Family Foundation. (2005, March). *Key findings from new research on children's media use*. Retrieved August 23, 2009, from http://www.kaiser network.org/

Kalyanaraman, S., & Ivory, J. D. (2009). Enhanced information scent, selective discounting, or consummate breakdown: The psychological effects of Web-based search results. *Media Psychology, 12*, 295–319.

Kamhawi, R., & Weaver, D. (2003). Mass communication research trends from 1980 to 1999. *Journalism & Mass Communication Quarterly, 80*, 7–27.

Kaminsky, S. M. (1974). *American film genres. Cincinnati,* OH: Pflaum.

Kang, S., & Gearhart, S. (2010). E-government and civic engagement: How is citizens' use of city web sites related with civic involvement and political behaviors? *Journal of Broadcasting & Electronic Media, 54,* 443–462.

Kaplan, D. (1972). The psychopathology of TV watching. *Performance,* July/August.

Katz, E. (1987). Communication research since Lazarsfeld. *Public Opinion Quarterly, 51*(Suppl.), S25–S45.

Katz, E., Blumler, J. G., & Gurevitch, M. (1974). Utilization of mass communication by the individual. In J. G. Blumler & E. Katz (Eds.) *The uses of mass communication* (pp. 19–32). Beverly Hills, CA: Sage.

Katz, E., & Gurevitch, M. (1976). *The secularization of leisure: Culture and communication in Israel*. Cambridge, MA: Harvard University Press.

Katz, E., & Lazarsfeld, P. F. (1955). *Personal influence: The part played by people in the flow of mass communications*. Glencoe, IL: Free Press.

Kawamoto, K. (2003). *Media and society in the digital age*. Boston: Allyn & Bacon.

Kaye, B. K., & Sapolsky. (1997). Electronic monitoring of in-home television RCD use. *Journal of Broadcasting and Electronic Media, 41,* 214–228.

Keane, J. (1995). Structural transformations of the public sphere. *Communication Review, 1*(1), 1–22.

Keller, K. L. (1991). Memory and evaluation effects in competitive advertising environments. *Journal of Consumer Research, 17*(4), 463–476.

Kennedy, M. G., O'Leary, A., Beck, V., Pollard, K., & Simpson, P. (2004). Increases in calls to the CDC National STD and AIDS hotline following AIDS-related episodes in a soap opera. *Journal of Communication, 54,* 287–301.

Kent, R. J., & Machleit, K. A. (1992). The effects of postexposure test expectation in advertising experiments utilizing recall and recognition measures. *Marketing Letters, 3*(1), 17–26.

Kepplinger, H. M., & Daschmann, G. (1997). Today's news–tomorrow's context: A dynamic model of news processing. *Journal of Broadcasting & Electronic Media, 41*, 548–565.

Key, V. O. (1961). *Public opinion and American democracy*. New York: Alfred A. Knopf.

Kim, J., & Morris, J. D. (2007). The power of affective response and cognitive structure in product-trial attitude formation. *Journal of Advertising, 36,* 95–106.

Kim, K. K. (1994, July). *Is there any diversity in the global advertising industry? The recent consolidation process of large U.S. advertising agencies and the current structure of the industry*. Paper presented at the annual conference of the International Communication Association, Sydney, Australia.

Kim, S-H., Scheufele, D. A., & Shanahan, J. (2002). Think about it this way: Attribute agenda-setting function of the press and the public's evaluation of a local issue. *Journalism and Mass Communication Quarterly, 79,* 7–25.

Kim, S-H, Scheufele, D. A., & Shanahan, J. (2005). Who cares about the issues? Issue voting and the role of news media during the 2000 U.S. presidential election. *Journal of Communication, 55,* 103–121.

Kim, S. T., Weaver, D., & Willnat, L. (2000). Media reporting and perceived credibility of online polls. *Journalism & Mass Communication Quarterly, 77,* 846–864.

Kim, Y. M., & Vishak, J. (2008). Just laugh! You don't need to remember: The effects of entertainment media on political information acquisition and information processing in political judgment. *Journal of Communication, 58,* 338–360.

King, C. M. (2000). Effects of humorous heroes and villains in violent action films. *Journal of Communication, 50*(1), 5–25.

King, P.M. (1986). Formal reasoning in adults: A review and critique. In R.A. Milnes & K. S. Kitchenor (Eds.), *Adult cognitive development: Methods and models* (pp. 1–21). New York: Praeger.

Kintsch, W. (1977). On comprehending stories. In P. Carpenter & M. Just (Eds.), *Cognitive processes in comprehension.* Hillsdale, NJ: Erlbaum.

Kiousis, S., & McCombs, M. (2004). Agenda-setting effects and attitude strength: Political figures during the 1996 presidential election. *Communication Research, 31,* 36–57.

Kiousis, S., & McDevitt, M. (2008). Agenda setting in civic development: Effects of curricula and issue importance on youth voter turnout. *Communication Research, 35,* 481–502.

Kirsh, S. J., & Olczak, P. V. (2000). Violent comic books and perceptions of ambiguous provocation situations. *Media Psychology, 2,* 47–62.

Kirsh, S. J., Olczak, P. V., & Mounts, J. R. W. (2005). Violent video games induce an affect processing bias. *Media Psychology, 7,* 239–250.

Kisielius, J., & Sternthal, B. (1984). Detecting and explaining vividness effects in attitudinal judgments. *Journal of Marketing Research, 21,* 54–64.

Klapper, J. T. (1949). *The effect of mass media.* New York: Bureau of Applied Social Research, Columbia University.

Klapper, J. T. (1960). *The effects of mass communication.* Glencoe, IL: Free Press.

Klein, P. (1971). The men who run TV aren't stupid. *New York,* 20–29.

Knobloch, S. (2003). Mood adjustment via mass communication. *Journal of Communication, 53,* 233–250.

Knobloch, S., Callison, Coy, Chen, L., Fritzsche, A., & Zillmann, D. (2005). Children's sex-stereotyped self-socialization through selective exposure to entertainment: Cross-cultural experiments in Germany, China, and the United States. *Journal of Communication, 55,* 122–138.

Knobloch, S., Patzig, G., Mende, A-M., & Hastall, M. (2004). Effects of discourse structure in narratives on suspense, curiosity, and enjoyment while reading news and novels. *Communication Research, 31,* 259–287.

Knobloch-Westerwick, S. (2007). Gender differences in selective media use for mood management and mood adjustment. *Journal of Broadcasting & Electronic Media, 51,* 73–92.

Knobloch-Westerwick, S., & Alter, S. (2006). Mood adjustment to social situations through mass media use: HOW men ruminate and women dissipate angry moods. *Human Communication Research 32,* 58–73.

Knobloch-Westerwick, S., David, P., Eastin, M. S., Tamborini, R., & Greenwood, D. (2009). Sports spectators' suspense: Affect and uncertainty in sports entertainment. *Journal of Communication, 59,* 750–767.

Knobloch-Westerwick, S., & Hastall, M. R. (2006). Social comparisons with news personae: Selective exposure to news portrayals of same-sex and same-age characters. *Communication Research, 33,* 262–285.

Knobloch-Westerwick, S., Hastall, M. R., & Rossmann, M. (2009). Coping or escaping? Effects of life dissatisfaction on selective exposure. *Communication Research, 36,* 207–228.

Knobloch-Westerwick, S., & Meng, J. (2009). Looking the other way: Selective exposure to attitude-consistent and counterattitudinal political information. *Communication Research, 36,* 426–448.

Kolter, P. (1988). *Marketing management* (6th ed.) Englewood Cliffs, NJ: Prentice Hall.

Konijn, E. A., & Hoorn, J. F. (2005). Some like it bad: Testing a model for perceiving and experiencing fictional characters. *Media Psychology, 7,* 107–144.

Koolstra, C. M., & Van der Voort, T. H. A. (1996). Longitudinal effects of television on children's leisure-time reading: A test of three explanatory models. *Human Communication Research, 23,* 4–35.

Koriat, A., Melkman, R., Averill, J. R., & Lazarus, R. S. (1972). The self-control of emotional reactions to a stressful film. *Journal of Personality, 40,* 601–619.

Kraus, R. (2009). Thou shall not take the name of thy god in vain: Washington offices' use of religious language to shape public and political agendas. *Journal of Media & Religion, 8,* 115–137.

Krcmar, M. (1996). Family communication patterns, discourse behavior, and child television viewing. *Human Communication Research, 23* (2), 251–277.

Krcmar, M. (1998). The contribution of family communication patterns to children's interpretations of television violence. *Journal of Broadcasting & Electronic Media, 42,* 250–264.

Krcmar, M., & Cantor, J. (1997). The role of television advisories and ratings in parent-child discussion of television viewing choices. *Journal of Broadcasting & Electronic Media, 41,* 393–411.

Krcmar, M., & Cooke, M. C. (2001). Children's moral reasoning and their perceptions of television violence. *Journal of Communication, 51,* 300–316.

Krcmar, M., & Greene, K. (1999). Predicting exposure to and uses of television violence. *Journal of Communication, 49,* 24–45.

Krcmar, M., & Greene, K. (2000). Connections between violent television exposure and adolescent risk taking, *Media Psychology, 2,* 195–217.

Krcmar, M., & Kean, L. G. (2005). Uses and gratifications of media violence: Personality correlates of viewing and liking violent genres. *Media Psychology, 7,* 399–420.

Krcmar; M., & Lachlan, K. (2009). Aggressive outcomes and videogame play: The role of length of play and the mechanisms at work. *Media Psychology, 12,* 249–267.

Krcmar, M., & Vieira, E. T. Jr. (2005). Imitating life, imitating television: The effects of family and television models on children's moral reasoning. *Communication Research, 32,* 267–294.

Krotz, F., & Eastman, S. T. (1999). Orientations toward television outside the home. *Journal of Communication, 49,* 5–27.

Kruglanski, A. W., & Stroebe, W. (2005). The influence of beliefs and goals on attitudes: Issues of structure, function, and dynamics. In D. Albarracin, B. T. Johnson, & M. P. Zanna (Eds.), *The handbook of attitudes* (pp. 323–368). Mahwah, NJ: Erlbaum.

Ku, G., Kaid, L. L., & Pfau, M. (2003). The impact of web site campaigning on traditional news media and public information processing. *Journalism & Mass Communication Quarterly, 80,* 528–547.

Kwak, H., Zinkhan, G. M., & Dominick, J. R. (2002). The moderating role of gender and compulsive buying tendencies in the cultivation effects of TV shows and TV advertising: A cross cultural study between the United States and South Korea. *Media Psychology, 4,* 77–111.

Lachlan, K. A., & Tamborini, R. (2008). The effect of perpetrator motive and dispositional attributes on enjoyment of television violence and attitudes toward victims. *Journal of Broadcasting & Electronic Media, 52,* 136–152.

Lacy, S., & Riffe, D. (1994). The impact of competition and group ownership on radio news. *Journalism & Mass Communication Quarterly, 71,* 583–593.

Lambe, J. L., & McLeod, D. M. (2005). Understanding third-person perception processes: Predicting perceived impact on self and others for multiple expressive contexts. *Journal of Communication, 55,* 277–291.

Lang, A. (1990). Involuntary attention and physiological arousal evoked by structural features and emotional content in TV commercials. *Communication Research, 17,* 275–299.

Lang, A. (Ed.). (1994a). *Measuring psychological responses to media.* Hillsdale, NJ: Erlbaum.

Lang, A. (1994b). What can the heart tell us about thinking? In A. Lang (Ed.), *Measuring psychological responses to media* (pp. 99–111). Hillsdale, NJ: Erlbaum.

Lang, A. (1995). Defining audio/video redundancy from a limited-capacity information processing perspective. *Communication Research, 22,* 86–115.

Lang, A. (2000). The limited capacity model of mediated message processing. *Journal of Communication, 50,* 46–70.

Lang, A., Bolls, P., Potter, R. F., & Kawahara, K. (1999). The effects of production pacing and arousing content on the information processing of television messages. *Journal of Broadcasting & Electronic Media, 43,* 451–475.

Lang, A., Dhillon, K., & Dong, Q. (1995). The effects of emotional arousal and valence on television viewers' cognitive capacity and memory. *Journal of Broadcasting & Electronic Media, 39,* 313–327.

Lang, A., Newhagen, J., & Reeves, B. (1996). Negative video as structure: Emotion, attention, capacity, and memory. *Journal of Broadcasting & Electronic Media, 40,* 460–477.

Lang, A., Schwartz, N., Chung, Y., & Lee, S. (2004). Processing substance abuse messages: Production pacing, arousing content, and age. *Journal of Broadcasting & Electronic Media, 48,* 61–88.

Lang, A., Shin, M., Bradley, S. D., Wang, Z., Lee, S., & Potter, D. (2005). Wait! Don't turn that dial! More excitement to come! The effects of story length and production pacing in local television news on channel changing behavior and information processing in a free choice environment. *Journal of Broadcasting & Electronic Media, 49,* 3–22.

Lang, A., & Yegiyan, N. S. (2008). Understanding the interactive effects of emotional appeal and claim strength in health messages. *Journal of Broadcasting & Electronic Media, 52,* 432–447.

Lang, A., Zhou, S. Schwartz, N., Bolls, P. D., & Potter, R. F. (2000). The effects of edits on arousal, attention and memory for television messages: When an edit is an edit can an edit be too much? *Journal of Broadcasting & Electronic Media, 44,* 94–109.

Lang, G. E., & Lang, A. (1981). Watergate: An exploration of the agenda-building process. In G. C. Wilhoit & H. DeBock (Eds.), *Mass communication review yearbook 2* (pp. 447–468). Newbury Park, CA: Sage.

Lang, G. E., & Lang, K. (1983). *The battle for public opinion*. New York: Columbia University Press.

Lang, G. E., & Lang, A. (1991). *Obscenity, censorship and public opinion in the NEA controversy*. Paper presented at the meeting of American Association for Public Opinion Research.

Langer, E. J., & Piper, A. (1988). Television from a mindful/mindless perspective. In S. Oskamp (Ed.), *Television as a social issue* (pp. 247–260). Newbury Park, CA: Sage.

LaRose, R., & Eastin, M. S. (2002). Is on-line buying out of control? Electronic commerce and consumer self-regulation. *Journal of Broadcasting and Electronic Media, 45* (4), 549–564.

LaRose, R., & Eastin, M. S. (2004). A social cognitive theory of Internet uses and gratifications: Toward a new model of media attendance. *Journal of Broadcasting & Electronic Media, 48,* 358–377.

LaRose, R., Lin, C. A., & Eastin, M. S. (2003). Unregulated Internet usage: Addiction, habit, or deficient self-regulation? *Media Psychology, 5,* 225–253.

Lasch, C. (1978). *The culture of narcissism*. New York: Norton.

Lasswell, H. D. (1948). The structure and function of communication in society. In L. Bryson (Ed.), *The communication of ideas* (pp. 37–51). New York: Harper.

Lasswell, H. W. (1927). *Propaganda techniques in the World War*. New York: Peter Smith.

L.A. Times publisher errs, apologizes. (1999, October 31). *Tallahassee Democrat*, p. 5B.

Lazarsfeld, P. F. (1948). Communication research and the social psychologist. In W. Dennis (Ed.), *Current trends in social psychology* (pp. 218–273). Pittsburgh: University of Pittsburgh Press.

Lazarsfeld, P. F., Berelson, B., & Gaudet, H. (1944). *The people's choice: How the voter makes up his mind in a presidential campaign*. New York: Duell, Sloan & Pearce.

Lazarus, R. S., & Alfert, E. (1964). The short-circuiting of threat by experimentally altering cognitive appraisal. *Journal of Abnormal and Social Psychology, 69,* 195–205.

Lazarus, R. S., Opton, E. M., Nomikos, M. S., & Rankin, N. O. (1965). The principle of short-circuiting of threat: Further evidence. *Journal of Personality, 33,* 622–635.

Lazarus, R. S., Speisman, J. C., Mordkoff, A. M., & Davidson, L. A. (1962). A laboratory study of psychological stress produced by a motion picture film. *Psychological Monographs: General & Applied, 76*(34), Whole No. 553.

LeDoux, J. (1996). *The emotional brain: The mysterious underpinnings of emotional life*. New York: Simon & Schuster.

Lee, B., & Tamborini, R. (2005). Third-person effect and internet pornography: The influence of collectivism and internet self-efficacy. *Journal of Communication, 55,* 292–310.

Lee, K-M., & Nass, C. (2005). Social-psychological origins of feelings of presence: Creating social presence with machine-generated voices. *Media Psychology, 7,* 31–45.

Lee, S., & Barnes, J. H. Jr. (1990). Using color preferences in magazine advertising. *Journal of Advertising Research, 29*(6), 25–30.

Lee, S., & Lang, A. (2009). Discrete emotion and motivation: Relative activation in the appetitive and aversive motivational systems as a function of anger, sadness, fear, and joy during televised information campaigns. *Media Psychology, 12,* 148–170.

Lee, T-T. (2005). The liberal media myth revisited: An examination of factors influencing perceptions of media bias. *Journal of Broadcasting & Electronic Media, 49,* 43–64.

Lemmens, J. S., Valkenburg, P. M., & Peter, J. (2009). Development and validation of a game addiction scale for adolescents. *Media Psychology, 12,* 77–95.

Leone, R., Peek, W. C., & Bissell, K. L. (2006). Reality television and third-person perception. *Journal of Broadcasting & Electronic Media, 50,* 253–269.

Lerner, D. (1958). *The passing of traditional society: Modernizing the Middle East*. Glencoe, IL: Free Press.

Levin, D. T., & Simons, D. J. (2000). Perceiving stability in a changing world: Combining shots and integrating views in motion pictures and the real world. *Media Psychology, 2,* 357–380.

Levy, S. (2007, August 27). Facebook grows up. *Newsweek,* pp. 40–46.

Lewis, C. (2000, September/October). Media money. *Columbia Journalism Review,* 20–27.

Li, X. (2008). Third-person effect, optimistic bias, and sufficiency resource in Internet use. *Journal of Communication, 58,* 568–587.

Liebert, R. M., & Baron, R. A. (1972). Short-term effects of television aggression on children's aggressive behavior. In J. P. Murray, E. A. Rubinstein, & G. A. Comstock (Eds.), *Television and social behavior: Reports and papers, Volume 2: Television and social learning.* Washington, DC: U.S. Government Printing Office.

Liebert, R. M., & Baron, R. A. (1973). Some immediate effects of televised violence on children's behavior. *Developmental Psychology, 6,* 469–475.

Liebert, R. M., Neale, J. M., & Davidson, E. A. (1973). *The early window: Effects of television on children and youth.* Elmsford, NY: Pergamon.

Liebert, R. M., & Schwartzberg, N. S. (1977). Effects of mass media. *Annual Review of Psychology, 28,* 141–173.

Liebert, R. M., & Sprafkin, J. (1988). *The early window: Effects of television on children and youth* (3rd ed.). New York: Pergamon.

Lim, S., & Reeves, B. (2009). Being in the game: Effects of avatar choice and point of view on psychophysiological responses during play. *Media Psychology, 12,* 348–370.

Lin, C. A. (1995). Network prime-time programming strategies in the 1980s. *Journal of Broadcasting & Electronic Media, 39,* 482–495.

Lind, R. A., & Rockler, N. (2001). Competing ethos: Reliance on profit versus social responsibility by laypeople planning a television newscast. *Journal of Broadcasting & Electronic Media, 45,* 118–134.

Lind, R. A., & Salo, C. (2002). The framing of feminists and feminism in news and public affairs programs in U.S. electronic media. *Journal of Communication, 52*(1), 211–228.

Lippmann, W. (1922). *Public opinion.* New York: Macmillan.

Lo, V.-H., & Wei, R. (2002). Third-person effect, gender, and pornography on the Internet. *Journal of Broadcasting & Electronic Media, 46,* 13–33.

Lo, V.-H., & Wei, R. (2005). Exposure to Internet pornography and Taiwanese adolescents' sexual attitudes and behavior. *Journal of Broadcasting & Electronic Media, 49,* 221–237.

Lombard, M. (1995). Direct responses to people on the screen: Television and personal space. *Communication Research, 22,* 288–324.

Lombard, M., Reich, R. D., Grabe, M. E., Bracken, C. C., & Ditton, T. B. (2000). Presence and television: The role of screen size. *Human Communication Research, 26,* 75–98.

Lovaas, O. I. (1961). Effect of exposure to symbolic aggression on aggressive behavior. *Child Development, 32,* 37–44.

Lowrey, T. M. (2006). The relation between script complexity and commercial memorability. *Journal of Advertising, 35*(3), 7–15.

Lowrey, W., & Kim, K. S. (2009). Online news media and advanced learning: A test of cognitive flexibility theory. *Journal of Broadcasting & Electronic Media, 53,* 547–566.

Lowry, D. T., Ching, T., Nio, J., & Leitner, D. W. (2003). Setting the public fear agenda: A longitudinal analysis of network TV crime reporting, public perceptions of crime, and FBI crime statistics. *Journal of Communication, 53,* 61–73.

Lowry, D. T., & Shidler, J. A. (1995). The sound bites, the biters, and the bitten: An analysis of network TV news bias in campaign '92. *Journalism & Mass Communication Quarterly, 72,* 147–157.

Lucas, C. J., & Schmitz, C. D. (1988). Communication media and current events knowledge among college students. *Higher Education Amsterdam, 17*(2), 139–149.

Lucas, K., & Sherry, J. L. (2004). Sex differences in video game play: A communication-based explanation. *Communication Research, 31,* 499–523.

Lyman, P., & Varian, H. R. (2003, October 27). *How much information?* Retrieved July 10, 2006, from http://www.sims.berkeley.edu/

Maccoby, E. E. (1954). Why do children watch TV? *Public Opinion Quarterly, 18,* 239–244.

Maccoby, E. E. (1964). Effects of the mass media. In M. L. Hoffman & L. W. Hoffman (Eds.), *Review of child development research* (pp. 323–348). New York: Russell Sage Foundation.

Magee, R. G., & Kalyanaraman, S. (2009). Effects of worldview and mortality salience in persuasion processes. *Media Psychology, 12,* 171—194.

Makovsky, D. (1999, May 24). Getting into the ring: Wealthy American and other foreigners played a quiet role in Israel's election. *U.S. News & World Report,* p. 43.

Malamuth, N. M. (1984). Aggression against women: Cultural and individual causes. In N. M. Malamuth

& E. Donnerstein (Eds.), *Pornography and sexual aggression*. Orlando, FL: Academic Press.

Malamuth, N. M., & Check, J.V.P. (1980). Penile tumescence and perceptual responses to rape as a function of victim's perceived reactions. *Journal of Applied Social Psychology, 10,* 528–547.

Mander, J. (1978). *Four arguments for the elimination of television*. New York: William Morrow.

Mansfield, E. (1970). *Microeconomics: Theory and applications* (2nd ed.). New York: Norton.

Marcuse, H. (1964). *One-dimensional man: Studies in the ideology of advanced industrial society.* Boston: Beacon Press.

Mares, M-L., (1996). The role of source confusions in television's cultivation of social reality judgments. *Human Communication Research, 23,* 278–297.

Mares,M-L., & Acosta, E. E. (2008). Be kind to three-legged dogs: Children's literal interpretations of TV's moral lessons. *Media Psychology, 11,* 377–399.

Mares, M-L., & Cantor, J. (1992). Elderly viewers' responses to televised portrayals of old age: Empathy and mood management versus social comparison, *Communication Research, 19,* 459–478.

Mares, M-L., Oliver. M. B., & Cantor, J. (2008). Age differences in adults' emotional motivations for exposure to films. *Media Psychology, 11,* 488–511.

Mares, M-L., & Woodard, E. H. (2001). Prosocial effects on children's social interactions. In D. G. Singer & J. L. Singer (Eds.), *Handbook of children and the media* (pp. 183–205). Thousand Oaks, CA: Sage.

Mares, M-L., & Woodard, E. (2005). Positive effects of television on children's social interactions: A meta-analysis. *Media Psychology, 7,* 301–322.

Mares, M-L., & Woodard, E. H. IV. (2006). In search of the older audience: Adult age differences in television viewing. *Journal of Broadcasting & Electronic Media, 50,* 595–614.

Marsh, K. L., & Wallace, H. M. (2005). The influence of attitudes on beliefs: Formation and change. In D. Albarracin, B. T. Johnson, & M. P. Zanna (Eds.). *The handbook of attitudes* (pp. 369–395). Mahwah, NJ: Erlbaum.

Mastin, T. (2000). Media use and civic participation in the African-American population: Exploring participation among professionals and nonprofessionals. *Journalism & Mass Communication Quarterly, 77,* 115–127.

Mastro, D., Lapinski, M. K., Kopacz, M. A., & Behm-Morawitz, E. (2009). The influence of exposure to depictions of race and crime in TV news on viewer's social judgments. *Journal of Broadcasting & Electronic Media, 53,* 615–635.

Mastro, D. E., Tamborini, R., & Hullett, C. R. (2005). Linking media to prototype activation and subsequent celebrity attraction: An application of self-categorization theory. *Communication Research, 32,* 323–349.

Matei, S., & Ball-Rokeach, S. (2003). The Internet in the communication of infrastructure of urban residential communities: Macro- or mesolinkage? *Journal of Communication, 53,* 642–657.

Matthes, J., Morrison, K. R., & Schemer, C. (2010). A spiral of silence for some: Attitude certainty and the expression of political minority opinions. *Communication Research, 37,* 774–800.

Maurer, M., & Reinemann, C. (2006). Learning versus knowing: Effects of misinformation in televised debates. *Communication Research, 33,* 489–506.

Mayer, J. D., & Cornfield, M. (2008). The Internet and the future of media politics. In M. J. Rozell & J. D. Mayer (Eds.), *Media power, media politics* (2nd ed., pp. 319–337). New York: Rowman & Littlefield.

McCombs, M. E., & Shaw, D. L. (1972). The agenda setting function of the press. *Public Opinion Quarterly, 36,* 176–187.

McCombs, M. E., & Shaw, D. L. (1993). The evolution of agenda setting theory: 25 years in the marketplace of ideas. *Journal of Communication, 43*(2), 58–66.

McGuire, W. J. (1969). The nature of attitudes and attitude change. In G. Lindzey & E. Aronson (Eds.), *The handbook of social psychology, Vol. 3 The individual in a social context* (pp. 136–314). Reading, MA: Addison-Wesley.

McGuire, W. J. (1985). Attitudes and attitude change. In G. Lindzey & E. Aronson (Eds.), *Handbook of social psychology, Vol. 2* (pp. 233–246). New York: Random House.

McGuire, W. J. (1990). Dynamic operations of thought systems. *American Psychologist, 45,* 504–512.

McIlwraith, R. D. (1998). "I'm addicted to television": The personality, imagination, and TV watching patterns of self-identified TV addicts. *Journal of Broadcasting & Electronic Media, 42,* 371–386.

McIntosh, W. D., Schwegler, A. F., & Terry-Murray, R. M. (2000). Threat and television viewing in the United States, 1960–1990. *Media Psychology, 2,* 35–46.

McLeod, D. M. (1995). Communicating deviance: The effects of television news coverage of social protest. *Journal of Broadcasting and Electronic Media, 39,* 4–19.

McLeod, D. M., & Detenber, B. H. (1999). Framing effects of television news coverage of social protest. *Journal of Communication, 49,* 3–23.

McLeod, D. M., Detenber, B. H., & Eveland, W. P. Jr. (2001). Behind the third-person effect: Differentiating perceptual processes for self and others, *Journal of Communication, 51*, 678–695.

McLeod, J. M., & Becker, L. B. (1974). Testing the validity of gratification measures through political effects analysis. In J. G. Blumler & E. Katz (Eds.), *The uses of mass communications: Current perspectives on gratifications research* (pp. 137–164). Beverly Hills, CA: Sage.

McLeod, J. M., Sotirovic, M., Voakes, P. S., Guod, Z, & Huang, K-Y. (1998). A model of public support for First Amendment rights. *Communication Law & Policy, 3*, 479–514.

McLeod, J. M., Ward, L. S., & Tancill, K. (1965). Alienation and uses of mass media. *Public Opinion Quarterly, 29*, 583–594.

McLuhan, M. (1962). *The Gutenberg galaxy: The making of typographic man.* Toronto: University of Toronto Press.

McLuhan, M. (1964). *Understanding media.* London: Routledge & Kegan Paul.

McLuhan, M., & Fiore, Q. (1967). *The medium is the message: An inventory of effects.* New York: Bantam.

McManus, J. H. (1994). *Market-driven journalism: Let the citizen beware?* Thousand Oaks, CA: Sage.

McPhee, W. N. (1963). *Formal theories of mass behavior.* New York: Free Press.

McQuail, D. (1987). *Mass communication theory: An introduction* (2nd ed.). London: Sage.

McQuail, D., & Windahl, S. (1981). *Communication models for the study of mass communications.* London: Longman.

McQuail, D., & Windahl, S. (1993). *Communication models for the study of mass communication* (2nd ed.). London: Longman.

McQuarrie, E. F., & Phillips, B. J. (2005). Indirect persuasion in advertising: How consumers process metaphors presented in pictures and words. *Journal of Advertising, 34*(2), 7–20.

Mead, G. H. (1934). *Mind, self and society.* Chicago: University of Chicago Press.

Media and eating disorders. (n.d.). Retrieved August 26, 2007, from http://www.raderprograms.com/media.aspx

Medrich, E. A., Roizen, J. A., Rubin, V., & Buckley, S. (1982). *The serious business of growing up: A study of children's lives outside school.* Berkeley: University of California Press.

Meffert, M. F., Chung, S., Joiner, A. J., Waks, L., & Garst, J. (2006). The effects of negativity and motivated information processing during a political campaign. *Journal of Communication, 56*, 27–51.

Mehta, A., & Davis, C. M. (1990, August). *Celebrity advertising: Perception, persuasion and processing.* Paper presented to the Association for Education in Journalism and Mass Communication, Minneapolis.

Meijer, M-M., & Kleinnijenhuis, J. (2006). Issue news and corporate reputation: Applying the theories of agenda setting and issue ownership in the field of business communication. *Journal of Communication, 56*, 543–559.

Meirick, P. C. (2004). Topic-relevant reference groups and dimensions of distance: Political advertising and first- and third-person effects. *Communication Research, 31*, 234–255.

Meirick, P. C. (2005). Rethinking the target corollary: The effects of social distance, perceived exposure, and perceived predispositions on first-person and third-person perceptions. *Communication Research, 32*, 822–844.

Meirick, P. C. (2008). Targeted audiences in anti-drug ads: Message cues, perceived exposure, perceived effects, and support for funding. *Media Psychology, 11*, 283–309.

Melican, D. B., & Dixon, T. L. (2008). News on the Net: Credibility, selective exposure, and racial prejudice. *Communication Research, 35*, 151–168.

Mendelsohn, H. (1966). *Mass entertainment.* New Haven, CT: College & University Press.

Mendelson, A. (2001). Effects of novelty in news photographs on attention and memory. *Media Psychology, 3*, 119-157.

Mendelson, A. L., & Thorson, E. (2004). How verbalizers process the newspaper environment. *Journal of Communication, 54*, 474–491.

Merton, R. K. (1949). *Social theory and social structure.* Glencoe, IL: Free Press.

Messner, S. F. (1986). Television violence and violent crime: An aggregate analysis. *Social Problems, 33*(3), 218–235.

Metallinos, N. (1996). *Television aesthetics: Perceptual, cognitive, and compositional bases.* Mahwah, NJ: Erlbaum.

Metzger, M. J. (2000). When no news is good news: Inferring closure for news issues. *Journalism & Mass Communication Quarterly, 77*, 760–787.

Metzger, M. J., Flanagin, A. J., & Medders, R. B. (2010). Social and heuristic approaches to credibility evaluation online. *Journal of Communication, 60*, 413–439.

Meyrowitz, J. (1985). *No sense of place.* New York: Oxford University Press.

Meyrowitz, J., & Maguire, J. (1993). Media, place and multiculturalism. *Society, 30*(5), 41–48.

Miller, N. E., & Dollard, J. (1941). *Social learning and imitation.* New Haven, CT: Yale University Press.

Mills, C. W. (1957). *The power elite.* New York: Oxford University Press.

Mills, C. W. (1959). *The sociological imagination.* New York: Oxford University Press.

Miron, D., Bryant, J., & Zillmann, D. (2001). Creating vigilance for better learning from television. In D. G. Singer & J. L. Singer (Eds.), *Handbook of children and the media* (pp. 153–181). Thousand Oaks, CA: Sage.

Mollison, T. A. (1998). Television broadcasting leads Romania's march toward an open, democratic society. *Journal of Broadcasting & Electronic Media, 42*, 128–141.

Moorman, M., Neijens, P. C., & Smit, E. G. (2007). The effects of program involvement on commercial exposure and recall in a naturalistic setting. *Journal of Advertising, 36*, 121–137.

Morgan, M., & Gross, L. (1982). Television and educational achievement and aspirations. In D. Pearl, L. Bouthilet, & J. Lazar (Eds.), *Television and behavior: Ten years of scientific progress and implications for the eighties* (pp. 78–90). Washington, DC: Government Printing Office.

Morgan, S. E., Movius, L., & Cody, M. J. (2009). The power of narratives: The effect of entertainment television organ donation storylines on the attitudes, knowledge, and behaviors of donors and nondonors. *Journal of Communication, 59,* 135–151.

Morgan, S. E., Palmgren, Stephenson, M. T., Hoyle, R. H., & Lorch, E. P. (2003). Associations between message features and subjective evaluations of the sensation value of antidrug public service announcements. *Journal of Communication, 53,* 512–526.

Moriarty, C. M., & Harrison, K. (2008). Television exposure and disordered eating among children: A longitudinal panel study. *Journal of Communication, 58,* 361–381.

Morley, D. (1980). *The "nationwide" audience: Structure and decoding.* London: BFI.

Morris, C. (1946). *Signs, language, and behavior.* New York: Braziller.

Moy, P., Domke, D., & Stamm, K. (2001). The spiral of silence and public opinion on affirmative action. *Journalism & Mass Communication Quarterly, 78,* 7–25.

Moy, P., McCluskey, M. R., McCoy, K., & Spratt, M. A. (2004). Political correlates of local news media use. *Journal of Communication, 54,* 532–546.

Moy, P., Pfau, M., & Kahlor, L. (1999). Media use and public confidence in democratic institutions. *Journal of Broadcasting & Electronic Media, 43,* 137–158.

Moy, P., & Scheufele, D. A. (2000). Media effects on political and social trust. *Journalism & Mass Communication Quarterly, 77,* 744–759.

Moy, P., Torres, M., Tanaka, K., & McCluskey, M. R. (2005). Knowledge or trust? Investigating linkages between media reliance and participation. *Communication Research, 32,* 59–96.

Moyer-Gusé, E., & Nabi, R. L. (2010). Explaining the effects of narrative in an entertainment television program: Overcoming resistance to persuasion. *Human Communication Research, 36,* 26–52.

Mulholland, T. (1973). Objective EEG methods for studying covert shifts of visual attention. In F. G. McGuigan & R. A. Schoonauer (Eds.), *The psychophysiology of thinking* (pp. 109–151). New York: Academic Press.

Mullin, C., Imrich, D. J., & Linz, D. (1995). The impact of acquaintance rape stories and case-specific pretrial publicity on juror decision making. *Communication Research, 23,* 100–135.

Mullin, C. R., & Linz, D. (1995). Desensitization and resensitization to violence against women: Effects of exposure to sexually violent films on judgments of domestic violence victims. *Journal of Personality & Social Psychology, 69,* 449–459.

Mumford, L. (1970). *The myth of the machine.* New York: Harcourt, Brace & World.

Murdock, G. (1990). Redrawing the map of the communication industries. In M. Ferguson (Ed.), *Public communication* (pp. 1–15). London: Sage.

Nabi, R. L. (1999). A cognitive-functional model for the effects of discrete negative emotions on information processing, attitude change, and recall. *Communication Theory, 9,* 292–320.

Nabi, R. L. (2003). "Feeling" resistance: Exploring the role of emotionally evocative visuals in inducing inoculation. *Media Psychology, 5,* 199–223.

Nabi, R. L., & Clark, S. (2008). Exploring the limits of social cognitive theory: Why negatively reinforced behaviors on TV may be modeled anyway. *Journal of Communication, 58,* 407–427.

Nabi, R. L., Finnerty, K., Domschke, T., & Hull, S. (2006). Does misery love company? Exploring the therapeutic effects of TV viewing on regretted experiences. *Journal of Communication, 56,* 689–706.

Nabi, R. L., & Hendriks, A. (2003). The persuasive effect of host and audience reaction shots in television talk shows. *Journal of Communication, 53,* 527–543.

Nabi, R. L., & Krcmar, M. (2004). Conceptualizing media enjoyment as attitude: Implications for mass media effects research. *Communication Theory, 14,* 288–310.

Nabi, R. L., & Riddle, K. (2008). Personality traits, television viewing, and the cultivation effect. *Journal of Broadcasting & Electronic Media, 52,* 327–348.

Nabi, R. L. & Sullivan, J. L. (2001). Does television relate to engagement in protective behavior and crime? A cultivation analysis from a theory of reasoned action perspective. *Communication Research, 28,* 802–825.

Nan, X. (2008). The influence of liking for a public service announcement on issue attitude. *Communication Research, 35,* 503–528.

Naples, M. J. (1981). *Effective frequency: The relationship between frequency and advertising effectiveness.* New York: Association of National Advertisers.

Napoli, P. M. (1999). The marketplace of ideas metaphor in communications regulation. *Journal of Communication, 49*(4), 151–169.

Neely, S. M., & Schumann, D. W. (2004). Using animated spokes-characters in advertising to young children: Does increasing attention to advertising necessarily lead to product preference? *Journal of Advertising, 33*(3), 7–23.

Neuman, W. R. (1991). *The future of the mass audience.* New York: Cambridge University Press.

Newcomb, T. (1953). An approach to the study of communicative acts. *Psychological Review, 60,* 393–404.

Newhagen, J. E. (1994). Self efficacy and call-in political television show use. *Communication Research, 21,* 366–379.

Newhagen, J. E. (1998). TV news images that induce anger, fear, and disgust: Effects on approach-avoidance and memory. *Journal of Broadcasting & Electronic Media, 42,* 265–276.

Niederdeppe, J., Davis, K. C., Farrelly, M. C., & Yarsevich, J. (2007). Stylistic features, need for sensation, and confirmed recall of national smoking prevention advertisements. *Journal of Communication, 57,* 272–292.

Nisbet, M. C., Scheufele, D. A., Shanahan, J. Moy, P., Brossard, D., & Lewenstein, B. V. (2002). Knowledge, reservations, or promise? A media effects model for public perceptions of science and technology. *Communication Research, 29,* 584–608.

Noam, E. (2009). *Media ownership and concentration in America.* New York: Oxford University Press.

Noelle-Neumann, E. (1974). The spiral of silence: A theory of public opinion. *Journal of Communication, 24,* 24–51.

Noelle-Neumann, E. (1984). *The spiral of silence: Public opinion--our social skin.* Chicago: University of Chicago Press.

Noelle-Neumann, E. (1991). The theory of public opinion: The concept of spiral of silence. In J. Anderson (Ed.), *Communication yearbook 14* (pp. 256–287). Newbury Park, CA: Sage.

Nomikos, M., Opton, E., Averill, J., & Lazarus, R. (1968). Surprise versus suspense in the production of stress reaction. *Journal of Personality & Social Psychology, 8,* 204–208.

Nowak, K. L., Hamilton, M. A., & Hammond, C. C. (2009). The effect of image features on judgments of homophily, credibility, and intention to use as avatars in future interactions. *Media Psychology, 12,* 50–76.

Ogles, R. M., & Hoffner, C. (1987). Film violence and perceptions of crime: The cultivation effect. In M. L. McLaughlin (Ed.), *Communication yearbook 10* (pp. 384–394). Thousand Oaks, CA: Sage.

Ohman, A. ((1979). The orienting response, attention, and learning: An information processing perspective. In H. D. Kimmel, E. H. van Olst, & J. F. Orlebeke (Eds.), *The orienting reflex in humans* (pp. 443–471). Hillsdale, NJ: Erlbaum.

O'Keefe, D. J., & Jensen, J. D. (2009). The relative persuasiveness of gain-framed and loss-framed messages for encouraging disease detection behaviors: A meta-analytic review. *Journal of Communication, 59,* 296–316.

Oliver, M. B. (1999). Caucasian viewers' memory of Black and White criminal suspects in the news. *Journal of Communication, 49,* 46–60.

Oliver, M. B. (2008). Tender affective states as predictors of entertainment preference. *Journal of Communication, 58,* 40–61.

Oliver, M. B., & Bartsch, A. (2010). Appreciation as audience response: Exploring entertainment gratifications beyond hedonism. *Human Communication Research, 36,* 53–81.

Oliver, M. B., & Fonash, D. (2002). Race and crime in the news: White's identification and misidentification of violent and nonviolent criminal suspects. *Media Psychology, 4,* 137–156.

Oliver, M. B., Jackson, R. L. II, Moses, N. N., & Dangerfield, C. L. (2004). The face of crime: Viewers' memory of race-related facial features of individuals pictured in the news. *Journal of Communication, 54,* 88–104.

Oliver, M. B., Weaver, J. B. III, & Sargent, S. L. (2000). An examination of factors related to sex differences in enjoyment of sad films. *Journal of Broadcasting & Electronic Media, 44,* 282–300.

Oliver, M. B., Yang, H., Ramasubramanian, S., Kim, J., & Lee, S. (2008). Exploring implications of perceived media reinforcement on third-person perceptions. *Communication Research, 35*, 745–769.

Olson, J. M., & Stone, J. (2005). The influence of behavior on attitudes. In D. Albarracin, B. T. Johnson, & M. P. Zanna (Eds.), *The handbook of attitudes* (pp. 223–271). Mahwah, NJ: Erlbaum.

Osborn, D. K., & Endsley, R. C. (1971). Emotional reactions of young children to TV violence. *Child Development, 42*, 321–331.

Ostman, R. E., & Parker, J. L. (1987). Impact of education, age, newspapers, and television on environmental knowledge, concerns and behaviors. *Journal of Environmental Education, 19*(1), 3–9.

Packard, V. (1957). *The hidden persuaders.* New York: David McKay.

Paek, H-J., Pan, Z., Sun, Y., Abisaid, J., & Houden, D. (2005). The third-person perception as social judgment: An exploration of social distance and uncertainty in perceived effects of political attack ads. *Communication Research, 32*, 143–170.

Page, B. I., & Shapiro, R. Y. (1992). *The rational public: Fifty years of trends in American's policy preferences.* Chicago: University of Chicago Press.

Page, D., & O'Neal, E. (1977). "Weapons effect" without demand characteristics. *Psychological Reports, 41*, 29–30.

Paik, H., & Comstock, G. (1994). The effects of television violence on antisocial behavior: A meta-analysis. *Communication Research, 21*, 516–546.

Palmgren, P., & Rayburn, J. D. (1982). Gratifications sought and media exposures: An expectancy value model. *Communication Research, 9*, 561–580.

Palmgren, P., & Rayburn, J. D. (1985). An expectancy-value approach to media gratifications. In K. E. Rosengren (Ed.), *Media gratification research* (pp. 61–72). Beverly Hills, CA: Sage.

Pan, Z., & Kosicki, G. M. (1996). Assessing news media influences on the formation of Whites' racial policy preferences. *Communication Research, 23*, 147–178.

Papacharissi, Z., & Mendelson, A. L. (2007). An exploratory study of reality appeal: Uses and gratifications of reality TV shows. *Journal of Broadcasting & Electronic Media, 51*, 355–370.

Park, C. W., & Young, S. M. (1986). Consumer response to television commercials: The impact of involvement and background music on brand attitude formation. *Journal of Marketing Research, 23*, 11–24.

Park, E., & Kosicki, G. M. (1995). Presidential support during the Iran-Contra affair: People's reasoning process and media influence. *Communication Research, 22*, 207–236.

Park, S-Y. (2005). The influence of presumed media influence on women's desire to be thin. *Communication Research, 32*, 594–614.

Parks, M. R., & Floyd, K. (1996). Making friends in cyberspace. *Journal of Communication, 46*(1), 80–97.

Pasek, J., Kenski, K., Romer, D., & Jamieson, K. H. (2006). America's youth and community engagement: How use of mass media is related to civic activity and political awareness in 14- to 22-year-olds. *Communication Research, 33*, 115–135.

Pashler, H. E. (1998). *The psychology of attention.* Cambridge, MA: MIT Press.

Patterson, T. (1980). *The mass media election: How Americans choose their president.* New York: Praeger.

Patterson, T. (1993). *Out of order.* New York: Knopf.

Paul, B., & Linz, D. G. (2008). The effects of exposure to virtual child pornography on viewer cognitions and attitudes toward deviant sexual behavior. *Communication Research, 35*, 3–38.

Paul, B., Salwen, M. B., & Dupagne, M. (2000). The third-person effect: A meta-analysis of the perceptual hypothesis. *Mass Communication & Society, 3*, 57–85.

Peiser, W., & Peter, J. (2000). Third-person perception of television-viewing behavior. *Journal of Communication, 50*, 25–45.

Peiser, W., & Peter, J. (2001). Explaining individual differences in third-person perception: A limits/possibilities perspective. *Communication Research, 28*, 156–180.

Peña, J., Hancock, J. T., & Merola, N. A. (2009). The priming effects of avatars in virtual settings. *Communication Research, 36*, 838–856.

Peri, Y. (1999). The media and collective memory of Yitzhak Rabin's remembrance. *Journal of Communication, 49*(3), 106–124.

Perkins, K. (1996, November 27). Statistics blur image of American family. *Santa Barbara News-Press,* pp. A1, A2.

Perloff, R. M. (2002). The third-person effect. In J. Bryant & D. Zillmann (Eds.), *Media effects: Advances in theory and research* (2nd ed., pp. 489–506). Mahwah, NJ: Erlbaum.

Perry, D. K. (1990). News reading, knowledge about, and attitudes toward foreign countries. *Journalism Quarterly, 67*, 353–358.

Perry, S. D., & Gonzenbach, W. J. (1997). Effects of news exemplification extended: Considerations of controversiality and perceived future opinion. *Journal of Broadcasting & Electronic Media, 41*, 229–244.

Peter, J., & Valkenburg, P. M. (2006). Adolescents' exposure to sexually explicit online material and recreational attitudes toward sex. *Journal of Communication, 56,* 639–660.

Peter, J., & Valkenburg, P. M. (2008a). Adolescents' exposure to sexually explicit internet material and sexual preoccupancy: A three-wave panel study. *Media Psychology, 11,* 207–234.

Peter, J., & Valkenburg, P. M. (2008b). Adolescents' exposure to sexually explicit internet material, sexual uncertainty, and attitudes toward uncommitted sexual exploration: Is there a link? *Communication Research, 35,* 579–601.

Peter, J., & Valkenburg, P. M. (2009a). Adolescents' exposure to sexually explicit internet material and sexual satisfaction: A longitudinal study. *Human Communication Research, 35,* 171–194.

Peter, J., & Valkenburg, P. M. (2009b). Adolescents' exposure to sexually explicit internet material and notions of women as sex objects: Assessing causality and underlying processes. *Journal of Communication, 59,* 407–433.

Peterson, E. M., & Raney, A. A. (2008). Reconceptualizing and reexamining suspense as a predictor of mediated sports enjoyment. *Journal of Broadcasting & Electronic Media, 52,* 544–562.

Petrevu, S. (2004). Communicating with the sexes: Male and female responses to print advertisements. *Journal of Advertising, 33*(3), 51–62.

Petty, R. E., & Cacioppo, J. T. (1981). *Attitudes and persuasion: Classic and contemporary approaches.* Dubuque, IA: W. C. Brown.

Petty, R. E., & Cacioppo, J. T. (1986). *Communication and persuasion: Central and peripheral routes to attitude change.* New York: Springer-Verlag.

Petty, R. E., Priester, J. R., & Brinol, P. (2002). Mass media attitude change: Implications of the elaboration likelihood model of persuasion. In J. Bryant & D. Zillmann (Eds.), *Media effects: Advances in theory and research* (2nd ed., pp. 155–198). Mahwah, NJ: Erlbaum.

Pfau, M., Compton, J., Parker, K. A., Wittenberg, E. M., An, C., Ferguson, M., et al. (2004). The traditional explanation for resistance versus attitude accessibility: Do they trigger distinct or overlapping processes of resistance? *Human Communication Research, 30,* 329–360.

Pfau, M., Haigh, M. M., Shannon, T., Tones, T., Mercurio, D., Williams, R., et al. (2008). The influence of television news depictions of the images of war on viewers. *Journal of Broadcasting & Electronic Media, 52,* 303–322.

Pfau, M., Holbert, R. L., Zubric, S. J., Pasha, N. H., & Lin, W-K. (2000). Role and influence of communication modality in the process of resistance to persuasion. *Media Psychology, 2,* 1–33.

Pfau, M., Mullen, L. J., Deidrich, T., & Garrow, K. (1995). Television viewing and public perceptions of attorneys. *Human Communication Research, 21,* 307–330.

Pfau, M., Szabo, A. Anderson, J., Morrill, J., Zubric, J., & Wan, H-H. (2001). The role and impact of affect in the process of resistance to persuasion. *Human Communication Research, 27,* 216–252.

Phillips. D. P. (1983). The impact of mass media violence on U.S. homicides. *American Sociological Review, 48,* 560–568.

Phillips, D. P., & Hensley, J. E. (1984). When violence is rewarded or punished: The impact of mass media stories on homicide. *Journal of Communication, 34,* 101–116.

Phillips, L. E. (2010, December 28). *Trends in consumers' time spent with media.* Retrieved January 5, 2011, from http://www.emarketer.com/

Picard, R. (1989). *Media economics.* Newbury Park, CA: Sage.

Picard, R. G., Winter, J. P., McCombs, M., & Lacy, S. (Eds.). (1988). *Press concentration and monopoly: New perspectives on newspaper ownership and operation.* Norwood, NJ: Ablex.

Pifer, L. K. (1991, November). *Scientific literacy and political participation.* Paper presented at the annual conference of the Midwest Association of Public Opinion Research, Chicago.

Pinkleton, B. E. (1998). Effects of print comparative political advertising on political decision-making and participation. *Journal of Communication, 48*(4), 24–36.

Pinkleton, B. E., Austin, E. W., & Fortman, K. K. J. (1998). Relationships of media use and political disaffection to political efficacy and voting behavior. *Journal of Broadcasting & Electronic Media, 42,* 34–49.

Pipher, M. (1996). *The shelter of each other.* New York: Putnam.

Plack, C. J. (2005). Auditory perception. In K. Lamberts & R. L. Goldstone (Eds.), *Handbook of cognition* (pp. 71–104). London: Sage.

Pool, M. M., Koolstra, C. M., & van der Voort, T. H. A. (2003). The impact of background radio and television on high school students' homework performance. *Journal of Communication, 53,* 74–87.

Postman, N. (1985). *Amusing ourselves to death.* New York: Penguin.

Potter, R. F. (2000). The effects of voice changes on orienting and immediate cognitive overload in radio listeners. *Media Psychology, 2,* 147–177.

Potter, R. F. (2009). Double the units: How increasing the number of advertisements while keeping the overall duration of commercial breaks constant affects radio listeners. *Journal of Broadcasting & Electronic Media, 53,* 584–598.

Potter, W. J. (1988). Perceived reality in television effects research. *Journal of Broadcasting & Electronic Media, 32,* 23–41.

Potter, W. J. (1991). Examining cultivation from a psychological perspective: Component subprocesses. *Communication Research, 18,* 77–102.

Potter, W. J. (1994). A methodological critique of cultivation research. *Journalism Monographs.*

Potter, W. J. (2011). *Media literacy* (5th ed.). Thousand Oaks, CA: Sage.

Potter, W. J., Cooper, R., & Dupagne, M. (1993). The three paradigms of mass media research in mainstream journals. *Communication Theory, 3,* 317–335.

Potter, W. J., Pashupati, K., Pekurny, R. B., Hoffman, E., & Davis, K. (2002). Perceptions of television: A schema explanation. *Media Psychology, 4,* 27-50.

Potter, W. J., & Riddle, K. (2006, November). *A content analysis of the mass media effects literature.* Paper presented at the annual convention of the National Communication Association, San Antonio.

Potter, W. J., & Riddle K. (2007). A content analysis of the media effects literature. *Journalism & Mass Communication Quarterly, 84,* 90–104.

Potter, W. J., & Tomasello, T. K. (2003). Building upon the experimental design in media violence research: The importance of including receiver interpretations. *Journal of Communication, 53,* 315–329.

Price, V., & Czilli, E. J. (1996). Modeling patterns of news recognition and recall. *Journal of Communication, 46,* 55–78.

Price, V., & Tewksbury, D. (1997). New values and public opinion: A theoretical account of media priming and framing. In G. A. Barnett & F. J. Boster (Eds.), *Progress in communication sciences: Advances in persuasion* (Vol. 13, pp. 173–212). Greenwich, CT: Ablex.

Price, V., Tewksbury, D., & Huang, L-N. (1998). Third-person effects on publication of a Holocaust-denial advertisement. *Journal of Communication, 48*(2), 3–26.

Prior, M. (2009). The immensely inflated news audience: Assessing bias in self-reported news exposure. *Public Opinion Quarterly, 73,* 130–143.

Protess, D. L., Cook, F. L., Doppelt, J. C., Ettema, J. S., Gordon, M. T., Leff, D. R., & Miller, P. (1991). *The journalism of outrage: Investigative reporting and agenda building in America.* New York: Guilford.

Pulaski, M. A. S. (1980). *Understanding Piaget: An introduction to children's cognitive development* (Rev. and exp. ed.). New York: Harper & Row.

Putnam, R. D. (2000). *Bowling alone: The collapse and revival of American community.* New York: Simon & Schuster.

Quick, B. L. (2009). The effects of viewing *Grey's Anatomy* on perceptions of doctors and patient satisfaction. *Journal of Broadcasting & Electronic Media, 53,* 38–55.

Radway, D. J. (1984). *Reading the romance.* Chapel Hill: University of North Carolina Press.

Rains, S. A. (2008). Health at high speed: Broadband Internet access, health communication, and the digital divide. *Communication Research, 35,* 283–297.

Rakow, L. F. (1992). *Gender on the line: Women, the telephone, and community life.* Urbana: University of Illinois Press.

Raney, A. A. (2004). Expanding disposition theory: Reconsidering character liking, moral evaluations, and enjoyment. *Communication Theory, 14,* 348–369.

Raney, A. A. (2005). Punishing media criminals and moral judgment: The impact on enjoyment. *Media Psychology, 7,* 145–163.

Raney, A. A., & Bryant, J. (2002). Moral judgment and crime drama: An integrated theory of enjoyment. *Journal of Communication, 52,* 402–415.

Ravaja, N. (2004a). Contributions of psychophysiology to media research: Review and recommendations. *Media Psychology, 6,* 193–235.

Ravaja, N. (2004b). Effects of image motion on a small screen on emotion, attention, and memory: Moving-face versus static-face newscaster. *Journal of Broadcasting & Electronic Media, 48,* 108–133.

Ravaja, N. (2009). The psychophysiology of digital gaming: The effect of a non-co-located opponent. *Media Psychology, 12,* 268–294.

Reagan, J. (1996). The "repertoire" of information sources. *Journal of Broadcasting & Electronic Media, 40,* 112–121.

Reeves, B., Newhagen, J., Maibach, E., Basil, M., & Kurz, K. (1991). Negative and positive television messages. *American Behavioral Scientist, 34*(6), 679–694.

Reeves, B., Thorson, E., Rothschild, M., McDonald, D., Hirsch, J., & Goldstein, R. (1985). Attention to television: Intrastimulus effects of movement and score changes on alpha variation over time. *International Journal of Neuroscience, 25,* 241–255.

Reid, S. A., & Hogg, M. A. (2005). A self-categorization explanation for the third-person effect. *Human Communication Research, 31,* 129–161.

Reiss, S., & Wiltz, J. (2004). Why people watch reality TV. *Media Psychology, 6,* 363–378.

Reith, M. (1999). Viewing of crime drama and authoritarian aggression: An investigation of the relationship between crime viewing, fear, and aggression. *Journal of Broadcasting & Electronic Media, 43,* 211–221.

Renner, R., & Lynch, G. P. (2008). A little knowledge is a dangerous thing: What we know about the role of the media in state politics. In M. J. Rozell & J. D. Mayer (Eds.), *Media power, media politics* (2nd ed., pp. 137–155). New York: Rowman & Littlefield.

Ressmeyer, T. J., & Wallen, D. J. (1991, November). *Where do people go to learn about science? Informal science education in Europe and the United States.* Paper presented at the annual conference of the Midwest Association for Public Opinion Research, Chicago.

Rhee, J. W. (1997). Strategy and issue frames in election campaign coverage: A social cognitive account of framing effects. *Journal of Communication, 47*(3), 26–48.

Richardson, J. D. (2005). Switching social identities: The influence of editorial framing on reader attitudes toward affirmative action and African Americans. *Communication Research, 32,* 503–528.

Rice, R. E. (1994). Examining constructs in reading comprehension using two presentation modes: Paper vs. computer. *Journal of Educational Computing Research, 11,* 153–178.

Rice, R. E., & Atkin, C. (1989). *Public communication campaigns* (2nd ed.). Newbury Park, CA: Sage.

Richardson, J. D. (2005). Switching social identities: The influence of editorial framing on reader attitudes toward affirmative action and African Americans. *Communication Research, 32,* 503–529.

Riddle, K. Eyal, K., Mahood, C., & Potter, W. J. (2006). Judging the degree of violence in media portrayals: A cross-genre comparison. *Journal of Broadcasting & Electronic Media, 50,* 270–286.

Riffe, D., & Freitag, A. (1997). A content analysis of content analyses: Twenty-five years of *Journalism Quarterly. Journalism & Mass Communication Quarterly, 74,* 873–882.

Riggs, K. E. (1996). Television use in a retirement community. *Journal of Communication, 46*(1), 144–156.

Riley, J. W., & Riley, M. W. (1959). Mass communication and the social system. In R. K. Merton et al (Eds.) *Sociology today.* New York: Basic Books.

Rimal, R. N., & Real, K. (2003). Perceived risk and efficacy beliefs as motivators of change: Use of the risk perception attitude (RPA) framework to understand health behaviors. *Human Communication Research, 29,* 370–399.

Roberts, D. F., & Maccoby, N. (1985). Effects of mass communication. In G. Lindzey & E. Aronson (Eds.), *Handbook of social psychology* (3rd ed., Vol. 2, pp. 539–599). New York: Random House.

Roberts, M., Wanta, W., & Dzwo, T-H. (2002). Agenda setting and issue salience online. *Communication Research, 29,* 452–465.

Robinson, J. P., & Davis, D. K. (1990). Television news and the informed public: An information-processing approach. *Journal of Communication, 40*(3), 106–119.

Robinson, M. J. (1976). Public affairs television and the growth of political malaise: The case of 'The selling of the Pentagon.' *American Political Science Review, 70,* 409–432.

Rodgers, S., & Thorson, E. (2003). A socialization perspective on male and female reporting. *Journal of Communication, 53,* 658–675.

Roe, K., & Minnebo, J. (2007). Antecedents of adolescents' motives for television use. *Journal of Broadcasting & Electronic Media, 51,* 305–315.

Rogers, E. M. (1962). *Diffusion of innovations.* New York: Free Press.

Rogers, E. M. (1983). *Diffusion of innovations* (3rd ed.). New York: Free Press.

Rogers, E. M. (1993). Looking back, looking forward: A century of communication research. In P. Gaunt (Ed.), *Beyond agendas: New directions in communication research* (pp. 19–40). New Haven, CT: Greenwood.

Rogers, E. M. (1995). *Diffusion of innovations* (4th ed.). New York: Free Press.

Rogers, E. M. (2000). Reflections on news event diffusion research. *Journalism & Mass Communication Quarterly, 77,* 561–576.

Rogers, E. M., & Shoemaker, F. (1971). *Communication of innovations: A cross-cultural approach.* New York: Free Press.

Romer, D., Jamieson, K. H., & Aday, S. (2003). Television news and the cultivation of fear of crime. *Journal of Communication, 53,* 88–104.

Romer, D., Jamieson, P. E., & Jamieson, K. H. (2006). Are news reports of suicide contagious? A stringent test in six U. S. cities. *Journal of Communication, 56,* 253–270.

Rosekrans, M. A., & Hartup, W. W. (1967). Imitative influences of consistent and inconsistent response consequences to a model on aggressive behavior in children. *Journal of Personality & Social Psychology, 7,* 429–434.

Rosengren, K. E. (1974). Uses and gratifications: A paradigm outlined. In J. G. Blumler & E. Katz (Eds.), *The uses of mass communications: Current perspectives of gratifications research* (pp. 269–286). Beverly Hills, CA: Sage.

Rosengren, K. E., Johnsson-Smaragdi, U., & Sonesson, I. (1994). For better and for worse: Effects studies and beyond. In K. E. Rosengren (Ed.), *Media effects and beyond: Culture socializations, and lifestyles* (pp. 133–149). London: Routledge.

Rosengren, K. E., Wenner, L. A., & Palmgreen, P. (Eds.) (1985). *Media gratifications research: Current perspectives*. Beverly Hills, CA: Sage.

Rosengren, K. E., & Windahl, S. (1989). *Media matter*. Norwood, NJ: Ablex.

Rosenstein, A. W., & Grant, A. E. (1997). Reconceptualizing the role of habit: A new model of television audience activity. *Journal of Broadcasting & Electronic Media, 41,* 324–344.

Roskos-Ewoldsen, D. R., Roskos-Ewoldsen, B., & Carpentier, F. R. D. (2002). Media priming: A synthesis. In J. Bryant & D. Zillmann (Eds.), *Media effects: Advances in theory and research* (2nd ed., pp. 97–120). Mahwah, NJ: Erlbaum.

Rossler, P., & Brosius, H-B. (2001). Do talk shows cultivate adolescents' views of the world? A prolonged-exposure experiment. *Journal of Communication, 51,* 143–163.

Rothenbuhler, E. W. (1993). Argument for a Durkheimian theory of the communicative. *Journal of Communication, 43,* 158–163.

Rozell, M. J., & Semiatin, R. J. (2008). Congress and the news media. In M. J. Rozell & J. D. Mayer (Eds.), *Media power, media politics* (2nd ed., pp. 43–62). New York: Rowman & Littlefield.

Rubin, A. M. (2002). The uses-and-gratifications perspective of media effects. In J. Bryant & D. Zillmann (Eds.), *Media effects: Advances in theory and research* (2nd ed., pp. 525–548). Mahwah, NJ: Erlbaum.

Rubin, A. M., & Perse, E. M. (1987). Audience activity and television news gratifications. *Communication Research, 14,* 58–84.

Rubin, A. M., Perse, E. M., & Powell, E. (1990). Loneliness, parasocial interaction and local TV news viewing. *Communication Research, 14,* 246–268.

Rubin, A. M., & Windahl, S. (1986). The uses and dependency model of mass communication. *Critical Studies in Mass Communication, 3,* 184–199.

Rucinski, D. (2004). Community boundedness, personal relevance, and the knowledge gap. *Communication Research, 31,* 472–495.

Russell, C. A., & Stern, B. B. (2006). Consumers, characters, and products: A balance model of sitcom product placement effects. *Journal of Advertising, 35,* 7–21.

Russomanno, J. A., & Everett, S. E. (1995). Candidate sound bites: Too much concern over length? *Journal of Broadcasting & Electronic Media, 39,* 408–415.

Ryan, J., & Peterson, R. A. (1982). The product image: The fate of creativity in country music songwriting. In J. S. Ettema & D. Charles Whitney (Eds.) *Individuals in mass media organizations: Creativity and constraint* (pp. 11–32). Beverly Hills, CA: Sage.

Sallott, L. M. (2002). What the public thinks about public relations: An impression management experiment. *Journalism & Mass Communication Quarterly, 79,* 150–171.

Salwen, M. B., & Driscoll, P. D. (1997). Consequences of third-person perception in support of press restrictions in the O. J. Simpson trial. *Journal of Communication, 47*(2), 60–78.

Salwen, M. B., & Dupagne, M. (2001). Third-person perception of television violence: The role of self-perceived knowledge. *Media Psychology, 3,* 211–230.

Salwen, M. B., & Dupagne, M. (2003). News of Y2K and experiencing Y2K: Exploring the relationship between the third-person effect and optimistic bias. *Media Psychology, 5,* 57–82.

Samuelson, R. J. (2005, July 25). The world is still round. *Newsweek,* p. 49.

Samuelson, R. J. (2006, October 30). The next capitalism. *Newsweek,* p. 45.

Sander, I. (1995 MAY). *How violent is TV-violence? An empirical investigation of factors influencing viewers' perceptions of TV-violence.* Paper presented at the annual conference of the International Communication Association, Albuquerque, NM.

Sandman, P. M. (1994). Mass media and environmental risk: Seven principles. *Risk.* Retrieved August 26, 2007, from http://www.fplc.edu/RISK/

Sapolsky, B. S., & Zillmann, D. (1978). Experience and empathy: Affective reactions to witnessing childbirth. *Journal of Social Psychology, 105,* 131–144.

Schachter, S., & Singer, J. (1962). Cognitive, social, and physiological determinants of emotional state. *Psychological Review, 69,* 379–399.

Schaefer, H. H., & Colgan, A. H. (1977). The effect of pornography on penile tumescence as a function of reinforcement and novelty. *Behavior Therapy, 8,* 938–946.

Schaefer, R. J., & Martinez, T. J. (2009). Trends in network news editing strategies from 1969 through 2005. *Journal of Broadcasting & Electronic Media, 53,* 347–364.

Scharrer, E. (2001). Mens, muscles, and machismo: The relationship between television violence exposure and aggression and hostility in the presence of hypermasculinity. *Media Psychology, 3,* 159–188.

Scharrer, E. (2002). Third-person perception and television violence: The role of out-group stereotyping in perceptions of susceptibility to effects. *Communication Research, 29,* 681–704.

Scheufele, B., Haas, A., & Brosius, H.-B. (2011). Mirror or molder? A study of media coverage, stock prices, and trading volumes in Germany. *Journal of Communication, 61,* 48–70.

Scheufele, D. A. (1999). Framing as a theory of media effects. *Journal of Communication, 49,* 103–122.

Scheufele, D. A. (2002). Differential gains from mass media and their implications for participatory behavior. *Communication Research, 29* (1), 45–64.

Scheufele, D. A., Shanahan, J., & Kim, S. (2002). Who cares about the issues? Media influences on issue awareness, issue stance, and issue involvement. *Journalism & Mass Communication Quarterly, 79* (2), 427–444.

Scheufele, D. A., Shanahan, J., & Lee, E. (2001). Real talk: Manipulating the dependent variable in spiral of silence research. *Communication Research, 28* (3), 304–324.

Schiller, H. (1979). Transnational media and national development. In K. Nordenstreng & H. Schiller (Eds.), *National sovereignty and international communication* (pp. 21–32). Norwood, NJ: Ablex.

Schiller, H. I. (1969). *Mass communication and American empire.* New York: Kelley.

Schimel, J., Greenberg, J., Pyszczynski, T., O'Mahen, H., & Arndt, J. (2000). Running from the shadow: Psychological distancing from others to deny characteristics people fear in themselves. *Journal of Personality & Social Psychology, 78,* 446–462.

Schimmack, U., & Crites, S. L., Jr. (2005). The structure of affect. In D. Albarracin, B. T. Johnson, & M. P. Zanna (Eds.). *The handbook of attitudes* (pp. 397–435). Mahwah, NJ: Erlbaum.

Schmitt, K. L., Woolf, K. D., & Anderson, D. R. (2003). Viewing the viewers: Viewing behaviors by children and adults during television programs and commercials. *Journal of Communication, 53,* 265–281.

Schmitt, K. M., Gunther, A. C., & Liebhart, J. L. (2004). Why partisans see mass media as biased. *Communication Research, 31,* 623–641.

Schneider, E. F., Lang, A., Shin, M., & Bradley, S. D. (2004). Death with a story: How story impacts emotional, motivational, and physiological responses to first-person shooter video games. *Human Communication Research, 30,* 361–375.

Schramm, W. (1954). *The processes and effects of mass communication.* Urbana: University of Illinois Press.

Schramm, W. (1969). Aging and mass communication. In M. W. Riley, J. W. Riley, & M. E. Johnson (Eds.), *Aging and society: Vol. 2. Aging and the professions* (pp. 352–375). New York: Russell Sage Foundation.

Schudson, M. (1998). *The good citizen: A history of American civic life.* Cambridge, MA: Harvard University Press.

Schudson, M. (2003). *The sociology of news.* New York: Norton.

Schultze, Q. (1991). *Televangelism and American culture: The business of popular religion.* Grand Rapids, MI: Baker.

Schwartz, B. (2004). *The paradox of choice: Why more is less.* New York: HarperCollins.

Schwarz, N., & Bohner, G. (2001). The construction of attitudes. In A. Tesser & N. Schwarz (Eds.), *Blackwell handbook of social psychology: Intraindividual processes* (pp. 436–457). Oxford, UK: Blackwell.

Scott, D. W. (2003). Mormon "family values" versus television: An analysis of the discourse of Mormon couples regarding television and popular media culture. *Critical Studies in Media Communication, 20,* 317–333.

Segovia, K. Y., & Bailenson, J. N. (2009). Virtually true: Children's acquisition of false memories in virtual reality. *Media Psychology, 12,* 371–393.

Segrin, C., & Nabi, R. L. (2002). Does television viewing cultivate unrealistic expectations about marriage? *Journal of Communication, 52,* 247–263.

Shah, D., Cho, J., Eveland, W. P. Jr., & Kwak, N. (2005). Information and expression in a digital age: Modeling internet effects on civic participation. *Communication Research, 32,* 531–565.

Shah, D. V., Kwak, N., Schmierbach, M., & Zubric, J. (2004). The interplay of news frames on cognitive complexity. *Human Communication Research, 30,* 102–120.

Shah, D. V., McLeod, J. M., & Yoon, S-H. (2001). Communication, context, and community: An exploration of print, broadcast, and Internet influences. *Communication Research, 28,* 464–506.

Shanahan, J., Morgan, M., & Stenbjerre, M. (1997). Green or brown? Television and the cultivation of environmental concern. *Journal of Broadcasting & Electronic Media, 41,* 305–323.

Shannon, C., & Weaver, W. (1949). *The mathematical theory of communication.* Urbana, IL: University of Illinois Press.

Shapiro, M. A., & Chock, T. M. (2003). Psychological processes in perceiving reality. *Media Psychology, 5,* 163–198.

Shapiro, M. A., & Chock, T. M. (2004). Media dependency and perceived reality of fiction and news. *Journal of Broadcasting & Electronic Media, 48,* 675–695.

Shapiro, M. A., & Fox, J. R. (2002). The role of typical and atypical events in story memory. *Human Communication Research, 28,* 109–135.

Shapiro, S., & Krishnan, H. S. (2001). Memory-based measures for assessing advertising effects: A comparison of explicit and implicit memory effects. *Journal of Advertising, 30*(3), 1–13.

Sheafer, T. (2007). How to evaluate it: The role of story-evaluative tone in agenda setting and priming. *Journal of Communication, 57,* 21–39.

Shehata, A. (2010). Unemployment on the agenda: A panel study of agenda-setting effects during the 2006 Swedish national election campaign. *Journal of Communication, 60,* 182–203.

Shen, F. (2004). Chronic accessibility and individual cognitions: Examining the effects of message frames in political advertisements. *Journal of Communication, 54,* 123–137.

Shen, F. (2009). An economic theory of political communication effects: How the economy conditions political learning. *Communication Theory, 19,* 374–396.

Sherman, S. (1995). Determinants of repeat viewing to prime-time public television programming. *Journal of Broadcasting & Electronic Media, 39,* 472–481.

Shermer, M. (2002). *Why people believe weird things: Pseudoscience, superstition, and other confusions of our time* (2nd ed.). New York: Henry Holt and Company.

Sherry, J. L. (2001). The effects of violent video games on aggression: A meta-analysis. *Human Communication Research, 27,* 409–431.

Sherry, J. L. (2004). Flow and media enjoyment. *Communication Theory, 14,* 328–347.

Shoemaker, P. J., & Reese, S. D. (1991). Mediating the message: *Theories of influences on mass media content.* White Plains, NY: Longman.

Shoemaker, P. J., & Reese, S. D. (1996). *Mediating the message: Theories of influences on mass media content* (2nd ed.). White Plains, NY: Longman.

Shrum, L. J. (1995). Assessing the social influence of television: A social cognition perspective on cultivation effects. *Communication Research, 22,* 402–429.

Shrum, L. J. (2001). Processing strategy moderates the cultivation effect. *Human Communications Research, 27,* 94–120.

Shrum, L. J. (2002). Media consumption and perceptions of social reality: Effects and underlying processes. In J. Bryant & D. Zillmann (Eds.), *Media effects: Advances in theory and research* (2nd ed., pp. 69–95). Mahwah, NJ: Erlbaum.

Sicilia, M., Ruiz, S., & Munuera, J. L. (2005). Effects of interactivity in a web site: The moderating effect of need for cognition. *Journal of Advertising, 34*(3), 31–45.

Siebert, T. (2006, September 7). Marketing to college students: Go Web! *Media Daily News.* Retrieved October 30, 2006, from http://publications.mediapost.com/

Sigal, L. V. (1973). *Reporters and officials: The organization and politics of newsmaking.* Lexington, MA: D. C. Heath & Company.

Simon, A. F. (1997). Television news and international earthquake relief. *Journal of Communication, 47*(3), 82–93.

Simon, A. F., & Jerit, J. (2007). Toward a theory relating political discourse, media, and public opinion. *Journal of Communication, 57,* 254–271.

Simons, R. F., Detenber, B. H., Cuthbert, B. N., Schwartz, D. D., & Reiss, J. E. (2003). Attention to television: Alpha power and its relationship to image motion and emotional content. *Media Psychology, 5,* 283–301.

Simonson, P. (1999). Mediated sources of public confidence: Lazarsfeld and Merton revisited. *Journal of Communication, 49,* 109–122.

Sinclair, J. (2004). Globalization, supranational institutions, and media. In J. D. H. Downing, D. McQuail, P. Schlesinger, & E. Wartella (Eds.), *The Sage handbook of media studies* (pp. 65–82). Thousand Oaks, CA: Sage.

Singer, B. D. (1970). Mass media and communications processes in the Detroit riots of 1967. *Public Opinion Quarterly, 34,* 236–245.

Singer, E., & Endreny, P. J. (1994). Reporting risk: How the mass media portray accidents, diseases, disasters and other hazards. *Risk.* Retrieved August 26, 2007, from http://www.fplc.edu/RISK/

Singer, J. L. (1980). The power and limitations of television: A cognitive-affective analysis. In P. H. Tannenbaum (Ed.), *The entertainment functions of television* (pp. 31–65). Hillsdale, NJ: Erlbaum.

Sintchak, G., & Geer, J. (1975). A vaginal plethysymograph system. *Psychophysiology, 12,* 113–115.

Skinner, B. F. (1974). *About behaviorism.* New York: Knopf.

Slater, M. D. (2003). Alienation, aggression, and sensation seeking as predictors of adolescent use of violent film, computer, and website content. *Journal of Communication, 53,* 105–121.

Slater, M. D., Goodall, E. E., & Hayes, A. F. (2009). Self-reported news attention does assess differential processing of media content: An experiment on risk perceptions utilizing a random sample of U.S. local crime and accident news. *Journal of Communication, 59,* 117–134.

Slater, M. D., Hayes, A. F., Reineke, J. B., Long, M., & Bettinghaus, E. P. (2009). Newspaper coverage of cancer prevention: Multilevel evidence for knowledge-gap effects. *Journal of Communication, 59,* 514–533.

Slater, M. D., Henry, K. L., Swaim, R. C., & Cardador, J. M. (2004). Vulnerable teens, vulnerable times: How sensation seeking, alienation, and victimization moderate the violent media content-aggressiveness relation. *Communication Research, 31,* 642–668.

Slater, M. D., & Rouner, D. (1996). Value-affirmative and value-protective processing of alcohol education messages that include statistical evidence or anecdotes. *Communication Research, 23,* 210–235.

Slater, M. D., & Rouner, M. (2002). Entertainment education and elaboration likelihood: Understanding the presence of narrative persuasion. *Communication Theory, 12* (2), 173–199.

Slater, M. D., Rouner, D., & Long, M. (2006). Television dramas and support for controversial public policies: Effects and mechanism. *Journal of Communication, 56,* 235–252.

Smith, M. E., & Gevins, A. (2004). Attention and brain activity while watching television: Components of viewer engagement. *Media Psychology, 6,* 285–305.

Smith, R. E., & Swinyard, W. R. (1982). Information response models: An integrated approach. *Journal of Marketing, 46,* 81–93.

Smith, R. E., & Swinyard, W. R. (1988). Cognitive response to advertising and trial: Belief strength, belief confidence and product curiosity. *Journal of Advertising, 17*(3), 3–14.

Smith, S. L., & Wilson, B. J. (2002). Children's comprehension of and fear reactions to television news. *Media Psychology, 4,* 1–26.

Snelson, J. S. (1993). The ideological immune system. *Skeptic, 1*(4), 44–45.

Solomon, D. S. (1989). A social marketing perspective on communication campaigns. In R. E. Rice & C. K. Atkin (Eds.), *Public communication campaigns* (2nd ed., pp. 87–104). Newbury Park, CA: Sage.

Sopory, P., & Dillard, J. P. (2002). The persuasive effects of metaphor: A meta-analysis. *Human Communication Research, 28,* 382–419.

Sotirovic, M. (2001). Effects of media use on complexity and extremity of attitudes toward the death penalty and prisoners' rehabilitation. *Media Psychology, 3,* 1–24.

Sparks, G. G. (1986). Developmental differences in children's reports of fear induced by the mass media. *Child Study Journal, 16,* 55–66.

Sparks, G. G., Nelson, C. L., & Campbell, R. G. (1997). The relationship between exposure to televised messages about paranormal phenomena and paranormal beliefs. *Journal of Broadcasting & Electronic Media, 41,* 345–359.

Sparks, G. G., Pellechia, M., & Irvine, C. (1999). The repressive coping style and fright reactions to mass media. *Communication Research, 26,* 176–192.

Sparks, G. G., Sparks, C. W., & Gray, K. (1995). Media impact on fright reactions and belief in UFOs: The potential role of mental imagery. *Communication Research, 22,* 3–23.

Speisman, J. C., Lazarus, R. S., Mordkoff, A., & Davison, L. (1964). Experimental reduction of stress based on ego-defense theory. *Journal of Abnormal & Social Psychology, 68,* 367–380.

Spilerman, S. (1976). Structural characteristics of cities and the and severity of racial disorders. *American Sociological Review, 41,* 771–793.

Stein, A. H., & Friedrich, L. K. (1975). Television content and young children's behavior. In J. P. Murray, E. A. Rubinstein, & G. A. Comstock (Eds.), *Television and social behavior, Vol. 2, Television and social learning.* Washington, DC: U.S. Government Printing Office.

Steiner, P. O. (1952). Program patterns and preferences, and the workability of competition in radio broadcasting. *Quarterly Journal of Economics, 66,* 194–223.

Stephenson, W. (1967). *Play theory of mass communication.* Chicago: University of Chicago Press.

Stephenson, M. T. (2003). Examining adolescents' responses to antimarijuana PSAs. *Human Communication Research, 29,* 343–369.

Stout, P. A., & Leckenby, J. D. (1986). Measuring emotional response to advertising. *Journal of Advertising, 15*(4), 35–42.

Stuckey, M. E., & Curry, K. E. (2008). Presidential elections and the media. In M. J. Rozell & J. D. Mayer (Eds.), *Media power, media politics* (2nd ed., pp. 175–198). New York: Rowman & Littlefield.

Sturgis, P., Roberts, C., & Allum, N. (2005). A different take on the deliberative poll. *Public Opinion Quarterly, 69,* 30–65.

Suckfill, M. (2000). Film analysis and psychophysiology: Effects of moments of impact and protagonists. *Media Psychology, 2,* 269–301.

Sujan, M. (1985). Consumer knowledge: Effects on evaluation strategies mediating consumer judgments. *Journal of Consumer Research, 12*(1), 31–46.

Sun, Y., Shen, L., & Pan, Z. (2008). On the behavioral component of the third-person effect. *Communication Research, 35,* 257–278.

Sundar, S. S., Narayan, S., Obregon, R., & Uppal, C. (1998). Does web advertising work? Memory for print vs. online media. *Journalism & Mass Communication Quarterly, 75,* 822–835.

Sundar, S. S., & Nass, C. (2001). Conceptualizing sources in online news. *Journal of Communication, 51* (1), 52–72.

Sundar, S. S., & Wagner, C. B. (2002). The world wide wait: Exploring physiological and behavioral effects of download speed. *Media Psychology, 4,* 173–206.

Surbeck, E. (1975). Young children's emotional reactions to T.V. violence: The effects of children's perceptions of reality. *Dissertation Abstracts International, 35,* 5139–A.

Sutherland, M., & Galloway, J. (1981). Role of advertising: Persuasion or agenda setting? *Journal of Advertising Research, 21*(5), 215–229.

Tal-Or, N., Boninger, D. S., Poran, A., & Gleicher, F. (2004). Counterfactual thinking as a mechanism in narrative persuasion. *Human Communication Research, 30,* 301–328.

Tal-Or, N., Tsfati, Y., & Gunther, A. C. (2009). The influence of presumed media influence: Origins of the third-person perception. In R. L. Nabi & M. B. Oliver (Eds.), *Media processes and effects* (pp. 99–112). Los Angeles, CA: Sage.

Tamborini, R., Eastin, M. S., Skalski, P., Lachlan, K., Fediuk, T. A., & Brady, R. (2004). Violent virtual video games and hostile thoughts. *Journal of Broadcasting & Electronic Media, 48,* 335–357.

Tan, A. S. (1981). *Mass communication theories and research.* New York: Grid Pub.

Tan, A. S. (1982). Television use and social stereotypes. *Journalism Quarterly, 59,* 119–122.

Tan, E. S-H. (2008). Entertainment is emotion: The functional architecture of the entertainment experience. *Media Psychology, 11,* 28—51.

Tannenbaum, P., & Gaer, E. P. (1965). Mood changes as a function of stress of protagonist and degree of identification in film-viewing situation. *Journal of Personality & Social Psychology, 2,* 612–616.

Tannenbaum, P. H., & Zillmann, D. (1975). Emotional arousal in the facilitation of aggression through communication. In L. Berkowitz (Ed.), *Advances in experimental social psychology* (Vol. 8, pp. 149–192). New York: Academic Press.

Tewksbury, D. (2003). What do Americans really want to know? Tracking the behavior of news readers on the Internet. *Journal of Communication, 53,* 694–710.

Tewksbury, D. (2005). The seeds of audience fragmentation: Specialization in the use of online news sites. *Journal of Broadcasting & Electronic Media, 49,* 332–348.

Tewksbury, D., Jones, J., Peske, M. W., Raymond, A., & Vig, W. (2000). The interaction of news and advocacy frames: Manipulating audience perceptions of a local public policy issue. *Journalism & Mass Communication Quarterly, 77,* 804–829.

Tewksbury, D., Moy, P., & Weis, D. S. (2004). Preparations for Y2K: Revisiting the behavioral components of the third-person effect. *Journal of Communication, 54,* 138–155.

Thomas, M. H. (1982). Physiological arousal, exposure to a relatively lengthy aggressive film, and aggressive behavior. *Journal of Research in Personality, 16,* 72–81.

Thomas, M. H., & Drabman, R. S. (1978). Effects of television violence on expectations of other's aggression. *Personality & Social Psychology Bulletin, 4,* 73–76.

Thomas, M. H., Horton, R. W., Lippincott, E. C., & Drabman, R. S. (1977). Desensitization to portrayals of real-life aggression as a function of exposure to television violence. *Journal of Personality & Social Psychology, 35,* 450–458.

Thompson, C. J., Locander, W. B., & Pollio, H. R. (1989). Putting consumer experience back into consumer research: The philosophy and method of existential-phenomenology. *Journal of Consumer Research, 16*(2), 133–146.

Thomsen, S. R., McCoy, J. K., Gustafson, R. L., & Williams, M. (2002). Motivations for reading beauty and fashion magazines and anorexic risk in college-age women. *Media Psychology, 4,* 113–135.

Tichenor, P., Donohue, G. A., & Olien, C. N. (1970). Mass media flow and differential growth of knowledge. *Public Opinion Quarterly, 34,* 159–170.

Tidhar, C. E., & Lemish, D. (2003). The making of television: Young viewers' developing perceptions. *Journal of Broadcasting & Electronic Media, 47,* 375–394.

Tsfati, Y. (2003). Does audience skepticism of the media matter in agenda setting? *Journal of Broadcasting & Electronic Media, 47,* 157–176.

Tsfati, Y., & Cappella, J. N. (2005). Why do people watch news they do not trust? The need for cognition as a moderator in the association between news media scepticism and exposure. *Media Psychology, 7,* 251–271.

Tsfati, Y., & Cohen, J. (2003). On the effect of the 'third-person effect': Perceived influence of media coverage and residential mobility intentions. *Journal of Communication, 53,* 711–727.

Tuchman, G. (1978). *Making news: A study in the construction of reality.* New York: Free Press.

Tuggle, C. A., & Huffman, S. (2001). Live reporting in television news: Breaking news or black holes? *Journal of Broadcasting & Electronic Media, 45,* 335–344.

Turner, V. (1977). Process, system, and symbol: A new anthropological synthesis. *Daedalus, Summer,* 61–80.

Turow, J. (1984). *Media industries: The production of news and entertainment.* New York: Longman.

Tversky, A., & Kahneman, D. (1973). Availability: A heuristic for judging frequency and probability. *Cognitive Psychology, 4,* 207–232.

U.S. Bureau of the Census. (2000). *Statistical abstract of the United States: 1999.* Washington, DC: Department of Commerce.

U.S. Census Bureau (2011a). Table 588: Employment status of persons 18 and older. *The 2011 Statistical Abstract.* Washington, DC: Department of Commerce.

U.S. Census Bureau (2011b). Table 75: Self described religious identification of the adult population. *The 2011 Statistical Abstract.* Washington, DC: Department of Commerce.

U.S. divorce statistics. (2002). Retrieved July 19, 2004, from http://divorcemagazine.com/statistics/

Valentino, N. A., Buhr, T. A., & Beckmann, M. N. (2001). When the frame is the game: Revisiting the impact of "strategic" campaign coverage on citizens' information retention. *Journalism & Mass Communication Quarterly, 78,* 93–112.

Valentino, N. A., Hutchings, V. L., & Williams, D. (2004). The impact of political advertising on knowledge, Internet information seeking, and candidate preference. *Journal of Communication, 54,* 337–354.

Valkenburg, P. M., & Beentjes, J. W. J. (1997). Children's creative imagination in response to radio and television stories. *Journal of Communication, 47* (2), 21–38.

Valkenburg, P. M., & Janssen, S. C. (1999). What do children value in entertainment programs? A cross-cultural investigation. *Journal of Communication, 49,* 3–21.

Valkenburg, P. M., & Van der Voort, T.H.A. (1995). The influence of television on children's daydreaming styles: A one-year panel study. *Communication Research, 22,* 267–287.

Valkenburg, P. M., & Vroone, M. (2004). Developmental changes in infants' and toddlers' attention to television entertainment. *Communication Research, 31,* 288–311.

Vandewater, E. A., Lee, J. H., & Shim, M-S. (2005). Family conflict and violent electronic media use in school-aged children. *Media Psychology, 7,* 73–86.

van der Molen, J. H. W., & Klijn, M. E. (2004). Recall of television versus print news: Retesting the semantic overlap hypothesis. *Journal of Broadcasting & Electronic Media, 48,* 89–107.

Van der Molen, J. H. W., & van der Voort, T H.A. (2000). The impact of television, print, and audio on children's recall of the news: A study of three alternative explanations for the dual-coding hypothesis. *Human Communication Research, 26,* 3–26.

Van der Voort, T.H.A. (1986). *Television violence: A child's-eye view.* Amsterdam: North-Holland.

van Dijk, J. (2004). Digital media. In J. D. H. Downing, D. McQuail, P. Schlesinger, & E. Wartella (Eds.), *The SAGE handbook of media studies* (pp. 145–163). Thousand Oaks, CA: Sage.

van Evra, J. P. (1997). *Television and child development* (2nd ed.). Mahwah, NJ: Erlbaum.

van Zoonen, L. (1994). *Feminist media studies.* London: Sage.

Varan, D. (1998). The cultural erosion metaphor and the transcultural impact of media systems. *Journal of Communication, 48*(2), 58–85.

Vettehen, P. H., Nuijten, K., & Peeters, A. (2008). Explaining effects of sensationalism on liking of television news stories: The role of emotional arousal. *Communication Research, 35,* 319–338.

Vinson, C. D. (2008). Political parties and the media. In M. J. Rozell & J. D. Mayer (Eds.), *Media power, media politics* (2nd ed., pp. 159–173) New York: Rowman & Littlefield.

Vincent, R. C., & Basil, M. D. (1997). College students' news gratifications, media use, and current events knowledge. *Journal of Broadcasting & Electronic Media, 41,* 380–392.

von Feilitzen, C. (1975). Findings of Scandinavian research on child and television in the process of socialization. *Fernsehen und Bildung, 9,* 54–84.

Vorderer, P., Klimmt, C., & Ritterfeld, U. (2004). Enjoyment: At the heart of media entertainment. *Communication Theory, 14,* 388–408.

Vorderer, P., & Knobloch, S. (2000). Conflict and suspense in drama. In D. Zillmann & P. Vorderer (Eds.), *Media entertainment: The psychology of its appeal* (pp. 59–72). Mahwah, NJ: Erlbaum.

Vorderer, P., Knobloch, S., & Schramm, H. (2001). Does entertainment suffer from interactivity? The impact of watching an interactive TV movie on viewers' experience of entertainment. *Media Psychology, 3,* 343–363.

Waisbord, S. (2004). Media and the reinvention of the nation. In J. D. H. Downing, D. McQuail, P. Schlesinger, & E. Wartella (Eds.). *The SAGE handbook of media studies* (pp. 375–392). Thousand Oaks, CA: Sage.

Walker, J. (1980). Changes in EEG rhythms during television viewing. *Perceptual & Motor Skills, 51,* 255–261.

Wang, M. C. (1988, May 4). Commentary. *Education Week, 36,* 28.

Ward, L. M., & Rivadenrya, R. (1999). Contributions of entertainment television to adolescent's sexual attitudes and expectations: The role of viewing amount versus viewer involvement. *Journal of Sex Research, 36,* 237–249.

Ward, M. (2009). Dark preachers: The impact of radio consolidation on independent religious syndicators. *Journal of Media & Religion, 8,* 79—96.

Watanabe, T. (1999, July 27). The crisis facing the Good Book. *Los Angeles Times,* p. A1.

Weaver, D., & Wilhoit, C. G. (1986). *The American journalist in the 1990s: US news people at the end of an era.* Mahwah, NJ: Erlbaum.

Weaver, A. J., & Wilson, B. J. (2009). The role of graphic and sanitized violence in the enjoyment of television dramas. *Human Communication Research, 35,* 442–463.

Weber, R., Tamborini, R., Lee, H. E., & Stipp, H. (2008). Soap opera exposure and enjoyment: A longitudinal test of disposition theory. *Media Psychology, 11,* 462–487.

Weber, R., Tamborini, R., Westcott-Baker, A., & Kantor, B. (2009). Theorizing flow and media enjoyment as cognitive synchronization of attentional and reward networks. *Communication Theory, 19,* 397–422.

Webster, J. G., & Phalen, P. F. (1997). *The mass audience: Rediscovering the dominant model.* Mahwah, NJ: Erlbaum.

Wegener, D. T., & Carlston, D. E. (2005). Cognitive processes in attitude formation and change. In D. Albarracin, B. T. Johnson, & M. P. Zanna (Eds.), *The handbook of attitudes* (pp. 493–542). Mahwah, NJ: Erlbaum.

Wei, R., Lo, V-H., & Lu, H-Y. (2007). Reconsidering the relationship between the third-person perception and optimistic bias. *Communication Research, 34,* 665–685.

Weiss, A. J., & Wilson, B. J. (1998). Children's cognitive and emotional responses to the portrayal of negative emotions in family-formatted situation comedies. *Human Communication Research, 24,* 584–609.

Westley, B. H., & MacLean, M. (1957). A conceptual model for mass communication research. *Journalism Quarterly, 34,* 31–38.

Whipple, T. W., & Courtney, A. E. (1980). How to portray women in TV commercials. *Journal of Advertising Research, 20*(2), 53–59.

White, D. M. (1950). The gatekeepers: A case study in the selection of news. *Journalism Quarterly, 27,* 383–390.

Whitman, D. (1996, December 16). I'm OK, you're not. *U.S. News & World Report,* pp. 24–30.

Wiener, P. O. (Ed.). (1958). *Charles S. Peirce: Selected writings.* New York: Dover.

Wicks, R. (1992). Improvement over time in recall of media information: An exploratory study. *Journal of Broadcasting & Electronic Media, 36,* 287–302.

Wilcox, G. B., Murphy, J. H., & Sheldon, P. S. (1985). Effects of attractiveness of the endorser on the performance of testimonial ads. *Journalism Quarterly, 62,* 515–532.

Wilkins, K. G. (2000). The role of media in public disengagement from political life. *Journal of Broadcasting & Electronic Media, 44,* 569–580.

Will, G. F. (1996, April 15). Civic speech gets rationed. *Newsweek,* p. 78.

Williams, D. (2006a). Groups and goblins: The social and civic impact of an online game. *Journal of Broadcasting & Electronic Media 50,* 651–670.

Williams, D. (2006b). Virtual cultivation: Online worlds, offline perceptions. *Journal of Communication, 56,* 69–87.

Williams, R. (1961). *Culture and society.* Harmondsworth, UK: Penguin.

Winn, M. (1977). *The plug-in drug.* New York: Viking.

Wise, K., Bolls, P., Myers, J., & Sternadori, M. (2009). When words collide online: How writing style and video intensity affect cognitive processing of online news. *Journal of Broadcasting & Electronic Media, 53,* 532–546.

Wise, K., Bolls, P. D., & Schaefer, S. R. (2008). Choosing and reading online news: How available choice affects cognitive processing. *Journal of Broadcasting & Electronic Media, 52,* 69–85.

Wood, W., Wong, F. Y., & Chachere, J. G. (1991). Effects of media violence on viewers' aggression in unconstrained social interaction. *Psychological Bulletin, 109,* 371–383.

Woodward, K. L. (1990, December 17). A time to seek. *Newsweek,* pp. 50–56.

WorldWideWebSize.com. (2011, Jan. 5). *The size of the World Wide Web.* Retrieved January 5, 2011 from http://www.worldwidewebsize.com/

Wright, C. R. (1949). *Mass communication: A sociological perspective*. New York: Random House.

Wright, C. R. (1960). Functional analysis and mass communication. *Public Opinion Quarterly, 24,* 605–620.

Wright, J. C., & Huston, A. C. (1995). *Effects of educational TV viewing of lower income preschoolers on academic skills, school readiness, and school adjustment one to three years later: A report to the Children's Television Workshop.* Lawrence: University of Kansas, Center for Research on the Influences of Television on Children.

Wu, B. T. W., Crocker, K. E., & Rogers, M. (1989). Humor and comparatives in ads for high- and low-involvement products. *Journalism Quarterly, 66,* 653–661.

Wyer, R. S., & Srull, T. K. (1989). *Memory and cognition in its social context*. Hillsdale, NJ: Erlbaum.

Wyer, R. S. Jr., & Albarracin, D. (2005). Belief formation, organization, and change: Cognitive and motivational influences. In D. Albarracin, B. T. Johnson, & M. P. Zanna (Eds.), *The handbook of attitudes* (pp. 273–322). Mahwah, NJ: Erlbaum.

Yan, M. Z., & Park, Y. J. (2009). Duopoly ownership and local informational programming on broadcast television: Before-after comparisons. *Journal of Broadcasting & Electronic Media, 53,* 383–399.

Yang, M., Roskos-Ewoldsen, D. R., Dinu, L., & Arpan, L. M. (2006). The effectiveness of "in-game" advertising: Comparing college students' explicit and implicit memory for brand names. *Journal of Advertising, 35*(4), 143–152.

Yanich, D. (2010). Does ownership matter? Localism, content, and the Federal Communications Commission. *Journal of Media Economics, 23,* 51–67.

Yanovitzky, I. (2002). Effects of news coverage on policy attention and actions: A closer look into the media-policy connection. *Communication Research, 29,* 422–451.

Yaros, R. A. (2006). Is it the medium or the message? Structuring complex news to enhance engagement and situational understanding by nonexperts. *Communication Research, 33,* 285–310.

Yee, N., & Bailenson, J. N. (2009). The difference between being and seeing: The relative contribution of self-perception and priming to behavioral changes via digital self-representation. *Media Psychology, 12,* 195–209.

Yegiyan, N. S., & Grabe, M. E. (2007). An experimental investigation of source confusion in televised messages: News versus advertisements. *Human Communication Research, 33,* 379–395.

Young, D. G. (2004). Late-night comedy in election 2000: Its influence on candidate trait ratings and the moderating effects of political knowledge and partisanship. *Journal of Broadcasting & Electronic Media, 48,* 1–22.

Young, D. G. (2008). The privileged role of the late-night joke: Exploring humor's role in disrupting argument scrutiny. *Media Psychology, 11,* 119–142.

Yuan, E. J., & Webster, J. G. (2006). Channel repertoires: Using peoplemeter data in Beijing. *Journal of Broadcasting & Electronic Media, 50,* 524–536.

Zajonc, R. (1980). Feeling and thinking: Preferences need no inferences. *American Psychologist, 35,* 151–175.

Zhang, Y. B., & Harwood, J. (2002). Television viewing and perceptions of traditional Chinese values among Chinese college students. *Journal of Broadcasting & Electronic Media, 46,* 245–264.

Zhang, Y., Miller, L. E., & Harrison, K. (2008). The relationship between exposure to sexual music videos and young adults' sexual attitudes. *Journal of Broadcasting & Electronic Media, 52,* 368–386.

Zhao, X. (2009). Media use and global warming perceptions: A snapshot of the reinforcing spirals. *Communication Research, 36,* 698–723.

Zhou, S. (2004). Effects of visual intensity and audio-visual redundancy in bad news. *Media Psychology, 6,* 237–256.

Zhou, S. (2005). Effects of arousing visuals and redundancy on cognitive assessment of television news. *Journal of Broadcasting & Electronic Media, 49,* 23–42.

Zillmann, D. (1971). Excitation transfer in communication-mediate aggressive behavior. *Journal of Experimental Social Psychology, 7,* 419–434.

Zillman, D. (1978). Attribution and misattribution of excitatory reactions. In J. H. Harvey, W. Ickes, & Kidd, R. F. (Eds.), *New directions in attribution research* (pp. 335–368). New York: Wiley.

Zillmann, D. (1980). Anatomy of suspense. In P. H. Tannenbaum (Ed.), *The entertainment functions of television* (pp. 133–163). Hillsdale, NJ: Erlbaum.

Zillmann, D. (1982). Television viewing and arousal. In D. Pearl, Bouthilet, & J. Lazar (Eds.), *Television and behavior: Ten years of scientific progress and implications for the eighties: Vol. 2 Technical reviews* (pp. 53–67). Washington, DC: Government Printing Office.

Zillmann, D. (1983). Transfer of excitation in emotional behavior. In J. T. Cacioppo & R. E. Petty (Eds.), *Social psychophysiology: A sourcebook* (pp. 215–242). New York: Guilford.

Zillmann, D. (1988). Mood management through communication choices. *American Behavioral Scientist, 31,* 327–340.

Zillmann, D. (1991a). The logic of suspense and mystery. In J. Bryant & D. Zillmann (Eds.), *Responding to the screen: Reception and reaction processes* (pp. 281–303). Hillsdale, NJ: Erlbaum.

Zillmann, D. (1991b). Television viewing and physiological arousal. In J. Bryant & D. Zillmann (Eds.), *Responding to the screen: Reception and reaction processes* (pp. 103–133). Hillsdale, NJ: Erlbaum.

Zillmann, D. (1996). The psychology of suspense in dramatic exposition. In P. Vorderer, H. J. Wulff, & M. Friedrichsen (Eds.), *Suspense: Conceptualizations, theoretical analyses, and empirical explorations* (pp. 199–232). Mahwah, NJ: Erlbaum.

Zillmann, D. (1999). Exemplification theory: Judging the whole by some of its parts. *Media Psychology, 1,* 69–94.

Zillmann, D. (2002). Exemplification theory of media influence. In J. Bryant & D. Zillmann (Eds.), *Media effects: Advances in theory and research* (2nd ed., pp. 19–41). Mahwah, NJ: Erlbaum.

Zillmann, D., & Brosius, H-B. (2000). *Exemplification in communication: The influence of case reports on the perception of issues.* Mahwah: NJ: Erlbaum.

Zillmann, D., & Bryant, J. (1994). Entertainment as media effect. In J. Bryant & D. Zillmann (Eds.), *Media effects: Advances in theory and research* (pp. 437–461). Hillsdale, NJ: Erlbaum.

Zillmann, D., Bryant, J., Comisky, P. W., & Medoff, N. J. (1981). Excitation and hedonic valence in the effect of erotica on motivated intermale violence. *European Journal of Social Psychology, 11,* 233–352.

Zillmann, D., Callison, C., & Gibson, R. (2009). Quantitative media literacy: Individual differences in dealing with numbers in the news. *Media Psychology, 12,* 394–416.

Zillmann, D., & Cantor, J. R. (1976). A disposition theory of humour and mirth. In A. J. Chapman & H. C. Foot (Eds.), *Humour and laughter: Theory, research and applications* (pp. 93-115). London: Wiley.

Zillmann, D., & Cantor, J. B. (1977). Affective responses to the emotions of a protagonist. *Journal of Experimental Social Psychology, 13,* 155–165.

Zillmann, D., Chen, L., Knobloch, S., & Callison, C. (2004). Effects of lead framing on selective exposure to Internet news reports. *Communication Research, 31,* 58–81.

Zillmann, D., & Cantor, J. R. (1972). Directionality of transitory dominance as a communication variable affecting humor appreciation. *Journal of Personality & Social Psychology, 24,* 191–198.

Zillmann, D., & Sapolsky, B. S. (1977). What mediates the effect of mild erotica on annoyance and hostile behavior in males? *Journal of Personality & Social Psychology, 35,* 587–596.

Zillmann, D., Taylor, K., & Lewis, K. (1998). News as nonfiction theater: How dispositions toward the public cast of characters affect reactions. *Journal of Broadcasting & Electronic Media, 42,* 153–169.

Zillmann, D., & Weaver, J. B. (1997). Psychoticism in the effect of prolonged exposure to gratuitous media violence on the acceptance of violence as a preferred means of conflict resolution. *Personality & Individual Differences, 22,* 613–627.

Zubayr, C. (1999). The loyal viewer? Patterns of repeat viewing in Germany. *Journal of Broadcasting & Electronic Media, 43,* 346–363.

Zwarun, L., Linz, D., Metzger, M., & Kunkel, D. (2006). Effects of showing risk in beer commercials to young drinkers. *Journal of Broadcasting & Electronic Media, 50,* 52–77.

Index

About the Author

W. James Potter is a professor in the Department of Communication at the University of California at Santa Barbara, where he teaches courses in media literacy, media content, and media effects. A holder of a Ph.D. in communication and another in instructional systems, he has also taught at Western Michigan University, Florida State University, Indiana University, University of California-Los Angeles, and Stanford University. He is a former editor of the *Journal of Broadcasting & Electronic Media*. He is the author of numerous scholarly articles, book chapters, and more than a dozen books, including the Sage titles *Media Literacy* 6th edition, *On Media Violence, Theory of Media Literacy: A Cognitive Approach, How to Publish Your Communication Research* (edited with Alison Alexander), and *The 11 Myths of Media Violence.*

⑤SAGE research methods online

The essential tool for researchers . . .

. . . from the world's leading research methods publisher

Discover SRMO Lists— methods readings suggested by other SRMO users

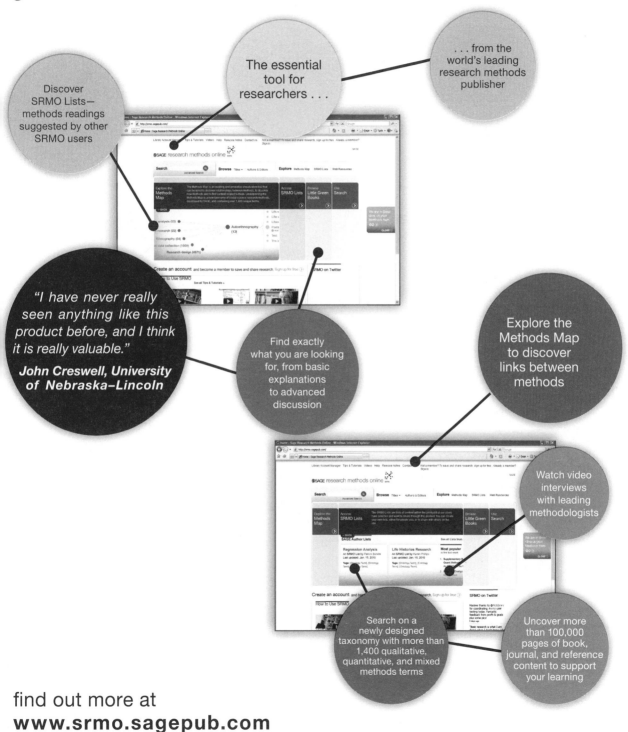

"I have never really seen anything like this product before, and I think it is really valuable."
John Creswell, University of Nebraska–Lincoln

Find exactly what you are looking for, from basic explanations to advanced discussion

Explore the Methods Map to discover links between methods

Watch video interviews with leading methodologists

Search on a newly designed taxonomy with more than 1,400 qualitative, quantitative, and mixed methods terms

Uncover more than 100,000 pages of book, journal, and reference content to support your learning

find out more at
www.srmo.sagepub.com